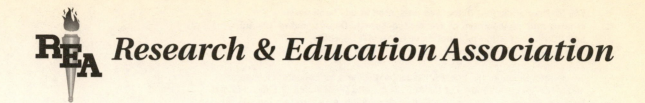

Research & Education Association

The Best Teachers' Test Preparation for the

MTEL™

Mathematics

(Fields 53, 47 & 09)

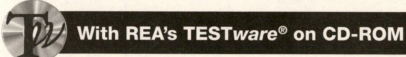

With REA's TESTware® on CD-ROM

Mel Friedman
Professor of Mathematics

And the Staff of
Research & Education Association

Visit our Educator Support Center at:
www.REA.com/teacher

The Mathematics Test Objectives presented in this book were
created and implemented by The Massachusetts Department of Education
and NES®. For further information visit the MTEL website
at *www.mtel.nesinc.com.*

For all references in this book, Massachusetts Tests for Educator Licensure®
and MTEL™ are trademarks of the Massachusetts Department of Education and
Pearson Education, Inc., or its affiliates. In addition, NES® and National Evaluation
Systems, Inc.™, are trademarks of Pearson Education, Inc.

Research & Education Association
61 Ethel Road West
Piscataway, New Jersey 08854
E-mail: info@rea.com

**The Best Teachers' Test Preparation for the
Massachusetts MTEL™ Mathematics Tests (Fields 53, 47 & 09)
With TEST*ware*® on CD-ROM**

Printed in the United States of America

Library of Congress Control Number 2007943562

ISBN-13: 978-0-7386-0416-9
ISBN-10: 0-7386-0416-X

Windows® is a registered trademark of Microsoft Corporation.

REA® and TEST*ware*® are registered trademarks of
Research & Education Association, Inc.

About Research & Education Association

Founded in 1959, Research & Education Association is dedicated to publishing the finest and most effective educational materials—including software, study guides, and test preps—for students in middle school, high school, college, graduate school, and beyond.

REA's Test Preparation series includes books and software for all academic levels in almost all disciplines. Research & Education Association publishes test preps for students who have not yet entered high school, as well as for high school students preparing to enter college. Students from countries around the world seeking to attend college in the United States will find the assistance they need in REA's publications. For college students seeking advanced degrees, REA publishes test preps for many major graduate school admission examinations in a wide variety of disciplines, including engineering, law, and medicine. Students at every level, in every field, with every ambition can find what they are looking for among REA's publications.

REA's practice tests are always based upon the most recently administered exams and include every type of question that you can expect on the actual exams.

REA's publications and educational materials are highly regarded and continually receive an unprecedented amount of praise from professionals, instructors, librarians, parents, and students. Our authors are as diverse as the fields represented in the books we publish. They are well-known in their respective disciplines and serve on the faculties of prestigious high schools, colleges, and universities throughout the United States and Canada.

Today, REA's wide-ranging catalog is a leading resource for teachers, students, and professionals.

We invite you to visit us at www.rea.com to find out how REA is making the world smarter.

Acknowledgments

We would like to thank REA's Carl Fuchs, President, for supervising development; Pam Weston, Vice President, Publishing, for setting the quality standards for production integrity and managing the publication to completion; Larry Kling, Vice President, Editorial, for his editorial direction; John Cording, Vice President, Technology, for coordinating the design, development, and testing of REA's TEST*ware*® software; Alice Leonard, Senior Editor, for project management and preflight editorial review; Diane Goldschmidt, Senior Editor, for post-production quality assurance; Sandra Rush for her editorial contributions; Heena Patel, Software Project Manager, for software testing; Christine Saul, Senior Graphic Artist, for cover design; and Jeff LoBalbo, Senior Graphic Artist, for post-production file mapping.

We also gratefully acknowledge Kathy Caratozzolo of Caragraphics for typesetting the manuscript.

CONTENTS

CHAPTER 1

INTRODUCTION: PASSING THE MTEL MATHEMATICS TESTS

FIELDS 53, 47 & 09 ....**3**
About This Book and TEST*ware*®..3
About the Tests...3
How to Use This Book and TEST*ware*® 5
About the Review Sections..6
Format of the MTEL Mathematics Tests 6
Scoring the MTEL Mathematics Tests 7
The Day of the Test 7
MTEL Study Schedule 9

CHAPTER 2

SUBAREA 1: NUMBER SENSE AND OPERATIONS

FIELDS 53, 47 & 09 ....**11**
Integers and Real Numbers..11
Rational and Irrational Numbers 12
Absolute Value 13
Order of Operations 14
Fractions 14
Decimals 18
Percentages 19
Radicals 21
Exponents 22
Scientific Notation 24
Estimation 25
Significant Digits 26
Real Numbers and Their Components 27
Complex Numbers 28

CHAPTER 3

SUBAREA II: PATTERNS, RELATIONS, AND ALGEBRA

FIELDS 53, 47 & 09 .... **33**
Algebra Vocabulary 33
Operations with Polynomials 33
Simplifying Algebraic Expressions 36
Linear Equations 38
Slope of the Line..38
Determining the Graph of a Linear Equation 40
Two Linear Equations 41
Quadratic Equations 44
Absolute Value Equations 54
Inequalities..55
Ratio, Proportion, and Variation..57
Elementary Functions 61
Properties of Functions...63
Graphing a Function...65
Polynomial Functions and Their Graphs 67

CHAPTER 4

SUBAREA III: GEOMETRY AND MEASUREMENT

FIELDS 53, 47 & 09 .... **79**
Points, Lines, and Angles...79
Congruent Angles and Congruent Line Segments........................90
Polygons..94
Triangles..97
Quadrilaterals 103
Circles..108
Solid Geometry 112
Coordinate Geometry..115

CHAPTER 5

SUBAREA IV: DATA ANALYSIS, STATISTICS AND PROBABILITY

FIELDS 09 & 47... **123**
Data Description: Graphs...123
Probability 129
Statistics..132
Measures of Variability 138
Sampling 140

CHAPTER 6

SUBAREA V: TRIGONOMETRY, CALCULUS, AND DISCRETE MATHEMATICS

FIELDS 09 & 47 ....**143**
Trigonometry 143
Calculus 154
Differentiation 156
Integration 163
Discrete/Finite Mathematics 167
Discrete Mathematics 172
Linear Equations and Matrices 173

PRACTICE TEST FOR ELEMENTARY TEST 53   **179**

Answer Sheets 181
Practice Test 185
Answer Key 203
Detailed Explanations of Answers 205

PRACTICE TEST FOR MIDDLE SCHOOL TEST 47   **219**

Formulas 221
Answer Sheets 222
Practice Test 227
Answer Key 242
Detailed Explanations of Answers 244

PRACTICE TEST FOR HIGH SCHOOL TEST 09   **259**

Formulas 261
Answer Sheets 262
Practice Test 267
Answer Key 285
Detailed Explanations of Answers 287

INDEX   **305**

INSTALLING REA'S TEST*ware*®   **312**

Mathematics Tests

Introduction

Introduction:

Passing the MTEL

Mathematics Tests

(Fields 53, 47 & 09)

About This Book and TEST*ware*®

REA's *The Best Teachers' Test Preparation for the MTEL Mathematics Test (Fields 53, 47 & 09)* is a comprehensive guide designed to assist you in preparing for the appropriate required test for your mathematics educator license in Massachusetts. To enhance your chances of success in this important step toward your career as a mathematics teacher, this test guide, along with REA's exclusive TEST*ware*®, comes packed with these features:

- Presents an accurate and complete overview of these three MTEL tests
- Identifies all of the important information and its representation on the test
- Provides a comprehensive review of every subarea on the test
- Provides three full-length practice tests (one for each test)
- Suggests tips and strategies for successfully completing standardized tests
- Replicates the format of the official tests, including levels of difficulty

- Supplies the correct answer and detailed explanations for each question on the practice tests, which enable you to identify correct answers and understand why they are correct and, just as important, why the other answers are incorrect.

This guide is the product of a review of the best resources available. REA editors considered the most recent test administrations and professional standards. We also researched information from the Massachusetts Department of Education, professional journals, textbooks, and educators. The result? The best test preparation materials based on the latest information available.

About the Tests

The MTEL mathematics tests are designed to assess the mathematical knowledge and competencies for a teacher of grades 5–8 and 8–12 (09), grades 5–8 only (47), and grades 1–6 (53). The following charts present a clear representation of the subareas, approximate number of questions, and the percentages of the total test that each subarea occupies. These subareas represent the combined expertise of Massachusetts educators, subject area specialists, and district-level educators who

An Overview of the MTEL Mathematics Tests

Mathematics (09)

	Subareas	Approx. Number of Questions	Approx. Test Weighting of Subareas
	Multiple-Choice:		
I.	Number Sense and Operations	14–16	12%
II.	Patterns, Relations, and Algebra	27–29	23%
III.	Geometry and Measurement	23–25	19%
IV.	Data Analysis, Statistics, and Probability	12–14	10%
V.	Trigonometry, Calculus, and Discrete Mathematics	19–21	16%
	Open-Response:		
VI.	Integration of Knowledge and Understanding	2	20%

Middle-School Mathematics (47)

	Subareas	Approx. Number of Questions	Approx. Test Weighting of Subareas
	Multiple-Choice:		
I.	Number Sense and Operations	18–20	15%
II.	Patterns, Relations, and Algebra	30–32	25%
III.	Geometry and Measurement	21–23	18%
IV.	Data Analysis, Statistics, and Probability	14–16	12%
V.	Trigonometry, Calculus, and Discrete Mathematics	12–14	10%
	Open-Response:		
VI.	Integration of Knowledge and Understanding	2	20%

Elementary Mathematics (53)

	Subareas	Approx. Number of Questions	Approx. Test Weighting of Subareas
	Multiple-Choice:		
I.	Number Sense, Operations, and Data Analysis	37–39	30%
II.	Patterns, Relations, and Algebra	30–32	25%
III.	Geometry and Measurement	30–32	25%
	Open-Response:		
IV.	Integration of Knowledge and Understanding	2	20%

worked to develop and validate these tests. This book contains a thorough review of all these subareas, as well as the specific skills that demonstrate each area.

Who Administers the Test?

All the MTEL tests are administered by the Massachusetts Department of Education.

Can I Retake the Test?

The MTEL can be taken as many times as needed to achieve a passing score.

When Should the MTEL Be Taken?

Candidates are typically nearing completion of or have completed their undergraduate work when they take MTEL tests.

MTEL tests are administered five times a year at six locations around the state. To receive information on upcoming administrations of the MTEL, consult the MTEL test date chart at the MTEL website. For all information, contact the Massachusetts Department of Education at:

Massachusetts Tests for Educator Licensure
National Evaluation Systems, Inc.
P.O. Box 660
Amherst, MA 01004-9013
Phone: (413) 256-2892
Fax: (413) 256-8221
Website: *www.mtel.nesinc.com* (refer to or download the "Registration Bulletin")

Is There a Registration Fee?

There is a fee for all MTEL tests. A complete summary of the registration fees is included in the MTEL Registration Bulletin at the MTEL website.

Calculator Usage

Examinees taking the MTEL Mathematics (09) will be offered a basic scientific calculator. You may not bring your own calculator to the test. Be sure to check the NES website for the latest information on this.

Examinees taking the MTEL for Middle School Mathematics (47) and Elementary Mathematics (53) will not use calculators.

How to Use This Book and TEST*ware*®

How Do I Begin Studying?

Identify which MTEL test you wish to prepare for, then review the table of contents of this test preparation guide.

1. To best utilize your study time, follow the MTEL Independent Study Schedule at the end of this chapter. This schedule is based on a six-week program, but can be condensed if necessary.

2. Take the practice test on CD-ROM for the MTEL you plan to take, score it according to the directions, then review the explanations to your answers carefully. Study the areas that your scores indicate need further review.

3. Review the format of the MTEL.

4. Review the test-taking advice and suggestions presented in this chapter.

5. Pay attention to the information about the objectives of the test.

6. Spend time reviewing topics that stand out as needing more study.

7. Take the practice test again this time in its printed version in this book, and follow the same procedure as #2 above.

8. Follow the suggestions at the end of this chapter for the day of the test.

Note: When taking the practice tests, remember that no calculators will be provided for the 47 and 53 tests, and only a basic scientific calculator will be provided for the 09 test.

When Should I Start Studying?

It is never too early to start studying for the MTEL. The earlier you begin, the more time you will have to sharpen your skills. Do not procrastinate!

A six-week study schedule is provided at the end of this chapter to assist you in preparing for the MTEL test you require. This schedule can be adjusted to meet your unique needs. If your test date is only four weeks away, you can halve the time allotted to each section, but keep in mind that this is not the most effective way to study. If you have several months before your test date, you may wish to extend the time allotted to each section. Remember, the more time you spend studying, the better your chances of achieving your goal of a passing score.

Studying for the MTEL Mathematics Tests

It is very important for you to choose the time and place for studying that works best for you. Some set aside a certain number of hours every morning to study, some choose the night before going to sleep, and still others study during the day, while waiting in line, or even while eating lunch. Choose a time when you can concentrate, and your study will be most effective. Be consistent and use your time wisely. Work out a study routine and stick to it.

When you take the practice test, simulate the conditions of the actual test as closely as possible. Turn your television and radio off and sit down at a quiet table with your calculator, if you will be using one. When you complete the practice test, score it, and then thoroughly review the explanations to the questions you answered incorrectly. Do not, however, review too much at any one time. Concentrate on one problem area at a time by examining the question and explanation, and by studying our review until you are confident that you have mastered the material. Keep track of your scores to discover areas of general weaknesses and to gauge your progress. Give extra attention to the review sections that cover your areas of difficulty, as this will build your skills in those areas.

About the Review Sections

The subject review in this book is designed to help you sharpen the basic skills needed to approach the MTEL test you are required to take, as well as to provide strategies for attacking the questions.

Each subarea is examined separately, clearly delineating the tests to which it applies. The skills required for all subareas fulfill the objectives of the Massachusetts Department of Education and are extensively discussed to optimize your understanding of what your specific MTEL test covers.

Your schooling has taught you most of what you need to succeed on the test. Our review is designed to help you fit the information you have acquired into specific subareas. Reviewing your class notes and textbooks together with our reviews will give you an excellent springboard for passing the test.

Format of the MTEL Mathematics Tests

The MTEL mathematics tests assess the candidate's proficiency and depth of understanding of the subject at the level required for a baccalaureate major, according to Massachusetts standards.

Referring to the previous charts, the MTEL Mathematics (09) and Middle School Mathematics (47) comprise six subarea sections, five of which total approximately 100 multiple-choice questions, and one of which involves two open-response questions. The MTEL Elementary Mathematics (53) has three multiple-choice subarea sections and one subarea containing two open-response questions. In all tests, the multiple-choice questions comprise 80% and the open-response questions comprise 20% of the total test.

Scoring the MTEL Mathematics Tests

Multiple-Choice Questions

A candidate's performance on subareas with multiple-choice questions is based strictly on the number of test questions answered correctly. Candidates do not lose any points for wrong answers. Each multiple-choice question counts the same toward the total score. These items are scored electronically and checked to verify accuracy.

Open-Response Questions

Open-response questions require a breadth of understanding of each test's field of mathematics and the ability to relate concepts from different aspects of the field. Open-response questions are scored holistically by two or more qualified educators. Scorers receive training in scoring procedures and are monitored for accuracy and consistency. Scorers are typically licensed teachers, administrators, arts and sciences faculty, teacher education faculty, and other content specialists.

Scorers judge the overall effectiveness of each response. That is, scorers are trained to provide an overall judgment, not to indicate specific errors.

A score is assigned to each response based on a scale that describes various levels of performance from weak to strong, or thorough. If your response is blank, unrelated to the assignment, illegible, or in a language other than the target language, you will receive no points for that question, and may or may not meet the qualifying score for the test, depending on your performance on the other questions.

You are given four hours to complete the test, so be aware of the amount of time you are spending on each question. Using the practice test will help you prepare to pace your time evenly, efficiently, and productively.

Score Results

After you have taken the MTEL, you will receive a score report indicating whether you met the qualifying score, your total test score, and information about your performance on the subareas of the test.

Score reports will be mailed to you, to the Massachusetts Department of Education, and to those you designate to receive them according to the schedule published in the MTEL Registration Bulletin. Your score will not be released via telephone or fax. There is a fee for each additional score report requested.

Each MTEL test has its own qualifying score set by the Massachusetts Commissioner of Education. Always check with them for the most current scale information.

The Day of the Test

Before the Test

On the day of the test, make sure to dress comfortably, so that you are not distracted by being too hot or too cold while taking the test. Plan to arrive at the test center early. This will allow you to collect your thoughts and relax before the test, and will also spare you the anguish that comes with being late.

You should check your MTEL Registration Bulletin and other registration information to find out what time to arrive at the testing center.

Before you leave for the testing center, make sure that you have your admission ticket and the following identification:

- One piece of current, government-issued identification, in the name in which you registered, bearing your photograph and signature

- One clear and legible photocopy of your original government-issued identification for each test session in which you are testing (i.e., one copy for the morning and/or one copy for the afternoon session)

- One additional piece of identification (with or without a photograph)

Note: If you do not have the required identification, you will be required to complete additional paperwork and have your photograph taken. This additional step will result in a reduction of your available testing time.

You must bring several sharpened no. 2 pencils with erasers, as none will be provided at the test center.

If you would like, you may wear a watch to the test center. However, you may not wear one that has a calculator, or one that makes noise. Dictionaries, textbooks, notebooks, briefcases, laptop computers, packages, and cell phones will not be permitted. Drinking, smoking, and eating are prohibited.

Test-Taking Tips

Some of you may not be familiar with tests such as the MTEL. This book will help acquaint you with this type of test and help alleviate your test-taking anxieties. Here are seven handy tips to help you be at your best:

Tip 1. Become comfortable with the format of the MTEL. When you are practicing, stay calm and pace yourself. After simulating the test only once, you will boost your chances of doing well, and you will be able to sit down for the actual test with much more confidence.

Tip 2. Read all of the possible answers. Just because you think you have found the correct response, do not automatically assume that it is the best answer. Read through each choice to be sure that you are not making a mistake by jumping to conclusions.

Tip 3. Use the process of elimination. Go through each answer to a question and eliminate as many of the answer choices as possible. By eliminating two answer choices, you have given yourself a better chance of getting the item correct since there will only be two choices left. Answer all the questions you can; you are not penalized for wrong answers, but you are rewarded for correct ones.

Tip 4. Place a question mark in your answer booklet next to the answers you guessed, then recheck them later if you have time.

Tip 5. Work quickly and steadily. Avoid focusing on any one problem too long. Taking the appropriate practice test in this book for your MTEL test will help you learn to efficiently budget your time.

Tip 6. Learn the directions and format of the test. This will not only save time, but will also help you avoid anxiety (and the mistakes caused by getting anxious).

Tip 7. Be sure that the answer circle you are marking corresponds to the number of the question in the test booklet. The test is multiple-choice, so it is graded by machine, and marking one answer in the wrong circle can throw off your answer key and your score. Be extremely careful.

During the Test

You are given four hours to complete the MTEL. Restroom breaks are allowed, but they count as testing time. Procedures will be followed to maintain test security. Once you enter the test center, follow all of the rules and instructions given by the test supervisor. If you do not, you risk being dismissed from the test and having your scores canceled.

When all of the materials have been distributed, the test instructor will give you directions for filling out your answer sheet. Fill out this sheet carefully. This information will be printed on your score report. Once the test begins, mark only one answer per question, completely erase unwanted answers and marks, and fill in answers darkly and neatly.

After the Test

When you finish your test, hand in your materials and you will be dismissed. Then, go home and relax—you deserve it!

MTEL Independent Study Schedule

The following study schedule allows for thorough preparation to pass your MTEL Mathematics test. This is a suggested six-week course of study. This schedule can, however, be condensed if you have less time available to study, or expanded if you have more time. Whatever the length of your available study time, be sure to keep a structured schedule by setting aside ample time each day to study. Depending on your schedule, you may find it easier to study throughout the weekend. No matter which schedule works best for you, the more time you devote to studying for the MTEL Mathematics test, the more prepared and confident you will be on the day of the test.

Week	Activity
1	Read and study Chapter 1, "Passing the MTEL Mathematics Tests (Fields 53, 47 & 09)." This chapter will introduce you to the format of the exam and give you an overview of the subareas tested on each mathematics exam. Consult the MTEL website at www.doe.mtel.nesinc.com for any further information you may need.
2 & 3	Study the review section of this book, Chapters 2 through 6. Take notes on the sections as you work through them, as writing will aid in your retention of information. Keep a list of the subject areas for which you may need additional aid. Textbooks for college mathematics will help in your preparation.
4	Condense your notes. Develop a structured outline detailing specific facts. It may be helpful to use index cards to aid yourself in memorizing important facts and concepts.
5	Take the practice test on CD-ROM for the MTEL Mathematics exam you plan to take. Review the explanations for the questions you answered incorrectly.
6	Restudy any areas you consider to be difficult by using your study materials, references, and notes. If you need a final confidence boost, take the test again, in its printed version in this book.

Chapter

SUBAREA I:

Number Sense

and Operations

Fields 53, 47 & 09
(For Field 53, also see Ch. 5 for Data Analysis)

Integers and Real Numbers

Most of the numbers used in algebra belong to a set called the **real numbers** or **reals**. This set can be represented graphically by the real number line.

Given the number line in Figure 2.1, we arbitrarily fix a point and label it with the number 0. In a similar manner, we can label any point on the line with one of the real numbers, depending on its position relative to 0. Numbers to the right of 0 are positive, and those to the left are negative. Value increases from left to right, so that if *a* is to the right of *b*, it is said to be greater than *b*.

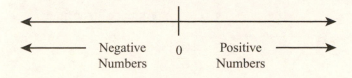

Figure 2.1

If we now divide the number line into equal segments, we can label the points on this line with real numbers. For example, the point 2 lengths to the left of zero is −2, and the point 3 lengths to the right of zero is +3 (the + sign is usually assumed, so +3 is written simply as 3). The number line now looks like Figure 2.2.

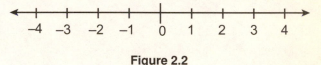

Figure 2.2

These boundary points represent the subset of the reals known as **integers**. The set of integers is made up of both the positive and negative whole numbers: {…, −4, −3, −2, −1, 0, 1, 2, 3, 4,…}. Some subsets of integers are:

Natural Numbers or Positive Numbers— the set of integers starting with 1 and increasing: $N = \{1, 2, 3, 4,…\}$.

Whole Numbers—the set of integers starting with 0 and increasing: $W = \{0, 1, 2, 3,…\}$.

Negative Numbers—the set of integers starting with −1 and decreasing: $Z = \{−1, −2, −3…\}$.

Prime Numbers—the set of positive integers greater than 1 that are divisible only by 1 and themselves: {2, 3, 5, 7, 11, …}.

Even Integers—the set of integers divisible by 2: {…, −4, −2, 0, 2, 4, 6,…}.

Odd Integers—the set of integers not divisible by 2: {…, −3, −1, 1, 3, 5, 7,…}.

Rational and Irrational Numbers

A **rational number** is any number that can be written in the form $\frac{a}{b}$, where a is any integer and b is any integer except zero. All rational numbers can be expressed as decimals by dividing b into a. The result is either a **terminating decimal**, meaning that b divides into a with a remainder of 0 after a certain point; or a **repeating decimal**, meaning that b continues to divide into a so that the decimal has a repeating pattern of integers. An **irrational number** is a number that cannot be written as a simple fraction. It is an infinite and nonrepeating decimal.

The tree diagram in Figure 2.3 shows the relationships between the different types of numbers.

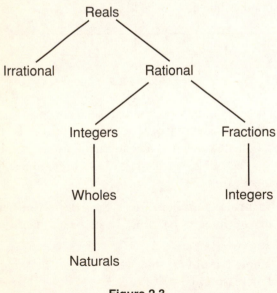

Figure 2.3

- **EXAMPLES**

Examples of rational numbers include:

2	3	5	10	32	−2	−4	−18	−25
$\frac{1}{4}$	$\frac{1}{2}$	$\frac{2}{3}$	$-\frac{1}{4}$	$-\frac{4}{7}$	$-\frac{10}{55}$	$\frac{21}{9}$	$\frac{101}{635}$	

- **EXAMPLES**

Examples of irrational numbers include:

π — approximately equal to 3.14159

e — approximately equal to 2.71828

$\sqrt{2}$ — approximately equal to 1.41421

$\sqrt{3}$ — approximately equal to 1.73205

$\sqrt{5}$ — approximately equal to 2.23607

PROBLEM

List the numbers shown below from least to greatest.
$\frac{1}{3}$, $\sqrt{3}$, 3, 0.3

SOLUTION

$\frac{1}{3} \approx 0.33333$

$\sqrt{3} \approx 1.73205$

Therefore, the numbers from least to greatest are:
0.3, $\frac{1}{3}$, $\sqrt{3}$, 3

A **prime** number is a number that has no factors other than itself and 1. For example, the numbers 1, 3, 5, and 7 are prime numbers.

PROBLEMS

Write each integer as a product of its primes: 2, 12, 5, 22, 18, 36.

SOLUTIONS

$2 = 2 \times 1$

$12 = 4 \times 3 = 2 \times 2 \times 3$

$5 = 5 \times 1$

$22 = 11 \times 2$

$18 = 6 \times 3 = 2 \times 3 \times 3$

$36 = 6 \times 6 = 3 \times 2 \times 3 \times 2$

or $18 \times 2 = 9 \times 2 \times 2 = 3 \times 3 \times 2 \times 2$

Absolute Value

The **absolute value** of a number is represented by two vertical lines around the number, and is equal to the given number, regardless of sign.

The absolute value of a real number A is defined as follows:

$$|A| = \begin{cases} A \text{ if } A \geq 0 \\ -A \text{ if } A < 0 \end{cases}$$

For example $|5| = 5$, $|-8| = -(-8) = 8$.

Absolute values follow the given rules:

(A) $|-A| = |A|$

(B) $|A| \geq 0$, equality holding only if $A = 0$

(C) $\left|\dfrac{A}{B}\right| = \dfrac{|A|}{|B|}$, $B \neq 0$

(D) $|AB| = |A| \times |B|$

(E) $|A|^2 = A^2$

Absolute value can also be expressed on the real number line as the distance of the point represented by the real number from the point labeled 0.

So $|-3| = 3$ because -3 is 3 units to the left of 0.

PROBLEMS

Classify each of the following statements as true or false. If it is false, explain why.

(1) $|-120| > 1$

(2) $|4 - 12| = |4| - |12|$

(3) $|4 - 9| = 9 - 4$

(4) $|12 - 3| = 12 - 3$

(5) $|-12a| = 12\,|a|$

SOLUTIONS

(1) True

(2) False, $|4 - 12| = |4| - |12|$

$|-8| = 4 - 12$

$8 \neq -8$

In general, $|a + b| \neq |a| + |b|$

(3) True

(4) True

(5) True

PROBLEM

Calculate the value of the following expression:

$$||2 - 5| + 6 - 14|$$

SOLUTION

Do the inside absolute value first.

$$||-3| + 6 - 14| = |3 + 6 - 14| = |9 - 14|$$

$$= |-5| = 5$$

PROBLEM

Using the number line in Figure 2.4, graph the solution to $-5 - (-3)$.

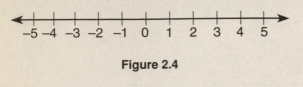

Figure 2.4

SOLUTION

Step 1 is to graph point -5 on the number line in Figure 2.5.

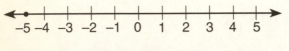

Figure 2.5

Step 2 is to move 3 units to the *right* of -5. In this problem we move to the right of -5 because a negative number is being subtracted, which is the same as adding its absolute value. Since -2 is 3 units to the right of -5, graph -2 on the number line. See Figure 2.6.

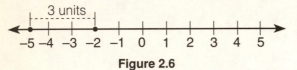

Figure 2.6

Order of Operations

When a series of operations involving addition, subtraction, multiplication, or division is indicated, first resolve any operations in parentheses, then resolve exponents, then resolve multiplication and/or division, and finally perform addition and/or subtraction. One way to remember this is to recite "Please excuse my dear Aunt Sally." The **P** stands for parentheses, the **E** for exponents, the **M** for multiplication, the **D** for division, the **A** for addition, and the **S** for subtraction.

Consider

$$60 - 25 \div 5 + 15 - 100 + 4 \times 10$$
$$= 60 - 25 \div 5 + 15 - 100 + 40$$
$$= 60 - 5 + 15 - 100 + 40$$
$$= 115 - 105$$
$$= 10$$

Notice that $25 \div 5$ could be evaluated at the same time that 4×10 is evaluated, since they are both part of the multiplication/division step.

Fractions

The fraction, $\dfrac{a}{b}$, where the **numerator** is a and the **denominator** is b, implies that a is being divided by b. The denominator of a fraction can never be zero since a number divided by zero is not defined. If the numerator is greater than the denominator, the fraction is called an **improper fraction**. A **mixed number** is the sum of a whole number and a fraction, so $4\dfrac{3}{8} = 4 + \dfrac{3}{8}$.

Operations with Fractions

(A) **To find the sum of two fractions having a common denominator,** simply add together the numerators of the given fractions and put this sum over the common denominator.

$$\frac{11}{3} + \frac{5}{3} = \frac{11 + 5}{3} = \frac{16}{3}$$

Similarly for subtraction,

$$\frac{11}{3} - \frac{5}{3} = \frac{11 - 5}{3} = \frac{6}{3} = 2$$

PROBLEM

Perform the following operation:

$$-\frac{8}{16} - \left(-\frac{4}{16}\right)$$

SOLUTION

Step 1 is to subtract the numerators.

$-8 - (-4) = -4$

Since the denominators in $-\dfrac{8}{16}$ and $-\dfrac{4}{16}$ are equal, keep the common denominator.

The correct answer is $-\dfrac{4}{16}$.

(B) **To find the sum of the two fractions having different denominators**, it is necessary to change the fractions so they have the same denominators, and proceed as in (A). We do this by finding the **lowest common denominator (LCD)** of the different denominators.

The LCD is the smallest whole number that is a multiple of the denominators. In other words, it is the smallest number that is divisible by each of the denominators.

(1) One way to find the LCD is to list the multiples of each denominator until you find the lowest common one.

For example, to find the LCD of $\dfrac{11}{6}$ and $\dfrac{5}{16}$, list the multiples of 6 and 16:

6: 6, 12, 18, 24, 30, 36, 42, 48, 54 . . .

16: 16, 32, 48

The LCD is thus 48.

The LCD is sometimes called the lowest common multiple, or LCM.

(2) Another way to find the LCD is by **factoring**. To **factor** a number means to find two numbers that when multiplied together have a product equal to the original number. These two numbers are then said to be factors of the original number. For example, the factors of 6 are 1 and 6, since $1 \times 6 = 6$, and 2 and 3, since $2 \times 3 = 6$.

Every number is the product of itself and 1. A **prime factor** is a number that does not have any factors beside itself and 1. This is important when finding the LCD of two fractions having different denominators.

To find the LCD of $\dfrac{11}{6}$ and $\dfrac{5}{16}$ by factoring, we must first find the prime factors of each of the two denominators.

$6 = 2 \times 3$

$16 = 2 \times 2 \times 2 \times 2$

The LCD is a product of the prime factors such that every prime factor is included.

$\text{LCD} = 2 \times 2 \times 2 \times 2 \times 3 = 48$

Note that we do not need to repeat the extra 2 that appears in both the factors of 6 and 16.

Once we have determined the LCD of the denominators, each of the fractions must be converted into equivalent fractions having the LCD as a denominator.

Rewrite $\dfrac{11}{6}$ and $\dfrac{5}{16}$ to have the LCD 48 as their denominators.

$6 \times ? = 48$	$16 \times ? = 48$
$6 \times 8 = 48$	$16 \times 3 = 48$

If the numerator and denominator of each fraction are multiplied (or divided) by the same number, the value of the fraction will not change. This is because a fraction, $\dfrac{b}{b}$, b being any number, is equal to the multiplicative identity, 1.

Therefore,

$$\frac{11}{6} \times \frac{8}{8} = \frac{88}{48} \qquad \frac{5}{16} \times \frac{3}{3} = \frac{15}{48}$$

We may now find

$$\frac{11}{6} + \frac{5}{16} = \frac{88}{48} + \frac{15}{48} = \frac{103}{48}$$

Similarly for subtraction,

$$\frac{11}{6} - \frac{5}{16} = \frac{88}{48} - \frac{15}{48} = \frac{73}{48}$$

PROBLEM

Find the lowest common denominator (LCD) for $\dfrac{5}{6}$, $\dfrac{4}{21}$, and $\dfrac{1}{7}$.

SOLUTION

Step 1 is to list multiples of each denominator.

$6 = 6, 12, 18, 24, 30, 36, 42, 48, 54, 60, 66, 72$

$21 = 21, 42, 63, 84, 105$

$7 = 7, 14, 21, 28, 35, 42, 49, 56, 63, 70$

The lowest common multiple of 6, 21, and 7 is 42. Since 42 is the lowest common multiple, it is also the LCD.

(C) **To find the product of two or more fractions,** simply multiply the numerators of the given fractions to find the numerator of the product and multiply the denominators of the given fractions to find the denominator of the product. For example,

$$\frac{2}{3} \times \frac{1}{5} \times \frac{4}{7} = \frac{2 \times 1 \times 4}{3 \times 5 \times 7} = \frac{8}{105}$$

If you are multiplying mixed numbers, you should **change the mixed number to an improper fraction.** To do this, simply multiply the whole number by the denominator of the fraction and add the numerator. This product becomes the numerator of the result and the denominator remains the same. For example,

$$5\frac{2}{3} = \frac{(5 \times 3) + 2}{3} = \frac{15 + 2}{3} = \frac{17}{3}$$

PROBLEM

Convert $2\frac{7}{8}$ into an improper fraction.

SOLUTION

Multiply the whole number "2" by the denominator "8".

$2 \times 8 = 16$

Next, add the numerator to the previous result.

$16 + 7 = 23$

The improper fraction is $\frac{23}{8}$.

(D) **To find the quotient of two fractions,** simply invert the divisor and multiply. e.g.,

$$\frac{8}{9} \div \frac{1}{3} = \frac{8}{9} \times \frac{3}{1} = \frac{24}{9}$$

PROBLEM

Find the solution to the following problem.

$$\frac{1}{4} \times \frac{6}{8} \div \frac{2}{3}$$

SOLUTION

Let's do the multiplication first.

$$\frac{1}{4} \times \frac{6}{8}$$

The answer is $\frac{6}{32}$.

Next, let's perform the division.

$$\frac{6}{32} \div \frac{2}{3}$$

Invert the divisor, and change the operation to multiplication.

$$\frac{6}{32} \times \frac{3}{2}$$

Next, multiply the numerators.

$6 \times 3 = 18$

And then multiply the denominators.

$32 \times 2 = 64$

The correct answer is $\frac{18}{64}$.

Note that if we did the division first $\left(\frac{6}{8} \div \frac{2}{3} \right)$ and then multiplied the result by $\frac{1}{4}$, the answer would be the same.

Simplifying Fractions

To **simplify** a fraction is to convert it into a form in which the numerator and denominator have no common factor other than 1.

A fraction can be simplified if both the numerator and denominator have a common factor. This factor is called the **greatest common factor** (GCF), also known as the **greatest common divisor** (GCD). If the numerator and denominator are divided by the same number, the GCF, the value of the fraction remains the same.

The GCF is the largest number that can divide into a group of numbers. In the case of a fraction, that would be the numerator and denominator.

You find the GCF by starting the same way you did to find the LCD, by writing each number as the product of its primes, except now you are looking for all of the *common* prime factors.

• **EXAMPLE**

Find the GCF for 12 and 24.

Write out each number as a product of primes.

$12 = 3 \times 2 \times 2$ $\qquad$ $24 = 3 \times 2 \times 2 \times 2$

The common factors in both sets of prime factors are $3 \times 2 \times 2 = 12$.

Therefore, 12 is the GCF.

• **EXAMPLE**

Simplify the fraction $\dfrac{8}{28}$.

Step 1 is to find the GCF:

$8 = 2 \times 2 \times 2$ $\qquad$ $28 = 7 \times 2 \times 2$

So the GCF is $2 \times 2 = 4$.

Step 2 is to divide the numerator and denominator of the fraction by the GCF = 4.

$$\frac{8 \div 4}{28 \div 4} = \frac{2}{7}$$

So $\dfrac{8}{28}$ simplifies into $\dfrac{2}{7}$.

Sometimes you can recognize a common factor just by looking at the numerator and denominator, and not have to go through formally finding the GCF.

So for $\dfrac{8}{28}$, if you recognized that 2 is a common factor (because the numerator and denominator are both even), you would get $\dfrac{4}{14}$, but 2 is a common factor again, and you would get $\dfrac{2}{7}$.

• **EXAMPLES**

Simplify the fractions found in the last section.

$$-\frac{4}{16} = -\frac{1}{4}$$

$$\frac{24}{9} = \frac{8}{3}$$

$$\frac{18}{64} = \frac{9}{32}$$

To change an improper fraction to a mixed number, simply divide the numerator by the denominator. The remainder becomes the numerator of the fractional part of the mixed number, and the denominator remains the same. For example,

$$\frac{35}{4} = 35 \div 4 = 8\frac{3}{4}$$

To check your work, change your result back to an improper fraction to see if it matches the original fraction.

A complex fraction is a fraction whose numerator and/or denominator is made up of fractions. To simplify the fraction, find the LCD of all the fractions. Multiply both the numerator and denominator by this number and simplify.

• **EXAMPLE**

Simplify: $\dfrac{1\frac{2}{3}}{\frac{4}{5}}$

First, change the mixed fraction to an improper fraction:

$$1\frac{2}{3} = \frac{5}{3}$$

The LCD of $\dfrac{5}{3}$ and $\dfrac{4}{5}$ is 15. Multiply numerator and denominator by 15.

$$\frac{\frac{5}{3} \times 15}{\frac{4}{5} \times 15} = \frac{25}{12} = 2\frac{1}{12}$$

Decimals

When we divide the denominator of a fraction into its numerator, the result is a **decimal**. The decimal is based upon a fraction with a denominator of 10, 100, 1,000, … and is written with a **decimal point**. Whole numbers are placed to the left of the decimal point, where the first place to the left is the units place, the second to the left is the tens, the third to the left is the hundreds, and so on. The fractional parts are placed on the right where the first place to the right is tenths; the second to the right is hundredths, etc.

- **EXAMPLES**

$$12\frac{3}{10} = 12.3 \qquad 4\frac{17}{100} = 4.17 \qquad \frac{3}{100} = .03$$

Operations With Decimals

(A) **To add numbers containing decimals**, write the numbers in a column, making sure the decimal points are lined up, one beneath the other. Add the numbers as usual, placing the decimal point in the sum so that it is still in line with the others. It is important not to mix the digits in the tenths place with the digits in the hundredths place, and so on. Note that if two numbers differ according to the amount of digits to the right of the decimal point, zeros must be added.

- **EXAMPLES**

$2.558 + 6.391$ $57.51 + 6.2$

$$\begin{array}{r} 2.558 \\ +6.391 \\ \hline 8.949 \end{array} \qquad \begin{array}{r} 57.51 \\ +\ 6.20 \\ \hline 63.71 \end{array}$$

Similarly with subtraction,

$78.54 - 21.33$ $7.11 - 4.2$

$$\begin{array}{r} 78.54 \\ -21.33 \\ \hline 57.21 \end{array} \qquad \begin{array}{r} 7.11 \\ -4.20 \\ \hline 2.91 \end{array}$$

$.63 - .214$ $15.224 - 3.6891$

$$\begin{array}{r} .630 \\ -.214 \\ \hline .416 \end{array} \qquad \begin{array}{r} 15.2240 \\ -\ 3.6891 \\ \hline 11.5349 \end{array}$$

(B) **To multiply numbers with decimals**, simply multiply as usual. Then, to figure out the number of decimal places that belong in the product, find the total number of decimal places in the numbers being multiplied.

- **EXAMPLES**

$$\begin{array}{r} 6.555 \quad \text{(3 decimal places)} \\ \times \quad 4.5 \quad \text{(1 decimal place)} \\ \hline 32775 \\ 26220 \quad\quad\quad \\ \hline 294975 \\ 29.4975 \quad \text{(4 decimal places)} \end{array}$$

$$\begin{array}{r} 5.32 \quad \text{(2 decimal places)} \\ \times \quad .04 \quad \text{(2 decimal places)} \\ \hline 2128 \\ 000 \quad\quad \\ \hline 2128 \\ .2128 \quad \text{(4 decimal places)} \end{array}$$

(C) **To divide numbers with decimals**, you must first make the divisor a whole number by moving the decimal point the appropriate number of places to the right. The decimal point of the dividend should also be moved the same number of places. Place a decimal point in the quotient, directly in line with the decimal point in the dividend. Then divide as usual.

- **EXAMPLES**

$12.92 \div 3.4$ $40.376 \div 7.21$

$$\begin{array}{r} 3.8 \\ 3.4\,)\overline{12.9.2} \\ -102 \\ \hline 272 \\ -272 \\ \hline 0 \end{array} \qquad \begin{array}{r} 5.6 \\ 7.21\,)\overline{40.37.6} \\ -3605 \\ \hline 4326 \\ -4326 \\ \hline 0 \end{array}$$

Comparing and Rounding Decimals

(A) When **comparing** two numbers with decimals to see which is the larger, first look at the tenths place. The larger digit in this place represents the larger number. If the two digits are the same, take a look at the digits in the hundredths place, and so on.

- **EXAMPLES**

  Which is larger, .518 or .216?

  5 is larger than 2, therefore

  .518 is larger than .216

  Which is larger, .723 or .726?

  The 7's in the tenths place are equal, so look at the hundredths place. The 2's in the hundedth place are equal, so look at the thousandths place.

  6 is larger than 3; therefore,

  .726 is larger than .723

(B) The method of **rounding** decimals has two components:

  (1) identifying which digit is to be rounded

  (2) determining whether it should be rounded "up" or left as is, by examining the next digit to the right.

  If the next digit to the right is less than 5, drop it and all digits to the right of it. If the next digit to the right is 5 or more, add 1 to the digit to be rounded and then drop all digits to the right of it.

- **EXAMPLE**

  2.3472 rounded to the nearest thousandth is 2.347; rounded to the nearest hundredth, it is 2.35; rounded to the nearest tenth, it is 2.3 (in the original number the next digit is 4).

PROBLEM

Round the following decimal to the nearest thousandth: 0.9196.

SOLUTION

Step 1 is to determine the digit that will be rounded.

0.9196

Since the digit "9" is in the thousandths' place, it will be rounded.

Step 2 is to locate the digit to the right of "9."

0.9196

The digit "6" is to the right of "9."

Step 3 is to determine if the decimal will be rounded up or down. Since 6 is greater than 5, the decimal will be rounded up. To do this, increase 9 by 1. Since 9 increased by 1 is 10, carry the addition over to the remaining decimal places.

0.920

The correct answer is 0.920.

Percentages

A **percentage** is a way of expressing the relationship between part and whole, where "whole" is defined as 100%. The symbol % means per hundred. Therefore, a percentage can be defined by a fraction with a denominator of 100, so $5\% = \dfrac{5}{100}$. Decimals can also represent a percentage. For instance,

$$56\% = \frac{56}{100} = 0.56$$

PROBLEMS

Compute the values of

(1) 90% of 400   (3) 50% of 500

(2) 180% of 400   (4) 200% of 4

SOLUTIONS

(1)   90% of 400 = $\dfrac{90}{100} \times 400 = 90 \times 4 = 360$

(2)   180% of 400 = $\dfrac{180}{100} \times 400 = 180 \times 4$
$= 720$

(3)   50% of 500 = $\dfrac{50}{100} \times 500 = 50 \times 5 = 250$

(4)   200% of 4 = $\dfrac{200}{100} \times 4 = 2 \times 4 = 8$

To determine what percentage of a number is represented by another number, divide the two. Remember that the "of" number is always the denominator.

PROBLEMS

(1)   What percentage of 100 is 99.5?

(2)   4 is what percentage of 200?

SOLUTIONS

(1) $\dfrac{99.5}{100} = .995 = 99.5\%$

(2) $\dfrac{4}{200} = .02 = 2\%$

Some problems may call for converting numbers into an equivalent or simplified form in order to make the solution more convenient.

(A) **To convert a fraction to a decimal**, divide the numerator by the denominator. For example, for $\dfrac{1}{2}$,

$$
\begin{array}{r}
.50 \\
2\overline{)1.00} \\
-10 \\
\hline
00
\end{array}
$$

So $\dfrac{1}{2} = 0.50$

(B) **To convert a number to a percentage**, multiply by 100. For example,

$0.50 = (0.50 \times 100)\% = 50\%$

(C) **To convert a percentage to a decimal**, divide by 100. For example,

$$30\% = \dfrac{30}{100} = 0.30$$

(D) **To convert a decimal to a fraction**, write the decimal as its fractional equivalent and then simplify. For example,

$$0.500 = \dfrac{500}{1000} = \dfrac{1}{2}$$

PROBLEMS

Express

(1)   1.65 as a percentage of 100

(2)   0.7 as a fraction

(3) $-\dfrac{10}{20}$ as a decimal

(4) $\dfrac{4}{2}$ as an integer

SOLUTIONS

(1) $\left(\dfrac{1.65}{100}\right) \times 100 = 1.65\%$

(2) $0.7 = \dfrac{7}{10}$

(3) $-\dfrac{10}{20} = -0.5$

(4) $\dfrac{4}{2} = 2$

PROBLEM

Convert the following fraction to a percentage: $\dfrac{17}{20}$.

SOLUTION

Divide the fraction and convert the decimal to a percentage: $17 \div 20 = .85 = 85\%$.

PROBLEM

Convert the following decimal to a percentage: 12.69

SOLUTION

Step 1 is to multiply the decimal by 100.

$12.69 \times 100 = 1,269.00$

Step 2 is to write the answer as a percentage.

$1,269.00 = 1,269\%$

The correct answer is 1,269%.

PROBLEM

Convert the following percentage to a decimal: 0.009%.

SOLUTION

Step 1 is to write the percentage as a real number.

$0.009\% = 0.009$

Step 2 is to divide the real number by 100.

$0.009 \div 100 = 0.00009$

The correct answer is 0.00009.

PROBLEM

Which of the following statements is true?

(a) $0.002\% = 0.200$ (c) $-0.95 > -93\%$

(b) $1.967 = 196.7\%$ (d) $1.00 < 100\%$

SOLUTION

Statement (a) is incorrect because 0.200 multiplied by 100 is 20, or 20%. Since 20% does not equal 0.002%, this statement cannot be true.

Statement (b) is correct. 1.967 multiplied by 100 is equivalent to 196.7%.

Statement (c) is incorrect because -0.95 is equivalent to -95%. Since -95% is not greater than -93%, this statement is not true.

Statement (d) is incorrect because 1.00 is exactly equivalent to 100%, not less than 100%.

The only correct statement is statement (b).

Radicals

Definitions

A **radical sign** indicates that the root of a number or expression will be taken. The **radicand** is the number from which the root will be taken. The **index** tells how many times the root needs to be multiplied by itself to equal the radicand.

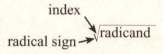

The **square root** of a number is a number that when multiplied by itself results in the original number. Usually, the "2" index for a square root is omitted. The square root of 81 is 9 since $9 \times 9 = 81$. However, -9 is also a square root of 81 since $(-9)(-9) = 81$. Every positive number will have two square roots. The principal square root is the positive one. Zero has only one square root, and negative numbers do not have real numbers as their square roots.

- **EXAMPLES**

(1) $\sqrt[3]{64}$;

3 is the index and 64 is the radicand. Since $4 \times 4 \times 4 = 64$, $\sqrt[3]{64} = 4$.

(2) $\sqrt[5]{32}$;

5 is the index and 32 is the radicand. Since $2 \times 2 \times 2 \times 2 \times 2 = 32$, $\sqrt[5]{32} = 2$.

Operations with Radicals

(A) **To multiply two or more numbers that contain radicals**, we utilize the law that states,

$$\sqrt{a} \times \sqrt{b} = \sqrt{ab}.$$

Simply multiply the whole numbers as usual. Then, multiply the radicands, put the product under the radical sign, and simplify.

- **EXAMPLES**

  (1) $\sqrt{12} \times \sqrt{5} = \sqrt{60} = \sqrt{4} \times \sqrt{5} = 2\sqrt{15}$

  (2) $3\sqrt{2} \times 4\sqrt{8} = 12\sqrt{16} = 12 \times 4 = 48$

Likewise, some square roots can be expressed as a product of two or more square roots. For example,

$$\sqrt{50} = \sqrt{(2 \times 25)} = \sqrt{2}\sqrt{25}$$

Since we know that $\sqrt{25} = 5$, we can rewrite the radical as

$$\sqrt{50} = 5\left(\sqrt{2}\right)$$

For example,

$$2\sqrt{10} \times 6\sqrt{5} = 12\sqrt{50} = 12 \times \sqrt{25} \times \sqrt{2} = 60\sqrt{2}$$

(B) **To divide radicals**, simplify both the numerator and the denominator. By multiplying the radical in the denominator by itself, you can make the denominator a rational number. The numerator must also be multiplied by this radical so that the value of the expression does not change. This is called rationalizing the denominator. You must choose as many factors as necessary to rationalize the denominator.

- **EXAMPLES**

  (1) $\dfrac{\sqrt{128}}{\sqrt{2}} = \dfrac{\sqrt{64} \times \sqrt{2}}{\sqrt{2}} = \dfrac{8\sqrt{2}}{\sqrt{2}} = 8$

  (2) $\dfrac{\sqrt{10}}{\sqrt{3}} = \dfrac{\sqrt{10} \times \sqrt{3}}{\sqrt{3} \times \sqrt{3}} = \dfrac{\sqrt{30}}{3}$

  (3) $\dfrac{\sqrt{8}}{2\sqrt{3}} = \dfrac{\sqrt{8} \times \sqrt{3}}{2\sqrt{3} \times \sqrt{3}} = \dfrac{\sqrt{24}}{2 \times 3} = \dfrac{2\sqrt{6}}{6} = \dfrac{\sqrt{6}}{3}$

(C) **To add two or more radicals**, the radicals must have the same index and the same radicand. You may have to simplify the radicals to determine if they are the same.

- **EXAMPLES**

  (1) $6\sqrt{2} + 2\sqrt{2} = (6 + 2)\sqrt{2} = 8\sqrt{2}$

  (2) $\sqrt{27} + 5\sqrt{3} = \sqrt{9}\sqrt{3} + 5\sqrt{3} = 3\sqrt{3} + 5\sqrt{3} = 8\sqrt{3}$

  (3) $7\sqrt{3} + 8\sqrt{2} + 5\sqrt{3} = 12\sqrt{3} + 8\sqrt{2}$

Use a similar method for subtraction.

- **EXAMPLES**

  (1) $12\sqrt{3} - 7\sqrt{3} = (12 - 7)\sqrt{3} = 5\sqrt{3}$

  (2) $\sqrt{80} - \sqrt{20} = \sqrt{16}\sqrt{5} - \sqrt{4}\sqrt{5}$
  $$= 4\sqrt{5} - 2\sqrt{5} = 2\sqrt{5}$$

  (3) $\sqrt{50} - \sqrt{3} = \sqrt{25}\sqrt{2} - \sqrt{3} = 5\sqrt{2} - \sqrt{3}$

PROBLEM

Find the solution to the following problem: $\sqrt[3]{-1}$.

SOLUTION

Step 1 is to determine what the base would be if you raise a number to the power of "3" to get -1.

Base $= -1$

Step 2 is to raise the base "–1" to the exponent "3" to verify the solution,

$$-1 \times -1 \times -1 = -1$$

The correct answer is -1.

Exponents

Definitions

When a number is multiplied by itself a specific number of times, it is said to be **raised to a power**. The way this is written is $a^n = b$ where a is the number, or **base**, n is the **exponent**, or **power**, that indicates the number of times the base is to be multiplied by itself, and b is the product of this multiplication.

In the expression 3^2, 3 is the base and 2 is the exponent. This means that 3 is multiplied by itself 2 times and the product is 9.

An exponent can be either positive or negative. A negative exponent implies a fraction. So, if n is a positive integer,

$$a^{-n} = \frac{1}{a^n}, a \neq 0. \text{ So, } 2^{-4} = \frac{1}{2^4} = \frac{1}{16}.$$

An exponent that is zero gives a result of 1, assuming that the base is not equal to zero.

$$a^0 = 1, a \neq 0.$$

An exponent can also be a fraction. If m and n are positive integers,

$$a^{\frac{m}{n}} = \sqrt[n]{a^m}.$$

The numerator remains the exponent of a, but the denominator tells what root to take. For example,

(1) $4^{\frac{3}{2}} = \sqrt[2]{4^3} = \sqrt{64} = 8$

(2) $3^{\frac{4}{2}} = \sqrt[2]{3^4} = \sqrt{81} = 9$

Any time a base is raised to a fractional exponent, the problem should be rewritten as a root.

If a fractional exponent were negative, the same operation would take place, but the result would be a fraction. For example,

$$27^{-\frac{2}{3}} = \frac{1}{27^{\frac{2}{3}}} = \frac{1}{\sqrt[3]{27^2}} = \frac{1}{\sqrt[3]{729}} = \frac{1}{9}$$

PROBLEMS

Simplify the following expressions:

(1) -3^{-2} (3) $\dfrac{-3}{4^{-1}}$

(2) $(-3)^{-2}$

SOLUTIONS

(1) Here the exponent applies only to 3. Since

$$x^{-y} = \frac{1}{x^y}, -3^{-2} = -(3)^{-2} = -\frac{1}{3^2} = -\frac{1}{9}$$

(2) In this case the exponent applies to the negative base. Thus,

$$(-3)^{-2} = \frac{1}{(-3)^2} = \frac{1}{(-3)(-3)} = \frac{1}{9}$$

(3) $\dfrac{-3}{4^{-1}} = \dfrac{-3}{\left(\frac{1}{4}\right)^1} = \dfrac{-3}{\frac{1^1}{4^1}} = \dfrac{-3}{\frac{1}{4}}$

Division by a fraction is equivalent to multiplication by that fraction's reciprocal; thus,

$$\frac{-3}{\frac{1}{4}} = -3 \times \frac{4}{1} = -12, \text{ and } \frac{-3}{4^{-1}} = -12$$

General Laws of Exponents

(A) $a^p a^q = a^{p+q}$

   $4^2 4^3 = 4^{2+3} = 4^5 = 1{,}024$

(B) $(a^p)^q = a^{pq}$

   $(2^3)^2 = 2^6 = 64$

(C) $\dfrac{a^p}{a^q} = a^{p-q}$

   $\dfrac{3^6}{3^2} = 3^4 = 81$

(D) $(ab)^p = a^p b^p$

   $(3 \times 2)^2 = 3^2 \times 2^2 = (9)(4) = 36$

(E) $\left(\dfrac{a}{b}\right)^p = \dfrac{a^p}{b^p}, b \neq 0$

   $\left(\dfrac{4}{5}\right)^2 = \dfrac{4^2}{5^2} = \dfrac{16}{25}$

PROBLEM

Find the value of the following expression: $(-3^1)^2$.

SOLUTION

Step 1 is to identify the base and the exponents. In this problem, "–3" is the base, "1" and "2" are the exponents.

Step 2, since this problem raises an exponent to an exponent, multiply the exponents.

$1 \times 2 = 2$

Step 3 is to rewrite the problem.

$(-3)^2$

Step 4 is to set up the multiplication. Multiply the base, "–3," with itself.

-3×-3

Step 5 is to perform the operation.

$-3 \times -3 = 9$

The correct answer is 9.

PROBLEM

Find the value of the following expression:

$$\left(\frac{6^6}{6^4}\right)$$

SOLUTION

Step 1 is to identify the base and the exponents. In this problem, "6" is the common base. "6" and "4" are the exponents.

Step 2, since the problem contains a common base, is to subtract the exponents.

$6 - 4 = 2$

Step 3 is to rewrite the problem using the new exponent.

6^2

Step 4 is to perform the operation.

$6 \times 6 = 36$

The correct answer is 36.

PROBLEM

Find the equivalent of $(3^2)^4$.

SOLUTION

$(3^2)^4 = 3^{(4 \times 2)} = 3^8$

To check that this is correct, remember that an exponent shows the number of times the base is to be taken as a factor. Note in this case that 3^2 is considered the base. Thus,

$(3^2)^4 = 3^2 \times 3^2 \times 3^2 \times 3^2$

Also, in multiplication we add exponents. Thus,

$3^2 \times 3^2 \times 3^2 \times 3^2 = 3^{(2+2+2+2)} = 3^8$

Note: To find the power of a power, multiply the exponents; this is the only case in which multiplication of exponents is performed.

Scientific Notation

Scientists, technicians, engineers, and others engaged in scientific work are often required to solve problems involving very large and very small numbers. Problems such as

$$\frac{22,684 \times 0.00189}{0.0713 \times 83 \times 7}$$

are not uncommon. Solving such problems by the rules of ordinary arithmetic is laborious and time consuming. Moreover, the tedious arithmetic process lends itself to operational errors. Also, there is difficulty in locating the decimal point in the result. These difficulties can be greatly reduced by a knowledge of the powers of 10 and their use.

The laws of exponents form the basis of scientific notation, or calculation using powers of 10. The following list includes several decimals and whole numbers expressed as powers of 10:

10,000	$= 10^4$	0.1	$= 10^{-1}$
1,000	$= 10^3$	0.01	$= 10^{-2}$
100	$= 10^2$	0.001	$= 10^{-3}$
10	$= 10^1$	0.0001	$= 10^{-4}$
1	$= 10^0$		

The concept of scientific notation may be demonstrated as follows:

$$60,000 = 6.0000 \times 10,000$$
$$= 6 \times 10^4$$
$$538 = 5.38 \times 100$$
$$= 5.38 \times 10^2$$

Notice that the final expression in each of the foregoing examples involves a number between 1 and 10, multiplied by a power of 10. Furthermore, in each case the exponent of the power of 10 is a number equal to the number of digits between the new position of the decimal point and the original position (understood) of the decimal point.

We apply this reasoning to write any number in scientific notation; that is, as a number between 1 and 10 multiplied by the appropriate power of 10. The appropriate power of 10 is found by the following mechanical steps:

1. Shift the decimal point to standard position, which is the position immediately to the right of the first nonzero digit.

2. Count the number of digits between the new position of the decimal point and its original position. This number indicates the value of the exponent for the power of 10.

3. If the decimal point is shifted to the left, the sign of the exponent of 10 is positive; if the decimal point is shifted to the right, the sign of the exponent of 10 is negative.

The validity of this rule, for those cases in which the exponent of 10 is negative, is demonstrated as follows.

$$0.00657 = 6.57 \times 0.001$$
$$= 6.57 \times 10^{-3}$$

$$0.348 = 3.48 \times 0.1$$
$$= 3.48 \times 10^{-1}$$

Further examples of the use of scientific notation are given as follows:

$$543,000,000 = 5.43 \times 10^{8}$$
$$186 = 1.86 \times 10^{2}$$
$$243.01 = 2.4301 \times 10^{2}$$
$$0.0000007 = 7 \times 10^{-7}$$
$$0.00023 = 2.3 \times 10^{-4}$$

Estimation

Sometimes just an estimate of an answer is all that is needed. Then round the numbers and avoid a lot of unnecessary calculation.

•   **EXAMPLE**

Jim is hosting a pizza party for 11 of his close friends. He wants to serve each guest a mini-pizza. Mini-pizzas cost $6.79 each. Estimate the total cost.

Round 11 to 10. Round $6.79 to $7.00. Now, multiply $7 times 10. The estimated cost is $70.00.

Note: The exact cost is $74.69.

•   **EXAMPLE**

Table 2.1 shows the number of fishing lures a factory produced over a 6-year period.

Table 2.1

Year	Fishing Lures
2000	6,257
2001	10,374
2002	5,890
2003	12,125
2004	9,642
2005	13,092

Estimate the total number of fishing lures produced from 2000 through 2005.

First, round each number to the thousands. Then, add the rounded numbers to find the estimate.

$$6,000 + 10,000 + 6,000 + 12,000 + 10,000 +$$
$$13,000 = 57,000 \text{ lures}$$

Note: The actual number of lures is 57,380.

PROBLEM

A rectangular duck pond (43 feet by 47 feet) is on a lot that measures 108 feet by 96 feet, as shown in Figure 2.7. The rest of the lot is a flower garden. Estimate the size of the flower garden in square feet.

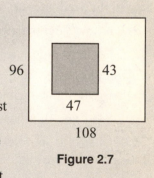

Figure 2.7

SOLUTION

First, estimate the area of the duck pond. Round 47 to 50 and 43 to 40. Now, multiply: $50 \times 40 = 2,000$. The area of the duck pond is about 2,000 square feet. Now, calculate the area of the lot. Round 96 to 100 and

108 to 100. Multiply: $100 \times 100 = 10,000$. To find the approximate area of the flower garden, subtract the area of the duck pond from the area of the lot. $10,000 - 2,000 = 8,000$. The flower garden is about 8,000 square feet.

Note: The actual area of the flower garden is 8,347 square feet.

Significant Digits

The number of significant digits in a measurement is critical, especially in chemistry. It is the number of digits that are believed to be correct. The more significant digits in a measurement, the more precise it is.

The basic rules for significant digits are:

(1)   All nonzero digits are significant.

(2)   All zeros between significant digits are significant.

(3)   Final zeros to the right of the decimal point are significant.

• **EXAMPLES**

815.85 has five significant digits. (All of the numbers give useful information.)

7.48629 has six significant digits.

600 has one significant digit. (Only the 6 is important. You don't know anything about the tens or the ones place, so the zeros are just seen as placeholders.)

240 has two significant digits.

542 has three significant digits.

0.7500 has four significant digits. (Final zeros that lie to the right of the decimal point are significant.)

0.008 has one significant digit.

5,006 has four significant digits. (All zeros between significant digits are significant.)

56,000 has two significant digits.

PROBLEM

How many significant digits are in the number 720?

SOLUTION

There are two significant digits in the number 720. The zero is just a placeholder.

PROBLEM

How many significant digits are in the number 28.05?

SOLUTION

There are four significant digits in the number 28.05. The zero counts because it is between two significant digits.

PROBLEM

How many significant digits are in the number 3,001?

SOLUTION

There are four significant digits in the number 3,001. The zeros count because they are between two significant digits.

PROBLEM

How many significant digits are in the number 0.00017?

SOLUTION

There are two significant digits in the number 0.00071. The zeros to the right of the decimal point are placeholders.

PROBLEM

How many significant digits are in the number 8,000?

SOLUTION

There is one significant digit in the number 8,000. Only the 8 is important. Without any other information about the measurement, the zeros are seen as placeholders.

Real Numbers and Their Components

Real Number Properties of Equality

The standard properties of equality involving real numbers are:

Reflexive Property of Equality

For each real number a,

$$a = a$$

Symmetric Property of Equality

For each real number a, and for each real number b,

if $a = b$, then $b = a$

Transitive Property of Equality

For each real number a, for each real number b, and for each real number c,

if $a = b$ and $b = c$, then $a = c$

Real Number Operations and Their Properties

The operations of addition and multiplication are of particular importance. As a result, many properties concerning those operations have been determined and named. Here is a list of the most important of these properties.

Closure Property of Addition

For every real number a, and for every real number b,

$$a + b \text{ is a real number}$$

Closure Property of Multiplication

For every real number a, and for every real number b,

$$ab \text{ is a real number}$$

Commutative Property of Addition

For every real number a, and for every real number b,

$$a + b = b + a$$

Commutative Property of Multiplication

For every real number a, and for every real number b,

$$ab = ba$$

Associative Property of Addition

For every real number a, and for every real number b, and for every real number c,

$$(a + b) + c = a + (b + c)$$

Associative Property of Multiplication

For every real number a, for every real number b, and for every real number c,

$$(ab)c = a(bc)$$

Identity Property of Addition

For every real number a,

$$a + 0 = 0 + a = a$$

Identity Property of Multiplication

For every real number a,

$$a \times 1 = 1 \times a = a$$

Inverse Property of Addition

For every real number a, there is a real number $-a$ such that

$$a + -a = -a + a = 0$$

Inverse Property of Multiplication

For every real number a, $a \neq 0$, there is a real number a^{-1} such that

$$a \times a^{-1} = a^{-1} \times a = 1$$

Distributive Property

For every real number a, for every real number b, and for every real number c,

$$a(b + c) = ab + ac$$

Subtraction and Division Operations

The operations of subtraction and division are also important, but less important than addition and multiplication. Here are the definitions for these operations.

For every real number a, for every real number b, and for every real number c,

$$a - b = c \text{ if and only if } b + c = a$$

For every real number a, for every real number b, and for every real number c,

$$a \div b = c \text{ if and only if } c \text{ is the unique real}$$
$$\text{number such that } bc = a$$

The definition of division eliminates division by 0. For example, $4 \div 0$ is undefined, $0 \div 0$ is undefined, but $0 \div 4 = 0$.

In many instances, it is possible to perform subtraction by first converting a subtraction statement to an addition statement. This is illustrated below.

For every real number a, and for every real number b,

$$a - b = a + (-b)$$

In a similar way, every division statement can be converted to a multiplication statement. Use the following model:

For every real number a, and for every real number b, with $b \neq 0$,

$$a \div b = a \times b^{-1}$$

Complex Numbers

A **complex number** is a number that can be written in the form $a + bi$, where a and b are real numbers and $i = \sqrt{-1}$. The number a is the **real part,** and the number b is the **imaginary part** of the complex number.

Returning momentarily to real numbers, the square of a real number cannot be negative. More specifically, the square of a positive real number is positive, the square of a negative real number is positive, and the square of 0 is 0. Then i is defined to be a number with a property that

$$i^2 = -1.$$

Obviously i is not a real number. C is then used to represent the set of all complex numbers, or

$$C = \{a + bi \mid a \text{ and } b \text{ are real numbers}\}$$

All the properties of real numbers described in the previous section carry over to complex numbers; therefore, those properties will not be stated again.

If a is a real number, then a can be expressed in the form $a = a + 0i$. Hence, every real number is a complex number and $R \subseteq C$.

The following are examples of addition, subtraction, and multiplication of complex numbers.

Suppose $a + bi$ and $c + di$ are complex numbers. Then to add, subtract, or multiply complex numbers, compute in the usual way, replace i^2 with -1, and simplify.

$$(a + bi) + (c + di) = (a + c) + (b + d)i$$
$$(a + bi) - (c + di) = (a - c) + (b - d)i$$
$$(a + bi)(c + di) = a\,(c + di) + bi\,(c + di)$$
$$= ac + adi + bci + bdi^2$$
$$= ac - bd + (ad + bc)i$$

PROBLEM

Simplify the following: $(3 + i)(2 + i)$.

SOLUTION

$$(3 + i)(2 + i) = 3(2 + i) + i(2 + i)$$
$$= 6 + 3i + 2i + i^2$$
$$= 6 + (3 + 2)i + (-1)$$
$$= 5 + 5i$$

Division of two complex numbers is usually accomplished with a special procedure that involves the conjugate of a complex number. The conjugate of $a + bi$ is denoted by

$$\overline{a + bi} = a - bi.$$

Also, $(a + bi)(a - bi) = a^2 + b^2$.

The usual procedure for division is illustrated below.

$$\frac{x + yi}{z + wi} = \frac{x + yi}{z + wi} \times \frac{z - wi}{z - wi}$$

$$= \frac{(xz + yw) + (-xw + yz)i}{z^2 + w^2}$$

$$= \frac{xz + yw}{z^2 + w^2} + \frac{-xw + yz}{z^2 + w^2}i$$

PROBLEMS

Evaluate the following:

(1) $3i^3$
(2) $2i^7$
(3) $-4i^4$
(4) $-5i^6$
(5) $(3 + 2i)(2 + 3i)$
(6) $(2 - i)(2 + i)$
(7) $(5 - 4i)^2$

SOLUTIONS

(1) $3i^3 = 3i(i)^2$
$$= 3i(-1) = -3i$$

(2) $2i^7 = 2i(i^2)(i^2)(i^2)$
$$= 2i(-1)(-1)(-1)$$
$$= -2i$$

(3) $-4i^4 = -4(i^2)(i^2)$
$$= -4(-1)(-1)$$
$$= -4$$

(4) $-5i^6 = -5(i^2)(i^2)(i^2)$
$$= -5(-1)(-1)(-1)$$
$$= 5$$

(5) $(3 + 2i)(2 + 3i) = 6 + \underbrace{9i + 4i}_{} + 6i^2$
$$= 6 + \quad 13i \quad - 6$$
$$= 13i$$

(6) $(2 - i)(2 + i) = 4 + 2i - 2i - i^2$
$$= 4 + 0 - (-1)$$
$$= 5$$

(7) $(5 - 4i)^2 = (5 - 4i)(5 - 4i)$
$$= (25 - 20i - 20i + 16i^2)$$
$$= 25 - 40i + 16(-1)$$
$$= 9 - 40i$$

Drill: Real and Complex Numbers

DIRECTIONS: Solve the following equations.

1. Which of the following is not a rational number:

   (A) $\dfrac{5}{9}$ (C) $-\sqrt{8}$

   (B) 4   (D) 0.375

2. If $|-a| = -a$, which of the following is false?

   (A) $a > 0$ (C) $a < 0$

   (B) $a = 0$ (D) a doesn't exist

3. $9 + \dfrac{4}{15} \times \dfrac{1}{3} \div \dfrac{4}{5} =$

   (A) 1   (C) $\dfrac{139}{36}$

   (B) $9\dfrac{1}{9}$ (D) $9\dfrac{16}{225}$

4. What percentage of 225 is 15?

   (A) $\dfrac{1}{15}\%$ (C) 15%

   (B) $6\dfrac{2}{3}\%$ (D) 150%

5. Simplify: $\left(2a^{\frac{2}{3}}\right)^{6} - 2a^{0} - (2a)^{0} =$

   (A) $16a^4 - 3$ (C) $16a^4 - 2$

   (B) $64a^4 - 2$ (D) $64a^4 - 3$

6. Evaluate $\dfrac{3}{2+i}$.

   (A) $2 - i$ (C) $6 - 2i$

   (B) $3(2 - i)$ (D) $6 - 3i$

ANSWER KEY

1. (C)
2. (A)
3. (B)

4. (A)
5. (D)
6. (A)

Detailed Explanations of Answers

Drill: Real and Complex Numbers

1. (C)

All of the other numbers can be expressed as fractions or terminating decimals.

2. (A)

If $a > 0$, then $-a$ would be a negative number, and absolute values cannot be negative.

3. (B)

The multiplication and division should be done before the addition. Remember when dividing to invert and multiply.

$$9 + \frac{4}{15} \times \frac{1}{3} \div \frac{4}{5} = 9 + \frac{4}{45} \div \frac{4}{5}$$

$$= 9 + \frac{4}{45} \times \frac{5}{4}$$

$$= 9 + \frac{1}{9}$$

$$= 9\frac{1}{9}$$

4. (A)

$$\frac{15}{225} = .06\frac{2}{3} = 6\frac{2}{3}\%$$

5. (D)

$$\left(2a^{\frac{2}{3}}\right)^6 - 2a^0 - (2a)^0 = 2^6 a^{\frac{2}{3} \times 6} - 2(1) - 1$$

$$= 64a^4 - 3$$

6. (A)

$$\frac{3}{2+i} \times \frac{2-i}{2-i} = \frac{3(2-i)}{2^2 - (-1)^2}$$

$$= \frac{3(2-i)}{4-1}$$

$$= \frac{3(2-i)}{3}$$

$$= 2 - i$$

SUBAREA II:
Patterns, Relations, and Algebra
Fields 53, 47 & 09

Algebra Vocabulary

In algebra, letters or variables are used to represent numbers. A **variable** is defined as a placeholder, which can take on any of several values at a given time. A **constant**, on the other hand, is a symbol that takes on only one value at a given time. A **term** is a constant, a variable, or a combination of constants and variables. For example: 7.76, $3x$, xyz, $\dfrac{5z}{x}$, and $(0.99)x^2$ are terms. If a term is a combination of constants and variables, the constant part of the term is referred to as the **coefficient** of the variable. If a variable is written without a coefficient, the coefficient is assumed to be 1.

• **EXAMPLES**

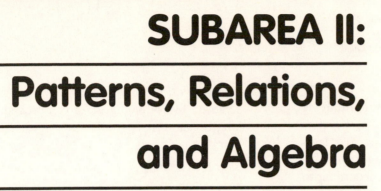

$3x^2$	y^3
coefficient: 3	coefficient: 1
variable: x	variable: y

An **expression** is a collection of one or more terms. If the number of terms is greater than 1, the expression is said to be the sum of the terms.

• **EXAMPLES**

$9, 9xy, 6x + \dfrac{x}{3}, 8yz - 2x$

An algebraic expression consisting of only one term is called a **monomial**, two terms is called a **binomial**, and three terms is called a **trinomial**. In general, an algebraic expression consisting of two or more terms is called a **polynomial**.

Operations with Polynomials

(A) **Addition of polynomials** is achieved by combining like terms, terms that differ only in their numerical coefficients, such as

$$P(x) = (x^2 - 3x + 5) + (4x^2 + 6x - 3)$$

Note that the parentheses are used to distinguish the polynomials.

By using the commutative and associative laws, we can combine like terms and rewrite $P(x)$ as:

$$P(x) = (x^2 + 4x^2) + (6x - 3x) + (5 - 3)$$

Using the distributive law, $ab + ac = a(b + c)$, yields:

$$(1 + 4)x^2 + (6 - 3)x + (5 - 3) = 5x^2 + 3x + 2$$

(B) **Subtraction of two polynomials** is achieved by first changing the sign of all terms in the expression that is being subtracted, and then adding this result to the other expression. For example,

$$(5x^2 + 4y^2 + 3z^2) - (4xy + 7y^2 - 3z^2 + 1)$$

$$= 5x^2 + 4y^2 + 3z^2 - 4xy - 7y^2 + 3z^2 - 1$$

$$= 5x^2 + (4y^2 - 7y^2) + (3z^2 + 3z^2) - 4xy - 1$$

$$= 5x^2 + (-3y^2) + 6z^2 - 4xy - 1$$

(C) **Multiplication of two or more monomials** is achieved by using the laws of exponents, the rules of signs, and the commutative and associative laws of multiplication. Begin by multiplying the coefficients and then multiply the variables according to the laws of exponents. For example,

$$(y^2)\,(5)\,(6y^2)\,(yz)\,(2z^2)$$

$$= (1)\,(5)\,(6)\,(1)\,(2)\,(y^2)\,(y^2)\,(yz)\,(z^2)$$

$$= 60[(y^2)\,(y^2)\,(y)]\,[(z)\,(z^2)]$$

$$= 60(y^5)\,(z^3)$$

$$= 60y^5z^3$$

(D) **Multiplication of a polynomial by a monomial** is achieved by multiplying each term of the polynomial by the monomial and combining the results. For example,

$$(4x^2 + 3y)\,(6xz^2) = (4x^2)\,(6xz^2) + (3y)\,(6xz^2)$$

$$= 24x^3z^2 + 18xyz^2$$

(E) **Multiplication of a polynomial by a polynomial** is achieved by multiplying each of the terms of one polynomial by each of the terms of the other polynomial and combining the result. For example,

$$(5y + z + 1)\,(y^2 + 2y)$$

$$= [(5y)\,(y^2) + (5y)\,(2y)] + [(z)\,(y^2) + (z)\,(2y)] +$$

$$[(1)\,(y^2) + (1)\,(2y)]$$

$$= (5y^3 + 10y^2) + (y^2z + 2yz) + (y^2 + 2y)$$

$$= (5y^3) + (10y^2 + y^2) + (y^2z) + (2yz) + (2y)$$

$$= 5y^3 + 11y^2 + y^2z + 2yz + 2y$$

(F) **Division of a monomial by a monomial** is achieved by first dividing the constant coefficients and the variable factors separately, and then multiplying these quotients. For example,

$$6xyz^2 \div 2y^2z = \left(\frac{6}{2}\right)\left(\frac{x}{1}\right)\left(\frac{y}{y^2}\right)\left(\frac{z^2}{z}\right)$$

$$= 3xy^{-1}z$$

$$= \frac{3xz}{y}$$

(G) **Division of a polynomial by a polynomial** is achieved by following the given procedure, called long division. It is similar to long division of real numbers.

Step 1: The terms of both the polynomials are arranged in order of ascending or descending powers of one variable.

Step 2: The first term of the dividend is divided by the first term of the divisor, which gives the first term of the quotient.

Step 3: This first term of the quotient is multiplied by the entire divisor and the result is subtracted from the dividend.

Step 4: Using the remainder obtained from Step 3 in the new dividend, Steps 2 and 3 are repeated until the remainder is zero or the degree (highest power of the variable) of the remainder is less than the degree of the divisor.

Step 5: The result is written as follows:

$$\frac{\text{dividend}}{\text{divisor}} = \text{quotient} + \frac{\text{remainder}}{\text{divisor}}$$

The divisor must not be 0.

- **EXAMPLE**

$$(2x^2 + x + 6) \div (x + 1)$$

$$
\begin{array}{r}
2x - 1 \\
x + 1 \overline{)\, 2x^2 + x + 6} \\
-(2x^2 + 2x) \\
\hline
-x + 6 \\
-(-x - 1) \\
\hline
7
\end{array}
$$

The result is:

$$(2x^2 + x + 6) \div (x + 1) = 2x - 1 + \frac{7}{x + 1}$$

Drill: Operations with Polynomials

DIRECTIONS: Perform the indicated operations.

1. $9a^2b + 3c + 2a^2b + 5c =$

   (A) $19a^2bc$
   (C) $11a^4b^2 + 8c^2$
   (B) $11a^2b + 8c$
   (D) $19a^4b^2c^2$

2. $14m^2n^3 + 6m^2n^3 + 3m^2n^3 =$

   (A) $20m^2n^3$
   (C) $23m^2n^3$
   (B) $23m^6n^9$
   (D) $32m^6n^9$

3. $3x + 2y + 16x + 3z + 6y =$

   (A) $19x + 8y$
   (C) $19x + 8y + 3z$
   (B) $19x + 11yz$
   (D) $11xy + 19xz$

4. $(4d^2 + 7e^3 + 12f) + (3d^2 + 6e^3 + 2f) =$

   (A) $23d^2e^3f$
   (C) $33d^4e^6f^2$
   (B) $33d^2e^3f$
   (D) $7d^2 + 13e^3 + 14f$

5. $3ac^2 + 2b^2c + 7ac^2 + 2ac^2 + b^2c =$

   (A) $12ac^2 + 3b^2c$
   (C) $11ac^2 + 4ab^2c$
   (B) $14ab^2c^2$
   (D) $15ab^2c^2$

6. $14m^2n - 6m^2n =$

   (A) $20m^2n$
   (C) $8m$
   (B) $8m^2n$
   (D) 8

7. $3x^3y^2 - 4xz - 6x^3y^2 =$

   (A) $-7x^2y^2z$
   (C) $-3x^3y^2 - 4xz$
   (B) $3x^3y^2 - 10x^4y^2z$
   (D) $-x^2y^2z - 6x^3y^2$

8. $9g^2 + 6h - 2g^2 - 5h =$

   (A) $15g^2h - 7g^2h$
   (C) $11g^2 + 7h$
   (B) $7g^4h^2$
   (D) $7g^2 + h$

9. $7b^3 - 4c^2 - 6b^3 + 3c^2 =$

   (A) $b^3 - c^2$
   (C) $13b^3 - c$
   (B) $-11b^2 - 3c^2$
   (D) $7b - c$

10. $11q^2r - 4q^2r - 8q^2r =$

    (A) $22q^2r$
    (C) $-2q^2r$
    (B) q^2r
    (D) $-q^2r$

11. $5p^2t \times 3p^2t =$

    (A) $15p^2t$
    (C) $15p^4t^2$
    (B) $15p^4t$
    (D) $8p^2t$

12. $(2r + s)\,14r =$

    (A) $28rs$
    (C) $16r^2 + 14rs$
    (B) $28r^2 + 14sr$
    (D) $28r + 14sr$

13. $(4m + p)(3m - 2p) =$

    (A) $12m^2 + 5mp + 2p^2$

    (B) $12m^2 - 2mp + 2p^2$

    (C) $7m - p$

    (D) $12m^2 - 5mp - 2p^2$

14. $(2a + b)(3a^2 + ab + b^2) =$

    (A) $6a^3 + 5a^2b + 3ab^2 + b^3$

    (B) $5a^3 + 3ab + b^3$

    (C) $6a^3 + 2a^2b + 2ab^2$

    (D) $3a^2 + 2a + ab + b + b^2$

15. $(6t^2 + 2t + 1)\,3t =$

    (A) $9t^2 + 5t + 3$
    (C) $9t^3 + 6t^2 + 3t$
    (B) $18t^2 + 6t + 3$
    (D) $18t^3 + 6t^2 + 3t$

16. $(x^2 + x - 6) \div (x - 2) =$

    (A) $x - 3$
    (C) $x + 3$
    (B) $x + 2$
    (D) $x - 2$

17. $24b^4c^3 \div 6b^2c =$

    (A) $3b^2c^2$
    (C) $4b^3c^2$
    (B) $4b^4c^3$
    (D) $4b^2c^2$

18. $(3p^2 + pq - 2q^2) \div (p + q) =$

    (A) $3p + 2q$ (C) $3p - q$

    (B) $2q - 3p$ (D) $3p - 2q$

19. $(y^3 - 2y^2 - y + 2) \div (y - 2)$

    (A) $(y - 1)^2$

    (B) $y^2 - 1$

    (C) $(y + 2)(y - 1)$

    (D) $(y + 1)^2$

20. $(m^2 + m - 14) \div (m + 4) =$

    (A) $m - 2$ (C) $m - 3 + \dfrac{4}{m + 4}$

    (B) $m - 3 + \dfrac{-2}{m + 4}$ (D) $m - 3$

Simplifying Algebraic Expressions

To factor a polynomial completely is to find the prime factors of the polynomial with respect to a specified set of numbers.

The following concepts are important when factoring or simplifying expressions.

(A) The factors of an algebraic expression consist of two or more algebraic expressions that, when multiplied together, produce the given algebraic expression.

(B) A **prime factor** is a polynomial with no factors other than itself and 1. The **least common multiple (LCM)** for a set of numbers is the smallest quantity divisible by every number of the set. For algebraic expressions, the least common numerical coefficients for each of the given expressions will be a factor.

(C) The **greatest common factor (GCF)** for a set of numbers is the largest factor that is common to all members of the set.

(D) For algebraic expressions, the greatest common factor is the polynomial of highest degree and the largest numerical coefficient that is a factor of all the given expressions.

Some important formulas, useful for factoring polynomials, are listed below. It is important to know the first five of these; most of the others are variations of these five and the last two.

$ac + ad = a(c + d)$ (common factor)

$a^2 - b^2 = (a + b)(a - b)$ (difference of two squares)

$a^2 + 2ab + b^2 = (a + b)(a + b) = (a + b)^2$
  (square of a sum)

$a^2 - 2ab + b^2 = (a - b)(a - b)$
$\qquad\qquad = (a - b)^2$
  (square of a difference)

$x^2 + (a + b)x + ab = (x + a)(x + b)$
  (simple quadratic)

$acx^2 + (ad + bc)x + bd = (ax + b)(cx + d)$

$ac + bc + ad + bd = (a + b)(c + d)$

$a^3 + 3a^2b + 3ab^2 + b^3 = (a + b)(a + b)(a + b)$
$\qquad\qquad = (a + b)^3$

$a^3 - 3a^2b + 3ab^2 - b^3 = (a - b)(a - b)(a - b)$
$\qquad\qquad = (a - b)^3$

$a^3 - b^3 = (a - b)(a^2 + ab + b^2)$

$a^3 + b^3 = (a + b)(a^2 - ab + b^2)$

$a^2 + b^2 + c^2 + 2ab + 2ac + 2bc = (a + b + c)^2$

$a^4 - b^4 = (a - b)(a^3 + a^2b + ab^2 + b^3)$

$a^5 - b^5 = (a - b)(a^4 + a^3b + a^2b^2 + ab^3 + b^4)$

$a^6 - b^6 = (a - b)(a^5 + a^4b + a^3b^2 + a^2b^3 + ab^4 + b^5)$

$a^n - b^n = (a - b)(a^{n-1} + a^{n-2}b + a^{n-3}b^2 + \ldots$
$\qquad + ab^{n-2} + b^{n-1})$

where n is any positive integer $(1, 2, 3, 4, \ldots)$.

$a^n + b^n = (a + b)(a^{n-1} - a^{n-2}b + a^{n-3}b^2 - \ldots$
$\qquad - ab^{n-2} + b^{n-1})$

where n is any positive odd integer $(1, 3, 5, 7, \ldots)$.

The procedure for factoring an algebraic expression completely is as follows:

Step 1: First find the greatest common factors if there are any. Combine any like terms.

Step 2: Continue factoring the factors obtained in Step 1 by using the formulas or GCFs until all factors other than monomial factors are prime.

• **EXAMPLE**

Factoring $4 - 16x^2$,

$4 - 16x^2 = 4(1 - 4x^2)$

Recognizing $(1 - 4x^2)$ as the difference between two squares yields

$4(1 + 2x)(1 - 2x)$

PROBLEMS

Express each of the following in simplest terms.

(1) $3x^2 + 2x^2 - 4x^2$

(2) $5axy^2 - 7axy^2 - 3xy^2$

SOLUTIONS

(1) Factor x^2 in the expression.

$3x^2 + 2x^2 - 4x^2 = (3 + 2 - 4)x^2 = 1x^2 = x^2$

(2) Factor xy^2 in the expression and then factor a.

$5axy^2 - 7axy^2 - 3xy^2 = (5a - 7a - 3)xy^2$

$= [(5 - 7)a - 3]xy^2$

$= (-2a - 3)xy^2$

PROBLEM

Simplify $\dfrac{\frac{1}{x-1} - \frac{1}{x-2}}{\frac{1}{x-2} - \frac{1}{x-3}}$.

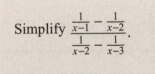

SOLUTION

Simplify the expression in the numerator by using the addition rule:

$\dfrac{a}{b} + \dfrac{c}{d} = \dfrac{ad + bc}{bd}$

Notice bd is the least common denominator, LCD. For the numerator, we obtain

$\dfrac{x - 2 - (x - 1)}{(x - 1)(x - 2)} = \dfrac{-1}{(x - 1)(x - 2)}.$

Repeat this procedure for the expression in the denominator:

$\dfrac{x - 3 - (x - 2)}{(x - 2)(x - 3)} = \dfrac{-1}{(x - 2)(x - 3)}$

We now have

$$\dfrac{\left(\dfrac{-1}{(x - 1)(x - 2)}\right)}{\left(\dfrac{-1}{(x - 2)(x - 3)}\right)}$$

which is simplified by inverting the fraction in the denominator, multiplying it by the numerator, and canceling like terms:

$$\dfrac{-1}{(x - 1)(x - 2)} \times \dfrac{(x - 2)(x - 3)}{-1} = \dfrac{x - 3}{x - 1}$$

Drill: Simplifying Algebraic Expressions

DIRECTIONS: Simplify the following expressions.

1. $16b^2 - 25z^2 =$

   (A) $(4b - 5z)^2$ (C) $(4b - 5z)(4b + 5z)$

   (B) $(4b + 5z)^2$ (D) $(16b - 25z)^2$

2. $x^2 - 2x - 8 =$

   (A) $(x - 4)^2$ (C) $(x + 4)(x - 2)$

   (B) $(x - 6)(x - 2)$ (D) $(x - 4)(x + 2)$

3. $2c^2 + 5cd - 3d^2 =$

   (A) $(c - 3d)(c + 2d)$

   (B) $(2c - d)(c + 3d)$

   (C) $(c - d)(2c + 3d)$

   (D) $(2c + d)(c + 3d)$

4. $4t^3 - 20t =$

  (A) $4t(t^2 - 5)$ (C) $4t(t + 4)(t - 5)$

  (B) $4t^2(t - 20)$ (D) $2t(2t^2 - 10)$

5. $x^2 + xy - 2y^2 =$

  (A) $(x - 2y)(x + y)$ (C) $(x + 2y)(x + y)$

  (B) $(x - 2y)(x - y)$ (D) $(x + 2y)(x - y)$

Linear Equations

A **linear equation** with one unknown is one that can be put into the form $ax + b = 0$, where a and b are constants, $a \neq 0$.

To solve a linear equation means to transform it into the form $x = \dfrac{-b}{a}$.

(A) If the equation has unknowns on both sides of the equality, it is convenient to put similar terms on the same sides.

•   **EXAMPLE**

$$4x + 3 = 2x + 9$$
$$4x + 3 - 2x = 2x + 9 - 2x$$
$$(4x - 2x) + 3 = (2x - 2x) + 9$$
$$2x + 3 = 0 + 9$$
$$2x + 3 - 3 = 0 + 9 - 3$$
$$2x = 6$$
$$\frac{2x}{2} = \frac{6}{2}$$
$$x = 3$$

(B) If the equation appears in fractional form, it is necessary to transform it, using cross-multiplication, and then repeat the same procedure as in (A).

•   **EXAMPLE**

To solve $\dfrac{3x + 4}{3} = \dfrac{7x + 2}{5}$, use cross-multiplication:

$$\frac{3x + 4}{3} \diagup\!\!\!\!\diagdown \frac{7x + 2}{5}$$

to obtain

$$3(7x + 2) = 5(3x + 4)$$

This is equivalent to:

$$21x + 6 = 15x + 20$$

which can be solved as in (A).

$$21x + 6 = 15x + 20$$
$$21x - 15x + 6 = 15x - 15x + 20$$
$$6x + 6 - 6 = 20 - 6$$
$$6x = 14$$
$$x = \frac{14}{6}$$
$$x = \frac{7}{3}$$

(C) If there are radicals in the equation, it is necessary to square both sides and then apply (A).

$$\sqrt{3x + 1} = 5$$
$$(\sqrt{3x + 1})^2 = 5^2$$
$$3x + 1 = 25$$
$$3x + 1 - 1 = 25 - 1$$
$$3x = 24$$
$$x = \frac{24}{3}$$
$$x = 8$$

Slope of the Line

The **slope** of the line containing two points, (x_1, y_1) and (x_2, y_2), is given by:

$$\text{Slope} = m = \frac{y_2 - y_1}{x_2 - x_1}$$

Horizontal lines have a slope of zero, and the slope of vertical lines is undefined. Parallel lines have equal slopes and perpendicular lines have slopes that are negative reciprocals of each other.

The equation of a line with slope m passing through a point $Q(x_0, y_0)$ is of the form:

$$y - y_0 = m(x - x_0)$$

This is called the **point-slope form** of a linear equation.

The equation of a line passing through $Q(x_1, y_1)$ and $P(x_2, y_2)$ is given by:

$$\frac{y - y_1}{x - x_1} = \frac{y_2 - y_1}{x_2 - x_1}$$

This is the **two-point form** of a linear equation.

The equation of a line intersecting the x-axis at $(x_0, 0)$ and the y-axis at $(0, y_0)$ is given by:

$$\frac{x}{x_0} + \frac{y}{y_0} = 1$$

This is the **intercept form** of a linear equation.

The equation of a line with slope m intersecting the y-axis at $(0, b)$ is given by:

$$y = mx + b$$

This is the **slope-intercept form** of a linear equation.

PROBLEM

Find the slope, the y-intercept, and the x-intercept of the equation $2x - 3y - 18 = 0$.

SOLUTION

The equation $2x - 3y - 18 = 0$ can be written in the form of the general linear equation, $ax + by = c$.

$$2x - 3y - 18 = 0$$

$$2x - 3y = 18$$

To find the slope and y-intercept, we derive them from the formula of the general linear equation $ax + by = c$. Dividing by b and solving for y, we obtain:

$$\frac{a}{b}x + y = \frac{c}{b}$$

$$y = \frac{c}{b} - \frac{a}{b}x$$

where $\frac{-a}{b}$ = slope and $\frac{c}{b}$ = y-intercept.

To find the x-intercept, solve for x when $y = 0$:

$$x = \frac{c}{a} - \frac{b}{a}y$$

$$x = \frac{c}{a}$$

In this form we have $a = 2$, $b = -3$, and $c = 18$. Thus,

$$\text{slope} = -\frac{a}{b} = -\frac{2}{-3} = \frac{2}{3}$$

$$y\text{-intercept} = \frac{c}{b} = \frac{18}{-3} = -6$$

$$x\text{-intercept} = \frac{c}{a} = \frac{18}{2} = 9$$

PROBLEM

Find the equation for the line passing through $(3, 5)$ and $(-1, 2)$.

SOLUTION

Method 1:

Use the two-point form with $(x_1, y_1) = (3, 5)$ and $(x_2, y_2) = (-1, 2)$. Then

$$\frac{y - y_1}{x - x_1} = \frac{y_2 - y_1}{x_2 - x_1}$$

$$\frac{y_2 - y_1}{x_2 - x_1} = \frac{2 - 5}{-1 - 3}$$

Thus

$$\frac{y - 5}{x - 3} = \frac{-3}{-4}$$

Cross multiply: $\quad -4(y - 5) = -3(x - 3)$

Distribute: $\quad -4y + 20 = -3x + 9$

Place in general form: $\quad 3x - 4y = -11$

Method 2:

Let $(x_1, y_1) = (-1, 2)$ and $(x_2, y_2) = (3, 5)$. Then

$$\frac{y_2 - y_1}{x_2 - x_1} = \frac{5 - 2}{3 - (-1)}$$

Thus

$$\frac{y - 2}{x + 1} = \frac{3}{4}$$

Cross multiply:　　　　$4(y - 2) = 3(x + 1)$

Distribute:　　　　　$3x - 4y = -11$

Place in general form:　$3x - 4y = -11$

Hence, either method results in the same equation. Keep in mind that the coefficient of the x-term should always be positive.

PROBLEMS

(a) Find the equation of the line passing through $(2, 5)$ with slope 3.

(b) Suppose a line passes through the y-axis at $(0, b)$. How can we write the equation if the point-slope form is used?

SOLUTIONS

(a) In the point-slope form, let $x_1 = 2, y_1 = 5, m = 3$.
　　The point-slope form of a line is:

$$y - y_1 = m(x - x_1)$$
$$y - 5 = 3(x - 2)$$
$$y - 5 = 3x - 6 \qquad \text{Distributive property}$$
$$y = 3x - 1 \qquad \text{Transposition}$$

(b)　　$y - b = m(x - 0)$
$$y = mx + b.$$

Notice that this is the slope-intercept form for the equation of a line.

PROBLEM

Construct the graph of the function defined by $y = 3x - 9$.

SOLUTION

This linear equation is in the slope-intercept form, $y = mx + b$.

Determining the Graph of a Linear Equation

A line can be determined by two points. Let us choose the intercepts. The x-intercept lies on the x-axis and the y-intercept is on the y-axis.

We can find the y-intercept by assigning 0 to x in the given equation and then find the x-intercept by assigning 0 to y. It is helpful to have a third point. We find a third point by assigning some value, say 4, to x and solving for y. Thus, we get Table 3.1 showing corresponding numbers:

Table 3.1

x	$y = 3x - 9$	y
0	$y = 3(0) - 9$	-9
3	$0 = 3x - 9, x = \dfrac{9}{3} = 3$	0
4	$y = 3(4) - 9$	3

The three points are $(0, -9)$, $(3, 0)$, and $(4, 3)$. Draw a line through them as in Figure 3.1 below.

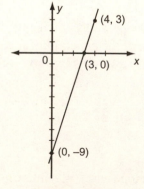

Figure 3.1

PROBLEM

Graph the function defined by $3x - 4y = 12$.

SOLUTION

Solve for y:

$$3x - 4y = 12$$
$$-4y = 12 - 3x$$
$$y = -3 + \frac{3}{4}x$$
$$y = \frac{3}{4}x - 3$$

The graph of this function is a straight line since it is of the form $y = mx + b$. The y-intercept crosses (intersects) the y-axis at the point $(0, -3)$ since for $x = 0$, $y = b = -3$. The x-intercept crosses (intersects) the x-axis at the point $(4, 0)$ since $x = (y + 3) \times \frac{4}{3}$, and for $y = 0$, $x = 3 \times \frac{4}{3} = 4$. These two points, $(0, -3)$ and $(4, 0)$ are sufficient to determine the graph (see Figure 3.2). A third point, $(8, 3)$, satisfying the equation of the function is plotted as a partial check of the intercepts. Note that the slope of the line is $m = \frac{3}{4}$. This means that y increases three units as x increases four units anywhere along the line.

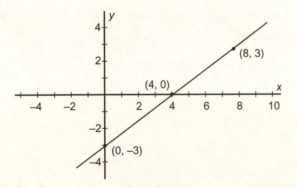

Figure 3.2

Two Linear Equations

Equations of the form $ax + by = c$, where a, b, and c are constants and a, $b \neq 0$ are called **linear equations** with two unknown variables.

There are several ways to solve systems of two linear equations with two variables.

Method 1: **Addition or subtraction**—If necessary, multiply the equations by numbers that will make the coefficients of one unknown in the resulting equations numerically equal. If the signs of equal coefficients are the same, subtract the equations; otherwise, add.

The result is one equation with one unknown; we solve it and substitute the value into the original equations to find the unknown that we first eliminated.

Method 2: **Substitution**—Find the value of one unknown in terms of the other. Substitute this value in the other equation and solve.

Method 3: **Graph**—Graph both equations. The point of intersection of the drawn lines is a simultaneous solution for the equations, and its coordinates correspond to the answer that would be found analytically.

Note: If the lines are parallel they have no simultaneous solution.

Dependent equations are equations that represent the same line; therefore, every point on the line of each dependent equation represents a solution. Since there are an infinite number of points on a line, there are an infinite number of simultaneous solutions. For example,

$$\begin{cases} 2x + y = 8 \\ 4x + 2y = 16 \end{cases}$$

are dependent equations. Since they represent the same line, all points that satisfy either of the equations are solutions of the system.

A system of linear equations is **consistent** if there is only one solution for the system.

A system of linear equations is **inconsistent** if it does not have any solutions.

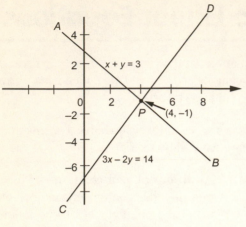

Figure 3.3

• **EXAMPLE**

Find the point of intersection of the graphs of the equations shown in Figure 3.3.

$$x + y = 3$$

$$3x - 2y = 14$$

To solve these linear equations, solve for y in terms of x. The equations will be in the form $y = mx + b$, where m is the slope and b is the intercept on the y-axis.

$$x + y = 3$$

Subtract x from both sides: $y = 3 - x$

Subtract $3x$ from both sides: $3x - 2y = 14$

Divide by -2: $-2y = 14 - 3x$

$$y = -7 + \frac{3}{2}x$$

The graphs of the linear functions, $y = 3 - x$ and $y = 7 + \frac{3}{2}x$ can be determined by plotting only two points. For example, for $y = 3 - x$, let $x = 0$, then $y = 3$. Let $x = 1$, then $y = 2$. The two points on this first line are $(0, 3)$ and $(1, 2)$. For $y = -7 + \frac{3}{2}x$, let $x = 0$, then $y = -7$. Let $x = 1$, then $y = -5\frac{1}{2}$. The two points on this second line are $(0, -7)$ and $(1, -5\frac{1}{2})$.

To find the point of intersection P of

$$x + y = 3 \text{ and } 3x - 2y = 14,$$

you can solve the equations algebraically. Multiply the first equation by 2. Add these two equations to eliminate the variable y.

$$
\begin{aligned}
2x + 2y &= 6 \\
3x - 2y &= 14 \\
\hline
5x &= 20
\end{aligned}
$$

Solve for x to obtain $x = 4$. Substitute this into $y = 3 - x$ to get $y = 3 - 4 = -1$. P is $(4, -1)$.

In Figure 3.3, AB is the graph of the first equation and CD is the graph of the second equation. The point of intersection P of the two graphs is the only point on both lines. The coordinates of P satisfy both equations and represent the desired solution of the problem. From the graph, P seems to be the point $(4, -1)$. These coordinates satisfy both equations, and hence are the exact coordinates of the point of intersection of the two lines.

To show that $(4, -1)$ satisfies both equations, substitute this point into both equations.

$x + y = 3$	$3x - 2y = 14$
$4 + (-1) = 3$	$3(4) - 2(-1) = 14$
$4 - 1 = 3$	$12 + 2 = 14$
$3 = 3$	$14 = 14$

• **EXAMPLE**

Solve the equations $2x + 3y = 6$ and $4x + 6y = 7$ simultaneously.

We have two equations and two unknowns,

$$2x + 3y = 6 \qquad (1)$$

and

$$4x + 6y = 7 \qquad (2)$$

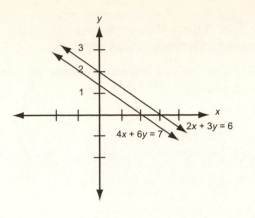

Figure 3.4

There are several methods to solve this problem. We have chosen to multiply each equation by a different number so that when the two equations are added, one of the variables drops out. Thus,

Multiply equation (1) by 2: $\quad 4x + 6y = 12 \quad$ (3)

Multiply equation (2) by -1: $\underline{-4x - 6y = -7} \quad$ (4)

Add equations (3) and (4): $\qquad 0 = 5$

We obtain a peculiar result!

Actually, what we have shown in this case is that if there were a simultaneous solution to the given equations, then 0 would equal 5. But the conclusion is impossible; therefore, there can be no simultaneous solution to these two equations, hence no point satisfying both.

The straight lines that are the graphs of these equations must be parallel if they never intersect, but not identical, which can be seen from the graph of these equations (see Figure 3.4).

• **EXAMPLE**

Solve the equations $2x + 3y = 6$ and $y = -\left(\dfrac{2x}{3}\right) + 2$ simultaneously.

We have two equations and two unknowns.

$2x + 3y = 6 \qquad\qquad$ (1)

and

$$y = -\left(\frac{2x}{3}\right) + 2 \qquad\qquad (2)$$

There are several methods of solution for this problem. Since equation (2) already gives us an expression for y, we use the method of substitution.

Substitute $-\left(\dfrac{2x}{3}\right) + 2$ for y in the first equation:

$$2x + 3(-\frac{2x}{3} + 2) = 6$$

Distribute: $\qquad 2x - 2x + 6 = 6$

$$6 = 6$$

The result $6 = 6$ is true, but indicates no solution. Actually, our work shows that no matter what real number x is, if y is determined by the second equation, then the first equation will always be satisfied.

The reason for this peculiarity may be seen if we take a closer look at the equation $y = -\left(\dfrac{2x}{3}\right) + 2$. It is equivalent to $3y = -2x + 6$, or $2x + 3y = 6$.

In other words, the two equations are equivalent. Any pair of values of x and y that satisfy one satisfy the other.

It is hardly necessary to verify that in this case the graphs of the given equations are identical lines, and that there are an infinite number of simultaneous solutions to these equations.

A system of three linear equations in three unknowns is solved by eliminating one unknown from any two of the three equations and solving them. After finding two unknowns, substitute them in any of the equations to find the third unknown.

PROBLEM

Solve the system

$2x + 3y - 4z = -8 \qquad\qquad$ (1)

$x + y - 2z = -5 \qquad\qquad$ (2)

$7x - 2y + 5z = 4 \qquad\qquad$ (3)

SOLUTION

We cannot eliminate any variable from two pairs of equations by a single multiplication. However, both x and z may be eliminated from equations (1) and (2) by multiplying equation (2) by -2, and then adding.

$$2x + 3y - 4z = -8 \qquad (1)$$

$$-2x - 2y + 4z = 10 \qquad (4)$$

By addition, we have $y = 2$. Although we may now eliminate either x or z from another pair of equations, we can more conveniently substitute $y = 2$ in equations (2) and (3) to get two equations in two variables. Thus, making the substitution $y = 2$ in equations (2) and (3), we have

$$x - 2z = -7 \qquad (5)$$

$$7x + 5z = 8 \qquad (6)$$

Multiply equation (5) by 5 and multiply (6) by 2. Then add the two new equations to get $x = -1$. Substitute $x = -1$ into either equation (5) or (6) to find $z = 3$.

The solution of the system is $x = -1$, $y = 2$, and $z = 3$. Check by substitution.

Homogeneous Systems

A system of equations that has all constant terms $b_1, b_2, \ldots, b_n$ equal to zero is said to be a **homogeneous** system.

$$\begin{cases} a_{11}x_1 + a_{12}x_2 + \ldots + a_{1n}x_m = b_1 \\ a_{21}x_1 + a_{22}x_2 + \ldots + a_{2n}x_m = b_2 \\ \vdots \qquad \vdots \qquad \qquad \vdots \\ a_{n1}x_1 + a_{n2}x_2 + \ldots + a_{nn}x_m = b_n \end{cases}$$

A homogeneous system (one in which each variable can be replaced by a constant and the constant can be factored out) always has at least one solution, which is called the trivial solution; that is, $x_1 = 0, x_2 = 0, \ldots, x_m = 0$.

For any given homogeneous system of equations, in which the number of variables is greater than or equal to the number of equations, there are nontrivial solutions.

Two systems of linear equations are said to be **equivalent** if and only if they have the same solution set.

DIRECTIONS: Find the solution set for each pair of equations.

1. $3x + 4y = -2$
    $x - 6y = -8$

    (A) $(2, -1)$ (C) $(-2, -1)$

    (B) $(1, -2)$ (D) $(-2, 1)$

2. $2x + y = -10$
    $-2x - 4y = 4$

    (A) $(6, -2)$ (C) $(-2, 6)$

    (B) $(-6, 2)$ (D) $(2, 6)$

3. $6x + 5y = -4$
    $3x - 3y = 9$

    (A) $(1, -2)$ (C) $(2, -1)$

    (B) $(1, 2)$ (D) $(-2, 1)$

4. $4x + 3y = 9$
    $2x - 2y = 8$

    (A) $(-3, 1)$ (C) $(3, 1)$

    (B) $(1, -3)$ (D) $(3, -1)$

5. $x + y = 7$
    $x = y - 3$

    (A) $(5, 2)$ (C) $(2, 5)$

    (B) $(-5, 2)$ (D) $(-2, 5)$

Quadratic Equations

A second-degree equation in x of the type $ax^2 + bx + c = 0$, where $a \neq 0$, and a, b, and c are real numbers, is called a **quadratic equation**.

Solving a quadratic equation means finding the values of x that satisfy $ax^2 + bx + c = 0$. These values of x are called **solutions**, or **roots**, of the equation.

A quadratic equation has a maximum of two roots. The methods of solving quadratic equations include:

(A) Direct solution: Given $x^2 - 9 = 0$.

We can solve directly by isolating the variable x:

$x^2 = 9$

$x = \pm 3$

(B) Factoring: Given a quadratic equation $ax^2 + bx + c = 0$, $a, b, c \neq 0$, to factor means to express it as the product $a(x - r_1)(x - r_2) = 0$, where r_1 and r_2 are the two roots.

Some helpful hints to remember are:

(a) $r_1 + r_2 = \dfrac{-b}{a}$.

(b) $r_1 \times r_2 = \dfrac{c}{a}$.

• **EXAMPLE**

Given $x^2 - 5x + 4 = 0$, find x.

Since $r_1 + r_2 = \dfrac{-b}{a} = \dfrac{-(-5)}{1} = 5$, the possible solutions are $(3, 2)$, $(4, 1)$, and $(5, 0)$. Also, $r_1 r_2 = \dfrac{c}{a} = \dfrac{4}{1} = 4$. So this equation is satisfied only by the second pair, $r_1 = 4$, $r_2 = 1$.

If the coefficient of x^2 is not 1, it is necessary to divide the equation by this coefficient and then factor.

• **EXAMPLE**

Given $2x^2 - 12x + 16 = 0$, find x.

Dividing by 2, we obtain:

$x^2 - 6x + 8 = 0$

Since $r_1 + r_2 = \dfrac{-b}{a} = 6$, the possible solutions are $(6, 0)$, $(5, 1)$, $(4, 2)$, and $(3, 3)$. Also, $r_1 r_2 = 8$, so the only possible answer is $(4, 2)$ and the expression $x^2 - 6x + 8 = 0$ can be factored as $(x - 4)(x - 2)$, with roots $x = 4$, $x = 2$.

(C) Completing the square: If it is difficult to factor the quadratic equation by using the previous method (B), we can complete the square by isolating the constant term on the right-hand side of the equation and then making the left-hand side a perfect square by taking half the coefficient of the x term, squaring it, and adding this to both sides of the equation. Then, recognizing that the left-hand side of the equation is a perfect square, take the square root of both sides to find x. Remember that the square root can be positive or negative.

• **EXAMPLE**

Given $x^2 - 12x + 8 = 0$, find x by completing the square.

Isolate the constant term,

$x^2 - 12x = -8$

Half of 12 (the coefficient of the x term) is 6, $6^2 = 36$. Add 36 to both sides of the equation:

$x^2 - 12x + 36 = -8 + 36 = 28$

Now we use the method in (B) to factor the left side: $r_1 + r_2 = 12$, $r_1 r_2 = 36$ is satisfied by the pair $(6, 6)$, so we have:

$(x - 6)(x - 6) = (x - 6)^2 = 28$.

Now we take the square root of both sides and solve for x.

$(x - 6) = \pm\sqrt{28} = \pm 2\sqrt{7}$

$x = \pm 2\sqrt{7} + 6$

So the roots are: $x = 2\sqrt{7} + 6$, $x = -2\sqrt{7} + 6$

PROBLEM

Solve $2x^2 + 8x + 4 = 0$ by completing the square.

SOLUTION

Divide all terms by 2, the coefficient of x^2.

$x^2 + 4x + 2 = 0$

Subtract the constant term, 2, from both sides.

$x^2 + 4x = -2$

Add to each side the square of one-half the coefficient of the x-term.

$x^2 + 4x + 4 = -2 + 4$

Factor.

$(x + 2)(x + 2) = (x + 2)^2 = 2$

Set the square root of the left member (a perfect square) equal to ± the square root of the right member and solve for x.

$x + 2 = \sqrt{2}$ or $x + 2 = -\sqrt{2}$

The roots are $\sqrt{2} - 2$ and $-\sqrt{2} - 2$.

Check each solution.

$2(\sqrt{2} - 2)^2 + 8(\sqrt{2} - 2) + 4$

$\qquad = 2(2 - 4\sqrt{2} + 4) + 8\sqrt{2} - 16 + 4$

$\qquad = 4 - 8\sqrt{2} + 8 + 8\sqrt{2} - 16 + 4$

$\qquad = 0$

$2(-\sqrt{2} - 2)^2 + 8(-\sqrt{2} - 2) + 4$

$\qquad = 2(2 + 4\sqrt{2} + 4) - 8\sqrt{2} - 16 + 4$

$\qquad = 4 + 8\sqrt{2} + 8 - 8\sqrt{2} - 16 + 4$

$\qquad = 0$

If these three methods don't seem to work easily, the quadratic formula *always* works to solve a quadratic equation.

Quadratic Formula

Consider the polynomial:

$ax^2 + bx + c = 0$, where $a \neq 0$.

The roots of this equation can be determined in terms of the coefficients a, b, and c by the **quadratic formula**:

$$x = \frac{-b \pm \sqrt{b^2 - 4ac}}{2a}$$

where $(b^2 - 4ac)$ is called the **discriminant** of the quadratic equation.

Note that if the discriminant is less than zero ($b^2 - 4ac < 0$), the roots are complex numbers, since the discriminant appears under a radical, square roots of negatives are complex numbers, and a real number added to an imaginary number yields a complex number.

If the discriminant is equal to zero ($b^2 - 4ac = 0$), the result is one real root.

If the discriminant is greater than zero ($b^2 - 4ac > 0$), then the roots are real and unequal. Further, the roots are rational if and only if a and b are rational and ($b^2 - 4ac$) is a perfect square; otherwise, the roots are irrational.

• **EXAMPLES**

Compute the value of the discriminant and then determine the nature of the roots of each of the following four equations:

(1) $4x^2 - 12x + 9 = 0$

(2) $3x^2 - 7x - 6 = 0$

(3) $5x^2 + 2x - 9 = 0$

(4) $x^2 + 3x + 5 = 0$

(1) $4x^2 - 12x + 9 = 0$,

Here a, b, and c are integers,

$a = 4$, $b = -12$, and $c = 9$

Therefore,

$b^2 - 4ac = (-12)^2 - 4(4)(9) = 144 - 144 = 0$

Since the discriminant is 0, the roots are rational and equal.

(2) $3x^2 - 7x - 6 = 0$

Here a, b, and c are integers,

$a = 3$, $b = -7$, and $c = -6$

Therefore,

$$b^2 - 4ac = (-7)^2 - 4(3)(-6) = 49 + 72 = 121 = 11^2$$

Since the discriminant is a perfect square, the roots are rational and unequal.

(3) $5x^2 + 2x - 9 = 0$

Here a, b, and c are integers,

$$a = 5, b = 2, \text{ and } c = -9$$

Therefore,

$$b^2 - 4ac = 2^2 - 4(5)(-9) = 4 + 180 = 184$$

Since the discriminant is greater than zero, but not a perfect square, the roots are irrational and unequal.

(4) $x^2 + 3x + 5 = 0$

Here a, b, and c are integers,

$$a = 1, b = 3, \text{ and } c = 5$$

Therefore,

$$b^2 - 4ac = 3^2 - 4(1)(5) = 9 - 20 = -11$$

Since the discriminant is negative, the roots are imaginary.

- **EXAMPLE**

Find the equation whose roots are $\dfrac{\alpha}{\beta}, \dfrac{\beta}{\alpha}$.

The roots of the equation are $x = \dfrac{\alpha}{\beta}$ and $x = \dfrac{\beta}{\alpha}$.

Subtract $\dfrac{\alpha}{\beta}$ from both sides of the first equation:

$$x - \frac{\alpha}{\beta} = \frac{\alpha}{\beta} - \frac{\alpha}{\beta} = 0, \quad \text{or} \quad x - \frac{\alpha}{\beta} = 0$$

Subtract $\dfrac{\beta}{\alpha}$ from both sides of the second equation:

$$x - \frac{\beta}{\alpha} = \frac{\beta}{\alpha} - \frac{\beta}{\alpha} = 0, \quad \text{or} \quad x - \frac{\beta}{\alpha} = 0$$

Therefore:

$$\left(x - \frac{\alpha}{\beta}\right)\left(x - \frac{\beta}{\alpha}\right) = (0)(0),$$

or

$$\left(x - \frac{\alpha}{\beta}\right)\left(x - \frac{\beta}{\alpha}\right) = 0. \tag{1}$$

Equation (1) is of the form:

$$(x - c)(x - d) = 0, \text{ or}$$
$$x^2 - cx - dx + cd = 0, \text{ or}$$
$$x^2 - (c + d)x + cd = 0. \tag{2}$$

Note that c corresponds to the root $\dfrac{\alpha}{\beta}$ and d corresponds to the root $\dfrac{\beta}{\alpha}$. The sum of the roots is:

$$c + d = \frac{\alpha}{\beta} + \frac{\beta}{\alpha} = \frac{\alpha(\alpha)}{\alpha(\beta)} + \frac{\beta(\beta)}{\beta(\alpha)} = \frac{\alpha^2}{\alpha\beta} + \frac{\beta^2}{\alpha\beta}$$

$$= \frac{\alpha^2 + \beta^2}{\alpha\beta}$$

The product of the roots is:

$$c \times d = \frac{\alpha}{\beta} \times \frac{\beta}{\alpha} = \frac{\alpha\beta}{\beta\alpha} = \frac{\alpha\beta}{\alpha\beta} = 1$$

Using the form of equation (2):

$$x^2 - \left(\frac{\alpha^2 + \beta^2}{\alpha\beta}\right)x + 1 = 0. \tag{3}$$

Multiply both sides of equation (3) by $\alpha\beta$

$$\alpha\beta\left[x^2 - \left(\frac{\alpha^2 + \beta^2}{\alpha\beta}\right)x + 1\right] = \alpha\beta(0)$$

Distribute to get

$$\alpha\beta x^2 - (\alpha^2 + \beta^2)x + \alpha\beta = 0$$

which is the equation whose roots are $\dfrac{\alpha}{\beta}, \dfrac{\beta}{\alpha}$.

Radical Equation

An equation that has one or more unknowns under a radical is called a radical equation.

To solve a radical equation, isolate the radical term on one side of the equation and move all the other terms to the other side. Then both sides of the equation are raised to a power equal to the index of the isolated radical.

After solving the resulting equation, the roots obtained must be checked, since this method often introduces extraneous roots. These introduced roots must be excluded if they are not solutions.

• **EXAMPLE**

Given $\sqrt{x^2 + 2} + 6x = x - 4$, find x.

$$\sqrt{x^2 + 2} = x - 4 - 6x = -5x - 4$$

$$\left(\sqrt{x^2 + 2}\right)^2 = (-(5x + 4))^2$$

$$x^2 + 2 = (5x + 4)^2$$

$$x^2 + 2 = 25x^2 + 40x + 16$$

$$24x^2 + 40x + 14 = 0$$

Applying the quadratic formula, we obtain:

$$x = \frac{-40 \pm \sqrt{1600 - 4(24)(14)}}{2(24)} = \frac{-40 \pm 16}{48}$$

$$x_1 = \frac{-7}{6}, \quad x_2 = \frac{-1}{2}$$

Checking roots:

$$\sqrt{\left(\frac{-7}{6}\right)^2 + 2} + 6\left(\frac{-7}{6}\right) \stackrel{?}{=} \left(\frac{-7}{6}\right) - 4$$

$$\frac{11}{6} - 7 \stackrel{?}{=} \frac{-31}{6}$$

$$\frac{-31}{6} = \frac{-31}{6}$$

$$\sqrt{\left(\frac{-1}{2}\right)^2 + 2} + 6\left(\frac{-1}{2}\right) \stackrel{?}{=} \left(\frac{-1}{2}\right) - 4$$

$$\frac{3}{2} - 3 \stackrel{?}{=} \frac{-9}{2}$$

$$\frac{-3}{2} \neq \frac{-9}{2}$$

Hence, $-\frac{1}{2}$ is not a root of the equation, but $\frac{-7}{6}$ is a root.

PROBLEM

Solve for x: $4x^2 - 7 = 0$.

SOLUTION

This quadratic equation can be solved for x by using the quadratic formula, which applies to equations in the form $ax^2 + bx + c = 0$ (in our equation $b = 0$). However, our method (A) is easier:

Adding 7 to both sides, $4x^2 = 7$

Dividing both sides by 4, $x^2 = \frac{7}{4}$

Taking the square root of both sides, $x = \pm\sqrt{\frac{7}{4}} = \pm\frac{\sqrt{7}}{2}$.

The two roots of the equation are $+\frac{\sqrt{7}}{2}$ and $-\frac{\sqrt{7}}{2}$.

PROBLEM

Solve the equation $2x^2 - 5x + 3 = 0$.

SOLUTION

$$2x^2 - 5x + 3 = 0$$

The equation is a quadratic equation of the form $ax^2 + bx + c = 0$ in which $a = 2$, $b = -5$, and $c = 3$. Therefore, the quadratic formula $x = \frac{-b \pm \sqrt{b^2 - 4ac}}{2a}$ may be used to find the solutions of the given equation. Substituting the values for a, b, and c in the quadratic formula:

$$x = \frac{-(-5) \pm \sqrt{(-5)^2 - 4(2)(3)}}{2(2)}$$

$$x = \frac{5 \pm \sqrt{1}}{4}$$

$$x = \frac{5 + 1}{4} = \frac{3}{2} \text{ and } x = \frac{5 - 1}{4} = 1$$

Check: Substituting $x = \frac{3}{2}$ in the given equation,

$$2\left(\frac{3}{2}\right)^2 - 5\left(\frac{3}{2}\right) + 3 = 0$$

$$0 = 0$$

Substituting $x = 1$ in the given equation,

$$2(1)^2 - 5(1) + 3 = 0$$

$$0 = 0$$

So the roots of $2x^2 - 5x + 3 = 0$ are $x = \dfrac{3}{2}$ and $x = 1$.

PROBLEM

Solve the equation $x^2 - x + 1 = 0$.

SOLUTION

In this equation, $a = 1$, $b = -1$, and $c = 1$. Substitute into the quadratic formula.

$$x = \frac{-(-1) \pm \sqrt{(-1)^2 - 4(1)(1)}}{2(1)}$$

$$= \frac{1 \pm \sqrt{1 - 4}}{2}$$

$$= \frac{1 \pm \sqrt{-3}}{2}$$

$$= \frac{1 \pm i\sqrt{3}}{2}$$

$$x = \frac{1 + i\sqrt{3}}{2} \text{ or } x = \frac{1 - i\sqrt{3}}{2}$$

Quadratic Functions

The function $f(x) = ax^2 + bx + c$, $a \neq 0$, where a, b, and c are real numbers, is called a quadratic function (or a function of second degree) in one unknown.

The graph of $y = ax^2 + bx + c$ is a curve known as a **parabola**.

The vertex of the parabola is the point $\left(\dfrac{-b}{2a}, \dfrac{4ac - b^2}{4a}\right)$. The parabola's axis is the line $x = \dfrac{-b}{2a}$.

The graph of the parabola opens upward if $a > 0$ and downward if $a < 0$. If $a = 0$ the quadratic is reduced to a linear function whose graph is a straight line.

The graphs in Figure 3.5 show parabolas with $a > 0$ (left), and $a < 0$ (right).

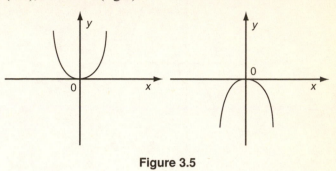

Figure 3.5

PROBLEM

Solve the system of equations

$$y = -x^2 + 7x - 5 \qquad (1)$$

$$y - 2x = 2 \qquad (2)$$

SOLUTION

Solving equation (2) for y yields an expression for y in terms of x. Substituting this expression in equation (1), we get

$$2x + 2 = -x^2 + 7x - 5 \qquad (3)$$

We now have a single equation, in terms of a single variable, to be solved. Writing equation (3) in standard quadratic form,

$$x^2 - 5x + 7 = 0 \qquad (4)$$

Since the equation is not factorable, the roots are not found by factoring. Evaluating the discriminant will indicate whether equation (4) has real roots. The discriminant, $b^2 - 4ac$, equals $(-5)^2 - 4(1)(7) = 25 - 28 = -3$. Since the discriminant is negative, equation (4) has no real roots, and therefore the system has no real solution. In terms of the graph, Figure 3.6 shows that the parabola and the straight line have no point in common.

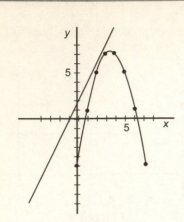

Figure 3.6

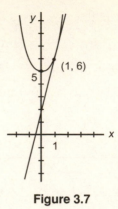

Figure 3.7

PROBLEM

Solve the system

$$y = 3x^2 - 2x + 5 \qquad (1)$$

$$y = 4x + 2 \qquad (2)$$

SOLUTION

To obtain a single equation with one unknown variable, x, substitute the value of y from equation (2) into equation (1),

$$4x + 2 = 3x^2 - 2x + 5 \qquad (3)$$

Writing equation (3) in standard quadratic form, we get

$$3x^2 - 6x + 3 = 0 \qquad (4)$$

We now may simplify equation (4) by dividing both members by 3, which is a factor common to each term:

$$x^2 - 2x + 1 = 0 \qquad (5)$$

To find the roots, factor and set each factor equal to 0. This may be done since if a product equals 0, then one or all of the factors must equal 0.

$$(x - 1)(x - 1) = 0$$
$$x - 1 = 0 \quad x - 1 = 0$$
$$x = 1 \qquad x = 1$$

Equation (5) has two equal roots, each equal to 1. For $x = 1$, from equation (2), we have $y = 4(1) + 2 = 6$. Therefore, the system has but one common solution:

$$x = 1, \quad y = 6$$

Figure 3.7 indicates that our solution is probably correct. We may also check to see whether our values satisfy equation (1) as well:

Substituting in: $y = 3x^2 - 2x + 5$

$$6 \overset{?}{=} 3(1)^2 - 2(1) + 5$$
$$6 \overset{?}{=} 3 - 2 + 5$$
$$6 = 6$$

Quadratic Equations in Two Unknowns and Systems of Equations

A quadratic equation in two unknowns has the general form:

$$ax^2 + bxy + cy^2 + dx + ey + f = 0$$

where a, b, and c are not all zero, and a, b, c, d, e, and f are constants.

If $b^2 - 4ac < 0$, $b \neq 0$, and $a \neq c$, the graph of $ax^2 + bxy + cy^2 + dx + ey + f = 0$ is a closed curve called an **ellipse**. If $b = 0$ and $a = c$, the graph $ax^2 + bxy + cy^2 + dx + ey + f = 0$ is a point or a **circle**, or else it does not exist.

If $b^2 - 4ac > 0$, the graph of $ax^2 + bxy + cy^2 + dx + ey + f = 0$ is a curve called a **hyperbola**.

If $b^2 - 4ac = 0$, the graph of $ax^2 + bxy + cy^2 + dx + ey + f = 0$ is a parabola or a pair of parallel lines that may be coincident, or else it does not exist.

Solving Systems of Equations Involving Quadratics

Some methods for solving systems of equations involving quadratics are given below:

(A) One linear and one quadratic equation

Solve the linear equation for one of the two unknowns, then substitute this value into the quadratic equation.

(B) Two quadratic equations

Eliminate one of the unknowns by using a method similar to that given for solving systems of linear equations.

- **EXAMPLE**

$$\begin{cases} x^2 + y^2 = 9 & (1) \\ x^2 + 2y^2 = 18 & (2) \end{cases}$$

By subtracting equation (1) from equation (2), we obtain $y^2 = 9$, and $y = \pm 3$.

By substituting the values of y into equation (1) or (2), we obtain:

$$x_1 = 0 \text{ and } x_2 = 0$$

So the solutions are:

$$x = 0, y = 3 \text{ and } x = 0, y = -3$$

(C) Two quadratic equations, one homogeneous

An equation is said to be **homogeneous** if it is of the form

$$ax^2 + bxy + cy^2 + dx + ey = 0$$

Consider the system

$$\begin{cases} x^2 + 3xy + 2y^2 = 0 & (1) \\ x^2 - 3xy + 2y^2 = 12 & (2) \end{cases}$$

Equation (1) can be factored into the product of two linear equations:

$$x^2 + 3xy + 2y^2 = (x + 2y)(x + y) = 0,$$

from which we determine that:

$x + 2y = 0 \Rightarrow x = -2y$ or
$x + y = 0 \Rightarrow x = -y$

By substituting $x = -2y$ into equation (2), we find:

$$(-2y)^2 - 3(-2y)y + 2y^2 = 12$$
$$4y^2 + 6y^2 + 2y^2 = 12$$
$$12y^2 = 12$$
$$y^2 = 1$$
$$y = \pm 1, \text{ so } x = \mp 2$$

Substituting $x = -y$ into equation (2) yields:

$$(-y)^2 - 3(-y)y + 2y^2 = 12$$
$$y^2 + 3y^2 + 2y^2 = 12$$
$$6y^2 = 12$$
$$y^2 = 2$$
$$y = \pm \sqrt{2}, \text{ so } x = \mp \sqrt{2}$$

Note: The sign $\mp$ means "minus or plus." Here, if y is positive, x is negative, and if y is negative, x is positive.

So the solutions of equations (1) and (2) are:

$x = 2, y = -1; x = -2, y = 1; x = \sqrt{2}, y = -\sqrt{2};$
and $x = -\sqrt{2}, y = \sqrt{2}$

(D) Two quadratic equations of the form

$$ax^2 + bxy + cy^2 = d$$

Combine the two equations to obtain a homogeneous quadratic equation, then solve the equations by the method given in (C).

(E) Two quadratic equations, each symmetrical in x and y

Note: An equation is said to be **symmetrical** in x and y if by exchanging the coefficients of x and y we obtain the same equation. An example would be $x^2 + y^2 = 9$.

To solve systems involving this type of equation, substitute $u + v$ for x and $u - v$ for y and solve the resulting equations for u and v.

- **EXAMPLE**

Given the system of symmetrical equations:

$$\begin{cases} x^2 + y^2 = 25 & (1) \\ x^2 + xy + y^2 = 37 & (2) \end{cases}$$

Substitute:

$x = u + v$

$y = u - v$

If we substitute the new values for x and y into equation (2) we obtain:

$(u + v)^2 + (u + v)(u - v) + (u - v)^2 = 37$

$u^2 + 2uv + v^2 + u^2 - v^2 + u^2 - 2uv + v^2 = 37$

$$3u^2 + v^2 = 37$$

If we substitute for x and y into equation (1), we obtain:

$$(u + v)^2 + (u - v)^2 = 25$$

$u^2 + 2uv + v^2 + u^2 - 2uv + v^2 = 25$

$$2u^2 + 2v^2 = 25$$

The "new" system is:

$3u^2 + v^2 = 37$
$2u^2 + 2v^2 = 25$

By now substituting $a = u^2$ and $b = v^2$, these equations become:

$3a + b = 37$
$2a + 2b = 25$

with solutions

$$a = \frac{9}{4}, \ b = \frac{1}{4}$$

Thus,

$$u^2 = \frac{49}{4} \ \text{and} \ v^2 = \frac{1}{4}$$

or

$$u = \pm\frac{7}{2} \ \text{and} \ v = \pm\frac{1}{2}$$

$$x = \frac{7}{2} + \frac{1}{2} = 4 \ \text{ or } \ \frac{-7}{2} - \frac{1}{2} = -4$$

$$y = \frac{7}{2} - \frac{1}{2} = 3 \ \text{ or } \ \frac{-7}{2} + \frac{1}{2} = -3$$

Since x and y are symmetrical, the possible solutions are $(4, 3)$, $(-4, -3)$, $(3, 4)$, $(-3, -4)$.

Note that if the equation is symmetrical, it is possible to interchange the solutions too. If $x = 3$, then $y = 4$ or vice versa.

PROBLEM

Solve the system:

$$2x^2 - 3xy - 4y^2 + x + y - 1 = 0$$

$$2x - y = 3$$

SOLUTION

A system of equations consisting of one linear and one quadratic is solved by expressing one of the unknowns in the linear equation in terms of the other and substituting the result in the quadratic equation. From the second equation, $y = 2x - 3$. Replacing y by this linear function of x in the first equation, we find

$2x^2 - 3x(2x - 3) - 4(2x - 3)^2 + x + (2x - 3) - 1 = 0$

$2x^2 - 3x(2x - 3) - 4(4x^2 - 12x + 9) + x + 2x - 3 - 1 = 0$

Distribute,

$2x^2 - 6x^2 + 9x - 16x^2 + 48x - 36 + x + 2x - 3 - 1 = 0$

Combine terms,

$-20x^2 + 60x - 40 = 0$

Divide both sides by –20,

$$\frac{-20x^2}{-20} + \frac{60x}{-20} - \frac{40}{-20} = \frac{0}{-20}$$

$x^2 - 3x + 2 = 0$

Factoring,

$(x - 2)(x - 1) = 0$

Setting each factor equal to zero, we obtain:

$x - 2 = 0$ $x - 1 = 0$

$x = 2$ $x = 1$

To find the corresponding y-values, substitute the x-values into $y = 2x - 3$:

when $x = 1$,   when $x = 2$,

$y = 2(1) - 3$ $y = 2(2) - 3$

$y = 2 - 3$ $y = 4 - 3$

$y = -1$ $y = 1$

Therefore, the two solutions of the system are

$(1, -1)$ and $(2, 1)$

and the solution set is $\{(1, -1), (2, 1)\}$.

PROBLEM

> Solve the system:
> $$2x^2 - 3xy + 4y^2 = 3 \quad (1)$$
> $$x^2 + xy - 8y^2 = -6 \quad (2)$$

SOLUTION

Multiply both sides of the first equation by 2.

$$2\left(2x^2 - 3xy + 4y^2\right) = 2(3)$$
$$4x^2 - 6xy + 8y^2 = 6 \quad (3)$$

Add equation (3) and equation (2):

$$
\begin{aligned}
x^2 + xy - 8y^2 &= -6 \\
4x^2 - 6xy + 8y^2 &= 6 \\
\hline
5x^2 - 5xy &= 0 \quad (4)
\end{aligned}
$$

Factoring out the common factor, $5x$, from the left side of equation (4):

$$5x(x - y) = 0$$

Whenever a product $ab = 0$, where a and b are any two numbers, either $a = 0$ or $b = 0$ or both. Hence, either

$5x = 0$ or $x - y = 0$

$x = \dfrac{0}{5}$ $x = y$

$x = 0$

Substituting $x = 0$ in equation (1):

$$2(0)^2 - 3(0)y + 4y^2 = 3$$
$$0 - 0 + 4y^2 = 3$$
$$4y^2 = 3$$
$$y^2 = \frac{3}{4}$$

$$y = \pm\sqrt{\frac{3}{4}}$$
$$= \pm\frac{\sqrt{3}}{\sqrt{4}}$$
$$= \pm\frac{\sqrt{3}}{2}$$

Hence, two solutions are $\left(0, \dfrac{\sqrt{3}}{2}\right), \left(0, -\dfrac{\sqrt{3}}{2}\right)$

Substituting x for y ($x = y$) in equation (1):

$$2x^2 - 3x(x) + 4(x)^2 = 3$$
$$2x^2 - 3x^2 + 4x^2 = 3$$
$$3x^2 = 3$$
$$x^2 = \frac{3}{3}$$
$$x^2 = 1$$
$$x = \pm\sqrt{1} = \pm 1$$

Therefore, when $x = 1$, $y = x = 1$. Also, when $x = -1$, $y = x = -1$. Hence, two other solutions are: $(1, 1)$ and $(-1, -1)$. Thus the four solutions of the system are

$$\left(0, \frac{\sqrt{3}}{2}\right), \left(0, -\frac{\sqrt{3}}{2}\right), (1, 1), \text{ and } (-1, -1)$$

Drill: Quadratic Equations

DIRECTIONS: Solve for all values of x.

1. $x^2 - 2x - 8 = 0$

   (A) 4 and –2   (C) 4

   (B) 4 and 8   (D) –2 and 8

2. $x^2 + 2x - 3 = 0$

   (A) –3 and 2   (C) 3 and 1

   (B) 2 and 1   (D) –3 and 1

3. $x^2 - 7x = -10$

   (A) –3 and 5   (C) 2

   (B) 2 and 5   (D) –2 and –5

4. $x^2 - 8x + 16 = 0$

   (A) 8 and 2   (C) 4

   (B) 1 and 16   (D) –2 and 4

5. $3x^2 + 3x = 6$

   (A) 3 and –6   (C) –3 and 2

   (B) 2 and 3   (D) 1 and –2

6. $x^2 + 16 = 0$

   (A) 64   (C) $4 \pm i$

   (B) $\pm 4i$ (D) $-4 \pm i$

7. $4y^2 + 1 = 0$

   (A) $\pm\dfrac{1}{2}$ (C) $-i \pm \dfrac{1}{2}$

   (B) $i \pm \dfrac{1}{2}$ (D) $\pm\dfrac{1}{2}i$

8. $x^2 - 4x + 13 = 0$

   (A) $3 \pm 2i$ (C) $\pm 5i$

   (B) $\pm 6i$ (D) $2 \pm 3i$

Absolute Value Equations

As shown earlier, the **absolute value** of a, $|a|$, is defined as

$|a| = a$ when $a > 0$,

$|a| = -a$ when $a < 0$,

$|a| = 0$ when $a = 0$.

When the definition of absolute value is applied to an equation, the quantity within the absolute value symbol is considered to have two values. This value can be either positive or negative before the absolute value is taken. As a result, each absolute value equation actually contains two separate equations, one using a positive value and one using a negative value.

The final step with an absolute value equation is to check the results to be sure the absolute value isn't negative.

• **EXAMPLE**

$|5 - 3x| = 7$ is valid if either

$$5 - 3x = 7 \qquad \text{or} \qquad 5 - 3x = -7$$
$$-3x = 2 \qquad\qquad\qquad -3x = -12$$
$$x = -\frac{2}{3} \qquad\qquad\qquad x = 4$$

The solution set is therefore $x = \left(-\dfrac{2}{3}, 4\right)$.

Remember, the absolute value of a number cannot be negative. So, for the equation $|5x + 4| = -3$, there would be no solution.

Drill: Absolute Value Equations

DIRECTIONS: Find the appropriate solutions.

1. $|4x - 2| = 6$

   (A) -2 and -1 (C) 2

   (B) -1 and 2   (D) No solution

2. $\left|3 - \dfrac{1}{2}y\right| = -7$

   (A) -8 and 20   (C) 2 and -5

   (B) 8 and -20 (D) No solution

3. $2|x + 7| = 12$

   (A) -13 and -1 (C) -1 and 13

   (B) -6 and 6   (D) No solution

4. $|5x| - 7 = 3$

   (A) 2 and 4   (C) -2 and 2

   (B) $\dfrac{4}{5}$ and 3   (D) No solution

5. $\left|\dfrac{3}{4}m\right| = 9$

   (A) 24 and -16 (C) -12 and 12

   (B) $\dfrac{4}{27}$ and $-\dfrac{4}{3}$ (D) No solution

Inequalities

An **inequality** is a statement in which the value of one quantity or expression is greater than ($>$), less than ($<$), greater than or equal to ($\geq$), less than or equal to ($\leq$), or not equal to ($\neq$) that of another.

• **EXAMPLE**

$5 > 4$

The expression above means that the value of 5 is greater than the value of 4.

Types of Inequalities

A **conditional inequality** is an inequality whose validity depends on the values of the variables in the expression. That is, certain values of the variables will make the expression true, and others will make it false.

$$3 - y > 3 + y$$

is a conditional inequality for the set of real numbers, since it is true for any replacement less than zero and false for all others.

$$x + 5 > x + 2$$

is an **absolute inequality** for the set of real numbers, meaning that for any real value x, the expression on the left is greater than the expression on the right.

$$5y < 2y + y$$

is inconsistent for the set of nonnegative real numbers. For any y greater than 0, the sentence is always false. An expression is **inconsistent** if it is always false when its variables assume allowable values.

The solution of a given inequality in one variable x consists of all values of x for which the inequality is true.

The graph of an inequality in one variable is represented by either a ray or a line segment on the real number line.

The endpoint is not a solution if the variable is strictly less than or greater than a particular value.

• **EXAMPLE**

$x > 2$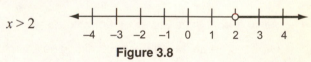

Figure 3.8

2 is not a solution and should be represented as shown in Figure 3.8.

The endpoint is a solution if the variable is either (1) less than or equal to or (2) greater than or equal to a particular value.

• **EXAMPLE**

$5 > x \geq 2$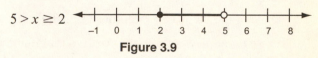

Figure 3.9

In this case, 2 is a solution and should be represented as shown in Figure 3.9.

Properties of Inequalities

If x and y are real numbers, then one and only one of the following statements is true.

$x > y$, $x = y$, or $x < y$.

This is the **order property of real numbers**.

If a, b, and c are real numbers, the following statements are true:

(A) If $a < b$ and $b < c$, then $a < c$.

(B) If $a > b$ and $b > c$, then $a > c$.

This is the **transitive property of inequalities**.

If a, b, and c are real numbers and $a > b$, then $a + c > b + c$ and $a - c > b - c$. This is the **addition property of inequality**.

Two inequalities are said to have the same **sense** if their signs of inequality point in the same direction.

The sense of an inequality remains the same if both sides are multiplied or divided by the same positive real number.

- **EXAMPLE**

$4 > 3$

If we multiply both sides by 5, we will obtain

$4 \times 5 > 3 \times 5$

$20 > 15$

The sense of the inequality does not change.

The sense of an inequality becomes opposite if each side is multiplied or divided by the same negative real number.

- **EXAMPLE**

$4 > 3$

If we multiply both sides by -5, we would obtain

$4 \times (-5) < 3 \times (-5)$

$-20 < -15$

The sense of the inequality becomes opposite.

If $a > b$ and a, b, and n are positive real numbers, then $a^n > b^n$ and $a^{-n} < b^{-n}$.

If $x > y$ and $q > p$, then $x + q > y + p$.

If $x > y > 0$ and $q > p > 0$, then $xq > yp$.

Inequalities that have the same solution set are called **equivalent inequalities.**

PROBLEM

Solve the inequality $2x + 5 > 9$.

SOLUTION

Add -5 to both sides: $2x + 5 + (-5) > 9 + (-5)$

Additive inverse property: $2x + 0 > 9 + (-5)$

Additive identity property: $2x > 9 + (-5)$

Combine terms: $2x > 4$

Multiply both sides by $\frac{1}{2}$: $\quad \frac{1}{2}(2x) > \frac{1}{2} \times 4$

$\qquad x > 2$

The solution set is

$X = \{x \,|\, 2x + 5 > 9\}$

$\quad = \{x \,|\, x > 2\}$

(that is, all x such that x is greater than 2).

Drill: Inequalities

DIRECTIONS: Find the solution set for each inequality.

1. $3m + 2 < 7$

(A) $m \geq \dfrac{5}{3}$ (C) $m < 2$

(B) $m > 2$ (D) $m < \dfrac{5}{3}$

2. $\dfrac{1}{2}x - 3 \leq 1$

(A) $-4 \leq x \leq 8$ (C) $x \leq 8$

(B) $x \geq -8$ (D) $2 \leq x \leq 8$

3. $-3p + 1 \geq 16$

(A) $p \geq -5$ (C) $p \leq \dfrac{-17}{3}$

(B) $p \geq \dfrac{-17}{3}$ (D) $p \leq -5$

4. $-6 < \dfrac{2}{3}r + 6 \le 2$

    (A) $-6 < r \le -3$ (C) $r \ge -6$

    (B) $-18 < r \le -6$ (D) $-2 < r \le -\dfrac{4}{3}$

5. $0 < 2 - y < 6$

    (A) $-4 < y < 2$ (C) $-4 < y < -2$

    (B) $-4 < y < 0$ (D) $-2 < y < 4$

Ratio, Proportion, and Variation

The **ratio** of two numbers x and y, written $x{:}y$, is the fraction $\dfrac{x}{y}$, where $y \ne 0$. A **proportion** is an equality of two ratios. The laws of proportion are listed below:

If $\dfrac{a}{b} = \dfrac{c}{d}$, then:

(A) $ad = bc$

(B) $\dfrac{b}{a} = \dfrac{d}{c}$

(C) $\dfrac{a}{c} = \dfrac{b}{d}$

(D) $\dfrac{a+b}{b} = \dfrac{c+d}{d}$

(E) $\dfrac{a-b}{b} = \dfrac{c-d}{d}$

Given a proportion $a{:}b = c{:}d$, then a and d are called the extremes, b and c are called the means, and d is called the fourth proportional to a, b, and c.

PROBLEM

Solve the proportion $\dfrac{x+1}{4} = \dfrac{15}{12}$.

SOLUTION

Cross multiply to determine x; that is, multiply the numerator of the first fraction by the denominator of the second, and equate this to the product of the numerator of the second and the denominator of the first.

$$(x+1)12 = 4 \times 15$$
$$12x + 12 = 60$$
$$x = 4$$

PROBLEM

If $\dfrac{a}{b} = \dfrac{c}{d}$, $a + b = 60$, $c = 3$, and $d = 2$, find b.

SOLUTION

We are given $\dfrac{a}{b} = \dfrac{c}{d}$. By cross multiplying, we obtain $ad = bc$.

By adding bd to both sides, we have $ad + bd = bc + bd$, which is equivalent to $d(a + b) = b(c + d)$ or

$$\dfrac{a+b}{b} = \dfrac{c+d}{d}$$

Replacing $(a + b)$ by 60, c by 3, and d by 2, we obtain

$$\dfrac{60}{b} = \dfrac{3+2}{2}$$
$$\dfrac{60}{b} = \dfrac{5}{2}$$

Cross multiplying, $5b = 120$
$$b = 24$$

Variation

(A) If x is directly proportional to y, written $x \propto y$, then $x = ky$ or $\dfrac{x}{y} = k$, where k is called the constant of proportionality or the constant of variation.

(B) If x varies inversely as y, then $x = \dfrac{k}{y}$.

(C) If x varies jointly as y and z, then $x = kyz$.

PROBLEM

> If y varies jointly as x and z, and $3x{:}1 = y{:}z$, find the constant of variation.

SOLUTION

If y varies jointly as x and z with k as the constant of variation, we can write

$y = kxz$

We are given

$3x{:}1 = y{:}z$

Expressing this ratio as a fraction,

$\dfrac{3x}{1} = \dfrac{y}{z}$

Solving for y by cross multiplying we get,

$y = 3xz$

Equating both relations for y, we have:

$kxz = 3xz$

Solving for the constant of variation, k, we divide both sides by xz, and

$k = 3$

PROBLEM

> If y varies directly with respect to x and $y = 3$ when $x = -2$, find y when $x = 8$.

SOLUTION

If y varies directly as x, then y is equal to some constant k times x; that is, $y = kx$, where k is a constant. We can now say $y_1 = kx_1$ and $y_2 = kx_2$ or $\dfrac{y_1}{x_1} = k$ and $\dfrac{y_2}{x_2} = k$, which implies $\dfrac{y_1}{x_1} = \dfrac{y_2}{x_2}$, a proportion. Thus,

$\dfrac{3}{-2} = \dfrac{y_2}{8}$.

Now we solve for y_2:

$8\left(\dfrac{3}{-2}\right) = 8\left(\dfrac{y_2}{8}\right)$

$-12 = y_2$

When $x = 8$, $y = -12$.

PROBLEM

> If y varies inversely as the cube of x, and $y = 7$ when $x = 2$, express y as a function of x.

SOLUTION

The relationship "y varies inversely with respect to x" is expressed as,

$y = \dfrac{k}{x}$

The inverse variation is now with respect to the cube of x, x^3, and we have,

$y = \dfrac{k}{x^3}$

Since $y = 7$ and $x = 2$ must satisfy this relation, we replace x and y by these values,

$7 = \dfrac{k}{2^3} = \dfrac{k}{8}$

and we find $k = 7 \times 8 = 56$. Substituting this value of k in the general relation, we get,

$y = \dfrac{56}{x^3}$

which expresses y as a function of x. We may now, in addition, find the value of y corresponding to any value of x. If we had the added requirement to find the value of y when $x = 1.2$, $x = 1.2$ would be substituted into the function to give

$y = \dfrac{56}{(1.2)^3} = \dfrac{56}{1.728} = 32.41$

Other expressions in use are "is proportional to" for "varies directly," and "is inversely proportional to" for "varies inversely."

Drill: Ratios and Proportions

DIRECTIONS: Find the appropriate solutions.

1. Solve for *n*: $\frac{4}{n} = \frac{8}{5}$.

    (A) 10   (C) 6

    (B) 8   (D) 2.5

2. Solve for *n*: $\frac{2}{3} = \frac{n}{72}$.

    (A) 12   (C) 64

    (B) 48   (D) 56

3. Solve for *n*. $n:12 = 3:4$.

    (A) 8   (C) 9

    (B) 1   (D) 4

4. Four out of every five students at West High take a mathematics course. If the enrollment at West is 785, how many students take mathematics?

    (A) 628   (C) 705

    (B) 157   (D) 655

5. At a factory, three out of every 1,000 parts produced are defective. In a day, the factory can produce 25,000 parts. How many of these parts would be defective?

    (A) 7   (C) 750

    (B) 75   (D) 7,500

6. A summer league softball team won 28 out of the 32 games they played. What is the ratio of games won to games played?

    (A) 4 : 5   (C) 7 : 8

    (B) 3 : 4   (D) 2 : 3

Real-World Problems Involving Proportion

PROBLEM

A chemist is preparing a chemical solution. She needs to add 3 parts sodium and 2 parts zinc to a flask of chlorine. If she has already placed 300 grams of sodium into the flask, how much zinc must she now add?

SOLUTION

Step 1 is to determine the ratio of sodium and zinc.

3 parts sodium, 2 parts zinc = 3:2

Step 2 is to write the problem as a proportion.

$$\frac{3}{2} = \frac{300}{?}$$

Step 3 is to put the proportion in the following format:

$AD = BC$ $3(?) = 2(300)$

Step 4 is to solve the right side of the proportion.

$2(300) = 600$

Step 5 is to rewrite the proportion.

$3(?) = 600$

Step 6 is to find the missing integer that solves the proportion. To do this, divide both sides by the known extreme, 3.

$$\frac{3(?)}{3} = \frac{600}{3} = 200$$

Step 7 is to rewrite the proportion.

$? = 200$

The solution is 200 grams of zinc.

PROBLEM

> An automobile dealer has to sell 3.5 cars for every 1 truck to achieve the optimum profit. This year, it is estimated that 3,500 cars will be sold. How many trucks must he sell to achieve the optimum profit?

SOLUTION

Step 1 is to determine the ratio of cars to trucks.

3.5 cars, 1 truck = 3.5:1

Make both sides of the ratio an integer. To do this, multiply both parts of the ratio by 2.

2(3.5):2(1) = 7:2

Step 2 is to write the problem as a proportion.

$$\frac{7}{2} = \frac{3,500}{?}$$

Step 3 is to put the proportion in the following format:

$AD = BC$ $7(?) = 2(3,500)$

Step 4 is to solve the right side of the proportion.

2(3,500) = 7,000

Step 5 is to rewrite the proportion.

7(?) = 7,000

Step 6 is to find the missing integer that solves the proportion. To do this, divide both sides by the known extreme, 7.

$$\frac{7(?)}{7} = \frac{7,000}{7} = 1,000$$

Step 7 is to rewrite the proportion.

? = 1,000

The solution is 1,000 trucks.

PROBLEM

> A baker is making a new recipe for chocolate chip cookies. He decides that for every 6 cups of flour, he needs to add 1 cup of sugar. He puts 30 cups of flour and 2 cups of sugar into the batter. How much more sugar does he need?

SOLUTION

Step 1 is to determine the ratio of flour to sugar.

6 cups flour, 1 cup sugar = 6:1

Step 2 is to write the problem as a proportion.

$$\frac{6}{1} = \frac{30}{?}$$

Step 3 is to put the proportion in the following format:

$AD = BC$ $6(?) = 1(30)$

Step 4 is to solve the right side of the proportion.

1(30) = 30

Step 5 is to rewrite the proportion.

6(?) = 30

Step 6 is to find the missing integer that solves the proportion.

To do this, divide both sides by the known extreme, 6.

$$\frac{6(?)}{6} = \frac{30}{6} = 5$$

Step 7 is to rewrite the proportion.

? = 5

The solution is that 5 cups of sugar must be added to the batter.

Step 8 is to determine how many more cups of sugar are needed, since 2 cups were already added.

5 − 2 = 3

The baker must still add 3 cups of sugar.

Elementary Functions

Table 3.2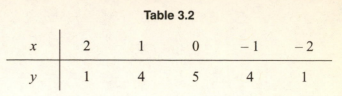

x	2	1	0	-1	-2
y	1	4	5	4	1

A **function** is any process that assigns a single value of y to each number of x. Because the value of x determines the value of y, y is called the **dependent variable** and x is called the **independent variable**. The set of all the values of x by which the function is defined is called the **domain** of the function. The set of corresponding values of y is called the **range** of the function.

The range is the set of real numbers less than or equal to 5, as can be seen from Table 3.2.

PROBLEM

PROBLEM

> Is $y^2 = x$ a function?

> Evaluate $f(1)$ for $y = f(x) = 5x + 2$.

SOLUTION

SOLUTION

Graph the equation (see Figure 3.10). Notice that x can have two values of y. Therefore, $y^2 = x$ is not a function.

$$f(x) = 5x + 2$$
$$f(1) = 5(1) + 2$$
$$= 5 + 2$$
$$= 7$$

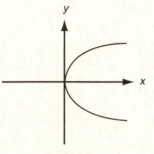

Figure 3.10

Functions can be added, subtracted, multiplied, or divided to form new functions.

(A) $(f + g)(x) = f(x) + g(x)$

(B) $(f - g)(x) = f(x) - g(x)$

(C) $(f \times g)(x) = f(x)\, g(x)$

(D) $\dfrac{f}{g}(x) = \dfrac{f(x)}{g(x)}$

PROBLEM

PROBLEMS

> Find the domain and range for $y = 5 - x^2$.

> Let $f(x) = 2x^2 - 1$ and $g(x) = 5x + 3$. Determine the following functions:
>
> (1) $f + g$ (3) $f \times g$
>
> (2) $f - g$ (4) $\dfrac{f}{g}$

SOLUTION

First determine if there are any values that would make the function undefined (i.e., dividing by 0). There are none. The domain is the set of real numbers. The range can be found by putting some values in for x.

SOLUTIONS

(1) $(f + g)(x) = f(x) + g(x) = 2x^2 - 1 + 5x + 3$
$$= 2x^2 + 5x + 2$$

(2) $(f - g)(x) = f(x) - g(x) = 2x^2 - 1 - (5x + 3)$
$$= 2x^2 - 1 - 5x - 3$$
$$= 2x^2 - 5x - 4$$

(3) $(f \times g)(x) = f(x) \, g(x) = (2x^2 - 1)(5x + 3)$
$$= 10x^3 + 6x^2 - 5x - 3$$

(4) $\left(\dfrac{f}{g}\right)(x) = \dfrac{f(x)}{g(x)} = \dfrac{(2x^2 - 1)}{5x + 3}$

Note the domain of (4) is for all real numbers except $-\dfrac{3}{5}$.

The **composite function** $f \circ g$ is defined as $(f \circ g)(x) = f(g(x))$.

PROBLEM

Given $f(x) = 3x$ and $g(x) = 4x + 2$.
Find $(f \circ g)(x)$ and $(g \circ f)(x)$.

SOLUTION

$(f \circ g)(x) = f(g(x)) = 3(4x + 2)$
$$= 12x + 6$$
$(g \circ f)(x) = g(f(x)) = 4(3x) + 2$
$$= 12x + 2$$

Note that $(f \circ g)(x) \neq (g \circ f)(x)$.

PROBLEM

Find $(f \circ g)(2)$ if
$f(x) = x^2 - 3$ and $g(x) = 3x + 1$

SOLUTION

$(f \circ g)(2) = f(g(2))$
$g(x) = 3x + 1$

Substitute 2 for the value of x.

$g(2) = 3(2) + 1$
$$= 7$$
$f(x) = x^2 - 3$

Substitute the value of $g(2)$ in $f(x)$.

$f(7) = (7)^2 - 3$
$$= 49 - 3$$
$$= 46$$

The **inverse** of a function, f^{-1}, is obtained from f by interchanging the x and y and then solving for y.

Two functions f and g are inverses of one another if $g \circ f = x$ and $f \circ g = x$. To find g when f is given, interchange x and y in the equation $y = f(x)$ and solve for $y = g(x)$. Then replace y with $f^{-1}(x)$.

PROBLEMS

Find the inverses of the functions:

(1) $f(x) = 3x + 2$

(2) $f(x) = x^2 - 3$

SOLUTIONS

(1) $f(x) = y = 3x + 2$

To find $f^{-1}(x)$, interchange x and y.

$$x = 3y + 2$$
$$3y = x - 2$$

Solve for y, then replace y with $f^{-1}(x)$.

$$f^{-1}(x) = \frac{x - 2}{3}$$

(2) $f(x) = y = x^2 - 3$.

To find $f^{-1}(x)$, interchange x and y.

$$x = y^2 - 3$$
$$y^2 = x + 3$$

Solve for y, then replace y with $f^{-1}(x)$.

$$f^{-1}(x) = \sqrt{x + 3}$$

Logarithms and Exponential Functions and Equations

An equation

$$y = b^x$$

(with $b > 0$ and $b \neq 1$) is called an **exponential function**. The exponential function with base b can be written as

$$y = f(x) = b^x.$$

The inverse of an exponential function is the **logarithmic function**,

$$f^{-1}(x) = \log_b x.$$

PROBLEM

Write the following equations in logarithmic form:

$3^4 = 81$ and $M^k = 5$.

SOLUTION

The expression $y = b^x$ is equivalent to the logarithmic expression $\log_b y = x$. Therefore, $3^4 = 81$ is equivalent to the logarithmic expression

$$\log_3 81 = 4$$

and $M^k = 5$ is equivalent to the logarithmic expression

$$\log_M 5 = k$$

PROBLEM

Find the value of $\log_5 25$ and $\log_4 x = 2$.

SOLUTION

$\log_5 25$ is equivalent to $5^x = 25$. Thus $x = 2$, since $5^2 = 25$.

$\log_4 x = 2$ is equivalent to $4^2 = x$, and $x = 16$.

Logarithm Properties

If M, N, p, and b are positive numbers and $b = 1$, then

(A) $\log_b 1 = 0$

(B) $\log_b b = 1$

(C) $\log_b b^x = x$

(D) $\log_b M N = \log_b M + \log_b N$

(E) $\log_b \dfrac{M}{N} = \log_b M - \log_b N$

(F) $\log_b M^p = p \log_b M$

PROBLEM

If $\log_{10} 3 = .4771$ and $\log_{10} 4 = .6021$, find $\log_{10} 12$.

SOLUTION

Since $12 = 4(3)$, $\log_{10} 12 = \log_{10}(4)(3)$

Remember

$$\log_b M N = \log_b M + \log_b N.$$

Therefore,

$$\log_{10} 12 = \log_{10} 4 + \log_{10} 3$$
$$= .6021 + .4771$$
$$= 1.0792$$

Properties of Functions

(A) A function F is **one-to-one** if for every range value there corresponds exactly one domain value of x.

(B) A function is said to be **even** if $f(-x) = f(x)$ or

$$f(x) + f(-x) = 2f(x).$$

(C) A function is said to be **odd** if $f(-x) = -f(x)$ or $f(x) + f(-x) = 0$.

(D) Periodicity

A function f with domain X is **periodic** if there exists a positive real number p such that $f(x + p) = f(x)$ for all $x \in X$.

The smallest number p with this property is called the **period** of f.

Over any interval of length p, the behavior of a periodic function can be completely described.

(E) Inverse of function

Assuming that f is a one-to-one function with domain X and range Y, then a function g having domain Y and range X is called the **inverse** function of f if:

$$f(g(y)) = y \text{ for every } y \in Y \text{ and}$$

$$g(f(x)) = x \text{ for every } x \in X$$

The inverse of the function f is denoted f^{-1}.

To find the inverse function f^{-1}, solve the equation $y = f(x)$ for x in terms of y.

Be careful: This solution must be a function.

(F) The **identity** function $f(x) = x$ maps every x to itself. See Figure 3.11(a).

(G) The **constant** function $f(x) = c$ for all $x \in R$. See Figure 3.11(b).

(H) The **zeros** of an arbitrary function $f(x)$ are particular values of x for which $f(x) = 0$. See Figure 3.11(c).

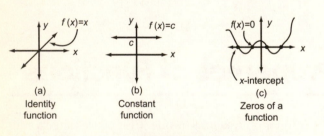

| (a) | (b) | (c) |
| Identity function | Constant function | Zeros of a function |

Figure 3.11

PROBLEM

Find the domain D and range R of the function

$$\left(x, \frac{x}{|x|} \right)$$

SOLUTION

Note that the y-value of any coordinate pair (x, y) is $\frac{x}{|x|}$. We can replace x in the formula $\frac{x}{|x|}$ with any number except 0, since the denominator, $|x|$, cannot equal 0. This is because division by 0 is undefined. Therefore, the domain D is the set of all real numbers except 0. If x is negative, i.e., $x < 0$, then $|x| = -x$ by definition. Hence, if x is negative, then $\frac{x}{|x|} = \frac{x}{-x} = -1$. If x is positive, i.e., $x > 0$, then $|x| = x$ by definition. Hence, if x is positive, then $\frac{x}{|x|} = \frac{x}{x} = 1$. (The case where $x = 0$ has already been found to be undefined). Thus, there are only two numbers, -1 and 1, in the range R of the function; that is, $R = \{-1, 1\}$.

PROBLEM

If $f(x) = 3x + 4$ and $D = \{x \mid -1 \le x \le 3\}$, find the range of $f(x)$.

SOLUTION

We first prove that the value of $3x + 4$ increases when x increases. If $X > x$, then we may multiply both sides of the inequality by a positive number to obtain an equivalent inequality. Thus, $3X > 3x$. We may also add a number to both sides of the inequality to obtain an equivalent inequality. Thus,

$$3X + 4 > 3x + 4.$$

Hence, if x belongs to D, the function value $f(x) = 3x + 4$ is least when $x = -1$ and greatest when $x = 3$. Consequently, since $f(-1) = -3 + 4 = 1$ and $f(3) = 9 + 4 = 13$, the range is all y from 1 to 13; that is,

$$R = \{y \mid 1 \le y \le 13\}.$$

Graphing a Function

The Cartesian Coordinate System

Consider two lines x and y drawn on a plane region called R.

Let the intersection of x and y be the origin and let us impose a coordinate system on each of the lines, as in Figure 3.12. This is called the **Cartesian coordinate system**.

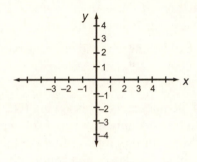

Figure 3.12

If (x, y) is a point or ordered pair on the coordinate plane R, then x is the first coordinate and y is the second coordinate.

To locate an ordered pair on the coordinate plane simply measure the distance of x units along the x-axis, then measure the y units vertically (parallel to the y-axis), as in Figure 3.13.

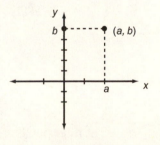

Figure 3.13

In Figure 3.14, I, II, III, and IV are called quadrants in the coordinate plane. (a, b) is an ordered pair with x-coordinate a and y-coordinate b.

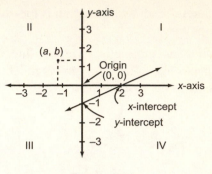

Figure 3.14

Drawing the Graph

There are several ways to plot the graph of a function. The process of computing and plotting points on the graph is always an aid in this endeavor. The more points we locate on the graph, the more accurate our drawing will be.

It is also helpful if we consider the symmetry of the function.

(A) Symmetry with respect to the y-axis occurs when both points $(-x, y)$ and (x, y) appear on the graph for every x and y in the graph (Figure 3.15(a)).

(B) A graph is symmetric with respect to the x-axis if whenever a point (x, y) is on the graph, then $(x, -y)$ is also on the graph (Figure 3.15(b)).

(C) When the simultaneous substitution of $-x$ for x and $-y$ for y does not change the solution of the equation, the graph is said to be symmetric about the origin (Figure 3.15(c)).

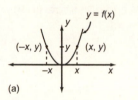

Symmetric about the y-axis

(a)

Symmetric about the x-axis
Note: This is not a function of x.

(b)

Symmetric about the origin

(c)

Figure 3.15

65

Another aid in drawing a graph is locating any vertical asymptotes.

A vertical asymptote is a vertical line $x = a$, such that the functional value $|f(x)|$ grows indefinitely large as x approaches the fixed value a.

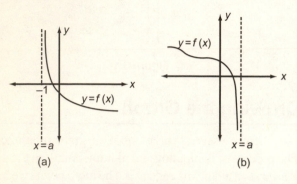

Figure 3.16

$x = a$ is a vertical asymptote for the functions in Figure 3.16.

The following steps encapsulate the procedure for drawing a graph:

(A) Determine the domain and range of the function.

(B) Find the intercepts of the graph and plot them.

(C) Determine the symmetries of the graph.

(D) Locate the vertical asymptotes and plot a few points on the graph near each asymptote.

(E) Plot additional points as needed.

PROBLEM

Construct the graph of the function defined by $y = 2x - 4$.

SOLUTION

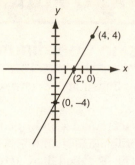

Figure 3.17

An equation of the form $y = mx + b$ is a linear equation; that is, the equation of a line.

A line can be determined by two points. Let us choose intercepts. The x-intercept lies on the x-axis and the y-intercept on the y-axis.

We find the intercepts by assigning 0 to x and solving for y and by assigning 0 to y and solving for x. It is helpful to have a third point. We find the third point by assigning a value, say 4, to x and solving for y. Thus we get Table 3.3 of corresponding numbers:

Table 3.3

x	$y = 2x - 4$	y
0	$y = 2(0) - 4 = 0 - 4 =$	-4
4	$y = 2(4) - 4 = 8 - 4 =$	4
2	$0 = 2x - 4 =$	0

Solving for x to get the x-intercept:

$$y = 2x - 4$$
$$y + 4 = 2x$$
$$x = \frac{y + 4}{2}$$

When $y = 0$, $x = \dfrac{4}{2} = 2$. The three points are $(0, -4)$, $(4, 4)$, and $(2, 0)$. Draw a line through them (see Figure 3.17).

PROBLEMS

Are the following points on the graph of the equation $3x - 2y = 0$?

(1) $(2, 3)$

(2) $(3, 2)$

(3) $(4, 6)$

SOLUTIONS

The point (a,b) lies on the graph of the equation $3x - 2y = 0$ if replacement of x and y by a and b, respectively, in the given equation results in an equation which is true.

(1) Replacing (x, y) by $(2, 3)$:

$$3x - 2y = 0$$

$$3(2) - 2(3) = 0$$

$$6 - 6 = 0$$

$$0 = 0, \text{ which is true.}$$

Therefore $(2, 3)$ is a point on the graph.

(2) Replacing (x, y) by $(3, 2)$:

$$3x - 2y = 0$$

$$3(3) - 2(2) = 0$$

$$9 - 4 = 5$$

$$5 = 0, \text{ which is not true.}$$

Therefore $(3, 2)$ is not a point on the graph.

(3) Replacing (x, y) by $(4, 6)$:

$$3x - 2y = 0$$

$$3(4) - 2(6) = 0$$

$$12 - 12 = 0$$

$$0 = 0, \text{ which is true.}$$

Therefore $(4, 6)$ is a point on the graph.

This problem may also be solved geometrically as follows: draw the graph of the line $3x - 2 = 0$ on the coordinate axes. This can be done by solving for y and plotting the points shown in Table 3.4:

Table 3.4

x	$y = \dfrac{3}{2}x$
0	0
1	$\dfrac{3}{2} = 1\dfrac{1}{2}$
2	3
−2	−3

(See Figure 3.18.)

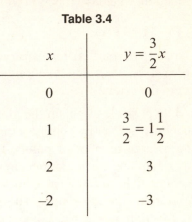

Figure 3.18

Observe that we obtain the same result as in our algebraic solution. The points $(2, 3)$ and $(4, 6)$ lie on the line $3x - 2y = 0$, whereas $(3, 2)$ does not.

Polynomial Functions and Their Graphs

A polynomial in x is an expression of the form

$$a_n x^n + a_{n-1} x^{n-1} + \ldots + a_1 x + a_0$$

where $a_1, a_2, \ldots,$ and a_n are real numbers and where all the exponents are positive integers. When $a_n \neq 0$, this polynomial is said to be of degree n. It is common to let $P(x)$ represent the polynomial. Then $y = P(x)$ is a polynomial function.

As discussed previously, a function with the property that

$$P(-x) = P(x)$$

is an even function, whereas a function with the property

$$P(-x) = -P(x)$$

is an odd function. Even functions are symmetric with respect to the y-axis, while odd functions are symmetric with respect to the origin.

It would be possible to obtain the graph of a polynomial function $y = P(x)$ by simply setting up a table and plotting a large number of points; this is how a computer or a graphing calculator operates. However, it is often desirable to have some basic information about the graph prior to plotting points. The graph of the polynomial function $y = a_0$ is a line parallel to the x-axis and $|a_0|$ units above or below the x-axis, depending on whether a_0 is positive or negative. A function of this type is called a constant function. The graph of the polynomial function

$$y = a_1 x + a_0$$

is a line with slope a_1 and with a_0 as the y-intercept. The graph of the polynomial function

$$y = a_2 x^2 + a_1 x + a_0$$

is a parabola.

It is much more difficult to graph a polynomial function with degree greater than two. The three items here should be investigated.

(1) Find lines (x-axis and y-axis) of symmetry and find out whether the origin is a point of symmetry.

(2) Find out about intercepts. The y-intercept is easy to find, but the x-intercepts are usually much more difficult to identify. If possible, factor $P(x)$.

(3) Find out what happens to $P(x)$ when $|x|$ is large.

This procedure is illustrated in the following example.

• **EXAMPLE**

Graph

$$y = x^4 - 5x^2 + 4$$

(1) The graph has symmetry with respect to the y-axis.

(2) The y-intercept is at 4. Since

$$x^4 - 5x^2 + 4 = (x^2 - 4)(x^2 - 1)$$
$$= (x - 2)(x + 2)(x - 1)(x + 1),$$

the x-intercepts are at 1, 2, –1, and –2.

(3) As $|x|$ gets large, $P(x)$ gets large.

Figure 3.19 is a sketch of the graph.

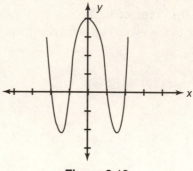

Figure 3.19

Rational Functions and Their Graphs

When $P(x)$ and $Q(x)$ are polynomials,

$$y = \frac{P(x)}{Q(x)}$$

is called a rational function. The domain of this function is the set of all real numbers x with the property that $Q(x) \neq 0$.

Graphing rational functions is rather difficult. As is the case for polynomial functions, it is desirable to have a general procedure for graphing rational functions. The suggested method for

$$y = \frac{P(x)}{Q(x)}$$

where $P(x) = a_n x^n + a_{n-1} x^{n-1} + \ldots + a_1 x + a_0$ and
$Q(x) = b_m x^m + b_{m-1} x^{m-1} + \ldots + b_1 x + b_0,$

is as follows:

(1) Find lines (x-axis and y-axis) of symmetry and determine whether the origin is a point of symmetry.

(2) Find out about intercepts. The y-intercept is at $\frac{a_0}{b_0}$ and the x-intercepts will be at values of x where $P(x) = 0$.

(3) Find vertical asymptotes. A line $x = c$ is a vertical asymptote whenever $Q(c) = 0$ and $P(c) \neq 0$.

(4) Find horizontal asymptotes

    (a) If $m = n$, then $y = \frac{a_n}{b_m}$ is the horizontal asymptote.

    (b) If $m > n$, then $y = 0$ is the horizontal asymptote.

    (c) If $m < n$, then there is no horizontal asymptote.

This procedure is illustrated in the following example.

• **EXAMPLE**

Graph

$$y = \frac{x}{(x-1)(x+3)}$$

(1) The axes are not lines of symmetry, nor is the origin a point of symmetry.

(2) The x-intercept and the y-intercept are both at the origin.

(3) The lines $x = 1$ and $x = -3$ are both vertical asymptotes.

(4) The line $y = 0$ is the horizontal asymptote.

Figure 3.20 is a sketch of the graph.

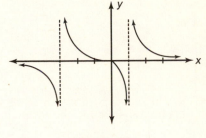

Figure 3.20

Special Functions and Their Graphs

It is possible to define a function by using different rules for different portions of the domain. The graphs of such functions are determined by graphing the different portions separately.

• **EXAMPLE**

Graph

$$f(x) = \begin{cases} x \text{ if } x \leq 1 \\ 2x \text{ if } x > 1 \end{cases}$$

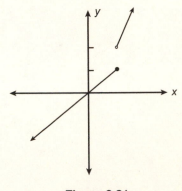

Figure 3.21

Notice on Figure 3.21 that point $(1,1)$ is part of the graph, but $(1, 2)$ is not.

Functions that involve absolute value can often be completed by translating them to a two-rule form. Consider this example.

•   **EXAMPLE**

Graph

$$f(x) = |x| - 1$$

Recall that

$$|x| = \begin{cases} x \text{ if } x \geq 0 \\ -x \text{ if } x < 0 \end{cases}$$

$f(x)$ can thus be translated to the following form.

$$f(x) = \begin{cases} x - 1 \text{ if } x \geq 0 \\ -x - 1 \text{ if } x < 0 \end{cases}$$

The graph is shown in Figure 3.22.

The greatest integer function, denoted by $f(x) = \big[|x| \big]$, is defined by $f(x) = j$, where j is the integer with the property that $j \leq x < j + 1$. The graph of this function is shown in Figure 3.23.

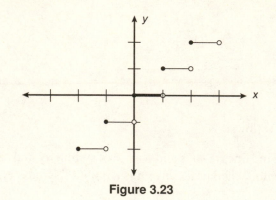

Figure 3.23

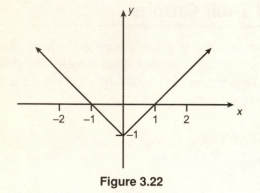

Figure 3.22

Algebra

ANSWER KEY

Drill: Operations with Polynomials

1. (B)	6. (B)	11. (C)	16. (C)
2. (C)	7. (C)	12. (B)	17. (D)
3. (C)	8. (D)	13. (D)	18. (D)
4. (D)	9. (A)	14. (A)	19. (B)
5. (A)	10. (D)	15. (D)	20. (B)

Drill: Simplifying Algebraic Expressions

1. (C)	3. (B)	5. (D)
2. (D)	4. (A)	

Drill: Two Linear Equations

1. (D)	3. (A)	5. (C)
2. (B)	4. (D)	

Drill: Quadratic Equations

1. (A)	3. (B)	5. (D)	7. (D)
2. (D)	4. (C)	6. (B)	8. (D)

Drill: Absolute Value Equations

1. (B)	3. (A)	5. (C)
2. (D)	4. (C)	

Drill: Inequalities

1. (D)	3. (D)	5. (A)
2. (C)	4. (B)	

Drill: Ratios and Proportions

1. (D)	3. (C)	5. (B)
2. (B)	4. (A)	6. (C)

Detailed Explanations of Answers

1. (B)

$$9a^2b + 3c + 2a^2b + 5c = (9a^2b + 2a^2b) + (3c + 5c)$$
$$= 11a^2b + 8c$$

2. (C)

$$14m^2n^3 + 6m^2n^3 + 3m^2n^3 = 23m^2n^3$$

3. (C)

$$3x + 2y + 16x + 3z + 6y = (3x + 16x) + (2y + 6y) + 3z$$
$$= 19x + 8y + 3z$$

4. (D)

$$(4d^2 + 7e^3 + 12f) + (3d^2 + 6e^3 + 2f) =$$
$$(4d^2 + 3d^2) + (7e^3 + 6e^3) + (12f + 2f) =$$
$$7d^2 + 13e^3 + 14f$$

5. (A)

$$3ac^2 + 2b^2c + 7ac^2 + 2ac^2 + b^2c =$$
$$(3ac^2 + 7ac^2 + 2ac^2) + (2b^2c + b^2c) =$$
$$12ac^2 + 3b^2c$$

6. (B)

$$14m^2n - 6m^2n = 8m^2n$$

7. (C)

$$3x^3y^2 - 4xz - 6x^3y^2 = (3x^3y^2 - 6x^3y^2) - 4xz$$
$$= -3x^3y^2 - 4xz$$

8. (D)

$$9g^2 + 6h - 2g^2 - 5h = (9g^2 - 2g^2) + (6h - 5h)$$
$$= 7g^2 + h$$

9. (A)

$$7b^3 - 4c^2 - 6b^3 + 3c^2 = (7b^3 - 6b^3) + (-4c^2 + 3c^2)$$
$$= b^3 - c^2$$

10. (D)

$$11q^2r - 4q^2r - 8q^2r = (11q^2r - 4q^2r) - 8q^2r$$
$$= 7q^2r - 8q^2r$$
$$= -q^2r$$

11. (C)

$$5p^2t \times 3p^2t = (5 \times 3)(p^2 \times p^2)(t \times t)$$
$$= 15p^4t^2$$

12. (B)

$$(2r + s)14r = (2r)(14r) + (s)(14r)$$
$$= 28r^2 + 14sr$$

13. (D)

$$(4m + p)(3m - 2p) = (4m)(3m) + (4m)(-2p)$$
$$+ (p)(3m) + (p)(-2p)$$
$$= 12m^2 [(-8mp) + 3mp] +$$
$$(-2p^2)$$
$$= 12m^2 - 5mp - 2p^2$$

14. (A)

$$(2a + b)(3a^2 + ab + b^2) = (2a)(3a^2) + (2a)(ab) +$$
$$(2a)(b^2) + (b)(3a^2) + (b)(ab) + (b)(b^2)$$
$$= 6a^3 + 2a^2b + 2ab^2 + 3a^2b$$
$$+ ab^2 + b^3 = 6a^3 + 5a^2b + 3ab^2 + b^3$$

15. (D)

$$(6t^2 + 2t + 1)(3t) = (6t^2)(3t) + (2t)(3t) + (1)(3t)$$
$$= 18t^3 + 6t^2 + 3t$$

16. (C)

$$(x^2 + x - 6) \div (x - 2) = \frac{x^2 + x - 6}{(x - 2)} = \frac{(x + 3)(x - 2)}{(x - 2)}$$

$$= x + 3$$

17. (D)

$$24b^4c^3 \div 6b^2c = \frac{\overset{4}{\cancel{24}} \, b^4 \, \overset{b^2 \, c^2}{\cancel{c^3}}}{\cancel{6} \, \cancel{b^2} \, \cancel{c}} = 4b^2c^2$$

18. (D)

$$(3p^2 + pq - 2q^2) \div (p + q) = \frac{3p^2 + pq - 2q^2}{(p + q)}$$

$$= \frac{(3p - 2q)(p + q)}{(p + q)}$$

$$= 3p - 2q$$

19. (B)

$$(y^3 - 2y^2 - y + 2) \div (y - 2) = y - 2 \overline{)\,y^3 - 2y^2 - y + 2\,}^{\displaystyle y^2 \quad\quad -1}$$

$$\underline{-(y^3 - 2y^2)}$$
$$0 - y + 2$$
$$\underline{-(-y + 2)}$$
$$0$$

20. (B)

$$(m^2 + m - 14) \div (m + 4) = m + 4 \overline{)\,m^2 + m - 14\,}^{\displaystyle m \quad\quad -3}$$

$$\underline{-(m^2 + 4m)}$$
$$-3m - 14$$
$$\underline{-(-3m - 12)}$$
$$-2$$

$$m - 3 + \frac{-2}{m + 4}$$

Drill: Simplifying Algebraic Expressions

1. (C)

$$16b^2 - 25z^2 = (4b + 5z)(4b - 5z)$$

2. (D)

$$x^2 - 2x - 8 = (x - 4)(x + 2)$$

3. (B)

$$2c^2 + 5cd - 3d^2 = (2c - d)(c + 3d)$$

4. (A)

$$4t^3 - 20t = 4t(t^2 - 5)$$

5. (D)

$$x^2 + xy - 2y^2 = (x - y)(x + 2y)$$

Drill: Two Linear Equations

1. (D)

Multiply the second equation by −3 and add to eliminate x.

$$
\begin{aligned}
3x + 4y &= -2 & = \quad\quad 3x + 4y &= -2 \\
-3(x - 6y &= -8) & = \quad\quad +\,-3x + 18y &= 24 \\
\hline
& & 0 + 22y &= 22 \\
& & y &= 1
\end{aligned}
$$

Substitute $y = 1$ in $x - 6y = -8$ to get

$$x - 6 = -8$$
$$\underline{+6 \quad +6}$$
$$x = -2$$

$$(-2, 1)$$

2. **(B)**

Add the equations to eliminate x.

$$2x + y = -10$$
$$\underline{-2x - 4y = 4}$$
$$0 - 3y = -6$$

$$\frac{-3y}{-3} = \frac{-6}{-3}$$

$$y = 2.$$

Substitute $y = 2$ in first equation to get

$$2x + 2 = -10$$
$$\underline{ - 2 = -2}$$
$$\frac{2x}{2} = \frac{-12}{2}$$

$$x = -6.$$

$$(-6, 2)$$

3. **(A)**

Multiply the second equation by -2 and add.

$$6x + 5y = -4 = 6x + 5y = -4$$
$$(3x - 3y = 9)(-2) = \underline{-6x + 6y = -18}$$
$$0 + 11y = -22$$
$$\frac{11y}{11} = \frac{-22}{11}$$
$$y = -2$$

Substitute $y = -2$ in the second equation to get

$$3x - 3(-2) = 9$$
$$3x + 6 = 9$$
$$\underline{ - 6 = -6}$$
$$\frac{3x}{3} = \frac{3}{3}$$
$$x = 1$$

$$(1, -2)$$

4. **(D)**

Multiply the second equation by -2 and add.

$$4x + 3y = 9 = 4x + 3y = 9$$
$$(2x - 2y = 8)(-2) = \underline{-4x + 4y = -16}$$
$$0 + 7y = -7$$
$$y = -1$$

Substitute $y = -1$ in the first equation to get

$$4x + 3(-1) = 9$$
$$4x - 3 = 9$$
$$\underline{ + 3 = +3}$$
$$\frac{4x}{4} = \frac{12}{4}$$
$$x = 3$$

$$(3, -1)$$

5. **(C)**

Rewrite the second equation in standard form and add.

$$x + y = 7 = x + y = 7$$
$$x = y - 3 = \underline{x - y = -3}$$
$$2x = 4$$
$$x = 2$$

Substitute $x = 2$ in the first equation to get

$$2 + y = 7$$

$$y = 5$$

$$(2, 5)$$

Drill: Quadratic Equations

1. **(A)**

$$(x^2 - 2x - 8) = 0$$
$$(x - 4)(x + 2) = 0$$

The values of x are 4 and -2.

2. (D)

$x^2 + 2x - 3 = 0$

$(x + 3)(x - 1) = 0$

The values of x are -3 and 1.

3. (B)

$x^2 - 7x = -10$

$x^2 - 7x + 10 = 0$

$(x - 5)(x - 2) = 0$

The values of x are 5 and 2.

4. (C)

$x^2 - 8x + 16 = 0$

$(x - 4)(x - 4) = 0$

$(x - 4)^2 = 0$

The value of x is 4.

5. (D)

$3x^2 + 3x = 6$

$3x^2 + 3x - 6 = 0$

$3(x^2 + x - 2) = 0$

$3(x + 2)(x - 1) = 0$

The values of x are -2 and 1.

6. (B)

$x^2 + 16 = 0$

$x^2 = -16$

$x^2 = (16)(-1)$

$x = \pm 4i$

7. (D)

$4y^2 + 1 = 0$

$4y^2 = -1 \Rightarrow y^2 = -\frac{1}{4} \quad y = \pm\frac{1}{2}i$

8. (D)

$x^2 - 4x + 13 = 0$

by the quadratic formula

$$\frac{-b \pm \sqrt{b^2 - 4ac}}{2a} = \frac{4 \pm \sqrt{16 - 4(1)(13)}}{2}$$

$$= \frac{4 \pm \sqrt{16 - 52}}{2}$$

$$= \frac{4 \pm \sqrt{-36}}{2}$$

$$= \frac{4 \pm 6i}{2}$$

$$= 2 \pm 3i$$

Drill: Absolute Value Equations

1. (B)

$|4x - 2| = 6 \quad 4x - 2 = 6 \text{ or } 4x - 2 = -6$

$4x = 8 \qquad 4x = -4$

$x = 2 \text{ or } \qquad x = -1$

2. (D)

$\left|3 - \frac{1}{2}y\right| = -7$

No solution. Absolute value must equal a positive number.

3. **(A)**

$$2|x + 7| = 12$$
$$|x + 7| = 6 \quad x + 7 = 6 \quad \text{or} \quad x + 7 = -6$$
$$x = -1 \quad \text{or} \quad x = -13$$

4. **(C)**

$$|5x| - 7 = 3$$
$$|5x| = 10 \quad 5x = 10 \quad \text{or} \quad 5x = -10$$
$$x = 2 \quad \text{or} \quad x = -2$$

5. **(C)**

$$\left|\frac{3}{4}m\right| = 9 \qquad \frac{3}{4}m = 9 \qquad \frac{3}{4}m = -9$$
$$\frac{4}{3}\left(\frac{3}{4}m\right) = 9\left(\frac{4}{3}\right) \quad \frac{4}{3}\left(\frac{3}{4}m\right) = (-9)\left(\frac{4}{3}\right)$$
$$m = 12 \qquad\qquad m = -12$$

Drill: Inequalities

1. **(D)**

$$3m + 2 < 7$$
$$\underline{\quad -2 \quad -2 \quad}$$
$$\left(\frac{1}{3}\right)3m \quad < 5\left(\frac{1}{3}\right)$$
$$m < \frac{5}{3}$$

2. **(C)**

$$\frac{1}{2}x - 3 \le 1$$
$$\underline{\quad +3 + 3 \quad}$$
$$\frac{1}{2}x \le 4$$
$$(2)\frac{1}{2}x \le 4(2)$$
$$x \le 8$$

3. **(D)**

$$-3p + 1 \ge 16$$
$$\underline{\quad -1 \quad -1 \quad}$$
$$-3p \ge 15$$
$$\left(-\frac{1}{3}\right)(-3p) \le 15\left(-\frac{1}{3}\right)$$
$$p \le -5$$

4. **(B)**

$$-6 < \frac{2}{3}r + 6 \le 2$$
$$\underline{-6 \qquad -6 - 6}$$
$$-12 < \frac{2}{3}r \le -4$$
$$\frac{3}{2}\left(-12 < \frac{2}{3}r \le -4\right)$$
$$-18 < r \le -6$$

5. **(A)**

$$0 < 2 - y < 6$$
$$\underline{-2 - 2 \qquad -2}$$
$$-2 < -y \quad < 4$$
$$-1(-2 < -y < 4)$$
$$2 > y > -4, \text{ or}$$
$$-4 < y < 2$$

Drill: Ratios and Proportions

1. **(D)**

$$\frac{4}{n} = \frac{8}{5} \qquad 5(4) = 8n$$
$$\left(\frac{1}{8}\right)20 = 8n\left(\frac{1}{8}\right)$$
$$\frac{20}{8} = n \Rightarrow 2.5 = n$$

2. (B)

$$\frac{2}{3} = \frac{n}{72} \qquad 2(72) = 3n$$

$$\frac{1}{3}(144) = (3n)\frac{1}{3}$$

$$(2)(24) = n$$

$$48 = n$$

5. (B)

$$3:1000 = y:25000 \Rightarrow \qquad \frac{3}{1000} = \frac{y}{25000}$$

$$(3)(25,000) = y(1000)$$

$$\frac{(3)(25,000)}{1000} = y$$

$$75 = y$$

3. (C)

$$n:12 = 3:4 \Rightarrow \quad \frac{n}{12} = \frac{3}{4}$$

$$4n = (12)(3)$$

$$4n = 36$$

$$n = 9$$

6. (C)

$$28:32 \Rightarrow \frac{28}{32} = \frac{7}{8} \Rightarrow 7:8$$

4. (A)

$$4:5 = x:785 \Rightarrow \qquad \frac{4}{5} = \frac{x}{785}$$

$$(785)(4) = 5x$$

$$\left(\frac{1}{5}\right)(785)(4) = (5x)\frac{1}{5}$$

$$(157)(4) = x$$

$$628 = x$$

SUBAREA III:
Geometry and Measurement

Fields 53, 47 & 09

Points, Lines, and Angles

Geometry is built upon a series of undefined terms. These terms are those that we accept as known in order to define other undefined terms.

(A) **Point:** Although we represent points on paper with small dots, a point has no size, thickness, or width.

(B) **Line:** A line is a series of adjacent points that extends indefinitely. A line can be either curved or straight; however, unless otherwise stated, the term "line" refers to a straight line.

(C) **Plane:** A plane is a collection of points lying on a flat surface that extends indefinitely in all directions.

Definitions

Definition 1

If A and B are two points on a line, then the **line segment** AB is the set of points on that line between A and B and including A and B, which are called the **endpoints**. The line segment is referred to as $\overline{AB}$, and is shown in Figure 4.1.

Figure 4.1

Definition 2

A **ray**, or **half-line**, is the set of all the points on a line on the same side of a dividing point. The dividing point is called the endpoint or the vertex of the ray. The ray AB shown in Figure 4.2 is denoted by $\overrightarrow{AB}$.

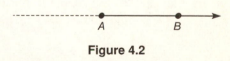

Figure 4.2

Definition 3

Three or more points are said to be **collinear** if and only if they lie on the same line.

Definition 4

Let X, Y, and Z be three collinear points, as shown in Figure 4.3. If Y is between X and Z, then $\overrightarrow{YX}$ and $\overrightarrow{YZ}$ are called **opposite rays.**

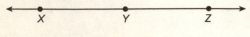

Figure 4.3

Definition 5

The **absolute value** of x, denoted by $|x|$, is defined as

$$|x| = \begin{cases} x & \text{if } x > 0 \\ 0 & \text{if } x = 0 \\ -x & \text{if } x < 0 \end{cases}$$

Definition 6

The absolute value of the difference of the coordinates of any two points on the real number line is the **distance** between those two points.

Definition 7

The **length** of a line segment is the distance between its endpoints.

Definition 8

Congruent segments are segments that have the same length. The sign for congruent is $\cong$.

Definition 9

The **midpoint** of a segment is defined as the point of the segment that divides the segment into two congruent segments. (The midpoint is said to **bisect** the segment.)

PROBLEM

Solve for x when $|x - 7| = 3$.

SOLUTION

This equation, according to the definition of absolute value, expresses the conditions that $x - 7$ must be 3 or -3, since in either case the absolute value is 3. If $x - 7 = 3$, we have $x = 10$; and if $x - 7 = -3$, we have $x = 4$. We see that there are two values of x that solve the equation.

PROBLEM

Find point C between A and B in Figure 4.4 such that $\overline{AC} \cong \overline{CB}$.

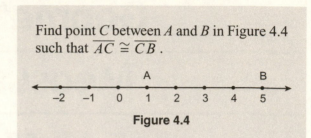

Figure 4.4

SOLUTION

We must determine point C in such a way that $\overline{AC} \cong \overline{CB}$, or $AC = CB$. We are first given that C is between A and B. Therefore, since the measure of the whole is equal to the sum of the measure of its parts:

$$AC + CB = AB \tag{1}$$

Using these two facts, we can find the length of AC. From that we can find C.

First, since $AC = CB$, we substitute AC for CB in equation (1):

$$AC + AC = AB$$

$$2(AC) = AB$$

Dividing by 2, we have

$$AC = \left(\frac{1}{2}\right) AB \tag{2}$$

To find AC, we must know AB. We can find AB from the coordinates of A and B. They are 1 and 5, respectively. Accordingly,

$$AB = |5 - 1|$$
$$= 4$$

Substitute 4 for *AB* in equation (2).

$$AC = \left(\frac{1}{2}\right)(4) \quad (4)$$

$$= 2$$

Therefore, *C* is 2 units from *A*. Since *C* is between *A* and *B*, the coordinate of *C* must be 3.

Definition 10

The **bisector** of a line segment is a line that divides the line segment into two congruent segments.

Definition 11

An **angle** is a collection of points that is the union of two rays having the same endpoint. An angle such as the one illustrated in Figure 4.5 can be referred to in any of the following ways:

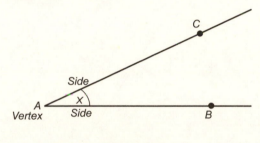

Figure 4.5

(A) By a capital letter that names its vertex, ∢*A*

(B) By a lowercase letter or number placed inside the angle, ∢*x*

(C) By three capital letters, where the middle letter is the vertex and the other two letters are not on the same ray. ∢*CAB* or ∢*BAC*, both represent the angle illustrated in Figure 4.5.

Definition 12

A set of points is **coplanar** if all the points lie in the same plane.

Definition 13

Two angles with a common vertex and a common side, but no common interior points, are called **adjacent angles.**

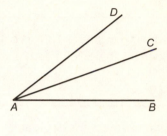

Figure 4.6

In Figure 4.6, ∢*DAC* and ∢*BAC* are adjacent angles; ∢*DAB* and ∢*BAC* are not adjacent angles.

Definition 14

Vertical angles are two angles with a common vertex and with sides that are two pairs of opposite rays.

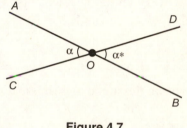

Figure 4.7

In Figure 4.7, ∢α and ∢α* are vertical angles.

Definition 15

An **acute angle** is an angle whose measure is larger than 0° but smaller than 90°.

Definition 16

An angle whose measure is 90° is called a **right angle**.

Definition 17

An **obtuse angle** is an angle whose measure is larger than 90° but less than 180°.

Definition 18

An angle whose measure is 180° is called a **straight angle**. Note: Such an angle is, in fact, a straight line.

Definition 19

An angle whose measure is greater than 180° but less than 360° is called a **reflex angle**.

Definition 20

Complementary angles are two angles, the sum of the measures of which equals 90°.

Definition 21

Supplementary angles are two angles, the sum of the measures of which equals 180°.

Definition 22

Congruent angles are angles of equal measure.

Definition 23

A ray **bisects** (is the bisector of) an angle if the ray divides the angle into two angles that have equal measure. In Figure 4.8, ray $\overrightarrow{AD}$ bisects ∡BAC.

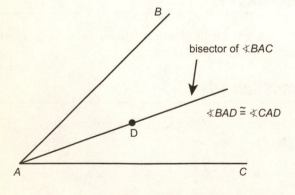

Figure 4.8

Definition 24

If the two noncommon sides of adjacent angles form opposite rays, then the angles are called a **linear pair.** Note that α and β are supplementary in Figure 4.9.

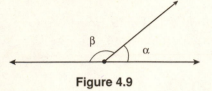

Figure 4.9

Definition 25

Two lines are said to be **perpendicular** if they intersect and form right angles. The symbol for perpendicular (or, is perpendicular to) is ⊥. $\overleftrightarrow{AB}$ is perpendicular to $\overleftrightarrow{CD}$, written as $\overleftrightarrow{AB} \perp \overleftrightarrow{CD}$, in Figure 4.10. Another word for perpendicular is **normal**.

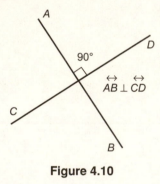

Figure 4.10

Definition 26

A line, a ray, or a line segment that bisects a line segment and is also perpendicular to that segment is called a **perpendicular bisector** of the line segment.

Definition 27

The **distance** from a point to a line is the measure of the perpendicular line segment from the point to that line. **Note:** This is the shortest possible distance from the point to the line.

Definition 28

Two or more distinct lines are said to be **parallel** (∥) if and only if they are coplanar and they do not intersect. $AB \parallel CB$ in Figure 4.11.

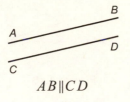

$$AB \parallel CD$$

Figure 4.11

Definition 29

The **projection of a given point** on a given line is the foot of the perpendicular drawn from the given point to the given line. It is the point where the perpendicular meets the line.

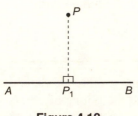

Figure 4.12

In Figure 4.12, P_1 is the projection of P on $\overleftrightarrow{AB}$.

Definition 30

The **projection of a segment** on a given line (when the segment is not perpendicular to the line) is a segment with endpoints that are the projections of the endpoints of the given line segment onto the given line.

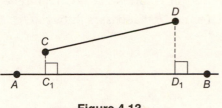

Figure 4.13

In Figure 4.13, $\overline{C_1 D_1}$ is the projection of $\overline{CD}$ onto $\overleftrightarrow{AB}$.

PROBLEM

The measure of the complement of a given angle is four times the measure of the angle. Find the measure of the given angle.

SOLUTION

By the definition of complementary angles, the sum of the measures of the two complements must equal 90°.

Accordingly,

(1) Let x = the measure of the angle

(2) Then $4x$ = the measure of the complement of this angle.

Therefore,

$$x + 4x = 90°$$
$$5x = 90°$$
$$x = 18°$$

The measure of the given angle is 18°.

PROBLEM

In Figure 4.14, we are given $\overleftrightarrow{AB}$ and triangle ABC. We are told that the measure of ∡1 is five times the measure of ∡2. Determine the measures of ∡1 and ∡2.

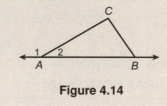

Figure 4.14

SOLUTION

Since ∡1 and ∡2 are adjacent angles whose non-common sides lie on a straight line, they are, by definition, supplementary. As supplements, their measures must sum to 180°.

If we let x = the measure of ∡1,

then $5x$ = the measure of ∡2.

To determine the respective angle measures, set $x + 5x = 180°$ and solve for x. $6x = 180°$. Therefore, $x = 30°$, and $5x = 150°$.

The measure of $\angle 1 = 150°$ and the measure of $\angle 2 = 30°$.

Postulates

Postulate 1 (The Point Uniqueness Postulate)

Let n be any positive number.

Then there exists exactly one point N on $\overrightarrow{AB}$ such that $AN = n$ (AN is the length of n). See Figure 4.15.

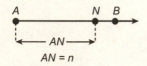

Figure 4.15

Postulate 2 (The Line Postulate)

Any two distinct points determine one and only one line that contains both points. See Figure 4.16.

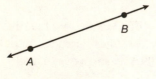

Figure 4.16

Postulate 3 (The Point Betweenness Postulate)

Let A and B be any two points. Then, there exists at least one point (and in fact an infinite number of such points) of $\overleftrightarrow{AB}$ such that P is between A and B, with $AP + PB = AB$. See Figure 4.17.

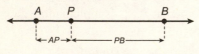

Figure 4.17

Postulate 4

Two distinct straight lines can intersect at most at only one point. See Figure 4.18.

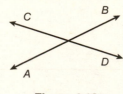

Figure 4.18

Postulate 5

The shortest line between any two points is a straight line. See Figure 4.19.

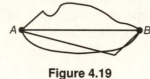

Figure 4.19

Postulate 6

There is a one-to-one correspondence between the real numbers and the points of a line. That is, to every real number, there corresponds exactly one point on the line, and to every point on the line, there corresponds exactly one real number. (In other words, a line has an infinite number of points between any two distinct points.)

Postulate 7

One and only one perpendicular can be drawn to a given line through any point on that line. Given point O on line $\overleftrightarrow{AB}$, in Figure 4.20, $\overleftrightarrow{OC}$ represents the only perpendicular to AB that passes through O.

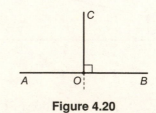

Figure 4.20

PROBLEM

In Figure 4.21, point B is between points A and C, and point E is between points D and F. Given that $\overline{AB} \cong \overline{DE}$ and $\overline{BC} \cong \overline{EF}$, prove that $\overline{AC} \cong \overline{DF}$.

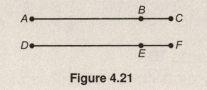

Figure 4.21

SOLUTION

Two important postulates are employed in this proof. The Point Betweenness Postulate states that if point Y is between points X and Z, then $XY + YZ = XZ$. Furthermore, the postulate states that the converse is also true—that is, if $XY + YZ = XZ$, then point Y is between points X and Z.

The Addition Postulate states that equal quantities added to equal quantities yield equal quantities. Thus, if $a = b$ and $c = d$, then $a + c = b + d$.

We present this solution as a formal proof.

Given: Point B is between A and C; point E is between points D and F; $\overline{AB} \cong \overline{DE}$; $\overline{BC} \cong \overline{EF}$

Prove: $\overline{AC} \cong \overline{DF}$.

Statement	Reason
1. (For the given, see above)	1. Given.
2. $AB = DE$ $BC = EF$	2. Congruent segments have equal lengths.
3. $AB + BC = DE + EF$	3. Addition Postulate.
4. $AC = DF$	4. Point Between Postulate.
5. $\overline{AC} \cong \overline{DF}$	5. Segments of equal length are congruent.

PROBLEM

Construct a line perpendicular to a given line through a given point on the given line.

SOLUTION

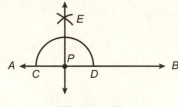

Figure 4.22

Let line $\overleftrightarrow{AB}$ and point P in Figure 4.22 be the given line and the given point, respectively.

We notice that $\sphericalangle APB$ is a straight angle. A line perpendicular to $\overleftrightarrow{AB}$ from point P will form adjacent congruent angles with $\overleftrightarrow{AB}$, by the definition of a perpendicular. Since $\sphericalangle APB$ is a straight angle, the adjacent angles will be right angles. As such, the required perpendicular is the angle bisector of $\sphericalangle APB$.

We can complete our construction by bisecting $\sphericalangle APB$.

1. Using P as the center and any convenient radius, construct an arc that intersects $\overleftrightarrow{AB}$ at points C and D.

2. With C and D as centers and with a radius greater in length than the one used in Step 1, construct arcs that intersect. The intersection point of these two arcs is point E.

3. Draw $\overleftrightarrow{EP}$.

$\overleftrightarrow{EP}$ is the required angle bisector and, as such, $\overleftrightarrow{EP} \perp \overleftrightarrow{AB}$.

PROBLEM

Present a formal proof of the following conditional statement:

If $\overleftrightarrow{CE}$ bisects $\sphericalangle ADB$, and if $\overleftrightarrow{FDB}$ and $\overleftrightarrow{CDE}$ are straight lines, then $\sphericalangle a \cong \sphericalangle x$. (Refer to Figure 4.23).

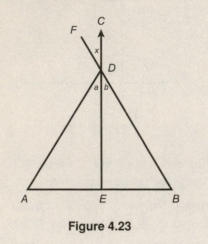

Figure 4.23

SOLUTION

In this problem, it will be necessary to recognize vertical angles and be knowledgeable of their key properties. Furthermore, we will need the definition of the bisector of an angle. The formal proof follows.

Statement	Reason
1. $\overleftrightarrow{CE}$ bisects $\sphericalangle ADB$	1. Given.
2. $\sphericalangle a \cong \sphericalangle b$	2. A bisector of an angle divides the angle into two congruent angles.
3. $\overleftrightarrow{FDB}$ and $\overleftrightarrow{CDE}$ are straight lines	3. Given.
4. $\sphericalangle x$ and $\sphericalangle b$ are vertical angles	4. Definition of vertical angles.
5. $\sphericalangle b \cong \sphericalangle x$	5. Vertical angles are congruent.
6. $\sphericalangle a \cong \sphericalangle x$	6. Transitivity property of congruence of angles.

Note that step 3 is essential because without $\overleftrightarrow{FDB}$ and $\overleftrightarrow{CDE}$ being straight lines, the definition of vertical angles would not be applicable to $\sphericalangle x$ and $\sphericalangle b$.

Postulate 8

The perpendicular bisector of a line segment is unique.

Postulate 9 (The Plane Postulate)

Any three non-collinear points determine one and only one plane that contains those three points.

Postulate 10 (The Points-in-a-Plane Postulate)

If two distinct points of a line lie in a given plane, then the line lies in that plane. See Figure 4.24.

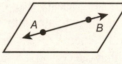

Figure 4.24

Postulate 11 (Plane Separation Postulate)

Any line in a plane separates the plane into two half planes.

Postulate 12

Given an angle, there exists one and only one real number between 0 and 180 corresponding to it.

Postulate 13 (The Angle Sum Postulate)

Referring to Figure 4.25, if A is in the interior of $\sphericalangle XYZ$, then

$$m\sphericalangle XYZ = m\sphericalangle XYA + m\sphericalangle AYZ.$$

Note: $m\sphericalangle A$ refers to the measurement of angle A.

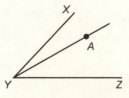

Figure 4.25

Postulate 14
(The Angle Difference Postulate)

Referring to Figure 4.26, if P is in the exterior of $\angle ABC$ and in the same half-plane (created by edge $\overleftrightarrow{BC}$) as A, then

$$m\angle ABP = m\angle PBC - m\angle ABC.$$

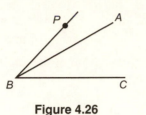

Figure 4.26

PROBLEM

In Figure 4.27, $\overline{SM}$ is the perpendicular bisector of $\overline{QR}$, and $\overline{SN}$ is the perpendicular bisector of $\overline{QP}$. Prove that $SR = SP$.

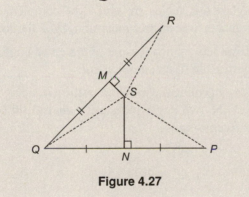

Figure 4.27

SOLUTION

Every point on the perpendicular bisector of a segment is equidistant from the endpoints of the segment.

Since point S is on the perpendicular bisector of $\overline{QR}$,

$$SR = SQ$$

Also, since point S is on the perpendicular bisector of $\overline{QP}$,

$$SQ = SP$$

By the transitive property (quantities equal to the same quantity are equal), we have:

$$SR = SP$$

PROBLEM

To construct an angle whose measure is equal to the sum of the measures of two given angles.

SOLUTION

To construct an angle equal to the sum of the measures of two given angles, we must invoke the theorem that states that the whole is equal to the sum of the parts. The construction, then, will duplicate the given angles in such a way as to form one larger angle equal in measure to the sum of the measures of the two given angles.

Two given angles, $\angle A$ and $\angle B$, are shown in Figure 4.28.

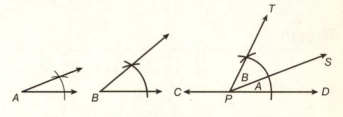

Figure 4.28

1. Construct any line $\overleftrightarrow{CD}$, and mark a point P on it.
2. At P, using $\overrightarrow{PD}$ as the base, construct $\angle DPS \cong \angle A$.
3. Now, using $\overrightarrow{PS}$ as the base, construct $\angle SPT \cong \angle B$ at point P.
4. $\angle DPT$ is the desired angle, equal in measure to $m\angle A + m\angle B$. This follows because the measure of the whole, $\angle DPT$, is equal to the sum of the measure of the parts, $\angle A$ and $\angle B$.

Theorems

Theorem 1

All right angles are equal.

Theorem 2

All straight angles are equal.

Theorem 3

Supplements of the same or equal angles are themselves equal.

Theorem 4

Complements of the same or equal angles are themselves equal.

Theorem 5

Vertical angles are equal.

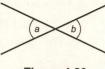

Figure 4.29

In Figure 4.29, $\angle a = \angle b$.

Theorem 6

Two supplementary angles are right angles if they have the same measure.

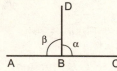

Figure 4.30

In Figure 4.30, $m\angle\alpha = m\angle\beta = 90°$.

Theorem 7

If two lines intersect and form one right angle, then the lines form four right angles.

PROBLEM

Find the measure of the angle whose measure is 40° more than the measure of its supplement.

SOLUTION

By the definition of supplementary angles, the sum of the measures of two supplements must equal 180°.

If we let x = the measure of the supplement of the angle, then $x + 40°$ = the measure of the angle.

Therefore, $x + (x + 40°) = 180°$

$$2x + 40° = 180°$$

$$2x = 140°$$

$$x = 70° \text{ and } x + 40° = 110°.$$

Therefore, the measure of the angle is 110°.

PROBLEM

What is the measure of a given angle whose measure is half the measure of its complement?

SOLUTION

When two angles are said to be complementary we know that their measures must sum, by definition, to 90°.

If we let x = the measure of the given angle, then $2x$ = the measure of its complement.

To determine the measure of the given angle, set the sum of the two angle measures equal to 90 and solve for x. Accordingly,

$$x + 2x = 90°$$

$$3x = 90°$$

$$x = 30°$$

Therefore, the measure of the given angle is 30° and its complement is 60°.

PROBLEM

Given that straight lines $\overleftrightarrow{AB}$ and $\overleftrightarrow{CD}$ intersect at point E, that $\angle BEC$ has measure 20° greater than 5 times a fixed quantity, and that $\angle AED$ has measure 60° greater than 3 times this same quantity: Find (a) the unknown fixed quantity, (b) the measure of $\angle BEC$, and (c) the measure of $\angle CEA$. (For the actual angle placement, refer to Figure 4.31.)

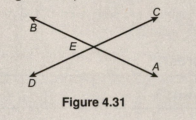

Figure 4.31

SOLUTION

(a) Since $\overleftrightarrow{AB}$ and $\overleftrightarrow{CD}$ are straight lines intersecting at point E, $\angle BEC$ and $\angle AED$ are, by definition, vertical angles. As such, they are congruent and their measures are equal. Therefore, if we let x represent the fixed quantity, $\angle BEC = 5x + 20$ and $\angle AED = 3x + 60$; according to the information given. We can then set up the following equality, and solve for the unknown quantity.

$$5x + 20 = 3x + 60$$
$$5x - 3x = 60 - 20$$
$$2x = 40$$
$$x = 20$$

Therefore, the value of the unknown quantity is 20°.

(b) From the information given about $\angle BEC$, we know that $m\angle BEC = (5x + 20)°$. By substitution, we have

$$m\angle BEC = 5(20°) + 20° = 100° + 20° = 120°.$$

Therefore, the measure of $\angle BEC$ is 120°.

(c) We know that $\overleftrightarrow{AB}$ is a straight line; therefore, $\angle CEA$ is the supplement of $\angle BEC$. Since the sum of the measure of two supplements is 180°, the following calculation can be made:

$$m\angle CEA + m\angle BEC = 180°$$
$$m\angle CEA = 180° - m\angle BEC.$$

Substituting in our value for $m\angle BEC$, we obtain:

$$m\angle CEA = 180° - 120° = 60°$$

Therefore, the measure of $\angle CEA$ is 60°.

Theorem 8

Any point on the perpendicular bisector of a given line segment is equidistant from the ends of the segment. In Figure 4.32, $\overline{PA} = \overline{PB}$.

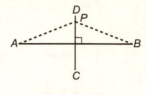

Figure 4.32

Theorem 9

If a point is equidistant from the ends of a line segment, this point must lie on the perpendicular bisector of the segment.

Theorem 10

If two points are equidistant from the ends of a line segment, these points determine the perpendicular bisector of the segment.

Theorem 11

Every line segment has exactly one midpoint.

Theorem 12

There exists one and only one perpendicular to a line through a point outside the line. In Figure 4.33, take point C outside line $\overleftrightarrow{AB}$. $\overrightarrow{OC}$ represents the only perpendicular to $\overleftrightarrow{AB}$ that passes through C.

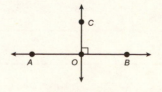

Figure 4.33

Theorem 13

If the exterior sides of adjacent angles are perpendicular to each other, then the adjacent angles are complementary.

In Figure 4.34, α and β are complementary.

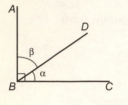

Figure 4.34

Theorem 14

Adjacent angles are supplementary if their exterior sides form a straight line.

In Figure 4.35, α and β are supplementary.

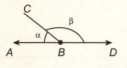

Figure 4.35

Theorem 15

Two angles that are equal and supplementary to each other are right angles.

Congruent Angles and Congruent Line Segments

Definitions

Definition 1

Two or more geometric figures are congruent when they have the same shape and size. Triangle *ABC*, congruent to triangle *DEF*, is written as $\triangle ABC \cong \triangle DEF$.

Definition 2

Two line segments are congruent if and only if they have the same measure.

Note: The expression "if and only if" can be used any time both a statement and the converse of that statement are true. We can rewrite this definition as "two line segments have the same measure if and only if they are congruent." The two statements are identical.

Definition 3

Two angles are congruent if and only if they have the same measure.

Theorems

Theorem 1

Every line segment is congruent to itself.

Theorem 2

Every angle is congruent to itself.

Let *R* be a relation on a set *A*. Then:

   R is reflexive if *aRa* for every *a* in *A*.

   R is symmetric if *aRb* implies *bRa*.

   R is antisymmetric if *aRb* and *bRa* imply *a* = *b*.

   R is transitive if *aRb* and *bRc* imply *aRc*.

Note: The term *aRa* means the relation *R* performed on *a* yields *a*. The term *aRb* means the relation *R* performed on *a* yields *b*.

Theorem 3

Given a line segment $\overline{AB}$ and a ray $\overrightarrow{XY}$, there exists one and only one point *O* on $\overrightarrow{XY}$ such that $\overline{AB} \cong \overline{XO}$. See Figure 4.36.

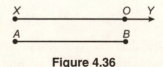

Figure 4.36

Theorem 4

If $\overline{AB} = \overline{CD}$, *Q* bisects $\overline{AB}$ and *P* bisects $\overline{CD}$, then

$\overline{AQ} \cong \overline{CP}$ and $\overline{AQ} = \overline{CP}$. See Figure 4.37.

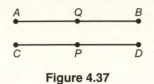

Figure 4.37

Theorem 5

If $m\angle ABC = m\angle DEF$, and $\overrightarrow{BX}$ and $\overrightarrow{EY}$ bisect $\angle ABC$ and $\angle DEF$, respectively, then $m\angle ABX = m\angle DEY = m\angle XBC = m\angle YEF$. See Figure 4.38.

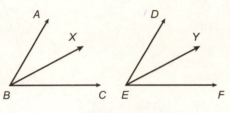

Figure 4.38

Theorem 6

Let P be in the interior of $\angle ABC$ and Q be in the interior of $\angle DEF$. If $m\angle ABP = m\angle DEQ$ and $m\angle PBC = m\angle QEF$, then $m\angle ABC = m\angle DEF$. See Figure 4.39.

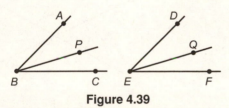

Figure 4.39

Theorem 7

Let P be in the interior of $\angle XYZ$ and Q be in the interior of $\angle ABC$. If $m\angle XYZ = m\angle ABC$ and $m\angle XYP = m\angle ABQ$ then $m\angle PYZ = m\angle QBC$. See Figure 4.40.

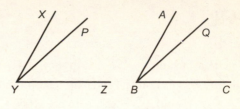

Figure 4.40

Postulates

By definition, a relation R is called an **equivalence relation** if relation R is reflexive, symmetric, and transitive.

Postulate 1

Congruence of segments is an equivalence relation.

(1) Congruence of segments is reflexive.
If $\overline{AB} \cong \overline{AB}$, $\overline{AB}$ is congruent to itself.

(2) Congruence of segments is symmetric.
If $\overline{AB} \cong \overline{CD}$, then $\overline{CD} \cong \overline{AB}$.

(3) Congruence of segments is transitive.
If $\overline{AB} \cong \overline{CD}$ and $\overline{CD} \cong \overline{EF}$, then $\overline{AB} \cong \overline{EF}$.

Postulate 2

Congruence of angles is an equivalence relation, that is, it is reflexive, symmetric, and transitive.

Postulate 3

Any geometric figure is congruent to itself.

Postulate 4

A geometric congruence may be reversed.

Postulate 5

Two geometric figures congruent to the same geometric figure are congruent to each other.

PROBLEM

Given triangle *RST* in Figure 4.41 with $\overline{RT} \cong \overline{ST}$. Points *A* and *B* lie at the midpoints of $\overline{RT}$ and $\overline{ST}$, respectively. Prove that $\overline{RA} \cong \overline{SB}$.

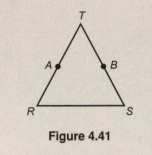

Figure 4.41

SOLUTION

This solution is best presented as a formal proof.

Statement	Reason
1. $\overline{RT} \cong \overline{ST}$ or $RT = ST$	1. Given.
2. *A* is the midpoint of $\overline{RT}$	2. Given.
3. $RA = \left(\dfrac{1}{2}\right)RT$	3. The midpoint of a line segment divides the line segment into two equal halves.
4. *B* is the midpoint of $\overline{ST}$	4. Given.
5. $SB = \left(\dfrac{1}{2}\right)ST$	5. The midpoint of a line segment divides the line segment into two equal halves.
6. $RA = SB$	6. Division Postulate: Halves of equal quantities are equal. (Statements 1, 3, and 5).
7. $\overline{RA} \cong \overline{SB}$	7. If two line segments are of equal length, then they are congruent.

Drill: Congruent Angles and Line Segments

1. Find *a* in Figure 4.42.

    (A) 38°
    (B) 68°
    (C) 78°
    (D) 90°

    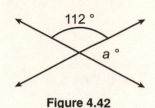

    Figure 4.42

2. Find *c* in Figure 4.43.

    (A) 32°
    (B) 48°
    (C) 58°
    (D) 82°

    Figure 4.43

3. Determine *x* in Figure 4.44.

    (A) 21°
    (B) 23°
    (C) 51°
    (D) 102°

    Figure 4.44

4. Find *z* in Figure 4.45.

    (A) 29°
    (B) 54°
    (C) 61°
    (D) 88°

    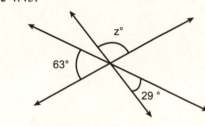

    Figure 4.45

5. In Figure 4.46, if $\overline{BD}$ is the bisector of angle ABC, and angle ABD is one-fourth the size of angle XYZ, what is the size of angle ABC?

    (A) 21°

    (B) 28°

    (C) 42°

    (D) 63°

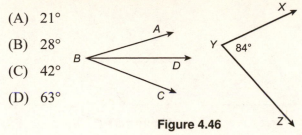

Figure 4.46

6. In Figure 4.47, $\overrightarrow{BA} \perp \overrightarrow{BC}$ and $m\angle DBC = 53°$. Find $m\angle ABD$.

    (A) 27°

    (B) 33°

    (C) 37°

    (D) 53°

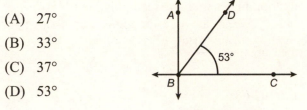

Figure 4.47

7. If $n \perp p$ in Figure 4.48, which of the following statements is true?

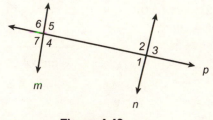

Figure 4.48

    (A) $\angle 1 \cong \angle 2$

    (B) $\angle 4 \cong \angle 5$

    (C) $m\angle 4 + m\angle 5 > m\angle 1 + m\angle 2$

    (D) $m\angle 3 > m\angle 2$

8. In Figure 4.49, if $p \perp t$ and $q \perp t$, which of the following statements is false?

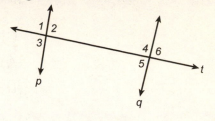

Figure 4.49

    (A) $\angle 1 \cong \angle 4$

    (B) $\angle 2 \cong \angle 3$

    (C) $m\angle 2 + m\angle 3 = m\angle 4 + m\angle 6$

    (D) $m\angle 2 > m\angle 5$

9. In Figure 4.50, if $a \| b$, find z.

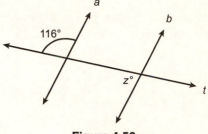

Figure 4.50

    (A) 26°   (C) 64°

    (B) 32°   (D) 86°

10. If $m \| n$ in Figure 4.51, which of the following statements is not necessarily true?

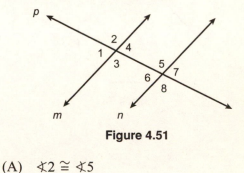

Figure 4.51

    (A) $\angle 2 \cong \angle 5$

    (B) $\angle 3 \cong \angle 6$

    (C) $m\angle 4 + m\angle 5 = 180°$

    (D) $\angle 1 \cong \angle 6$

Polygons

Regular Polygons (Convex)

A **polygon** is a closed figure with the same number of sides as angles.

An **equilateral polygon** is a polygon all of whose sides are of equal measure. See Figure 4.52.

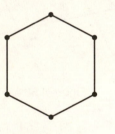

Figure 4.52

An **equiangular polygon** is a polygon all of whose angles are of equal measure. See Figure 4.53.

Figure 4.53

A **regular polygon** is a polygon that is both equilateral and equiangular. Examples of regular polygons are shown in Figure 4.54.

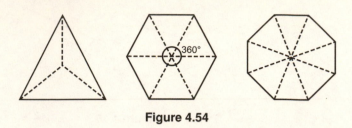

Figure 4.54

If any regular n-sided polygon is divided into n triangles whose sides are the radii and sides of the polygon, it can be seen (Figure 4.54) that the sum of the interior angles of an n-sided polygon is $180°n - 360° = (n-2)180°$, or any interior angle of an n-sided polygon measures $\dfrac{(n-2)180°}{n}$.

PROBLEM

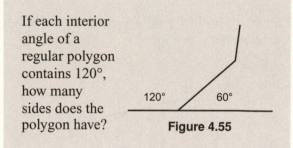

If each interior angle of a regular polygon contains 120°, how many sides does the polygon have?

Figure 4.55

SOLUTION

At each vertex of a polygon, we can draw an exterior angle that is supplementary to the interior angle, as shown in Figure 4.55.

Since we are told that the interior angle measures 120°, we can deduce that the exterior angle measures 60°.

Each exterior angle of a regular polygon of n sides measures $\dfrac{360°}{n}$ degrees. We know that each exterior angle measures 60°, and, therefore, by setting $\dfrac{360°}{n}$ equal to 60°, we can determine the number of sides in the polygon. The calculation is as follows:

$$\frac{360°}{n} = 60°$$

$$60°n = 360°$$

$$n = 6$$

Therefore, the regular polygon with interior angles of 120° has six sides and is called a hexagon.

The **perimeter** of a regular polygon is the product of the length of a side (*s*) and the number of sides (*n*), $p = ns$.

The area of a regular polygon can be determined by using the **apothem** and **radius** of the polygon. See Figure 4.56. The apothem (*a*) of a regular polygon is the segment from the center of the polygon perpendicular to a side of the polygon. The radius (*r*) of a regular polygon is the segment joining any vertex of a regular polygon with the center of that polygon.

(1) All radii of a regular polygon are congruent.

(2) All apothems of a regular polygon are congruent.

r   *a*

Figure 4.56

The area of a regular polygon equals one-half the product of the length of the apothem and the perimeter.

$$\text{Area} = \frac{1}{2}a \times p$$

Note: The radius of a regular hexagon is congruent to a side.

Drill: Regular Polygons (Convex)

DIRECTIONS: Find the appropriate solutions.

1. Find the measure of an interior angle of a regular pentagon.

   (A) 55°   (C) 90°

   (B) 72°   (D) 108°

2. Find the sum of the measures of the exterior angles of a regular triangle.

   (A) 90°   (C) 180°

   (B) 115°   (D) 360°

3. A regular triangle has sides of 24 mm. If the apothem is $4\sqrt{3}$ mm, find the area of the triangle.

   (A) 72 mm²   (C) 144 mm²

   (B) $96\sqrt{3}$ mm²   (D) $144\sqrt{3}$ mm²

4. Find the area of a regular hexagon with sides of 4 cm.

   (A) $12\sqrt{3}$ cm²   (C) $24\sqrt{3}$ cm²

   (B) 24 cm²   (D) 48 cm²

5. Find the area of a regular decagon with sides of length 6 cm and an apothem of length 9.2 cm.

   (A) 55.2 cm²   (C) 138 cm²

   (B) 60 cm²   (D) 276 cm²

Similar Polygons

Definition

Two polygons are similar if there is a one-to-one correspondence between their vertices such that all pairs of corresponding angles are congruent and the ratios of the measures of all pairs of corresponding sides are equal. Note that although they must have the same shape, they may have different sizes. See Figure 4.57.

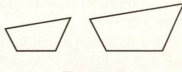

Figure 4.57

Theorem 1

The perimeters of two similar polygons have the same ratio as the measure of any pair of corresponding line segments of the polygons.

Theorem 2

The ratio of the lengths of two corresponding diagonals of two similar polygons is equal to the ratio of the lengths of any two corresponding sides of the polygons.

Theorem 3

Two polygons composed of the same number of triangles, similar each to each and similarly placed, are similar. See Figure 4.58.

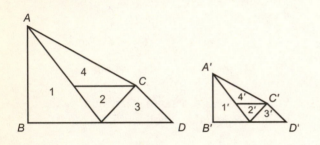

Figure 4.58

PROBLEM

> Prove that any two regular polygons with the same number of sides are similar.

SOLUTION

For any two polygons to be similar, their corresponding angles must be congruent and their corresponding sides proportional. It is necessary to show that these conditions always exist between regular polygons with the same number of sides.

Let us examine the corresponding angles first. For a regular polygon with n sides, each vertex angle is $\dfrac{(n-2)180}{n}$. Therefore, two regular polygons with the same number of sides will have corresponding vertex angles that are all of the same measure and, hence, are all congruent. This fulfills our first condition for similarity.

We must now determine whether the corresponding sides are proportional. It will suffice to show that the ratios of the lengths of every pair of corresponding sides are the same.

Since the polygons are regular, the sides of each one will be equal. Call the length of the sides of one polygon ℓ_1 and the length of the sides of the other polygon ℓ_2. Hence, the ratio of the lengths of corresponding sides will be $\ell_1 : \ell_2$. This will be a constant for any pair of corresponding sides and, hence, the corresponding sides are proportional.

Thus, any two regular polygons with the same number of sides are similar.

PROBLEM

> The lengths of two corresponding sides of two similar polygons are 4 and 7. If the perimeter of the smaller polygon is 20, find the perimeter of the larger polygon.

SOLUTION

We know, by theorem, that the perimeters of two similar polygons have the same ratio as the measures of any pair of corresponding sides.

If we let s and p represent the side and perimeter of the smaller polygon and s' and p' represent the corresponding side and perimeter of the larger one, we can then write the proportion

$$p : p' = s : s'$$

By substituting the given values, we can solve for p'.

$$20 : p' = 4 : 7$$
$$4\,p' = 140$$
$$p' = 35.$$

Therefore, the perimeter of the larger polygon is 35.

Triangles

A closed three-sided geometric figure is called a **triangle**. The points of the intersection of the sides of a triangle are called the **vertices** of the triangle. A **side** of a triangle is a line segment whose endpoints are the vertices of two angles of the triangle. In Figure 4.59, the vertices are *A*, *B*, and *C*, and the sides are *AB*, *BC*, and *CA*.

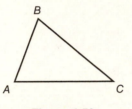

Figure 4.59

The **perimeter** of a triangle is the sum of the measures of the sides of the triangle.

A triangle with no equal sides is called a **scalene triangle**. Examples of scalene triangles are shown in Figure 4.60.

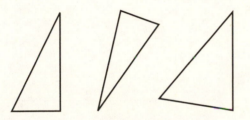

Figure 4.60

A triangle having at least two equal sides is called an **isosceles triangle** (see Figure 4.61). The third side is called the **base** of the triangle, and the base angles (the angles opposite the equal sides) are equal.

If two sides of a triangle are congruent, then the angles opposite them are congruent.

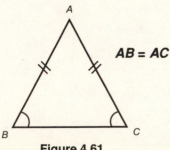

AB = AC

Figure 4.61

An **equilateral triangle** is a triangle having three equal sides. $\overline{AB} = \overline{AC} = \overline{BC}$. An equilateral, triangle is also **equiangular**, with each angle equaling 60°. Figure 4.62 shows an equilateral triangle.

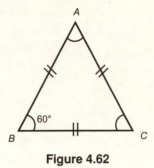

Figure 4.62

PROBLEM

In Figure 4.63, $\triangle ABC$ is an isosceles triangle, such that $\overline{BA} \cong \overline{BC}$. Line segment $\overline{AD}$ bisects $\sphericalangle BAC$ and $\overline{CD}$ bisects $\sphericalangle BCA$. Prove that $\triangle ADC$ is an isosceles triangle.

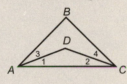

Figure 4.63

SOLUTION

In order to prove $\triangle ADC$ is isosceles, we must prove that two of its sides, $\overline{AD}$ and $\overline{CD}$, are congruent. To prove $\overline{AD} \cong \overline{CD}$ in $\triangle ADC$, we have to prove that the angles opposite $\overline{AD}$ and $\overline{CD}$, $\sphericalangle 1$ and $\sphericalangle 2$, are congruent.

Statement	Reason
1. $\overline{BA} \cong \overline{BC}$	1. Given.
2. $\sphericalangle BAC \cong \sphericalangle BCA$ or $m\sphericalangle BAC = m\sphericalangle BCA$	2. If two sides of a triangle are congruent, then the angles opposite them are congruent.
3. $\overline{AD}$ bisects $\sphericalangle BAC$ $\overline{CD}$ bisects $\sphericalangle BCA$	3. Given.

4. $m \angle 1 = \left(\dfrac{1}{2}\right) m \angle BAC$ 4. The bisector of an angle divides the angle into two angles whose measures are equal.

$m \angle 2 = \left(\dfrac{1}{2}\right) m \angle BCA$

5. $m \angle 1 = m \angle 2$ 5. Halves of equal quantities are equal.

6. $\angle 1 \cong \angle 2$ 6. If the measure of two angles are equal, then the angles are congruent.

7. $\overline{CD} \cong \overline{AD}$ 7. If two angles of a triangle are congruent, then the sides opposite these angles are congruent.

8. $\triangle ADC$ is an isosceles triangle.   8. If a triangle has two congruent sides, then it is an isosceles triangle.

A triangle with one obtuse angle (greater than 90°) is called an **obtuse triangle**. Figure 4.64 shows an obtuse triangle.

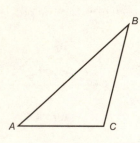

Figure 4.64

An **acute triangle** is a triangle with three acute angles (less than 90°). Figure 4.65 shows an acute triangle.

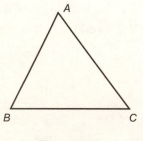

Figure 4.65

A triangle with a right angle is a **right triangle**, as shown in Figure 4.66. The side opposite the right angle

in a right triangle is called the **hypotenuse** of the right triangle. The other two sides are called arms or **legs** of the right triangle. By the **Pythagorean Theorem**, the lengths of the three sides of a right triangle are related by the formula

$$c^2 = a^2 + b^2$$

where c is the hypotenuse and a and b are the other sides (the legs).

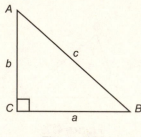

Figure 4.66

PROBLEM

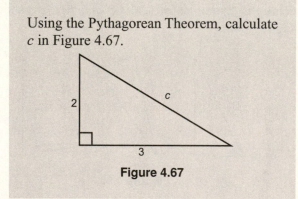

Using the Pythagorean Theorem, calculate c in Figure 4.67.

Figure 4.67

SOLUTION

(1) Write the Pythagorean Theorem.

$a^2 + b^2 = c^2$

(2) Substitute the values of a and b into the equation.

$(3)^2 + (2)^2 = c^2$

(3) Simplify the equation.

$9 + 4 = c^2$

(4) Combine like terms.

$13 = c^2$

(5) Solve for c.

$\sqrt{13} = c$

PROBLEM

Using the Pythagorean Theorem, calculate a in Figure 4.68.

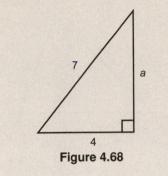

Figure 4.68

SOLUTION

(1) Write the Pythagorean Theorem.

$$a^2 + b^2 = c^2$$

(2) Substitute the values of b and c into the equation.

$$a^2 + (4)^2 = 7^2$$

(3) Simplify the equation.

$$a^2 + 16 = 49$$

(4) Subtract 16 from both sides and rewrite the equation.

$$a^2 = 33$$

(5) Solve for a.

$$a = \sqrt{33}$$

An **altitude** of a triangle is a line segment from a vertex of the triangle perpendicular to the opposite side, as shown in Figure 4.69.

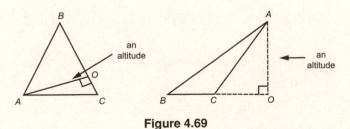

Figure 4.69

The **area** of a triangle is given by $A = \frac{1}{2}bh$, where h is the altitude and b is the base to which the altitude is drawn.

PROBLEM

Find the area of a regular hexagon if one side has length 6.

SOLUTION

Sketch the hexagon as in Figure 4.70. Since the length of a side equals 6, the radius also equals 6 and the perimeter equals 36. The base of the right triangle, formed by the radius and apothem, is half the length of a side, or 3. You can find the length of the apothem by using the Pythagorean Theorem.

$$a^2 + b^2 = c^2$$
$$a^2 + (3)^2 = (6)^2$$
$$a^2 = 36 - 9$$
$$a^2 = 27$$
$$a = 3\sqrt{3}$$

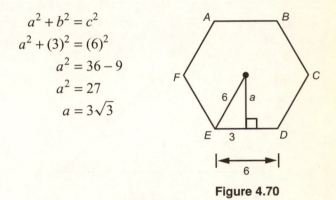

Figure 4.70

The apothem equals $3\sqrt{3}$. Therefore, the area of the hexagon

$$= \frac{1}{2}a \times p$$
$$= \frac{1}{2}(3\sqrt{3})(36)$$
$$= 54\sqrt{3}$$

A line segment connecting a vertex of a triangle and the midpoint of the opposite side is called a **median** of the triangle. In Figure 4.71, AO is a median.

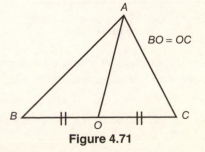

Figure 4.71

A line that bisects and is perpendicular to a side of a triangle is called a **perpendicular bisector** of that side. See Figure 4.72.

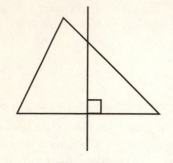

Figure 4.72

An **angle bisector** of a triangle is a line that bisects an angle and extends to the opposite side of the triangle. In Figure 4.73, *AO* is the angle bisector of ∢*A*, so $\angle \alpha = \angle \beta$.

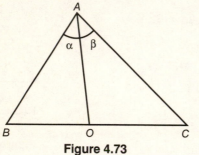

Figure 4.73

The line segment that joins the midpoints of two sides of a triangle is called a **midline** of the triangle. In Figure 4.74, the midline is *DE*, so *AD = DC* and *BE = EC*.

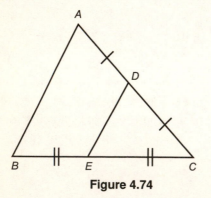

Figure 4.74

An **interior angle** of a triangle is an angle formed by two sides and includes the third side within its collection of points.

The sum of the measures of the interior angles of a triangle is 180°.

An **exterior angle** of a triangle is an angle formed outside a triangle by one side of the triangle and the extension of an adjacent side. In Figure 4.75, ∢ACB is an interior angle, and α is its exterior angle.

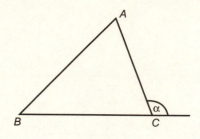

Figure 4.75

Three or more lines (or rays or segments) are **concurrent** if there exists one point common to all of them, that is, if they all intersect at the same point.

PROBLEM

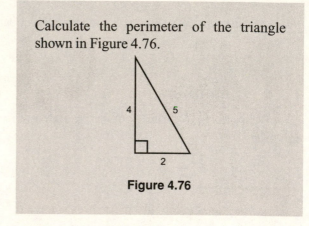

Calculate the perimeter of the triangle shown in Figure 4.76.

Figure 4.76

SOLUTION

(1) Write the formula for the perimeter of a triangle.

perimeter = length of side 1 + length of side 2 + length of side 3

(2) Substitute the known values into the formula.

perimeter = 4 + 2 + 5

(3) Solve the equation.

perimeter = 11

The perimeter of the triangle is 11.

PROBLEM

Calculate the area of the triangle shown in Figure 4.77.

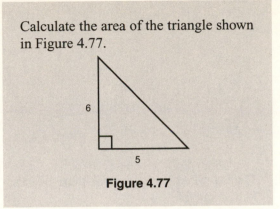

Figure 4.77

SOLUTION

(1) Write the formula for the area of a triangle.

$$A = \frac{1}{2}bh$$

(2) Substitute the known values into the formula. The base of the triangle is 5 and the height is 6.

$$A = \frac{1}{2}(5)(6)$$

(3) Solve the equation.

$$A = 15$$

The area of the triangle is 15.

PROBLEM

Calculate the area of the triangle shown in Figure 4.78.

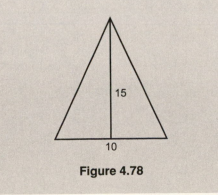

Figure 4.78

SOLUTION

(1) Write the formula for the area of a triangle.

$$A = \frac{1}{2}bh$$

(2) Substitute the known values into the formula. The base of the triangle is 10 and the height is 15.

$$A = \frac{1}{2}(10)(15)$$

(3) Solve the equation.

$$A = 75$$

The area of the triangle is 75.

PROBLEM

The measure of the vertex angle of an isosceles triangle exceeds the measurement of each base angle by 30°. Find the value of each angle of the triangle shown in Figure 4.79.

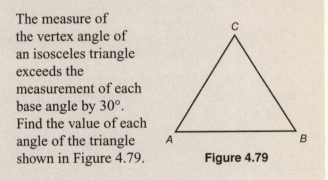

Figure 4.79

SOLUTION

We know that the sum of the values of the angles of a triangle is 180°. In an isosceles triangle, the angles opposite the congruent sides (the base angles) are, themselves, congruent and of equal value.

Therefore,

(1) Let x = the measure of each base angle.

(2) Then $x + 30$ = the measure of the vertex angle.

We can solve for x algebraically by keeping in mind the sum of all the measures will be 180°.

$$x + x + (x + 30) = 180$$
$$3x + 30 = 180$$
$$3x = 150$$
$$x = 50$$

Therefore, the base angles each measure 50°, and the vertex angle measures 80°.

Drill: Triangles

DIRECTIONS: Find the solutions.

1. In $\triangle PQR$, shown in Figure 4.80, $\angle Q$ is a right angle. Find $m\angle R$.

   (A) 27°   (C) 54°

   (B) 33°   (D) 67°

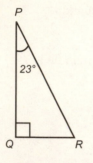

Figure 4.80

2. $\triangle MNO$ in Figure 4.81 is isosceles. If the vertex angle, $\angle N$, has a measure of 96°, find the measure of $\angle M$.

   (A) 21°

   (B) 42°

   (C) 64°

   (D) 84°

Figure 4.81

3. Find x in Figure 4.82.

   (A) 15°

   (B) 25°

   (C) 30°

   (D) 45°

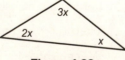

Figure 4.82

4. The two triangles shown in Figure 4.83 are similar. Find b.

   (A) $2\frac{2}{3}$

   (B) 3

   (C) 4

   (D) 16

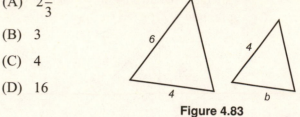

Figure 4.83

5. The two triangles shown in Figure 4.84 are similar. Find a and b.

   (A) 5 and 10   (C) $4\frac{2}{3}$ and $7\frac{1}{3}$

   (B) 4 and 8   (D) $5\frac{1}{3}$ and 8

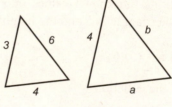

Figure 4.84

6. Find the area of $\triangle MNO$ in Figure 4.85.

   (A) 22

   (B) 49

   (C) 56

   (D) 84

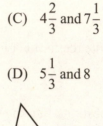

Figure 4.85

7. Find the area of $\triangle PQR$ in Figure 4.86.

   (A) 31.5

   (B) 38.5

   (C) 53

   (D) 77

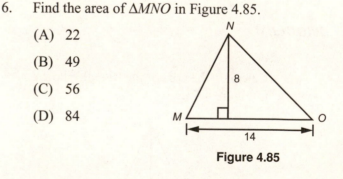

Figure 4.86

8. Find the area of ΔSTU in Figure 4.87.

    (A) $4\sqrt{2}$

    (B) $8\sqrt{2}$

    (C) $12\sqrt{2}$

    (D) $16\sqrt{2}$

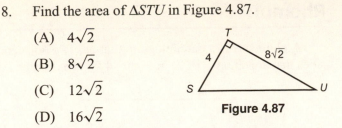

Figure 4.87

9. Find the area of ΔABC in Figure 4.88.

    (A) 54 cm²

    (B) 81 cm²

    (C) 108 cm²

    (D) 135 cm²

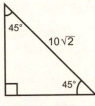

Figure 4.88

10. Find the area of ΔXYZ in Figure 4.89.

    (A) 20 cm²

    (B) 50 cm²

    (C) $50\sqrt{2}$ cm²

    (D) 100 cm²

Figure 4.89

Quadrilaterals

A **quadrilateral** is a polygon with four sides.

Parallelograms

A **parallelogram** is a quadrilateral whose opposite sides are parallel. *ABCD* in Figure 4.90 is a parallelogram if *AB* ‖ *CD* and *AD* ‖ *BC*.

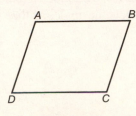

Figure 4.90

Two angles that have their vertices at the endpoints of the same side of a parallelogram are called consecutive angles.

The perpendicular segment connecting any point of a line containing one side of a parallelogram to the line containing the opposite side of the parallelogram is called the altitude of the parallelogram, as shown in Figure 4.91.

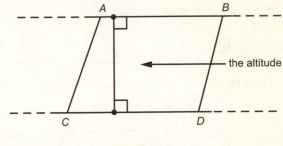

Figure 4.91

A diagonal of a parallelogram is a line segment joining any two nonconsecutive vertices.

The area of a parallelogram is given by the formula $A = bh$, where b is the base and h is the height drawn perpendicular to that base. Note that the height equals the altitude of the parallelogram shown in Figure 4.92.

$A = bh$

$A = (10)(3)$

$A = 30$

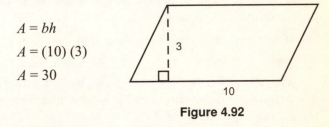

Figure 4.92

PROBLEM

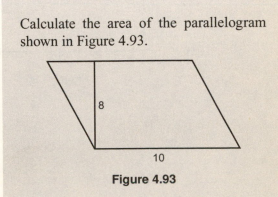

Calculate the area of the parallelogram shown in Figure 4.93.

Figure 4.93

103

SOLUTION

(1) Write the formula for the area of a parallelogram.

$A = bh$, where b is the base and h is the height.

(2) Substitute the known values into the formula.

$A = 10(8)$

(3) Solve the equation.

$A = 80$

The area of the parallelogram is 80.

Rectangles

A **rectangle** is a parallelogram with right angles, such as *ABCD* in Figure 4.94.

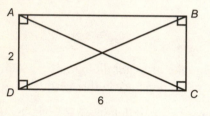

Figure 4.94

The diagonals of a rectangle are equal, so $AC = BD$.

If the diagonals of a parallelogram are equal, the parallelogram is a rectangle.

If a quadrilateral has four right angles, then it is a rectangle.

The area of a rectangle is given by the formula $A = lw$, where l is the length and w is the width. For the rectangle shown in Figure 4.95,

$A = lw$

$A = (3)(10)$

$A = 30$

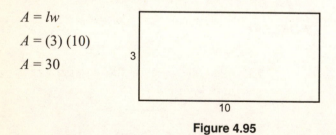

Figure 4.95

Rhombi

A **rhombus** is a parallelogram that has two adjacent sides that are equal. *ABCD* in Figure 4.96 is a rhombus.

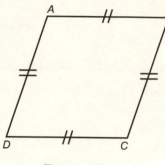

Figure 4.96

All sides of a rhombus are equal.

If a quadrilateral has four equal sides, then it is a rhombus.

The diagonals of a rhombus are perpendicular to each other. In Figure 4.97, $AC \perp BD$.

If the diagonals of a parallelogram are perpendicular, the parallelogram is a rhombus.

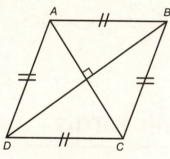

Figure 4.97

The area of a rhombus can be found by the formula $A = \frac{1}{2}(d_1 \times d_2)$ where d_1 and d_2 are the diagonals.

The diagonals of a rhombus bisect the angles of the rhombus.

A parallelogram is a rhombus if either diagonal of the parallelogram bisects the angles of the vertices it joins.

PROBLEM

Calculate the area of the rhombus shown in Figure 4.98.

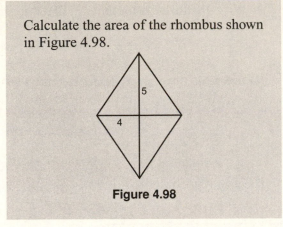

Figure 4.98

SOLUTION

(1) Write the formula for the area of a rhombus.

$A = \frac{1}{2}(d_1 \times d_2)$, where d_1 and d_2 are the diagonals of the rhombus.

(2) Substitute the known values into the formula.

$$A = \frac{1}{2}(5)(4)$$

(3) Solve the equation.

$$A = 10$$

The area of the rhombus is 10.

Squares

A **square** is a rhombus with a right angle. *ABCD* in Figure 4.99 is a square.

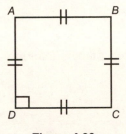

Figure 4.99

A rhombus is a square if one of its interior angles is a right angle.

A square is an equilateral quadrilateral.

A square has all the properties of parallelograms and rectangles.

In a square, the measure of either diagonal can be calculated by multiplying the length of any side by the square root of 2, as shown in Figure 4.100.

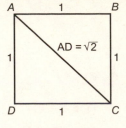

Figure 4.100

The area of a square is given by the formula $A = s^2$, where s is the side of the square. Since all sides of a square are equal, it does not matter which side is used. For the square shown in Figure 4.101,

$A = s^2$

$A = 6^2$

$A = 36$

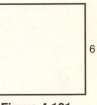

Figure 4.101

The area of a square can also be found by taking $\frac{1}{2}$ the product of the length of the diagonal squared. For the square shown in Figure 4.102,

$A = \frac{1}{2}d^2$

$A = \frac{1}{2}(8)^2$

$A = 32$

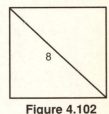

Figure 4.102

Trapezoids

A **trapezoid** is a quadrilateral with two and only two sides parallel. The parallel sides of a trapezoid are called **bases.**

The **median** of a trapezoid is the line joining the midpoints of the nonparallel sides, as shown in Figure 4.103.

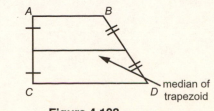

Figure 4.103

The perpendicular segment connecting any point in one base of the trapezoid to the other base is the **altitude** of the trapezoid, as shown in Figure 4.104.

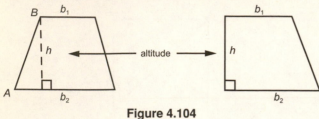

Figure 4.104

The area of a trapezoid equals one half the altitude times the sum of the bases, or $A = \frac{1}{2}h(b_1 + b_2)$.

An **isosceles trapezoid** is a trapezoid whose non-parallel sides are equal. A pair of angles including only one of the parallel sides is called a pair of base angles, as shown in Figure 4.105.

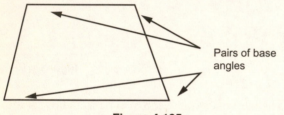

Pairs of base angles

Figure 4.105

The median of a trapezoid is parallel to the bases and equal to one-half their sum.

The base angles of an isosceles trapezoid are equal.

The diagonals of an isosceles trapezoid are equal.

The opposite angles of an isosceles trapezoid are supplementary.

PROBLEM

Calculate the area of the trapezoid shown in Figure 4.106.

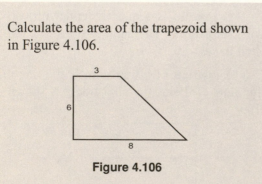

Figure 4.106

SOLUTION

(1) Write the formula for the area of a trapezoid.

$A = \frac{1}{2}h(b_1 + b_2)$, where b_1 and b_2 are the bases

(2) Substitute the known values into the formula.

$A = \frac{1}{2}(6)(3 + 8)$

(3) Solve the equation.

$A = 33$

The area of the trapezoid is 33.

Drill: Quadrilaterals

DIRECTIONS: Refer to the diagrams and find the appropriate solutions.

1. In Figure 4.107, quadrilateral *ABCD* is a parallelogram. If $m\angle B = (6x + 2)°$ and $m\angle D = 98°$, find *x*.

(A) 12

(B) 16

(C) $16\frac{2}{3}$

(D) 18

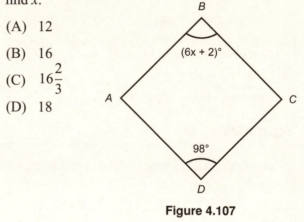

Figure 4.107

2. Find the area of parallelogram *STUV* in Figure 4.108.

(A) 56

(B) 90

(C) 108

(D) 162

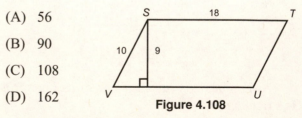

Figure 4.108

3. In Figure 4.109, in rectangle $ABCD$, $\overline{AD} = 6\,\text{cm}$ and $\overline{DC} = 8\,\text{cm}$. Find the length of the diagonal $\overline{AC}$.

　(A) 10 cm　　　　(C) 20 cm

　(B) 12 cm　　　　(D) 28 cm

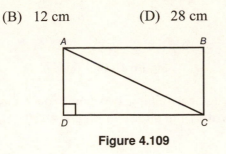

Figure 4.109

4. Find the area of rectangle $UVXY$ in Figure 4.110.

　(A) 17 cm²

　(B) 34 cm²

　(C) 35 cm²

　(D) 70 cm²

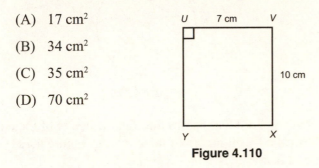

Figure 4.110

5. In Figure 4.111, find the length of $\overline{BO}$ in rectangle $BCDE$ if diagonal $\overline{EC}$ is 17 mm.

　(A) 6.55 mm

　(B) 8 mm

　(C) 8.5 mm

　(D) 17 mm

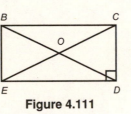

Figure 4.111

6. In rhombus $GHIJ$ in Figure 4.112, $\overline{GI} = 6\,\text{cm}$ and $\overline{HJ} = 8\,\text{cm}$. Find the length of $\overline{GH}$.

　(A) 3 cm

　(B) 4 cm

　(C) 5 cm

　(D) $4\sqrt{3}$ cm

Figure 4.112

7. Find the area of trapezoid $RSTU$ in Figure 4.113.

　(A) 80 cm²

　(B) 87.5 cm²

　(C) 140 cm²

　(D) 175 cm²

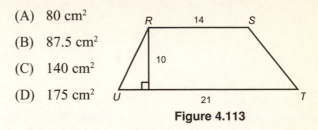

Figure 4.113

8. In Figure 4.114, $ABCD$ is an isosceles trapezoid. Find the perimeter.

　(A) 21 cm　　　　(C) 30 cm

　(B) 27 cm　　　　(D) 50 cm

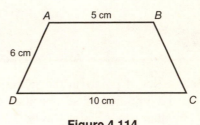

Figure 4.114

9. Find the area of trapezoid $MNOP$ in Figure 4.115.

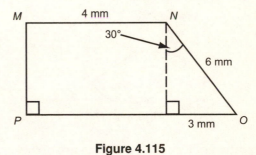

Figure 4.115

　(A) $(17 + 3\sqrt{3})\,\text{mm}^2$　　(C) $\dfrac{33\sqrt{3}}{2}\,\text{mm}^2$

　(B) $\dfrac{33}{2}\,\text{mm}^2$　　(D) 33 mm²

10. In Figure 4.116, trapezoid *XYZW* is isosceles. If $m \angle W = 58°$ and $m \angle Z = (4x - 6)°$, find *x*.

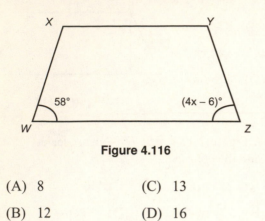

Figure 4.116

(A) 8   (C) 13

(B) 12   (D) 16

Circles

A **circle** is a set of points in the same plane equidistant from a fixed point, called its center. Circles are often named by their center point, circle *O*.

A **radius** of a circle is a line segment drawn from the center of the circle to any point on the circle, as shown in Figure 4.117.

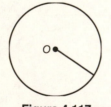

Figure 4.117

A portion of a circle is called an **arc** of the circle. In Figure 4.118, $\overset{\frown}{AB}$ is an arc.

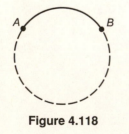

Figure 4.118

A line that intersects a circle in two points is called a **secant**. In Figure 4.119, $\overleftrightarrow{AB}$ is a secant.

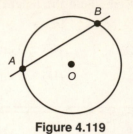

Figure 4.119

A line segment joining two points on a circle is called a **chord** of the circle. In Figure 4.120, $\overline{AB}$ is a chord.

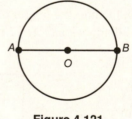

Figure 4.120

A chord that passes through the center of the circle is called a **diameter** of the circle. In Figure 4.121, $\overline{AB}$ is a diameter.

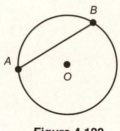

Figure 4.121

The line passing through the centers of two (or more) circles is called the **line of centers**, as shown in Figure 4.122.

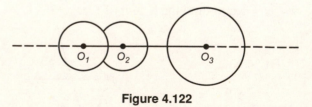

Figure 4.122

An angle whose vertex is on the circle and whose sides are chords of the circle is called an **inscribed angle**. ∡*BAC* in the diagrams in Figure 4.123 is an inscribed angle.

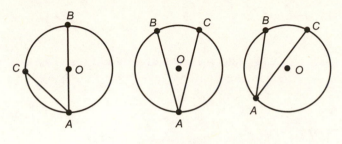

Figure 4.123

An angle whose vertex is at the center of a circle and whose sides are radii is called a **central angle**. The measure of a minor arc is the measure of the central angle that intercepts that arc. In Figure 4.124, $m\overset{\frown}{AB} = \alpha = m\angle AOB$.

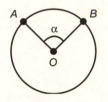

Figure 4.124

If the arc is equal to the radius (i.e., $\overset{\frown}{AB} = AO = BO$ in Figure 4.124) the central angle is one **radian**, by definition. In general, one radian is the ratio of the length of the enclosed arc to the radius. In Figure 4.124, if α were given in radions, $\alpha = \dfrac{\overset{\frown}{AB}}{AO}$.

The distance from a point P to a given circle is the distance from that point to the point where the circle intersects with a line segment with endpoints at the center of the circle and point P.

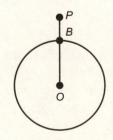

Figure 4.125

The distance of point P to the circle with center O in Figure 4.125 is the line segment $\overline{PB}$ of line segment $\overline{PO}$.

A line that has one and only one point of intersection with a circle is called a **tangent** to that circle, and their common point is called a **point of tangency.** In Figure 4.126, $\overleftrightarrow{QR}$ and $\overleftrightarrow{PR}$ are tangents and Q and P are each points of tangency.

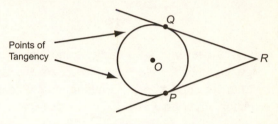

Figure 4.126

Congruent circles are circles whose radii are congruent. In Figure 4.127, if $O_1A_1 \cong O_2A_2$, then $O_1 \cong O_2$.

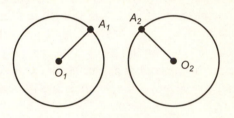

Figure 4.127

A **circumscribed circle** is a circle passing through all the vertices of a polygon. The polygon is said to be **inscribed** in the circle. See Figure 4.128.

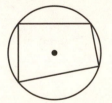

Figure 4.128

Circles that have the same center and unequal radii are called **concentric circles**, as shown in Figure 4.129.

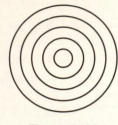

Figure 4.129

The **circumference** of a circle is the length of its outer edge, given by $C = \pi d = 2\pi r$, where r is the radius, d is the diameter, and π (pi) is a mathematical constant approximately equal to 3.14.

The **area** of a circle is given by $A = \pi r^2$.

A full circle is 360°. The measure of a semicircle is 180°.

The length of arc intercepted by a central angle has the same ratio to the circle's circumference as the measure of the arc has to 360°, the full circle. Therefore, arc length is given by $\frac{n}{360} \times 2\pi r$, where n = measure of the central angle. The measure of an arc in degrees, however, is the same as the measure of its central angle.

A sector is the portion of a circle between two radii. Its area is given by $A = \frac{n}{360}(\pi r^2)$, where n is the central angle formed by the radii.

PROBLEM

Calculate the circumference of a circle that has a radius of 12 inches.

SOLUTION

(1) Write the formula for the circumference of a circle.

$$C = 2\pi r$$

(2) Substitute the known values into the equation. π is approximately 3.14. The radius is 12.

$$C = 2(3.14)12$$

(3) Solve the equation.

$$C = 75.4$$

The circumference = 75.4 inches.

PROBLEM

Calculate the area of a circle that has a diameter of 10 meters.

SOLUTION

(1) Write the formula for the area of a circle.

$$A = \pi r^2.$$

(2) Substitute the known values into the equation. π is approximately 3.14. The diameter of the circle is 10 meters, so the radius is 5 meters.

$$A = \pi(5)^2$$

(3) Solve the equation.

$$A = 78.5$$

The area of the circle is 78.5 m².

PROBLEM

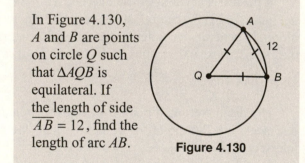

In Figure 4.130, A and B are points on circle Q such that $\triangle AQB$ is equilateral. If the length of side $\overline{AB} = 12$, find the length of arc AB.

Figure 4.130

SOLUTION

To find the arc length of arc AB, we must find the measure of the central angle $\angle AQB$ and the measure of the radius $\overline{QA}$. $\angle AQB$ is an interior angle of the equilateral triangle $\triangle AQB$. Therefore,

$$m\angle AQB = 60°.$$

Similarly, in the equilateral ΔAQB,

$$\overline{AQ} = \overline{AB} = \overline{QB} = 12.$$

Given radius, r, and central angle, n, arc length is given by

$$\frac{n}{360} \times 2\pi r.$$

Therefore, by substitution,

$$\angle AQB = \frac{60}{360} \times 2\pi \times 12 = \frac{1}{6} \times 2\pi \times 12 = 4\pi.$$

Therefore, the length of arc $AB = 4\pi$.

Drill: Circles

1. Find the circumference of circle A if its radius is 3 mm.

   (A) 3π mm   (C) 9π mm

   (B) 6π mm   (D) 12π mm

2. Find the area of circle I in Figure 4.131.

   (A) 22 mm²

   (B) 121 mm²

   (C) 121π mm²

   (D) 132 mm²

   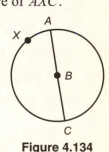

   Figure 4.131

3. The diameter of circle Z is 27 mm. Find the area of the circle.

   (A) 91.125 mm²   (C) 191.5π mm²

   (B) 182.25 mm²   (D) 182.25π mm²

4. The area of circle B is 225π cm². Find the length of the diameter of the circle.

   (A) 15 cm   (C) 30 cm

   (B) 20 cm   (D) 20π cm

5. The area of circle X is 144π mm², and the area of circle Y is 81π mm². Write the ratio of the radius of circle X to that of circle Y.

   (A) 3:4   (C) 9:12

   (B) 4:3   (D) 27:12

6. In Figure 4.132, the radius of the smaller of the two concentric circles is 5 cm, and the radius of the larger circle is 7 cm. Determine the area of the shaded region.

   (A) 7π cm²

   (B) 24π cm²

   (C) 25π cm²

   (D) 36π cm²

   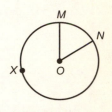

   Figure 4.132

7. In Figure 4.133, find the measure of $\overset{\frown}{MN}$ if $m\angle MON = 62°$.

   (A) 16°

   (B) 32°

   (C) 59°

   (D) 62°

   Figure 4.133

8. In Figure 4.134, find the measure of $\overset{\frown}{AXC}$.

   (A) 150°

   (B) 160°

   (C) 180°

   (D) 270°

   Figure 4.134

9. In Figure 4.135, find the measure of $\overset{\frown}{XY}$ in circle W.

   (A) 40°

   (B) 120°

   (C) 140°

   (D) 180°

   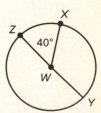

   Figure 4.135

10. Find the area of the sector shown in Figure 4.136.

    (A) 4 cm²

    (B) 2π cm²

    (C) 16 cm²

    (D) 8π cm²

Figure 4.136

Solid Geometry

Cubes, Cylinders

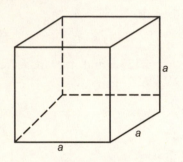

Figure 4.137

Figure 4.137 is a cube, a three-dimensional, 6-sided solid with equal edges and all angles equal to 90°.

The volume of a cube with edge *a* is

$$V = a^3$$

The surface area of a cube with edge *a* is

$$A = 6a^2$$

Figure 4.138 is a right circular cylinder.

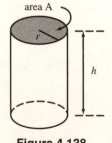

Figure 4.138

The volume of a right circular cylinder with radius *r* and height *h* is

$$V = \pi r^2 h$$

The surface area of a right circular cylinder with radius *r* and height *h* is

$$A = 2\pi r^2 + 2\pi rh$$

Intersecting Planes

If two different planes intersect, they intersect in a straight line.

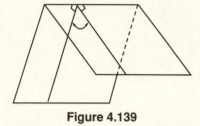

Figure 4.139

The angle between two planes is the angle between two rays on the two planes, each of which is perpendicular to the line of intersection of the planes. See Figure 4.139.

Volume and Surface Area

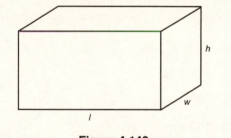

Figure 4.140

Figure 4.140 is a rectangular solid.

The volume of a rectangular solid with length *l*, width *w*, and height *h* is

$$V = lwh$$

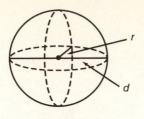

Figure 4.141

Figure 4.141 is a sphere.

The volume of a sphere with radius r is

$$V = \frac{4}{3}\pi r^3$$

The surface area of a sphere with radius r is

$$A = 4\pi r^2$$

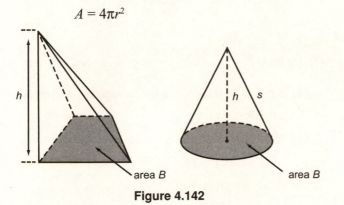

Figure 4.142

Figure 4.142 shows a pyramid (left) and a cone (right).

The volume of a pyramid or cone with base area B and height h is

$$V = \frac{1}{3}Bh.$$

If the base of the cone is a circle with radius r, then

$$A = \pi r^2,$$

so

$$V = \frac{1}{3}\pi r^2 h$$

The total area of a cone is the sum of the surface area of the conical part (πrs), where s is the slant height, plus the area of the circular base, so $A = \pi rs + \pi r^2$.

PROBLEM

Calculate the volume of a sphere that has a radius of 2 meters.

SOLUTION

(1) Write the formula for the volume of a sphere.

$$V = \frac{4}{3}\pi r^3$$

(2) Substitute the known values into the equation. π is approximately 3.14 and the radius is 2 meters.

$$V = \frac{4}{3}\pi(2)^3$$

(3) Solve the equation.

$$V = 33.49 \text{ or } \sim 33.5$$

The volume of the sphere is 33.5 m^3.

PROBLEM

Calculate the volume of the cube that has a length of 5, a height of 1.5, and a width of 4.

SOLUTION

(1) Write the formula for the volume of a cube.

$$V = l \times w \times h$$

(2) Substitute the known values into the formula.

$$V = 5 \times 4 \times 1.5$$

(3) Solve the equation.

$$V = 30$$

The volume of the cube = 30.

PROBLEM

Calculate the volume of a pyramid that has a height of 3 feet. The area of the base of the pyramid is 15 square feet.

SOLUTION

(1) Write the formula for the volume of a pyramid.

$V = \dfrac{1}{3}Bh$, where B is the area of the base of the pyramid, and h is the height.

(2) Substitute the known values into the formula.

$$V = \frac{1}{3}(15)(3)$$

(3) Solve the equation.

$V = 15$

The volume of the pyramid is 15 cubic feet.

PROBLEM

Calculate the volume of the cone shown in Figure 4.143.

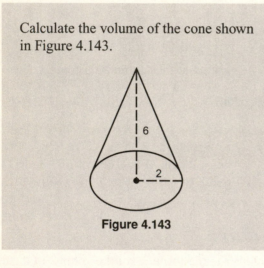

Figure 4.143

SOLUTION

(1) Write the formula for the volume of a cone.

$$V = \frac{1}{3}\pi r^2 h$$

(2) Substitute the known values into the equation.

$$V = \frac{1}{3}\pi (2)^2 (6)$$

(3) Solve the equation.

$V = 25.12$

The volume of the cone is 25.12.

PROBLEM

Calculate the volume of the cylinder shown in Figure 4.144.

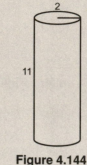

Figure 4.144

SOLUTION

(1) Write the formula for the volume of a cylinder.

$V = \pi r^2 h$

(2) Substitute the known values into the formula.

$V = \pi (2)^2 (11)$

(3) Solve the equation.

$V = 138.16$

The volume is 138.16.

PROBLEM

Calculate the total area of the cone shown in Figure 4.145. Round to the nearest whole number.

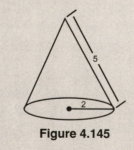

Figure 4.145

SOLUTION

(1) Write the formula for the total area of a cone.

$A = \pi rs + \pi r^2$, where s is the slant height

(2) Substitute the known values into the formula.

$A = \pi(2)(5) + \pi(2)^2$

(3) Solve the equation.

$A = 10\pi + 4\pi = \pi(10 + 4) = \pi(14)$

$A = 44$

The correct answer is 44.

Coordinate Geometry

Coordinate geometry refers to the study of geometric figures using algebraic principles.

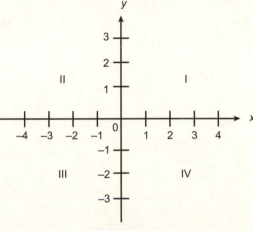

Figure 4.146

Figure 4.146 is called the Cartesian coordinate plane discussed in Chapter 3. The graph consists of a pair of perpendicular lines called **coordinate axes.** The **vertical axis** is the y-axis and the **horizontal axis** is the x-axis. The point of intersection of these two axes is called the **origin**; it is the zero point of both axes. Furthermore, points to the right of the origin on the x-axis and above the origin on the y-axis represent positive real numbers. Points to the left of the origin on the x-axis or below the origin on the y-axis represent negative real numbers.

The four regions cut off by the coordinate axes are, in counterclockwise direction from the top right, called the first, second, third, and fourth quadrants, respectively. The first quadrant contains all points with two positive coordinates.

Figure 4.147 shows two points, A and B. Points can be identified by the ordered pair (x, y) of numbers. The x-coordinate is the first number and the y-coordinate is the second number.

To plot a point on the graph when given the coordinates, draw perpendicular lines from the number-line coordinates to the point where the two lines intersect.

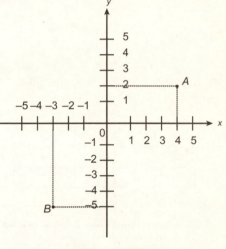

Figure 4.147

To find the coordinates of a given point on the graph, draw perpendicular lines from the point to the coordinates on the number line.

In Figure 4.147, point A has the coordinates $(4, 2)$ and point B has the coordinates of $(-3, -5)$.

For any two points A and B with coordinates (x_A, y_A) and (x_B, y_B), respectively, the distance between A and B is represented by:

$$d = \sqrt{(x_A - x_B)^2 + (y_A - y_B)^2}$$

This is commonly known as the distance formula, and is derived from the Pythagorean Theorem. See Figure 4.148.

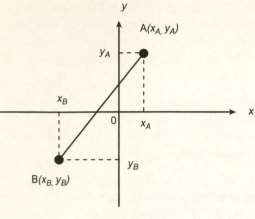

Figure 4.148

PROBLEM

In Figure 4.149, find the distance between point $A(1, 3)$ and $B(5, 3)$.

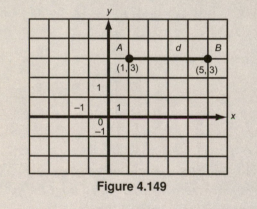

Figure 4.149

SOLUTION

In this case, where the ordinate of both points is the same, the distance between the two points is given by the absolute value of the difference between the two abscissas. In fact, this case reduces to merely counting boxes, as Figure 4.149 shows.

Let, x_1 = abscissa of A y_1 = ordinate of A
     x_2 = abscissa of B y_2 = ordinate of B
     d = the distance

Therefore, $d = |x_1 - x_2|$. By substitution, $d = |1 - 5|$ $= |-4| = 4$. This answer can also be obtained by applying the general formula for distance between any two points.

$$d = \sqrt{(x_1 - x_2)^2 + (y_1 - y_2)^2}$$

By substitution,

$$d = \sqrt{(1 - 5)^2 + (3 - 3)^2}$$

$$= \sqrt{(-4)^2 + (0)^2}$$

$$= \sqrt{16}$$

The distance is 4.

To find the midpoint of a segment between the two given endpoints, use the formula

$$MP = \left(\frac{x_1 + x_2}{2}, \frac{y_1 + y_2}{2}\right)$$

where x_1 and y_1 are the coordinates of one point, and x_2 and y_2 are the coordinates of the other point.

Geometry Review

ANSWER KEY

Drill: Regular Polygons (Convex)

1. (D)
2. (D)
3. (D)
4. (C)
5. (D)

Drill: Triangles

1. (D)
2. (B)
3. (C)
4. (A)
5. (D)

6. (C)
7. (B)
8. (D)
9. (A)
10. (B)

Drill: Quadrilaterals

1. (B)
2. (D)
3. (A)
4. (D)
5. (C)

6. (C)
7. (D)
8. (B)
9. (C)
10. (D)

Drill: Circles

1. (B)
2. (C)
3. (D)
4. (C)
5. (B)

6. (B)
7. (D)
8. (C)
9. (C)
10. (B)

Detailed Explanations of Answers

Drill: Regular Polygons (Convex)

1. (D)

A pentagon is five-sided. A regular pentagon is both equiangular and equilateral. Therefore, each exterior angle is $360° \div 5 = 72°$.

Since each exterior angle is supplementary to each interior angle, the interior angle is $180° - 72° = 108°$.

2. (D)

The sum of the measures of the exterior angles of any regular polygon is $360°$.

3. (D)

$$a = 4\sqrt{3} \text{ mm} \qquad p = \text{perimeter} = 3(24) = 72 \text{ mm}$$

$$A = \frac{1}{2}ap = \frac{1}{2}(4\sqrt{3})(72) = 144\sqrt{3} \text{ mm}^2$$

4. (C)

In a regular hexagon, $s = 4$ means the radius = 4 too, which, by the Pythagorean Theorem, makes the apothem

$$\sqrt{(4)^2 - (2)^2} = 2\sqrt{3}$$

$$A = \frac{1}{2}ap = \frac{1}{2}(2\sqrt{3})(6)(4) = 24\sqrt{3} \text{ cm}^2$$

5. (D)

A decagon has 10 sides.

$$A = \frac{1}{2}ap = \frac{1}{2}a(s)(10) = \frac{1}{2}(9.2)(6)(10) = 276 \text{ cm}^2$$

Drill: Triangles

1. (D)

Since $\angle Q$ is a right angle, $m\angle Q = 90°$. Therefore, $90° - 23° = 67°$

2. (B)

$$\frac{180° - 96°}{2} = \frac{84°}{2} = 42°$$

3. (C)

$$3x + 2x + x = 180°$$

$$6x = 180°$$

$$x = 30°$$

4. (A)

$$6:4 = 4:b \Rightarrow \frac{6}{4} = \frac{4}{b} \Rightarrow 6b = 16$$

$$b = \frac{16}{6} = 2\frac{4}{6} = 2\frac{2}{3}$$

5. (D)

$$3:6 = 4:b \qquad b = 8$$

$$3:4 = 4:a$$

$$\frac{3}{4} = \frac{4}{a}$$

$$3a = 16 \quad a = 16\left(\frac{1}{3}\right) = 5\frac{1}{3}$$

6. (C)

$$A = \frac{1}{2}bh = \frac{1}{2}(14)(8) = 56$$

7. (B)

$$A = \frac{1}{2}bh = \frac{1}{2}(11)(7) = 38\frac{1}{2}, \text{ or } 38.5$$

8. (D)

$$A = \frac{1}{2}bh = \frac{1}{2}(4)(8\sqrt{2}) = 16\sqrt{2}$$

9. (A)

Using the Pythagorean Theorem,

$$\overline{AB} = \sqrt{(\overline{AC})^2 - (\overline{BC})^2} = \sqrt{(15)^2 - (9)^2} = \sqrt{144} = 12$$

Then $A = \frac{1}{2}bh = \frac{1}{2}(9)(12) = 54 \text{ cm}^2$

10. (B)

This is an isosceles right triangle, so the legs are equal. Using the Pythagorean Theorem,

$$(10\sqrt{2})^2 = a^2 + a^2$$
$$200 = 2a^2$$
$$a^2 = 100$$
$$a = 10$$

So the sides are 10 cm each.

$$A = \frac{1}{2}bh = \frac{1}{2}(10)(10) = 50 \text{ cm}^2$$

Drill: Quadrilaterals

1. (B)

∡B and ∡D are opposite angles in the parallelogram and are equal. Therefore,

$$6x + 2 = 98$$
$$6x = 96$$
$$x = 16$$

2. (D)

$$A = bh = (18)(9) = 162$$

3. (A)

Using the Pythagorean Theorem,

$$\overline{AC} = \sqrt{(\overline{AD})^2 + (\overline{DC})^2}$$
$$= \sqrt{(6)^2 + (8)^2}$$
$$= \sqrt{36 + 64}$$
$$= \sqrt{100}$$
$$= 10 \text{ cm}$$

4. (D)

$$A = bh = (7)(10) = 70 \text{ cm}^2$$

5. (C)

$$\overline{EC} = \overline{BD} = 17$$
$$\overline{BO} = \frac{1}{2}\overline{BD} = \frac{1}{2}(17) = 8.5$$

6. (C)

Using the Pythagorean Theorem,

$$\overline{GH} = \sqrt{\left(\frac{1}{2}GI\right)^2 + \left(\frac{1}{2}HJ\right)^2}$$

$$= \sqrt{\left[\left(\frac{1}{2}\right)(6)\right]^2 + \left[\left(\frac{1}{2}\right)(8)\right]^2}$$

$$= \sqrt{(3)^2 + (4)^2}$$

$$= \sqrt{25} = 5$$

7. (D)

$$A = \frac{1}{2}(b_1 + b_2)h$$

$$= \frac{1}{2}(14 + 21)(10)$$

$$= \frac{1}{2}(35)(10)$$

$$= 175$$

8. (B)

$$\overline{BC} = \overline{AD} = 6$$

$$P = 6 + 6 + 5 + 10 = 27$$

9. (C)

Use the Pythagorean Theorem to find the height.

$h^2 = 6^2 - 3^2$

$h^2 = 27$

$h = 3\sqrt{3}$.

$$A = \frac{1}{2}(b_1 + b_2)h = \frac{1}{2}(4 + 7)(3\sqrt{3})$$

$$= \frac{1}{2}(11)(3\sqrt{3})$$

$$= \frac{33}{2}(\sqrt{3})$$

10. (D)

The base angles of an isosceles trapezoid are equal.

Therefore, $\angle W = \angle Z$, so

$$58 = 4x - 6$$

$$64 = 4x$$

$$16 = x$$

Drill: Circles

1. (B)

$$C = 2\pi r = 2(\pi)(3) = 6\pi$$

2. (C)

$$A = \pi r^2 = \pi(11)^2 = 121\pi$$

3. (D)

$$A = \pi r^2 \quad r = \frac{1}{2}d = \frac{1}{2}(27) = 13.5$$

$$A = \pi(13.5)^2 = 182.25\pi$$

4. (C)

$$A = 225\pi = \pi r^2, \text{ so } r = \sqrt{225} = 15$$

$$d = 2r = 2(15) = 30$$

5. (B)

$$C_X = \pi r^2 = 144\pi \quad r_X = 12$$

$$C_Y = \pi r^2 = 81\pi \quad r_Y = 9$$

$$r_X : r_Y = 12:9 = 4:3$$

6. (B)

Shaded Area = Larger Area − Smaller Area

$$= \pi r_1^{\,2} - \pi r_2^{\,2}$$

$$= \pi(7)^2 - \pi(5)^5$$

$$= 49\pi - 25\pi$$

$$= 24\pi$$

7. (D)

Measure of arc = measure of central angle

8. (C)

The measure of a semicircle is 180º. Therefore, $\overset{\frown}{AXC} = 180º$.

9. (C)

Since $\overset{\frown}{XYZ}$ is semicircle, $180º - 40º = 140º$

10. (B)

$$\frac{45}{360}\pi r^2 = \frac{1}{8}\pi(4)^2 = \frac{16}{8}\pi = 2\pi$$

SUBAREA IV:
Data Analysis, Statistics and Probability

Fields 09 & 47

Data Description: Graphs

Types of Data Presentation

Repeated measurements yield data, which must be organized according to some principle. The data should be arranged in such a way that each observation can fall into one, and only one, category. A simple graphical method of presenting data is the **pie chart**, which is a circle divided into parts that represent categories.

•   **EXAMPLE**

The pie chart in Figure 5.1 shows the following data.

2009 Budget

38% came from individual income taxes

28% from social insurance receipts

13% from corporate income taxes

12% from borrowing

5% from excise taxes

4% other

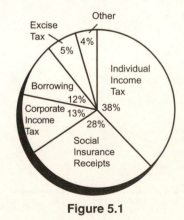

Figure 5.1

These data can also be presented in the form of a **bar chart** or **bar graph**, as shown in Figure 5.2.

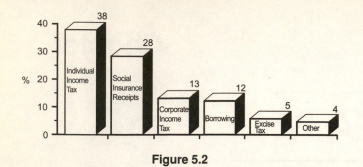

Figure 5.2

• EXAMPLE

The population of the United States for the years 1860 through 1960 is shown in Table 5.1.

Table 5.1

Year	Population in millions
1860	31.4
1870	39.8
1880	50.2
1890	62.9
1900	76.0
1910	92.0
1920	105.7
1930	122.8
1940	131.7
1950	151.1
1960	179.3

. . . in the graph shown in Figure 5.3,

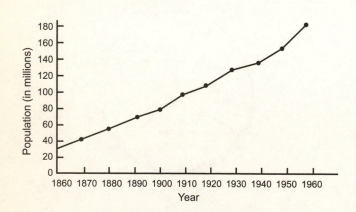

Figure 5.3

. . . and in the bar chart shown in Figure 5.4.

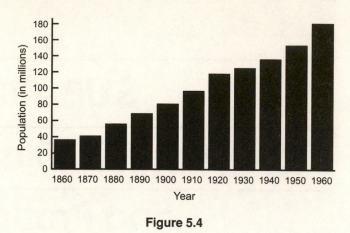

Figure 5.4

• EXAMPLE

A quadratic function is given by

$$y = x^2 + x - 2$$

We compute the values of y corresponding to various values of x, as shown in Table 5.2

Table 5.2

x	−3	−2	−1	0	1	2	3
y	4	0	−2	−2	0	4	10

From this table, we obtain the points of the graph in Figure 5.5.

$(-3, 4)\ (-2, 0)\ (-1, -2)\ (0, -2)\ (1, 0)\ (2, 4)\ (3, 10)$

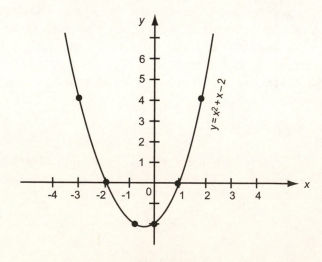

Figure 5.5

The curve shown is called a parabola. The general equation for a parabola is

$$y = ax^2 + bx + c, a \neq 0$$

where *a*, *b*, and *c* are constants.

PROBLEMS

Twenty students are enrolled in the foreign language department, and their major fields are as follows: Spanish, Spanish, French, Italian, French, Spanish, German, German, Russian, Russian, French, German, German, German, Spanish, Russian, German, Italian, German, and Spanish.

(a) Make a frequency distribution table.

(b) Make a frequency bar graph.

SOLUTIONS

(a) The frequency distribution table is constructed by writing down the major field and next to it the number of students, as shown in Table 5.3.

Table 5.3

Major Field	Number of Students
German	7
Russian	3
Spanish	5
French	3
Italian	2
Total	20

(b) The bar graph for these data is shown in Figure 5.6.

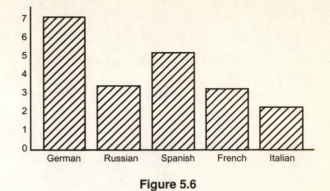

Figure 5.6

In a bar graph, the fields are listed and spaced evenly along the horizontal axis. Each specified field is represented by a rectangle, and all have the same width. The height of each, identified by a number on the vertical axis, corresponds to the frequency of that field.

A **box-and-whiskers** plot is a graph that displays five statistics. A minimum score, a maximum score, and three percentiles. A percentile value for a score tells you the percentage of scores lower than it. The beginning of the box is the score at the 25th percentile. The end of the box represents the 75th percentile. The score inside the box is the median, or the score at the 50th percentile. Attached to the box you will find two whiskers. The score at the end of the left whisker is the minimum score. The score at the end of the right whisker is the maximum score.

• EXAMPLE

In the box-and-whiskers plot shown in Figure 5.7, the minimum score is 70, the score at the 25th percentile is 78, the median score is 82, the score at the 75th percentile is 90, and the maximum score is 94.

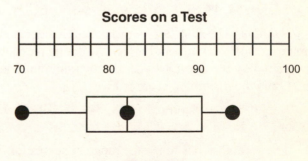

Figure 5.7

PROBLEM

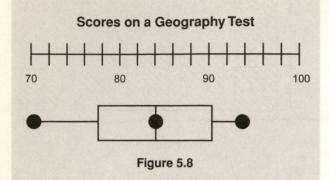

Scores on a Geography Test

70   80   90   100

Figure 5.8

Using the box-and-whiskers plot in Figure 5.8, what was the median score on the geography test?

SOLUTION

The median score is 84. On a box-and-whiskers plot, the median score is the score on the inside of the box.

• EXAMPLE

A **stem-and-leaf plot** is a way of displaying scores in groups. A stem-and-leaf plot gives you a picture of the scores, as well as the actual numbers themselves, in a compact form. In this type of plot, a score is broken into a stem and a leaf. The leaf consists of the smallest digit, and the stem consists of the remaining larger digits.

Task: Create a stem-and-leaf plot that uses the following scores.

Scores: 64, 48, 61, 81, 63, 59, 70, 54, 76, 61, 55, 31

Solution: The first step is to take these scores and create a set of "rank-ordered scores," ordering the scores from smallest to largest. Notice that the minimum score is 31, and the maximum score is 81.

Rank-Ordered Scores: 31, 48, 54, 55, 59, 61, 61, 63, 64, 70, 76, 81

The second step is to list the range of scores for the stems in a column. The stem of our smallest score (31) is 3, and that of our largest score (81) is 8. List all of the whole numbers between 3 and 8 as stems.

The third step is to put the leaves on the stems. Take each score, one at a time and put the last digit in a col-

umn next to its stem. For example, the last digit of 31 is 1, so put a 1 next to its stem of 3. The last digit of 48 is 8, so put an 8 next to its stem of 4. Do this for the remaining scores.

Stems	Leaves
8	1
7	0 6
6	1 1 3 4
5	4 5 9
4	8
3	1

A stem-and-leaf plot gives you a picture of how the scores are grouped so that you can begin to understand their meaning. In this example, you can see that 4 people got a score in the 60s, and that most of the scores are centered around the 50s and 60s. You can also see that the high score was 81, and the low score was 31.

PROBLEM

Stems	Leaves
6	5
5	3 6
4	0 1 7
3	2 9
2	4

This stem-and-leaf plot was created using what set of scores?

SOLUTION

In this stem-and-leaf plot, the stems are the first digit, and the leaves are the remaining digits. Starting from the bottom, the first score is 24, the second score is 32, then comes 39, 40, 41, 47, 53, 56, and 65.

• EXAMPLE

A **scatterplot** is a graph that shows the relationship between two variables. A scatterplot is a set of (x, y) coordinates. Each coordinate is a point on the graph. x represents a value of one variable, and y represents the value of another variable. Remember, a variable is just a measurement that can take on more than one value. A scatterplot is useful because in one picture you can see if there is a relationship between two variables. It has been said that, "A picture is worth a thousand words." Likewise, "A graph is worth a thousand numbers."

Given: Variable *x* represents grade level. Variable *y* represents hours of homework each week.

Task: Using the data shown in Table 5.4, construct a scatterplot.

Question: What is the relationship between these two variables?

Table 5.4

x	Grade Level	1	2	3	4	5	6	7	8	9	10	11	12
y	Hours of Homework	2	3	3	6	4	10	7	10	12	9	14	15

Answer: You can think of these two variables as one set of (*x*, *y*) coordinates on a graph. Remember, a coordinate is just a point. So the scatterplot is just a graph of the following points: (1, 2), (2, 3), (3, 3), (4, 6), (5, 4), (6, 10), (7, 7), (8, 10), (9, 12), (10, 9), (11, 14), and (12, 15) as shown in Figure 5.9. This graph shows that as grade level increases, the number of homework hours per week tends to increase.

Scatterplot

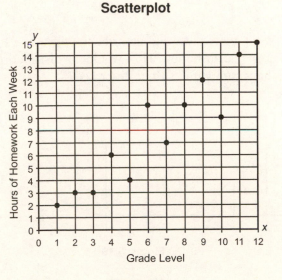

Figure 5.9

A statistic called **correlation** tells you whether two measurements go together along a straight line. A scat-

terplot is one way of looking at correlation. There are three different types of correlation: positive (Figure 5.10), none (Figure 5.11), and negative (Figure 5.12).

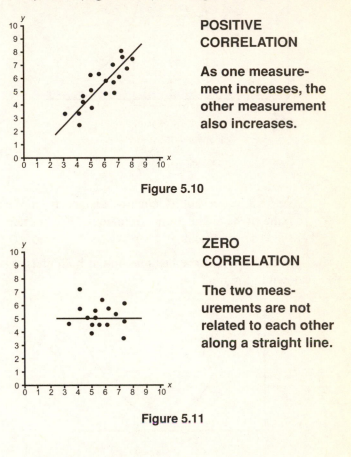

POSITIVE CORRELATION

As one measurement increases, the other measurement also increases.

Figure 5.10

ZERO CORRELATION

The two measurements are not related to each other along a straight line.

Figure 5.11

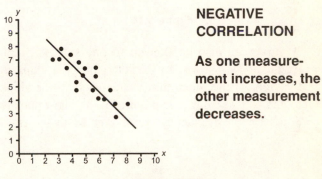

NEGATIVE CORRELATION

As one measurement increases, the other measurement decreases.

Figure 5.12

Types of Frequency Curves

In applications, we find that most of the frequency curves fall within one of the categories listed.

(A) One of the most popular is the **bell-shaped** or **symmetrical frequency curve**, shown in Figure 5.13.

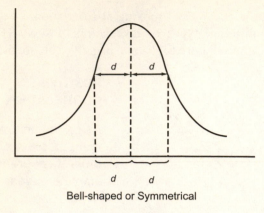

Bell-shaped or Symmetrical

Figure 5.13

Note that observations equally distant from the maximum have the same frequency. The normal curve is symmetrical.

(B) The **U-shaped curve** has maxima at both ends, as shown in Figure 5.14.

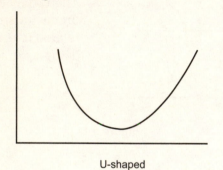

U-shaped

Figure 5.14

(C) A curve can also be **skewed** to one side. A graph is said to be skewed to the left when the slope to the right of the maximum is steeper than the slope to the left as shown in Figure 5.15. The opposite holds for the frequency curve skewed to the right (Figure 5.16).

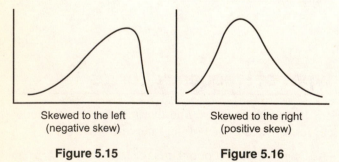

Skewed to the left
(negative skew)

Skewed to the right
(positive skew)

Figure 5.15   **Figure 5.16**

(D) A **J-shaped curve** has a maximum at one end, as shown in Figure 5.17.

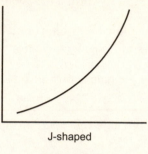

J-shaped

Figure 5.17

(E) A **multimodal frequency curve** has more than one maximum, as shown in Figure 5.18. A curve with two maxima is called bimodal.

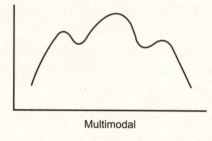

Multimodal

Figure 5.18

PROBLEM

What are two ways to describe the form of a frequency distribution? How would the distributions shown in Figure 5.19 be described?

(a)   (b)

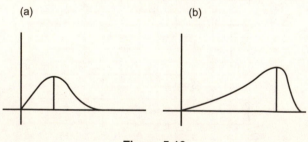

Figure 5.19

SOLUTION

The form of a frequency distribution can be described by its departure from symmetry or skewness and its degree of peakedness (kurtosis).

If the few extreme values are higher than most of the others, we say that the distribution is "positively skewed" or "skewed" to the right.

If the few extreme values are lower than most of the others, we say that the distribution is "negatively skewed" or "skewed" to the left.

(a) This distribution has extreme values in the upper half of the curve and is skewed to the right or positively skewed.

(b) The extreme values of this distribution are in the lower half of the curve. Thus, the distribution is negatively skewed or skewed to the left.

Probability

Probability is defined as the likelihood of the occurrence of an event or as the chance that some particular event will occur.

• EXAMPLE

A weather report might indicate the chance of rain to be 70%, which could be interpreted as the probability of rain = .70.

(A) Objective Probability (Calculated)

In most instances, the probability that an event will occur is determined by a mathematical formula and is based on empirical evidence.

$$P(X) = \frac{\text{No. of outcomes corresponding to event } X}{\text{Total no. of possible outcomes}}$$

• EXAMPLE

The probability of drawing a queen from a deck of cards is defined as:

$$P(\text{Queen}) = \frac{\text{No. of queens in the deck}}{\text{Total no. of cards in the deck}}$$

$$= \frac{4}{52} = \frac{1}{13}, \text{ or .077.}$$

(B) Subjective Probability

When the probability of an event occurring is based on the personal (or professional) judgment of an individual or group of individuals, the probability is referred to as "subjective."

• EXAMPLE

The probability that sales will increase by $500,000 next year if we increase our advertising expenditure by $10,000 is .25.

Properties of Probabilities

The following three properties are characteristics of all probabilities:

(A) $0 \leq P(X) \leq 1$; every probability is contained within the range 0 to 1, inclusive, where 0 represents absolute certainty that the event will not occur and 1 represents absolute certainty that the event will occur.

• EXAMPLE

$$P\,(\text{Head on Coin}) = \frac{1}{2}$$
$$P\,(6 \text{ on Die}) = \frac{1}{6}$$
$$P\,(\text{Ace of Spades}) = \frac{1}{52}$$

(B) $\sum_{i=1}^{n} P_i(X) = 1$; the probabilities of all possible simple events that can occur within a given experiment will sum to 1.

• EXAMPLE

coin: $P(\text{Head}) + P(\text{Tail}) = \dfrac{1}{2} + \dfrac{1}{2} = 1$

die: $P(1) + P(2) + P(3) + P(4) + P(5) + P(6)$
$$= \frac{1}{6} + \frac{1}{6} + \frac{1}{6} + \frac{1}{6} + \frac{1}{6} + \frac{1}{6} = 1$$

cards: $P(\text{Club}) + P(\text{Heart}) + P(\text{Spade}) + P(\text{Diamond})$
$$= \frac{1}{4} + \frac{1}{4} + \frac{1}{4} + \frac{1}{4} = 1$$

(C) $P(X) + P(\text{Not } X) = 1$; the probability that event X occurs plus the probability that event X does not occur sums to 1.

- **EXAMPLE**

  coin: $P(\text{Head}) + P(\text{Not a Head}) = \dfrac{1}{2} + \dfrac{1}{2} = 1$

  die: $P(6) + P(\text{Not a 6}) = \dfrac{1}{6} + \dfrac{5}{6} = 1$

  cards: $P(\text{Spade}) + P(\text{Not a Spade})$
  $= \dfrac{13}{52} + \dfrac{39}{52} = 1$, or $\dfrac{1}{4} + \dfrac{3}{4} = 1$

Methods of Computing Probabilities

(A) Computing Probabilities by Addition—"Or" Situations

(1) **Mutually Exclusive Events** - Events that cannot occur simultaneously are mutually exclusive. To determine the probability that either event X occurs *or* event Y occurs, the individual probabilities of event X and event Y are added.

$P(X \text{ or } Y) = P(X) + P(Y)$

- **EXAMPLE**

  The probability that either a club or a spade is drawn from a deck of cards in a single draw is defined as:

  $P(\text{Club or Spade}) = P(\text{Club}) + P(\text{Spade})$
  $= \dfrac{13}{52} + \dfrac{13}{52} = \dfrac{26}{52} = \dfrac{1}{2}$, or .5

  Note that this concept applies to three or more events as well.

2. **Nonmutually Exclusive Events** - Events that can occur simultaneously are nonmutually exclusive. To determine the probability that either event X occurs or event Y occurs, the individual probabilities of event X and event Y are added and the probability that the two occur simultaneously is subtracted from the total.

$$P(X \text{ or } Y) = P(X) + P(Y) - P(X \text{ and } Y)$$

- **EXAMPLE**

  The probability that either a queen or a spade is drawn from a deck of cards in a single draw is defined as:

  $P(\text{Queen or Spade}) = P(\text{Queen}) + P(\text{Spade}) -$
  $P(\text{Queen and Spade})$
  $= \dfrac{4}{52} + \dfrac{13}{52} - \dfrac{1}{52} = \dfrac{16}{52} = \dfrac{4}{13}.$

  Notice in this example that we must subtract $\dfrac{1}{52}$ from the total because the queen of spades is counted in the total number of queens and it is also counted in the total number of spades. If we do not subtract $P(\text{Queen and Spade})$, we are counting that one card twice.

(B) Computing Probabilities by Multiplication—"And" Situations

(1) Independent Events

Two (or more) events are independent if the occurrence of one event has no effect upon whether the other event occurs. To determine the probability that event X occurs *and* event Y occurs when X and Y are independent, the individual probabilities of event X and event Y are multiplied together.

$$P(X \text{ and } Y) = P(X) \times P(Y)$$

- **EXAMPLES**

(a) The probability of tossing a 6 on a single die followed by the toss of a 3 is:

  $P(6 \text{ and } 3) = P(6) \times P(3) = \dfrac{1}{6} \times \dfrac{1}{6} = \dfrac{1}{36}.$

(b) The probability of tossing three heads in three tosses of a coin:

  $P(H, H, H) = P(H) \times P(H) \times P(H)$
  $= \dfrac{1}{2} \times \dfrac{1}{2} \times \dfrac{1}{2} = \dfrac{1}{8}.$

(c) The probability of drawing a heart from a deck of cards, replacing the first card, and drawing a club on the second draw:

$$P(H \text{ and } C) = P(H) \times P(C)$$

$$= \frac{13}{52} \times \frac{13}{52} = \frac{1}{4} \times \frac{1}{4} = \frac{1}{16}.$$

Note that this concept applies to three or more events as well.

(2) Dependent Events

Two (or more) events are dependent if the occurrence of one event has some effect upon whether the other event occurs. To determine the probability that event X occurs *and* event Y occurs when X and Y are dependent, the formula is:

$$P(X \text{ and } Y) = P(X) \times P(Y \mid X)$$

or

$$P(X \text{ and } Y) = P(Y) \times P(X \mid Y)$$

where $P(Y \mid X)$ is read as "the probability that event Y will occur, given that event X has already occurred," and $P(X \mid Y)$ is read as "the probability that event X will occur given that event Y has already occurred."

• **EXAMPLES**

(a) A box contains 6 red balls, 4 green balls, and 5 purple balls. What is the probability that a red ball is drawn on the first draw and a purple ball is drawn on the second draw, if the first ball is not replaced prior to the second ball being drawn?

$$P(\text{Red and Purple}) = P(R) \times P(P \mid R)$$

$$= \frac{6}{15} \times \frac{5}{14} = \frac{30}{210} = \frac{1}{7}.$$

(b) Three cards are drawn from a deck. What is the probability that the first is a queen, the second is a queen, and the third is a king? Assume that each card is **not** replaced prior to the next one being drawn.

$$P(Q1, Q2, K) = P(Q1) \times P(Q2 \mid Q1) \times$$
$$P(K \mid Q1 \text{ and } Q2)$$

$$= \frac{4}{52} \times \frac{3}{51} \times \frac{4}{50} = \frac{48}{132,600} = .004$$

Probability Tables

A tabular approach is often easier to understand when calculating probabilities.

• **EXAMPLE**

Table 5.5

ASSEMBLED PARTS

		Good	Defective	Total
Worker	A	.5390	.0110	.55
	B	.4365	.0135	.45
TOTAL		.9755	.0245	1.00

The **cell** probabilities are referred to as **joint probabilities,** which represent the combined probability of the two events (row and column) occurring; for example, in Table 5.5, the probability that worker A assembled the part and it is good is .539. The **total** row and column probabilities are referred to as **marginal probabilities,** which are the sums of the joint probabilities over the rows or columns. For example, .45 is a marginal probability representing the probability that worker B assembled the part. It is the sum of .4365 (probability that worker B assembled it and it is good) plus .0135 (the probability that worker B assembled it and it is defective).

Statistics

$$\bar{x} = \frac{3 \times 3 + 7 \times 2 + 2 \times 1 + 8 \times 5 + 0 \times 10 + 4 \times 6}{3 + 2 + 1 + 5 + 10 + 6} \approx 3.3$$

Measures of Central Tendency

Central tendency is a term used for a statistic that represents an entire data set. The common measures of central tendency are the mean, the mode, and the median.

Mean

The **arithmetic mean**, or **mean**, of a set of measurements is the sum of the measurements divided by the total number of measurements. It is also called the "average."

The arithmetic mean of a set of numbers $x_1, x_2, \ldots, x_n$ is denoted by $\bar{x}$ (read "x bar").

$$\bar{x} = \frac{\sum_{i=1}^{n} x_i}{n} = \frac{x_1 + x_2 + \ldots + x_n}{n}$$

• EXAMPLE

The arithmetic mean of the numbers 3, 7, 1, 24, 11, and 32 is

$$\bar{x} = \frac{3 + 7 + 1 + 24 + 11 + 32}{6} = \frac{78}{6} = 13$$

Let $f_1, f_2, \ldots, f_n$ be the frequencies of the numbers $x_1, x_2, \ldots, x_n$ (i.e., number x_i occurs f_i times). The arithmetic mean is

$$\bar{x} = \frac{f_1 x_1 + f_2 x_2 + \ldots + f_n x_n}{f_1 + f_2 + \ldots + f_n} = \frac{\sum_{i=1}^{n} f_i x_i}{\sum_{i=1}^{n} f_i}$$

Note that the total frequency, that is, the total number of cases, is $\sum_{i=1}^{n} f_i$.

• EXAMPLE

If the measurements 3, 7, 2, 8, 0, and 4 occur with frequencies 3, 2, 1, 5, 10, and 6, respectively, then the arithmetic mean is

PROBLEM

The following measurements were taken by an antique dealer as he weighed to the nearest pound his prized collection of anvils. The weights were 84, 92, 37, 50, 50, 50, 84, 40, 92, and 98. What was the mean weight of the anvils?

SOLUTION

The average or mean weight of the anvils is

$$\bar{x} = \frac{\text{sum of observations}}{\text{number of observations}}$$

$$= \frac{84 + 92 + 37 + 50 + 50 + 50 + 84 + 40 + 92 + 98}{10}$$

$$= \frac{677}{10} = 67.7 \cong 68 \text{ pounds}$$

An alternate way to compute the sample mean is to rearrange the terms in the numerator, grouping the numbers that are the same. Thus,

$$\bar{x} = \frac{(84 + 84) + (92 + 92) + (50 + 50 + 50) + 37 + 40 + 98}{10}$$

We see that we can express the mean in terms of the frequency of observations. The frequency of an observation is the number of times a number appears in a sample.

$$\bar{x} = \frac{2(84) + 2(92) + 3(50) + 37 + 40 + 98}{10}$$

The observations 84 and 92 appear in the sample twice, and 50 appears three times, so they are each multiplied by their frequency.

Keep in mind that the arithmetic mean is strongly affected by extreme values.

EXAMPLE

Consider four workers whose annual bonuses are $2,500, $3,200, $3,700, and $48,000. The arithmetic mean of their bonuses is

$$\frac{\$57,400}{4} = \$14,350$$

The figure $14,350 can hardly represent the typical annual bonuses of the four workers.

The **deviation** d_i of x_i from its mean $\bar{x}$ is defined to be

$$d_i = x_i - \bar{x}$$

The sum of the deviations of x_1, x_2, ..., x_n from the mean $\bar{x}$ is equal to zero. Indeed,

$$\sum_{i=1}^{n} d_i = \sum_{i=1}^{n}(x_i - \bar{x}) = 0$$

We can show that this is true by the following:

$$\sum_{i=1}^{n}(x_i - \bar{x}) = \sum_{i=1}^{n} x_i - n\bar{x} = \sum x_i - n\frac{\sum x_i}{n}$$

$$= \sum x_i - \sum x_i = 0$$

The mean of a sum is equal to the sum of the means.

If $z_1 = x_1 + y_1$, . . ., $z_n = x_n + y_n$, then $\bar{z} = \bar{x} + \bar{y}$. Indeed,

$$\bar{x} = \frac{\sum x}{n}, \bar{y} = \frac{\sum y}{n}, \text{ and } \bar{z} = \frac{\sum z}{n}$$

We have

$$\bar{z} = \frac{\sum z}{n} = \frac{\sum(x+y)}{n} = \frac{\sum x}{n} + \frac{\sum y}{n} = \bar{x} + \bar{y}.$$

The arithmetic mean plays an important role in statistical inference. The sample mean $\bar{x}$ can be used to make inferences about the corresponding population mean, denoted by μ.

EXAMPLE

Suppose a bank has 500 savings accounts. We pick a sample of 12 accounts. The balance on each account in dollars is

657	284	51
215	73	327
65	412	218
539	225	195

The sample mean $\bar{x}$ is

$$\bar{x} = \frac{\sum_{i=1}^{12} x_i}{12} = \$271.75$$

The average amount of money for the 12 sampled accounts is $271.75. Using this information, we can estimate the total amount of money in the bank to be

$$\$271.25 \times 500 = \$135,875.$$

Means can also be computed for grouped data, that is, when data are presented in a frequency distribution. Then, all values within a given class interval are considered to be equal to the class mark, or midpoint, of the interval.

PROBLEM

Given the data shown in the bar graph of Figure 5.20, find the average value.

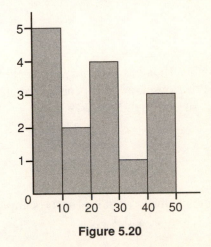

Figure 5.20

SOLUTION

To find the arithmetic mean, $\bar{x}$, multiply each different number by its associated frequency. The numbers are the midpoints of the intervals since we don't know the individual values. Add these products, then divide by the total number of numbers.

$$\bar{x} = [5(5) + 2(15) + 4(25) + 1(35) + 3(45)] \div 15$$
$$= (25 + 30 + 100 + 35 = 135) \div 15$$
$$= 325 \div 15 = 21.67$$

Mode

The **mode** of a set of numbers is the value that occurs most often (with the highest frequency).

Observe that the mode may not exist, for example, if each data point appears only once. Also, if the mode exists, it may not be unique. For example, for the numbers 1,1,2,2,3,4,5, the mode is not unique. This set of data has two modes, 1 and 2, which each appear twice, so this set of data is **bimodal**.

• EXAMPLE

The set of numbers 2, 2, 4, 7, 9, 9, 13, 13, 13, 26, and 29 has mode 13.

PROBLEM

Find the mode of the sample 14, 19, 16, 21, 18, 19, 24, 15, and 19.

SOLUTION

The number 19 is observed three times in this sample, and no other observation appears as frequently. The mode of this sample is therefore 19.

PROBLEM

Find the mode or modes of the sample 6, 7, 7, 3, 8, 5, 3, and 9.

SOLUTION

In this sample the numbers 7 and 3 both appear twice. There are no other observations that appear as frequently as these two. Therefore, 3 and 7 are the modes of this sample. The sample is bimodal.

PROBLEM

Find the mode of the sample 14, 16, 21, 19, 18, 24, and 17.

SOLUTION

In this sample all the numbers occur with the same frequency. There is no single number that is observed more frequently than any other. Thus, there is no mode or all observations are modes. The mode is not a useful concept here.

For grouped data—data presented in the form of a frequency table or histogram—we do not know the actual measurements, only how many measurements fall into each interval. In such a case, the mode is the midpoint of the class interval with the highest frequency.

• EXAMPLE

One can compute the mode from a histogram or frequency distribution.

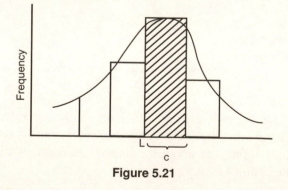

Figure 5.21

The shaded area in Figure 5.21 indicates the modal class, that is, the class containing the mode, or the class with the highest frequency.

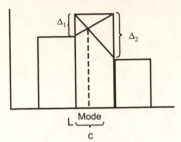

Figure 5.22

$$\text{Mode} = L + c\left(\frac{\Delta_1}{\Delta_1 + \Delta_2}\right)$$

where (see Figure 5.22)

L is the lower class boundary of the modal class

c is the size of the modal class interval

Δ_1 is the excess of the modal frequency over the frequency of the next lower class

Δ_2 is the excess of the modal frequency over the frequency of the next higher class

Median

The **median** of a set of numbers is defined as the middle value when the numbers are arranged in order of magnitude. The number of observations that lie above the median is the same as the number of observations that lie below it.

Usually, the median is used to measure the midpoint of a large set of numbers. For example, we can talk about the median age of people getting married. Here, the median reflects the central value of the data for a large set of measurements. For small sets of numbers, we use the following conventions:

- For an odd number of measurements, the median is the middle value.

- For an even number of measurements, the median is the average of the two middle values.

In both cases, the numbers have to be arranged in order of magnitude.

- **EXAMPLE**

The scores of a test are 78, 79, 83, 83, 87, 92, and 95. Hence, the median is 83.

- **EXAMPLE**

The median of the set of numbers 21, 25, 29, 33, 44, and 47 is $\frac{29 + 33}{2} = 31$.

PROBLEM

Find the median of the sample 34, 29, 26, 37, and 31.

SOLUTION

Arranged in order, we have 26, 29, 31, 34, and 37. The number of observations is odd, and thus the median is 31. Note that there are two numbers in the sample above 31 and two below 31.

PROBLEM

Find the median of the sample 34, 29, 26, 37, 31, and 34.

SOLUTION

The sample arranged in order is 26, 29, 31, 34, 34, and 37. The number of observations is even, and thus the median, or middle number, is chosen halfway between the third and fourth numbers. In this case, the median is

$$\frac{31 + 34}{2} = 32.5$$

It is more difficult to compute the median for grouped data. The exact value of the measurements is not known; hence, we know only that the median is located in a particular class interval. The problem is where to place the median within this interval.

For grouped data, the median obtained by interpolation is given by

$$\text{Median} = L + \frac{c}{f_{\text{median}}} \left[\frac{n}{2} - \left(\sum f \right)_{\text{cum}} \right]$$

where

L = the lower class limit of the interval that contains the median

c = the size of the median class interval

f_{median} = frequency of the median class

n = the total frequency

$\left(\sum f \right)_{\text{cum}}$ = the sum of frequencies (cumulative frequency) for all classes before the median class

• EXAMPLE

The weight of 50 men is depicted in Table 5.6 in the form of frequency distribution.

Table 5.6

Weight	Frequency
115 – 121	2
122 – 128	3
129 – 135	13
136 – 142	15
143 – 149	9
150 – 156	5
157 – 163	3
TOTAL	50

Class 136–142 has the highest frequency.

The mode is the midpoint of the class interval with the highest frequency.

$$\text{Mode} = \frac{135.5 + 142.5}{2} = 139$$

We can also use the formula

$$\text{Mode} = L + c \left(\frac{\Delta_1}{\Delta_1 + \Delta_2} \right)$$

where $L = 135.5$

$c = 7$

$\Delta_1 = 2 \ (15 - 13 = 2)$

$\Delta_2 = 6 \ (15 - 9 = 6)$

$$\text{Mode} = 135.5 + 7 \times \frac{2}{2 + 6} = 137.25$$

The median is located in class 136–142.

We have

$$\text{Median} = L + \frac{c}{f_{\text{median}}} \left[\frac{n}{2} - \left(\sum f \right)_{\text{cum}} \right]$$

where $L = 135.5$

$c = 7$

$f_{\text{median}} = 15$

$n = 50$

$\left(\sum f \right)_{\text{cum}} = 2 + 3 + 13 = 18$

Hence,

$$\text{Median} = 135.5 + \frac{7}{15} \left[\frac{50}{2} - 18 \right] = 138.77$$

To compute the arithmetic mean for grouped data, we compute the midpoint x_i of each of the intervals and use the formula

$$\bar{x} = \frac{\sum\limits_{i=1}^{n} f_i x_i}{\sum\limits_{i=1}^{n} f_i}$$

We have

$$\bar{x} = \frac{118 \times 2 + 125 \times 3 + 132 \times 13 + 139 \times 15 + 146 \times 9 + 153 \times 5 + 160 \times 3}{50}$$

$$= 139.42$$

For symmetrical curves, the mean, mode, and median all coincide, as shown in Figure 5.23.

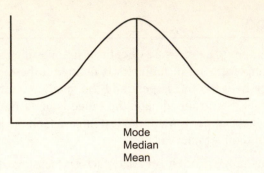

Mode
Median
Mean

Figure 5.23

For skewed distributions, we have the following.

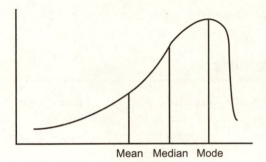

Mean   Median   Mode

Figure 5.24

The distribution in Figure 5.24 is skewed to the left.

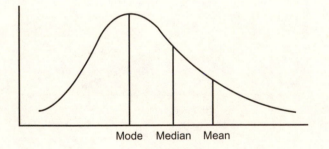

Mode   Median   Mean

Figure 5.25

The distribution in Figure 5.25 is skewed to the right.

PROBLEM

Find the median weight from Table 5.7.

Table 5.7	
Class Boundaries	**Frequencies**
58.5 – 61.5	4
61.5 – 64.5	8
64.5 –67.5	12
67.5 –70.5	13
70.5 –73.5	21
73.5 –76.5	15
76.5 –79.5	12
79.5 – 82.5	9
82.5 – 85.5	4
85.5 –88.5	2

SOLUTION

There are 100 observations in the sample. The median will be the 50th observation. When using an even-numbered sample of grouped data, the convention is to call the $\frac{n}{2}$th observation the median. There are 37 observations in the first four intervals, and the first five intervals contain 58 observations. The 50th observation is in the fifth class interval.

We use the technique of linear interpolation to estimate the position of the 50th observation within the class interval.

The width of the fifth class is 3 units, and there are 21 observations in that class interval. To interpolate, we imagine that each observation takes up $\frac{3}{21}$ units of the interval. There are 37 observations in the first four intervals, and thus the 13th observation in the fifth class will be the median. This 13th observation will be approximately $13\left(\frac{3}{21}\right)$ units from the lower boundary of the fifth class interval. The median is thus the lower boundary of the fifth class plus $13\left(\frac{3}{21}\right)$, or

$$\text{median} = 70.5 + \frac{13}{7} = 72.36$$

PROBLEM

A sample of drivers involved in motor vehicle accidents was categorized by age, as shown in Table 5.8:

Table 5.8

Age	Number of Accidents
16 – 25	28
26 – 35	13
36 – 45	12
46 – 55	8
56 – 65	19
66 – 75	20

What is the value of the median?

SOLUTION

The total number of accidents is 100. The median is the $\frac{100}{2}$ = 50th number when the numbers are arranged in ascending order. We seek the $\frac{100}{2}$ = 50th number, which appears in the third class (36–45). The two intervals 16–25 and 26–35 consist of 41 count. We need nine numbers from the interval 36–45. Use the lower boundary of this interval 36–45, which is 35.5, and add $\frac{9}{12}$ of the width of the interval (10).

Then

$$35.5 + \frac{9}{12}(10) = 43$$

Measures of Variability

Dispersion of the Data

The degree to which numerical data tend to spread about an average value is called the **variation** or **dispersion** of the data. We shall define various measures of dispersion here.

Range

The simplest measure of data variation is the **range**. The range of a set of numbers is defined to be the difference between the largest and the smallest numbers of the set. For grouped data, the range is the difference between the upper limit of the last interval and the lower limit of the first interval.

The range is not a very satisfactory measure of dispersion as it involves only two of the observations in the sample.

- **EXAMPLE**

The range of the numbers 3, 6, 21, 24, and 38 is 38 – 3 = 35.

Percentiles

The **nth percentile** of a set of numbers arranged in order of magnitude is the value that has n% of the numbers below it and $(100 - n)$% above it. Figure 5.26 shows the 70th percentile.

- **EXAMPLE**

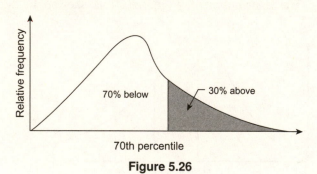

Figure 5.26

Percentiles are often used to describe the results of achievement tests; for example, saying that someone graduates in the top 10% of the class. Frequently used percentiles are the 25th, 50th and 75th percentiles, which are called the lower quartile, the middle quartile (median), and the upper quartile, respectively.

Interquartile Range

The **interquartile range**, abbreviated IQR, of a set of numbers is the difference between the upper and lower quartiles, as shown in Figure 5.27.

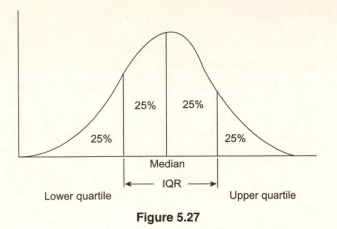

Figure 5.27

PROBLEM

Find the range of the sample composed of the observations 33, 53, 35, 37, and 49.

SOLUTION

In our sample, the largest observation is 53 and the smallest is 33. The difference is 53 – 33 = 20, and the range is 20.

PROBLEM

In a sample of data, the 75th percentile is the number 23. If the interquartile range is 10, what number represents the 25th percentile?

SOLUTION

The interquartile range = the difference between the 75th percentile and the 25th percentile. If x = 25th percentile, we have 23 – x = 10, so x = 13.

Deviations of the Data

The **deviation** of a number x from its mean $\bar{x}$ is defined to be

$$x - \bar{x}$$

Using deviations, we can construct many different measures of variability.

As discussed previously, the mean deviation for any set of measurements is always zero. Indeed, let $x_1, x_2, \ldots, x_n$ be measurements. Their mean is given by

$$\bar{x} = \frac{\sum x_i}{n}$$

The deviations are $x_1 - \bar{x}, x_2 - \bar{x}, \ldots, x_n - \bar{x}$, and the sum of the deviations is equal to

$$\sum_{i=1}^{n} (x_i - \bar{x}) = \sum_{i=1}^{n} x_i - n\bar{x} = \sum_{i=1}^{n} x_i - \sum_{i=1}^{n} x_i = 0$$

Standard Deviation

The **standard deviation**, σ, of a set $x_1, x_2, \ldots, x_n$ of n numbers is defined by

$$\sigma = \sqrt{\frac{\sum_{i=1}^{n}(x_i - \bar{x})^2}{n}}$$

The sample standard deviation is denoted by s, and the corresponding population standard deviation is denoted by σ. The difference between a sample and its corresponding population is discussed in the section "Sampling."

The sample standard deviation requires a denominator of $n - 1$ not n. For large values of n, the difference between the two definitions is negligible.

$$s = \sqrt{\frac{\sum_{i=1}^{n}(x_i - \bar{x})^2}{n - 1}}$$

Variance

The **variance** of a set of measurements is defined as the square of the standard deviation. Thus,

$$s^2 = \frac{\sum_{i=1}^{n}(x_i - \bar{x})^2}{n - 1}$$

Usually, the variance of the sample is denoted by s^2, and the corresponding population variance is denoted by σ^2.

• EXAMPLE

A simple manual task was given to six children, and the time each child took to complete the task was measured. Results are shown in Table 5.9.

Table 5.9

x_i	$x_i - \bar{x}$	$(x_i - \bar{x})^2$
12	2.5	6.25
9	−0.5	0.25
11	1.5	2.25
6	−3.5	12.25
10	0.5	0.25
9	−0.5	0.25
Total 57	0	21.5

For this sample, we shall find the standard deviation and variance.

The average $\bar{x}$ is 9.5.

$$\bar{x} = 9.5$$

The standard deviation is

$$s = \sqrt{\frac{21.5}{5}} = 2.07$$

and the variance is

$$s^2 = 4.3$$

PROBLEM

A couple has six children whose ages are 6, 8, 10, 12, 14, and 16. Find the variance in ages.

SOLUTION

The variance in ages is a measure of the spread or dispersion of ages about the sample mean.

To compute the variance, we first calculate the sample mean.

$$\bar{X} = \frac{\sum X_i}{n} = \frac{\text{sum of observations}}{\text{number of observations}}$$

$$= \frac{6 + 8 + 10 + 12 + 14 + 16}{6} = \frac{66}{6} = 11$$

The variance is defined to be

$$s^2 = \frac{\sum_{i=1}^{n}(X_i - \bar{X})^2}{n - 1}$$

$$= \frac{(6-11)^2 + (8-11)^2 + (10-11)^2 + (12-11)^2 + (14-11)^2 + (16-11)^2}{5}$$

$$= \frac{25 + 9 + 1 + 1 + 9 + 25}{5} = \frac{70}{5} = 14$$

Sampling

Sample quantities, such as sample mean, deviation, etc., are called **sample statistics** or **statistics**. Based on these quantities, we estimate the corresponding quantities for population, which are called **population parameters** or **parameters**. For two different samples, the difference between sample statistics can be due to chance variation or some significant factor. The latter case should be investigated, and possible mistakes corrected. The statistical inference is a study of inferences made concerning a population and based on the samples drawn from it.

Probability theory evaluates the accuracy of such inferences. The most important initial step is the choice of samples that are representative of a population. The methods of sampling are called the **design** of the experiment. One of the most widely used methods is random sampling.

Random Sampling

A sample of n measurements chosen from a population N ($N > n$) is said to be a **random** sample if it meets the following conditions:

(A) Equal Chance. A sample meets the condition of equal chance if it is selected in such a way that every observation in the entire population has an equal chance of being included in the sample.

(B) Independence. A sample meets this condition when the selection of any single observation does not affect the chances for selection of any other.

Samples that are not random are called **biased**.

One way to obtain a random sample is to assign a number to each member of the population. The population thus becomes a set of numbers. Then, using the random number table, we can choose a sample of desired size.

• EXAMPLE

Suppose 1,000 voters are registered and eligible to vote in an upcoming election. To conduct a poll, we need a sample of 50 persons, so we assign a number between 1 and 1,000 to each voter. Then, using the random number table or a computer program, we choose at random 50 numbers, which represent 50 voters. This is our required sample.

Sampling With and Without Replacement

From a bag containing ten numbers from 1 to 10, we have to draw three numbers. As the first step, we draw a number. Now, we have the choice of replacing or not replacing the number into the bag. If we replace the number, then this number can come up again. If the number is not replaced, then it can come up only once.

Sampling when each element of a population may be chosen more than once (i.e., where the chosen element is replaced) is called **sampling with replacement**. Sampling without replacement takes place when each element of a population can be chosen only once.

Remember that populations can be finite or infinite.

PROBLEM

Decide whether the following sampling procedure should be classified as producing a random sample or as producing a biased sample.

In order to solve a particular problem, an investigator selects 100 people, each of whom will provide 5 scores. The investigator will then take the average of each set of scores, which will yield 100 averages. Is this sample of average scores a random sample?

SOLUTION

The 100 elements are independent. When repeated measures can be converted to a single score, so that each individual observed contributes just one summary observation (such as an average), the independence condition is met. Use of an average often helps to reduce the effects of chance variation within an individual's performance. Also, any observation would have an equal chance of being chosen. The sample is random.

PROBLEM

A wheat researcher is studying the yield of a certain variety of wheat in the state of Colorado. She has at her disposal five farms scattered throughout the state on which she can plant the wheat and observe the yield. Describe the sample and the target population. Under what conditions will this be a random sample?

SOLUTION

The sample consists of the wheat yields on the five farms. The target population consists of the yields of wheat on every farm in the state. This sample will be random if (1) every farm in the state has an equal chance of being selected and (2) the selection of any particular farm is independent of the selection of any other farm.

Sampling Distributions

A population is given from which we draw samples of size n, with or without replacement. For each sample, we compute a statistic, such as the mean, standard deviation, variance, etc. These numbers will depend on the sample, and they will vary from sample to sample. In this way, we obtain a distribution of the statistic called the **sampling distribution**.

For example, if for each sample we measure its mean, then the distribution obtained is the sampling distribution of means. We obtain the sampling distributions of variances, standard deviations, medians, etc., in the same way.

SUBAREA V:

Trigonometry, Calculus, and Discrete Mathematics

Fields 09 & 47

Trigonometry

Trigonometry is a field of mathematics that basically is used to solve triangles. With trigonometry, we can find the missing measures (lengths of sides and angles) in a triangle if we have some information about the triangle. Extensions of the use of trigonometry include astronomy, geography, and even medical imaging. The values of trigonometric functions for any angle are available in "trig" tables or on most calculators.

Angles and Trigonometric Functions

The basic trigonometric functions are based on the right triangle, such as $\triangle ABC$, shown in Figure 6.1:

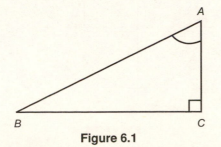

Figure 6.1

Sine

$$\sin \angle A = \frac{\text{measure of side opposite} \angle A}{\text{measure of hypotenuse}}$$
$$= \frac{BC}{AB}$$

Cosine

$$\cos \angle A = \frac{\text{measure of side adjacent to} \angle A}{\text{measure of hypotenuse}}$$
$$= \frac{AC}{AB}$$

Tangent

$$\tan \angle A = \frac{\text{measure of side opposite} \angle A}{\text{measure of side adjacent to} \angle A}$$
$$= \frac{BC}{AC}$$

Cotangent

$$\cot \angle A = \frac{\text{measure of side adjacent to} \angle A}{\text{measure of side opposite} \angle A}$$
$$= \frac{AC}{BC}$$

Secant

$$\sec \angle A = \frac{\text{measure of hypotenuse}}{\text{measure of side adjacent to} \angle A}$$

$$= \frac{AB}{AC}$$

Cosecant

$$\csc \angle A = \frac{\text{measure of hypotenuse}}{\text{measure of side opposite} \angle A}$$

$$= \frac{AB}{BC}$$

Table 6.1 gives the values of sine, cosine, tangent, and cotangent for some special angles. The angles are given in radians and in degrees. A **radian** is a measure of the central angle in a circle and is usually expressed in terms of π. A full circle has 360°, or 2π radians, or 1 radian = $\frac{180}{\pi}$ degrees.

Table 6.1

α	Sin α	Cos α	Tan α	Cot α
0°	0	1	0	∞
$\frac{\pi}{6} = 30°$	$\frac{1}{2}$	$\frac{\sqrt{3}}{2}$	$\frac{1}{\sqrt{3}}$	$\sqrt{3}$
$\frac{\pi}{4} = 45°$	$\frac{1}{\sqrt{2}}$	$\frac{1}{\sqrt{2}}$	1	1
$\frac{\pi}{3} = 60°$	$\frac{\sqrt{3}}{2}$	$\frac{1}{2}$	$\sqrt{3}$	$\frac{1}{\sqrt{3}}$
$\frac{\pi}{2} = 90°$	1	0	∞	0

A circle with center located at the origin of the rectangular coordinate axes with radius equal to one unit length is called a unit circle, as shown in Figure 6.2.

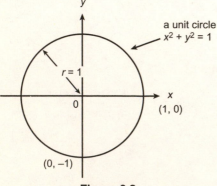

Figure 6.2

An angle whose vertex is at the origin of a rectangular coordinate system and whose initial side coincides with the positive *x*-axis is said to be in **standard position** with respect to the coordinate system.

A **quadrantal angle** is an angle in standard position whose terminal side lies on one of the axes of a Cartesian coordinate system. Thus quadrantal angles have measures of 0°, ± 90°, ± 180°, ± 270°, ± 360°, . . .

An angle in standard position with respect to a Cartesian coordinate system whose terminal side lies in the first (or second or third or fourth) quadrant is called a first (or second or third or fourth) quadrant angle.

If θ is a nonquadrantal angle in standard position and $P(x, y)$ is any point, distinct from the origin, on the terminal side of θ (see Figures 6.3 and 6.4), then the six trigonometric functions of θ are defined in terms of the **abscissa** (*x*-coordinate), **ordinate** (*y*-coordinate), and distance $\overline{OP}$ as follows:

$$\sin \theta = \frac{\text{ordinate}}{\text{distance}} = \frac{y}{r}$$

$$\cos \theta = \frac{\text{abscissa}}{\text{distance}} = \frac{x}{r}$$

$$\tan \theta = \frac{\text{ordinate}}{\text{abscissa}} = \frac{y}{x}$$

$$\cot \theta = \frac{\text{abscissa}}{\text{ordinate}} = \frac{x}{y}$$

$$\sec \theta = \frac{\text{distance}}{\text{abscissa}} = \frac{r}{x}$$

$$\csc \theta = \frac{\text{distance}}{\text{ordinate}} = \frac{r}{y}$$

Figure 6.3

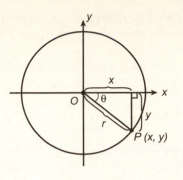

Figure 6.4

The signs of the functions in the quadrants depend on whether the ordinate or abscissa is positive or negative in that quadrant (the distance is always taken as positive). Thus, for $x < 90°$, if $\sin x = A$, $\sin (x + 180) = -A$, or $\sin x = -\sin (x + 180)$.

The values of the trigonometric functions of quadrantal angles are given in Table 6.2.

Table 6.2

θ	$\sin \theta$	$\cos \theta$	$\tan \theta$	$\cot \theta$	$\sec \theta$	$\csc \theta$
0°	0	1	0	$\pm\infty$	1	$\pm\infty$
90°	1	0	$\pm\infty$	0	$\pm\infty$	1
180°	0	−1	0	$\pm\infty$	−1	$\pm\infty$
270°	−1	0	$\pm\infty$	0	$\pm\infty$	−1

If θ is a first quadrant angle in standard position, then no special relationships are needed.

In the second quadrant,

$$\sin \theta = \sin (\theta + 90°) \qquad \cot \theta = -\cot (\theta + 90°)$$
$$\cos \theta = -\cos (\theta + 90°) \qquad \sec \theta = -\sec (\theta + 90°)$$
$$\tan \theta = -\tan (\theta + 90°) \qquad \csc \theta = \csc (\theta + 90°)$$

In the third quadrant,

$$\sin \theta = -\sin (\theta + 180°) \qquad \cot \theta = \cot (\theta + 180°)$$
$$\cos \theta = -\cos (\theta + 180°) \qquad \sec \theta = -\sec (\theta + 180°)$$
$$\tan \theta = \tan (\theta + 180°) \qquad \csc \theta = -\csc (\theta + 180°)$$

In the fourth quadrant,

$$\sin \theta = -\sin (\theta + 270°) \qquad \cot \theta = -\cot (\theta + 270°)$$
$$\cos \theta = \cos (\theta + 270°) \qquad \sec \theta = \sec (\theta + 270°)$$
$$\tan \theta = -\tan (\theta + 270°) \qquad \csc \theta = -\csc (\theta + 270°)$$

• **EXAMPLE**

In Figure 6.5, find $\sin \theta$, given $A = 30°$.

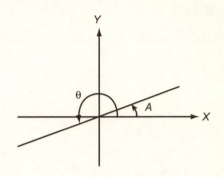

Figure 6.5

Obviously, $\theta = 180° + A = 210°$. Since sine is negative in the third quadrant, we have

$$\sin \theta = \sin 210° = -|\sin(210° - 180°)| = -\sin 30° = -\frac{1}{2}.$$

• **EXAMPLE**

If $\sin 2x = -\cos(-x + 9°)$, find x.

$$\sin 2x = -\cos(-x + 9°) = \cos(-x + 9° + 180°)$$
$$\text{So} \quad -x + 9° + 180° = 90° - 2x$$
$$x = -99°$$

Basic Identities

We can find all the trigonometric functions of an acute angle when the value of any one function of that angle is known by using basic trigonometric identities.

$$\tan \alpha = \frac{\sin \alpha}{\cos \alpha}$$

$$\cot \alpha = \frac{\cos \alpha}{\sin \alpha} = \frac{1}{\tan \alpha}$$

$$\csc \alpha = \frac{1}{\sin \alpha}$$

$$\sec \alpha = \frac{1}{\cos \alpha}$$

$$\sin^2\alpha + \cos^2\alpha = 1$$

$$1 + \tan^2\alpha = \sec^2\alpha$$

$$1 + \cot^2\alpha = \csc^2\alpha$$

• **EXAMPLES**

Given α is an acute angle and $\csc \alpha = 2$, then

$$\sin \alpha = \frac{1}{\csc \alpha} = \frac{1}{2}$$

$$\cos^2 \alpha + \sin^2 \alpha = 1, \text{ so}$$

$$\cos \alpha = \sqrt{1 - \sin^2 \alpha}$$

$$= \sqrt{1 - \left(\frac{1}{2}\right)^2}$$

$$= \sqrt{1 - \frac{1}{4}}$$

$$= \frac{\sqrt{3}}{2}$$

$$\tan \alpha = \frac{\sin \alpha}{\cos \alpha} = \frac{\frac{1}{2}}{\frac{\sqrt{3}}{2}} = \frac{1}{\sqrt{3}} = \frac{\sqrt{3}}{3}$$

$$\cot \alpha = \frac{1}{\tan \alpha} = \sqrt{3}$$

$$\sec \alpha = \frac{1}{\cos \alpha} = \frac{1}{\frac{\sqrt{3}}{2}} = \frac{2}{\sqrt{3}} = \frac{2\sqrt{3}}{3}$$

Formulas

The following trigonometric formulas are useful in solving problems. They are available in most reference books on trigonometry, so unlike the basic identities, which you should readily know, they are listed here for reference only. It would be useful, however, to readily know the sine functions here.

Addition and Subtraction Formulas

$$\sin(A \pm B) = \sin A \cos B \pm \cos A \sin B$$

$$\cos(A \pm B) = \cos A \cos B \mp \sin A \sin B$$

$$\tan(A \pm B) = \frac{\tan A \pm \tan B}{1 \mp \tan A \tan B}$$

$$\cot(A \pm B) = \frac{\cot A \cot B \mp 1}{\cot B \pm \cot A}$$

Note that $\mp$ means "minus or plus," and therefore $\cos(A + B) = \cos A \cos B - \sin A \sin B$.

Double-Angle Formulas

$$\sin 2A = 2 \sin A \cos A$$

$$\cos 2A = 2 \cos^2 A - 1$$

$$= 1 - 2 \sin^2 A$$

$$= \cos^2 A - \sin^2 A$$

$$\tan 2A = \frac{2 \tan A}{1 - \tan^2 A}$$

Half-Angle Formulas

$$\sin \frac{A}{2} = \pm \frac{\sqrt{1 - \cos A}}{2}$$

$$\cos \frac{A}{2} = \pm \frac{\sqrt{1 + \cos A}}{2}$$

$$\tan \frac{A}{2} = \pm \sqrt{\frac{1 - \cos A}{1 + \cos A}}$$

$$= \frac{1 - \cos A}{\sin A}$$

$$= \frac{\sin A}{1 + \cos A}$$

$$\cot \frac{A}{2} = \sqrt{\frac{1 + \cos A}{1 - \cos A}} = \frac{1 + \cos A}{\sin A} = \frac{\sin A}{1 - \cos A}$$

Sum and Difference Formulas

$$\sin \alpha + \sin \beta = 2 \sin \left(\frac{\alpha + \beta}{2} \right) \cos \left(\frac{\alpha - \beta}{2} \right)$$

$$\sin \alpha - \sin \beta = 2 \cos \left(\frac{\alpha + \beta}{2} \right) \sin \left(\frac{\alpha - \beta}{2} \right)$$

$$\cos \alpha + \cos \beta = 2 \cos \left(\frac{\alpha + \beta}{2} \right) \cos \left(\frac{\alpha - \beta}{2} \right)$$

$$\cos \alpha - \cos \beta = -2 \sin \left(\frac{\alpha + \beta}{2} \right) \sin \left(\frac{\alpha - \beta}{2} \right)$$

$$\tan \alpha + \tan \beta = \frac{\sin(\alpha + \beta)}{\cos \alpha \cos \beta}$$

$$\tan \alpha - \tan \beta = \frac{\sin (\alpha - \beta)}{\cos \alpha \cos \beta}$$

Product Formulas of Sines and Cosines

$$\sin A \sin B = \frac{1}{2}[\cos(A - B) - \cos(A + B)]$$

$$\cos A \cos B = \frac{1}{2}[\cos(A + B) + \cos(A - B)]$$

$$\sin A \cos B = \frac{1}{2}[\sin(A + B) + \sin(A - B)]$$

$$\cos A \sin B = \frac{1}{2}[\sin(A + B) - \sin(A - B)]$$

• **EXAMPLE**

If $\sin \alpha = \dfrac{3}{5}$ and $\cos \beta = \dfrac{3}{5}$, find $\cos(\alpha + \beta)$.

Since $\cos(\alpha + \beta) = \cos\alpha\cos\beta - \sin\alpha\sin\beta$, we need to find $\cos\alpha$ and $\sin\beta$ as follows:

$$\cos \alpha = \sqrt{1 - \sin^2 \alpha} = \sqrt{1 - \frac{9}{25}} = \sqrt{\frac{16}{25}} = \frac{4}{5}$$

$$\sin \beta = \sqrt{1 - \cos^2 \beta} = \sqrt{1 - \frac{9}{25}} = \sqrt{\frac{16}{25}} = \frac{4}{5}$$

So,

$$\cos(\alpha + \beta) = \frac{4}{5} \times \frac{3}{5} - \frac{3}{5} \times \frac{4}{5} = 0$$

Properties and Graphs of Trigonometric Functions

The **sine function** is the graph of $y = \sin x$. Other trigonometric functions are defined similarly. See Figure 6.6.

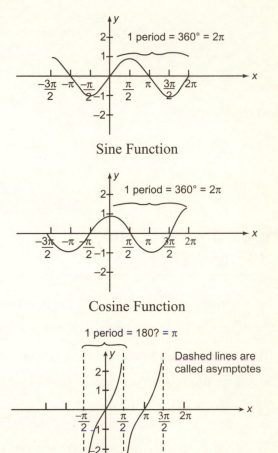

Sine Function

Cosine Function

Tangent Function

Figure 6.6

Periodicity

The **period** of a (repeating) function, f, is the smallest positive number p such that $f(x) = f(x + p)$ for all x. In other words, it is one complete graph of f without repeating itself.

The period of the tangent and cotangent function is π. This fact is clear from the graphs of the tangent and cotangent functions. Pick any angle, x, on the x-axis, and notice $x + \pi$ has the same tangent as x. The period of the other trigonometric functions is 2π.

If the period of a function f is p, and $g(x) = f(nx)$, then the period of g is $\frac{p}{n}$.

PROBLEM

> What is the period of $\sin 3x$?

SOLUTION

Since the period p of $\sin x$ is 2π, the period of $\sin 3x$ is $\frac{p}{n} = \frac{2\pi}{3}$.

Amplitude, Frequency, and Phase Shift

For the function $y = a \sin (bx + c)$, the **amplitude** a is the height of the peaks (or valleys) of the function; the **frequency** b is the number of cycles in an interval of 2π, and the **phase shift**, calculated from $-\frac{c}{b}$, is how many units the graph $y = a \sin bx$ is shifted horizontally.

Note that the graph of $y = \sin x$ is the same as the graph of $y = \cos x$ with a phase shift of $\frac{\pi}{2}$ to the right.

- **EXAMPLE**

Draw one period of the graph for the function $y = 0.5 \sin \left(4x + \frac{\pi}{6}\right)$ and indicate its amplitude, period, and phase shift.

At $x = 0$, $y = 0.5 \sin \frac{\pi}{6}$

At $x = \frac{\pi}{4}$, $y = 0.5 \sin(\pi + \frac{\pi}{6}) = -0.5 \sin \frac{\pi}{6}$

At $x = \frac{\pi}{2}$, $y = 0.5 \sin(2\pi + \frac{\pi}{6}) = -0.5 \sin \frac{\pi}{6}$

The graph is shown in Figure 6.7.

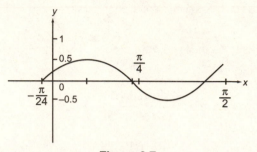

Figure 6.7

So, amplitude $= \frac{1}{2}$

period $= \frac{2\pi}{4} = \frac{\pi}{2}$

phase shift $= -\dfrac{\frac{\pi}{6}}{4} = -\frac{\pi}{24}$

Inverse Trigonometric Functions

If $-1 < x < 1$, then there are infinitely many angles whose sine is x, as we can see by looking at the graph of the sine function. Inverse trigonometric functions are denoted by "arc" and then the function, such as arcsin, or by using a -1 exponent, such as $\sin^{-1}$.

Definitions:

$\arcsin x =$ the angle between $-\frac{\pi}{2}$ and $\frac{\pi}{2}$ whose sine is x.

$\text{arccsc } x =$ the angle between $-\frac{\pi}{2}$ and $\frac{\pi}{2}$ whose cosecant is x.

$\arctan x =$ the angle between $-\frac{\pi}{2}$ and $\frac{\pi}{2}$ whose tangent is x.

arccos x = the angle between θ and π whose cosine is x.

arcsec x = the angle between θ and π whose secant is x.

arccot x = the angle between θ and π whose cotangent is x.

PROBLEM

Evaluate arcsin $\dfrac{1}{2}$.

SOLUTION

Since $\sin \dfrac{\pi}{6} = \dfrac{1}{2}, \arcsin \dfrac{1}{2} = \dfrac{\pi}{6}$. The sine function and the arcsine function (abbreviated arcsin or $\sin^{-1}$) are inverses of each other in the sense that the composition of the two functions is the identity function (that is the function that takes x back to x).

$\sin(\arcsin x) = x$

$\arcsin(\sin x) = x$

Use Trigonometry to Solve Right-Triangle Problems

PROBLEM

Determine the length of side AC in Figure 6.8.

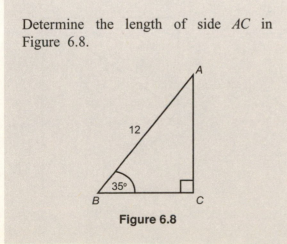

Figure 6.8

SOLUTION

1. Determine if sine, cosine, or tangent is needed.

Since the angle and hypotenuse are known, and the opposite side needs to be determined, use sine.

2. Write the ratio for sine.

$$\sin \angle B = \frac{\text{opposite side}}{\text{hypotenuse}}$$

3. Using a calculator, find the sine of $\angle B$.

$$\sin \angle B = \sin(35°) = 0.574$$

4. Rewrite the ratio.

$$0.574 = \frac{\text{opposite side}}{12}$$

5. Multiply both sides of the equation by 12 to determine the length of the opposite side.

$$6.88 = \text{length of } AC$$

The correct answer is that the length of AC is 6.88.

PROBLEM

Determine the length of side AB in Figure 6.9.

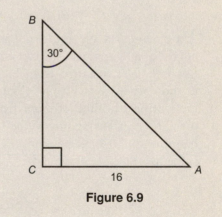

Figure 6.9

SOLUTION

1. Determine if sine, cosine, or tangent is needed. Since the angle and opposite side are known, and the hypotenuse needs to be determined, use sine.

2. Write the ratio for sine.

$$\sin \angle B = \frac{\text{opposite side}}{\text{hypotenuse}}$$

3. Using a calculator, find the sine of $\angle B$.

$$\sin \angle B = \sin(30) = 0.50$$

4. Rewrite the ratio.

$$0.50 = \frac{16}{\text{hypotenuse}}$$

5. Multiply both sides of the equation by the hypotenuse.

$$\text{hypotenuse}(0.50) = 16$$

6. Divide both sides of the equation by 0.50 to determine the length of the hypotenuse.

$$\text{hypotenuse} = 32$$

The correct answer is that the length of AB is 32.

Note: In a 30°–60°–90° triangle, the side opposite the 30° angle is always half the hypotenuse.

PROBLEM

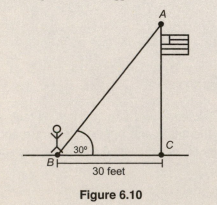

A carpenter is trying to determine the height of a flagpole so she can build a new flagpole. The distance from the flagpole to the carpenter is 30 feet. The angle of inclination (the line of sight from where the carpenter is standing to the top of the flagpole) is 30°. (See Figure 6.10.) What is the height of the flagpole?

Figure 6.10

SOLUTION

1. Determine if sine, cosine, or tangent is needed. Since the angle and adjacent side are known, and the opposite side needs to be determined, use tangent.

2. Write the ratio for tangent.

$$\tan \angle B = \frac{\text{opposite side}}{\text{adjacent side}}$$

3. Using a calculator, find the tangent of $\angle B$.

$$\tan \angle B = \tan(30) = 0.577$$

4. Rewrite the ratio. $0.577 = \dfrac{\text{opposite side}}{30 \text{ feet}}$

5. Multiply both sides of the equation by 30 to determine the length of AC.

$$17.31 = \text{length of } AC.$$

The correct answer is that the height of the flagpole is 17.31 feet.

PROBLEM

A man is playing billiards with his friend. The cue ball hits the 7 ball at point C. The ball travels to point B and is deflected toward point A (the pocket). If the distance of CB is 14 inches, angle C is 60°, and $\angle B$ is 90°, what is the length of AB? See Figure 6.11.

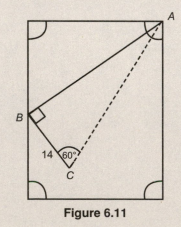

Figure 6.11

SOLUTION

1. Determine if sine, cosine, or tangent is needed. Since the angle and adjacent side are known, and the opposite side needs to be determined, use tangent.

2. Write the ratio for tangent.

$$\tan \angle C = \frac{\text{opposite side}}{\text{adjacent side}}$$

3. Using a calculator, find the tangent of $\angle C$.

$$\tan \angle C = \tan(60) = 1.73$$

4. Rewrite the ratio.

$$1.73 = \frac{\text{opposite side}}{14 \text{ inches}}$$

5. Multiply both sides of the equation by 14 to determine the length of AB.

$$24.22 = \text{length of } AB$$

The correct answer is that the distance to the pocket is 24.22 inches.

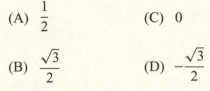

Drill: Trigonometry

1. $\tan^{-1}(-\sqrt{3}) =$

   (A) $-60°$ (C) $30°$

   (B) $60°$ (D) $-30°$

2. Calculate $\dfrac{\sin^{-1} \frac{1}{2}}{\tan^{-1} 1}$.

   (A) $\dfrac{1}{2}$ (C) $45°$

   (B) $30°$ (D) $\dfrac{2}{3}$

3. Find $\cos[\arcsin(-1)]$.

   (A) $\dfrac{1}{2}$ (C) 0

   (B) $\dfrac{\sqrt{3}}{2}$ (D) $-\dfrac{\sqrt{3}}{2}$

4. If x is inside $[0, 2\pi]$, one solution for the equation $\sqrt{1+\sin^2 x} = \sqrt{2}\sin x$ is

   (A) $\dfrac{5}{2}\pi$ (C) $\dfrac{3}{2}\pi$

   (B) $\dfrac{\pi}{6}$ (D) $\dfrac{\pi}{2}$

5. $\sec^2\theta - \tan^2\theta =$

   (A) $\dfrac{4}{5}$ (C) -1

   (B) $\dfrac{1}{2}$ (D) 1

6. $\dfrac{\sin(45° + x) + \sin(45° - x)}{\cos x} =$

   (A) $\sqrt{2}$ (C) $\dfrac{\sqrt{2}}{2}$

   (B) $\tan x$ (D) $\dfrac{\sqrt{2}}{2}\cos x$

7. The amplitude of $y = \dfrac{\sqrt{3}}{3}\sin x + \cos x$ is

   (A) $\dfrac{\sqrt{3}}{2}$ (C) $\dfrac{\sqrt{3}}{4}$

   (B) $\dfrac{\sqrt{2}}{2}$ (D) $\dfrac{2\sqrt{3}}{3}$

8. $\dfrac{\csc x}{2\cos x} =$

   (A) $\cos 3x$ (C) $\sin 2x$

   (B) $\tan 2x$ (D) $\csc 2x$

Trigonometry Review

ANSWER KEY

Drill: Trigonometry

1. (A)   5. (D)
2. (D)   6. (A)
3. (C)   7. (D)
4. (D)   8. (D)

Detailed Explanations of Answers

1. (A)

Using Table 6.1, we find $\tan^{-1}\left(\sqrt{3}\right) = 60°$, so $\tan^{-1}(-\sqrt{3}) = -60°$ in the 2nd or 4th quadrant. Remember that $\tan^{-1}$ is the same as arctan, or "the angle whose tangent is. . ."

2. (D)

$$\frac{\sin^{-1}\frac{1}{2}}{\tan^{-1}1} = \frac{30}{45} = \frac{2}{3}$$

3. (C)

$$\cos[\arcsin(-1)] = \cos(-90) = 0$$

4. (D)

$$\left[\sqrt{1+\sin^2 x}\right]^2 = \left[\sqrt{2}\sin x\right]^2 \Rightarrow 1 + \sin^2 x = 2\sin^2 x$$

Subtract $-2\sin^2 x$:

$$\frac{-2\sin^2 x}{1-\sin^2 x} = \frac{-2\sin^2 x}{0}$$
$$\cos^2 x = \quad 0$$

$$\cos x = 0 \text{ at } \frac{\pi}{2} \text{ or } \frac{3}{2}\pi$$

$\frac{3}{2}\pi$ doesn't satisfy the original equation, so $\frac{\pi}{2}$ is the answer.

5. (D)

$$\sec^2\theta - \tan^2\theta = (\tan^2\theta + 1) - \tan^2\theta = 1$$

6. (A)

$$\frac{\sin(45° + x) + \sin(45° - x)}{\cos x}$$

$$= \frac{\sin 45 \cos x + \cos 45 \sin x + \sin 45 \cos x - \cos 45 \sin x}{\cos x}$$

$$= \frac{2\sin 45 \cos x}{\cos x}$$

$$= 2\sin 45$$

$$= 2\left(\frac{\sqrt{2}}{2}\right)$$

$$= \sqrt{2}$$

7. (D)

$$y = \frac{\sqrt{3}}{3}\sin x + \cos x$$

Test reference angles 0, 30, 45, 60, and 90 to determine that 30 is the greatest value:

$$\frac{\sqrt{3}}{3}\sin(30) + \cos(30) = \frac{\sqrt{3}}{3}\left(\frac{1}{2}\right) + \left(\frac{\sqrt{3}}{2}\right)$$

$$= \frac{\sqrt{3}}{6} + \frac{\sqrt{3}}{2}$$

$$= \frac{\sqrt{3}}{6} + \frac{3\sqrt{3}}{6}$$

$$= \frac{4\sqrt{3}}{6}$$

$$= \frac{2\sqrt{3}}{3}$$

8. (D)

$$\frac{\csc x}{2\cos x} = \frac{\frac{1}{\sin x}}{2\cos x} = \frac{1}{2\sin x \cos x} = \frac{1}{\sin 2x} = \csc 2x$$

Calculus

Limits

Let f be a function that is defined on an open interval containing a, but possibly not defined at a itself. Let L be a real number. The statement

$$\lim_{x \to a} f(x) = L$$

defines the **limit** of the function $f(x)$ at the point a. Very simply, L is the value that the function has as the point a is approached.

PROBLEM

$$\lim_{x \to 2} f(x) = 2x + 1$$

SOLUTION

As $x \to 2$, $f(x) \to 5$. Therefore, $\lim_{x \to 2}(2x + 1) = 5$

PROBLEM

Find $\lim_{x \to 3} f(x) = \dfrac{x^2 - 9}{x + 1}$

SOLUTION

$$\lim_{x \to 3} = \frac{x^2 - 9}{x + 1} = \frac{0}{4} = 0.$$

Continuity

A function f is **continuous** at a point a if $\lim_{x \to a} f(x) = f(a)$.

This implies that three conditions are satisfied:

(A) $f(a)$ exists, that is, f is defined at a

(B) $\lim_{x \to a} f(x)$ exists

(C) the two numbers are equal

To test continuity at a point $x = a$, we test whether

$$\lim_{x \to a^+} F(x) = \lim_{x \to a^-} F(x) = F(a)$$

where the superscript "+" indicates values of x are approaching a from the right, and superscript "–" indicates approaching a from the left.

PROBLEM

Investigate the continuity of the function:

$$h(x) = \begin{cases} 3 + x & \text{if } x \le 1 \\ 3 - x & \text{if } 1 < x. \end{cases}$$

SOLUTION

Graph the function (see Figure 6.12).

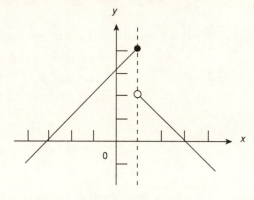

Figure 6.12

Because there is a break in the graph at the point $x = 1$, we investigate the three conditions for continuity at the point $x = 1$. The three conditions are: (1) $f(x_0)$ is defined, (2) $\lim_{x \to x_0} f(x)$ exists, and (3) $\lim_{x \to x_0} f(x) = f(x_0)$. At $x = 1$, $h(1) = 4$; therefore, condition (1) is satisfied.

$$\lim_{x \to 1^-} h(x) = \lim_{x \to 1^-} (3 + x) = 4$$

$$\lim_{x \to 1^+} h(x) = \lim_{x \to 1^+} (3 - x) = 2.$$

Because $\lim\limits_{x \to 1^-} h(x) \neq \lim\limits_{x \to 1^+} h(x)$, we conclude that $\lim\limits_{x \to 1} h(x)$ does not exist. Therefore, condition (2) fails to hold at $x = 1$.

Hence, h is discontinuous at 1.

PROBLEM

Investigate the continuity of:

$$F(x) = \begin{cases} |x - 3| & \text{if } x \neq 3 \\ 2 & \text{if } x = 3. \end{cases}$$

SOLUTION

Graph the function (Figure 6.13).

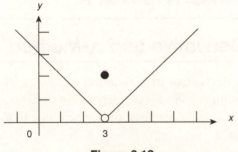

Figure 6.13

We investigate the three conditions for continuity at the point $x = 3$. The three conditions are:

(1) $f(x_0)$ is defined, (2) $\lim\limits_{x \to x_0} f(x)$ exists, (3) $\lim\limits_{x \to x_0} f(x) = f(x_0)$.

At $x = 3$ we have $F(3) = 2$; therefore, condition (1) is satisfied.

$\lim\limits_{x \to 3^-} F(x) = 0$ and $\lim\limits_{x \to 3^+} F(x) = 0$. Therefore, $\lim\limits_{x \to 3} F(x)$ exists and is 0; therefore, condition (2) is satisfied.

$\lim\limits_{x \to 3} F(x) = 0$ but $F(3) = 2$. Therefore, condition (3) is not satisfied. F is thus discontinuous at 3.

Theorems of Continuity

(A) A function defined in a closed interval $[a,b]$ is continuous in $[a,b]$ if and only if it is continuous in the open interval (a,b), as well as continuous from the right at "a" and from the left at "b." See Figure 6.14.

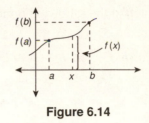

Figure 6.14

(B) If f and g are continuous functions at a, then so are the functions $f + g$, $f - g$, fg and $\dfrac{f}{g}$ where $g(a) \neq 0$.

(C) If $\lim\limits_{x \to a} g(x) = b$ and f is continuous at b, then $\lim\limits_{x \to a} f(g(x)) = f(b) = f[\lim\limits_{x \to a} g(x)]$.

(D) If g is continuous at a and f is continuous at $b = g(a)$, then $\lim\limits_{x \to a} f(g(x)) = f[\lim\limits_{x \to a} g(x)] = f(g(a))$.

(E) Intermediate Value Theorem. If f is continuous on a closed interval $[a, b]$ and if $f(a) \neq f(b)$, then f takes on every value between $f(a)$ and $f(b)$ in the interval $[a, b]$.

(F) $f(x) = k$, where k is a real number, is continuous everywhere.

(G) $f(x) = x$, the identity function, is continuous everywhere.

(H) If f is continuous at a, then $\lim\limits_{x \to \infty} f\left(a + \dfrac{1}{n}\right) = f(a)$.

(I) If f is continuous on an interval containing a and b, $a < b$, and if $f(a) \times f(b) < 0$, then there exists at least one point c, $a < c < b$ such that $f(c) = 0$.

PROBLEM

Let h be defined by:

$$h(x) = \begin{cases} 4 - x^2 & \text{if } x < 4 \\ 2 + x^2 & \text{if } 1 < x. \end{cases}$$

Find each of the following limits if they exist:

$$\lim_{x \to 1^-} h(x), \; \lim_{x \to 1^+} h(x), \; \lim_{x \to 1} h(x).$$

SOLUTION

It is desirable to sketch the given function to aid in visualizing the problem. See Figure 6.15.

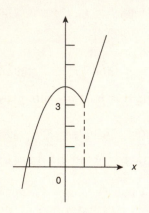

Figure 6.15

Now,

$$\lim_{x \to 1^-} h(x) = \lim_{x \to 1^-} -(4 - x^2) = 3$$

$$\lim_{x \to 1^+} h(x) = \lim_{x \to 1^+} +(2 + x^2) = 3$$

Therefore, $\lim_{x \to 1} h(x)$ exists and is equal to 3. Note that $h(1) = 3$. This holds because the function is continuous.

PROBLEM

If $h(x) = \sqrt{4 - x^2}$, prove that $h(x)$ is continuous in the closed interval $[-2, 2]$.

SOLUTION

To prove continuity we employ the definition stated earlier: A function defined in the closed interval $[a, b]$ is said to be continuous in $[a, b]$ if and only if it is continuous in the open interval (a, b), as well as continuous from the right at a and continuous from the left at b. The function h is continuous in the open interval $(-2, 2)$. We must show that the function is continuous from the right at -2 and from the left at 2. Therefore, we must show that $f(-2)$ is defined and $\lim_{x \to -2^+} f(x)$ exists and that these are equal. Similarly, we must show that $f(2) = \lim_{x \to 2^-} f(x)$. We have:

$$\lim_{x \to -2^+} \sqrt{4 - x^2} = 0 = h(-2),$$

and

$$\lim_{x \to -2^-} \sqrt{4 - x^2} = 0 = h(2).$$

Thus, h is continuous in the closed interval $[-2, 2]$.

Differentiation

The Derivative and Δ-Method

The **derivative** of a function expresses its rate of change with respect to an independent variable. The derivative is also the slope of the tangent line to the curve at any point.

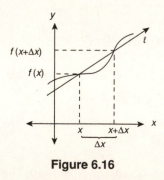

Figure 6.16

Consider the graph of the function f in Figure 6.16. Choosing a point x and a point $x + \Delta x$ (where Δx denotes a small distance on the x-axis), we can obtain both $f(x)$ and $f(x + \Delta x)$. By drawing a tangent line, l, of the curve through the points $f(x)$ and $f(x + \Delta x)$, we can measure the rate of change of this line.

The **average rate of change** of $y = f(x)$ is the slope of this line, or $\dfrac{\Delta y}{\Delta x} = \dfrac{f(x + \Delta x) - f(x)}{\Delta x}$. As we let the distance, Δx, approach zero, then the Δ—**method** gives us

$$\lim_{\Delta x \to 0} \frac{f(x + \Delta x) - f(x)}{\Delta x}$$

becomes the **instantaneous rate of change** of the function, or the derivative.

We denote the derivative of the function f as f'. So we have

$$f'(x) = \lim_{\Delta x \to 0} \frac{f(x + \Delta x) - f(x)}{\Delta x}$$

If $y = f(x)$, some common notations for the derivative are

$$y' = f'(x)$$

$$\frac{dy}{dx} = f'(x)$$

$$D_x y = f'(x) \text{ or } Df = f'$$

PROBLEM

Find the slope of each of the following curves at the given point, using the Δ-method.

(a) $y = 3x^2 - 2x + 4$ at $(1, 5)$

(b) $y = x^3 - 3x + 5$ at $(-2, 3)$

SOLUTION

The slope of a given curve at a specified point is the derivative, in this case $\dfrac{\Delta y}{\Delta x}$, evaluated at that point.

(a) From the Δ-method we know that:

$$\frac{\Delta y}{\Delta x} = \frac{f(x + \Delta x) - f(x)}{\Delta x}$$

For the curve $y = 3x^2 - 2x + 4$, we find:

$$\frac{\Delta y}{\Delta x} = \frac{3(x + \Delta x)^2 - 2(x + \Delta x) + 4 - (3x^2 - 2x + 4)}{\Delta x}$$

$$= \frac{3x^2 + 6x\Delta x + 3(\Delta x)^2 - 2x - 2\Delta x + 4 - 3x^2 + 2x - 4}{\Delta x}$$

$$= \frac{6x\Delta x + 3(\Delta x)^2 - 2\Delta x}{\Delta x}$$

$$= 6x + 3\Delta x - 2$$

So $\lim\limits_{\Delta x \to 0} \dfrac{\Delta y}{\Delta x} = \lim\limits_{\Delta x \to 0} (6x + 3\Delta x - 2) = 6x - 2$

At $(1, 5)$, $\dfrac{\Delta y}{\Delta x} = 6(1) - 2 = 4$ is the required slope.

(b) Again using the Δ-method, $\dfrac{\Delta y}{\Delta x}$ for the curve $y = x^3 - 3x + 5$ can be found as follows:

$$\frac{\Delta y}{\Delta x} = \frac{f(x + \Delta x) - f(x)}{\Delta x}$$

$$\frac{\Delta y}{\Delta x} = \frac{(x + \Delta x)^3 - 3(x + \Delta x) + 5 - (x^3 - 3x + 5)}{\Delta x}$$

$$= \frac{x^3 + 3x^2\Delta x + 3x(\Delta x)^2 + (\Delta x)^3 - 3x - 3\Delta x + 5 - x^3 + 3x - 5}{\Delta x}$$

$$= \frac{3x^2\Delta x + 3x(\Delta x)^2 + (\Delta x)^3 - 3\Delta x}{\Delta x}$$

$$= 3x^2 + 3x\Delta x + (\Delta x)^2 - 3$$

So $\lim\limits_{\Delta x \to 0} \dfrac{\Delta y}{\Delta x} = \lim\limits_{\Delta x \to 0} [3x^2 + 3x\Delta x + (\Delta x)^2 - 3] = 3x^2 - 3$

At $(-2, 3)$, $\dfrac{\Delta y}{\Delta x} = 3(-2)^2 - 3 = 9$ is the required slope.

PROBLEM

Find the average rate of change, by the Δ-method, for:

$$y = \frac{1}{x}.$$

SOLUTION

$$y = f(x) = \frac{1}{x}$$

The average rate of change is defined to be

$\frac{\Delta y}{\Delta x}$ with $\Delta y = f(x + \Delta x) - f(x)$.

Since

$$f(x) = \frac{1}{x}, \ f(x + \Delta x) = \frac{1}{x + \Delta x},$$

and

$$\Delta y = \frac{1}{x + \Delta x} - \frac{1}{x} = \frac{x - (x + \Delta x)}{x(x + \Delta x)}$$

$$= \frac{-\Delta x}{x(x + \Delta x)}.$$

Now,

$$\frac{\Delta y}{\Delta x} = \frac{-\Delta x}{x(x + \Delta x)\Delta x} = -\frac{1}{x(x + \Delta x)}$$

Therefore, the average rate of change is $\frac{-1}{x(x + \Delta x)}$.

The Derivative at a Point

If f is defined on an open interval containing "a," then

$$f'(a) = \lim_{x \to a} \frac{f(x) - f(a)}{x - a},$$

provided the limit exists.

PROBLEM

> Find the instantaneous rate of change of the function:
>
> $$y = \frac{2x}{x + 1}$$
>
> for any value of x and for $x = 2$.

SOLUTION

The instantaneous rate of change of a function is defined as

$$\lim_{\Delta x \to 0} \frac{\Delta y}{\Delta x} = \lim_{\Delta x \to 0} \frac{f(x + \Delta x) - f(x)}{\Delta x}$$

In this case,

$$f(x) = \frac{2x}{x + 1} \text{ and therefore,}$$

$$f(x + \Delta x) = \frac{2(x + \Delta x)}{x + \Delta x + 1}$$

Substituting, we have:

$$\Delta y = f(x + \Delta x) - f(x) = \frac{2x + 2 \cdot \Delta x}{x + \Delta x + 1} - \frac{2x}{x + 1}$$

$$= \frac{(2x + 2 \cdot \Delta x)(x + 1) - 2x(x + \Delta x + 1)}{(x + \Delta x + 1)(x + 1)}$$

$$= \frac{2x^2 + 2x \cdot \Delta x + 2x + 2 \cdot \Delta x - 2x^2 - 2x \cdot \Delta x - 2x}{(x + \Delta x + 1)(x + 1)}$$

$$= \frac{2 \cdot \Delta x}{(x + \Delta x + 1)(x + 1)}$$

$$\frac{\Delta y}{\Delta x} = \frac{2 \cdot \Delta x}{(x + \Delta x + 1)(x + 1)(\Delta x)}$$

$$= \frac{2}{(x + \Delta x + 1)(x + 1)}$$

Now,

$$\lim_{\Delta x \to 0} \frac{\Delta y}{\Delta x} = \lim_{\Delta x \to 0} \frac{2}{(x + \Delta x + 1)(x + 1)}$$

Substituting 0 for Δx, we have

$$\lim_{\Delta x \to 0} \frac{\Delta y}{\Delta x} = \frac{2}{(x + 1)^2}$$

the instantaneous rate of change for any value of x.

For $x = 2$, we have

$$\frac{2}{(x+1)^2} = \frac{2}{(2+1)^2} = \frac{2}{9}$$

PROBLEM

Find the rate of change of y with respect to x at the point $x = 5$, if

$$2y = x^2 + 3x - 1.$$

SOLUTION

Rate of change is defined as $\lim\limits_{\Delta x \to 0} \dfrac{\Delta y}{\Delta x}$, with $\Delta y = f(x + \Delta x) - f(x)$.

We have:

$$2\Delta y = (x + \Delta x)^2 + 3(x + \Delta x) - 1 - (x^2 + 3x - 1)$$
$$= x^2 + 2x \cdot \Delta x + (\Delta x)^2 + 3x + 3\Delta x - 1 - x^2 - 3x + 1$$
$$= 2x \cdot \Delta x + (\Delta x)^2 + 3\Delta x$$

Dividing by Δx,

$$\frac{2\Delta y}{\Delta x} = \frac{2x \cdot \Delta x}{\Delta x} + \frac{(\Delta x)^2}{\Delta x} + \frac{3\Delta x}{\Delta x}$$
$$= 2x + \Delta x + 3$$

and

$$\frac{\Delta y}{\Delta x} = x + \frac{\Delta x}{2} + \frac{3}{2}$$

Now,

$$\lim_{\Delta x \to 0} \frac{\Delta y}{\Delta x} = \lim_{\Delta x \to 0}\left(x + \frac{\Delta x}{2} + \frac{3}{2}\right) = x + \frac{3}{2}$$

For $x = 5$,

$$\lim_{\Delta x \to 0} \frac{\Delta y}{\Delta x} = 5 + \frac{3}{2} = 6\frac{1}{2}$$

Rules for Finding the Derivatives

(A) If f is a constant function, $f(x) = c$, then $f'(x) = 0$.

(B) If

$$f(x) = x, \text{ then } f'(x) = 1.$$

(C) If f is differentiable, then

$$(cf(x))' = cf'(x)$$

(D) **Power Rule:** If $f(x) = x^n$, where n is real, then

$$f'(x) = nx^{n-1}$$

if $n < 0$, then x^n is not defined at $x = 0$.

(E) If f and g are differentiable on the interval (a,b) then:

(1)

$$(f + g)'(x) = f'(x) + g'(x)$$

(2) **Product Rule:**

$$(fg)'(x) = f(x)g'(x) + g(x)f'(x)$$

(3) **Quotient Rule:**

$$\left(\frac{f}{g}\right)'(x) = \frac{g(x)f'(x) - f(x)g'(x)}{[g(x)]^2}$$

(F) **Polynomials:**

If $f(x) = (a_0 + a_1 x + a_2 x^2 + \ldots + a_n x^n)$ then $f'(x) = a_1 + 2a_2 x + 3a_3 x^2 + \ldots + na_n x^{n-1}$

This employs the power rule and the rules concerning constants.

(G) **Chain Rule:**

Let $f(u)$ be a composite function, where $u = g(x)$. Then

$$f'(u) = f'(u)g'(x)$$

or if $y = f(u)$ and $u = g(x)$ then
$$D_x y = (D_u y)(D_x u) = f'(u)g'(x)$$

- **EXAMPLE**

Find $f'(x)$ if $f(x) = (x^3 + 1)(2x^2 + 8x - 5)$.

$$f'(x) = (x^3 + 1)(4x + 8) + (2x^2 + 8x - 5)(3x^2)$$
$$= 4x^4 + 8x^3 + 4x + 8 + 6x^4 + 24x^3 - 15x^2$$
$$= 10x^4 + 32x^3 - 15x^2 + 4x + 8$$

- **EXAMPLE**

Find $f'(x)$ if $f(x) = \dfrac{3x^2 - x - 2}{4x^2 + 5}$.

$$f'(x) = \frac{(4x^2 + 5)(6x - 1) - (3x^2 - x + 2)(8x)}{(4x^2 + 5)^2}$$

$$= \frac{(24x^3 - 4x^2 + 30x - 5) - (24x^3 - 8x^2 + 16x)}{(4x^2 + 5)^2}$$

$$= \frac{4x^2 + 14x - 5}{(4x^2 + 5)^2}$$

PROBLEM

Find the derivative of: $y = x^{3b}$.

SOLUTION

Applying the power rule,

$$\frac{\Delta y}{\Delta x} = 3b \cdot x^{3b-1}.$$

PROBLEM

Find the derivative of: $y = (x^2 + 2)^3$.

SOLUTION

Method 1. Expand the cube and use the power rule:

$$\frac{dy}{dx} = \frac{d}{dx}[(x^2 + 2)^3] = \frac{d}{dx}(x^6 + 6x^4 + 12x^2 + 8)$$

$$= 6x^5 + 24x^3 + 24x$$

Method 2. Let $u = x^2 + 2$, then $y = (x^2 + 2)^3 = u^3$.

Using the chain rule, we have:

$$\frac{dy}{dx} = \frac{dy}{du} \cdot \frac{du}{dx} = \frac{d(u^3)}{du} \cdot \frac{d(x^2 + 2)}{dx} = 3u^2(2x)$$
$$= 3(x^2 + 2)^2 \cdot (2x) = 3(x^4 + 4x^2 + 4) \cdot (2x)$$
$$= 6x^5 + 24x^3 + 24x$$

Rectilinear Motion

When an object moves along a straight line, we call the motion rectilinear motion. Distance s, velocity v, and acceleration a, are the chief concerns of the study of motion.

Velocity is the proportion of distance over time.

$$\boxed{v = \frac{s}{t}}$$

$$\text{Average velocity} = \frac{s(t_2) - s(t_1)}{t_2 - t_1}$$

where t_1, t_2 are time instances and $s(t_2) - s(t_1)$ is the displacement of an object.

Instantaneous velocity at time t is defined as

$$\boxed{v = Ds(t) = \lim_{h \to 0} \frac{s(t + h) - s(t)}{h}}$$

We usually write $\boxed{v(t) = \dfrac{ds}{dt}}$

Acceleration, the rate of change of velocity with respect to time is

$$\boxed{a(t) = \frac{dv}{dt}}$$

It follows clearly that

$a(t) = v'(t) = s''(t)$, where the double prime indicates the second derivative, or the derivative of the derivative.

When motion is due to gravitational effects, $g = 32.2 \text{ ft/sec}^2$ or $g = 9.81 \text{ m/sec}^2$ is usually substituted for acceleration.

Speed at time t is defined as $|v(t)|$. The speed indicates how fast an object is moving without specifying the direction of motion.

PROBLEM

A rope attached to a boat is being pulled in at a rate of 10 ft/sec. If the water is 20 ft below the level at which the rope is being drawn in, how fast is the boat approaching the wharf when 36 ft of rope are yet to be pulled in?

SOLUTION

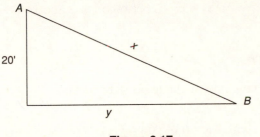

Figure 6.17

In the sketch of Figure 6.17, the length AB denotes the rope, and the position of the boat is at B. Since the rope is being drawn in at a rate of 10 ft/sec,

$$\frac{dx}{dt} = 10$$

To find how fast the boat is being towed in when 36 ft of rope are left,

$\frac{dy}{dt}$ must be found at $x = 36$.

From the Pythagorean Theorem, $20^2 + y^2 = x^2$, or $y = \sqrt{x^2 - 400}$. Differentiating with respect to t,

$$\frac{dy}{dt} = \frac{dy}{dx} \cdot \frac{dx}{dt} = \frac{1}{2}(x^2 - 400)^{\frac{1}{2}}(2x)\frac{dx}{dt} = \frac{x\frac{dx}{dt}}{\sqrt{x^2 - 400}}$$

Substituting the conditions that:

$$\frac{dx}{dt} = -10 \text{ and } x = 36,$$

$$\frac{dy}{dt} = \frac{-360}{\sqrt{896}} = -\frac{45}{\sqrt{14}}$$

It has now been found that, when there are 36 ft of rope left, the boat is moving in at the rate of:

$$\frac{45}{\sqrt{14}} \text{ ft /sec}$$

PROBLEM

A boat is being hauled toward a pier at a height of 20 ft above the water level. The rope is drawn in at a rate of 6 ft/sec. Neglecting sag, how fast is the boat approaching the base of the pier when 25 ft of rope remain to be pulled in?

SOLUTION

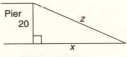

Figure 6.18

Formulating the given data, and from the sketch in Figure 6.18, we have:

$$\frac{dz}{dt} = 6, z = 25, \text{ and } \frac{dx}{dt} \text{ is to be found.}$$

At any time t we have, from the Pythagorean Theorem,

$$20^2 + x^2 = z^2$$

By differentiation, we obtain:

$$x\frac{dx}{dt} = z\frac{dz}{dt}$$

When $z = 25$, $x = \sqrt{25^2 - 20^2} = 15$; therefore

$$15\frac{dx}{dt} = 25(-6)$$

$$\frac{dx}{dt} = -10 \text{ ft/sec}$$

(The boat approaches the base at 10 ft/sec.)

Rate of Change and Related Rates

In the last section, we saw how functions of time can be expressed as velocity and acceleration. In general, we can speak about the rate of change of any function with respect to an arbitrary parameter (such as time in the previous section).

For linear functions $f(x) = mx + b$, the rate of change is simply the slope m.

For nonlinear functions we define the **average rate of change** between points c and d to be $\dfrac{f(d) - f(c)}{d - c}$ (see Figure 6.19), and the **instantaneous rate of change** of f at the point x to be $f'(x) = \lim\limits_{h \to 0} \dfrac{f(x+h) - f(x)}{h}$.

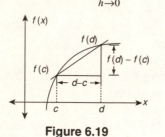

Figure 6.19

If the limit does not exist, then the rate of change of f at x is not defined.

The form, common to all related rate problems, is as follows:

(a) Two variables, x and y, are given. They are functions of time, but the explicit functions are not given.

(b) The variables, x and y, are related to each other by some equation, such as $x^2 + y^3 - 2x - 7y^2 + 2 = 0$.

(c) An equation that involves the rate of change, $\dfrac{dx}{dt}$ and $\dfrac{dy}{dt}$, is obtained by differentiating with respect to t and using the power rule.

As an illustration, the previous equation leads to

$$2x\frac{dx}{dt} + 3y^2\frac{dy}{dt} - 2\frac{dx}{dt} - 14y\frac{dy}{dt} = 0$$

The derivatives $\dfrac{dx}{dt}$ and $\dfrac{dy}{dt}$ in this equation are called the related rates.

PROBLEM

Compute the average rate of change of $y = f(x) = x^2 - 2$ between $x = 3$ and $x = 4$.

SOLUTION

Average rate of change is defined as:

$\dfrac{\Delta y}{\Delta x}$ with $\Delta y = f(x + \Delta x) - f(x)$.

Given: $x = 3$, $\Delta x = 4 - 3 = 1$,

$y = f(x) = f(3) = 3^2 - 2 = 7$

For $x = 4$,

$y + \Delta y = f(x + \Delta x) = 4^2 - 2 = 14$

So $\Delta y = f(x + \Delta x) - f(x) = f(4) - f(3)$

$\qquad = (4^2 - 2) - (3^2 - 2) = 14 - 7 = 7$

$\dfrac{\Delta y}{\Delta x} = \dfrac{7}{1} = $ the average rate of change.

PROBLEM

Find the rate of change of y with respect to x at the point $x = 5$ if $2y = x^2 + 3x - 1$.

SOLUTION

Rate of change is defined as

$$\lim_{\Delta x \to 0} \frac{\Delta y}{\Delta x} \text{ with}$$

$\Delta y = f(x + \Delta x) - f(x)$.

We have:

$$2\Delta y = (x + \Delta x)^2 + 3(x + \Delta x) - 1 - (x^2 + 3x - 1)$$

$$= x^2 + 2x \cdot \Delta x + (\Delta x)^2 + 3x + 3\Delta x - 1 - x^2 - 3x + 1$$

$$= 2x \cdot \Delta x + (\Delta x)^2 + 3\Delta x$$

Dividing by Δx,

$$\frac{2\Delta y}{\Delta x} = \frac{2x \cdot \Delta x}{\Delta x} + \frac{(\Delta x)^2}{\Delta x} + \frac{3\Delta x}{\Delta x}$$

$$= 2x + \Delta x + 3$$

so

$$\frac{\Delta y}{\Delta x} = x + \frac{\Delta x}{2} + \frac{3}{2}$$

Now,

$$\lim_{\Delta x \to 0} \frac{\Delta y}{\Delta x} = \lim_{\Delta x \to 0} x + \frac{\Delta x}{2} + \frac{3}{2} = x + \frac{3}{2}$$

For $x = 5$,

$$\lim_{\Delta x \to 0} \frac{\Delta y}{\Delta x} = 5 + \frac{3}{2} = 6\frac{1}{2}$$

This means that the instantaneous rate of change of the function represented by the curve at the point $x = 5$ is $6\frac{1}{2}$.

The function, it is seen, changes $6\frac{1}{2}$ times as fast as the independent variable x at $x = 5$.

The slope of the tangent at $x = 5$ is $6\frac{1}{2}$.

Integration

Indefinite Integrals

An **indefinite integral** can be thought of as an anti-derivative. If $f(x)$ is continuous, $F(x) = \int f(x) + C$. In other words, $F(x)$ is a function whose derivative $F'(x) = f(x)$, then $F(x)$ is called the indefinite integral of $f(x)$. This is the basis for the first part of the Fundamental Theorem of Calculus.

The indefinite integral deals with antidifferentiation of a function, and it is called "indefinite" because several antiderivatives can exist for one function. For example, the integral of $f(x) = \frac{3}{4}x^3$ can be $F(x) = \int \frac{3}{4}x^3 = 3x^4$, but it can also be $G(x) = 3x^4 + 7$ or $H(x) = 3x^4 - 5$, or an infinite number of other functions. This is the basis for Theorem 1.

THEOREM 1

If $F(x)$ and $G(x)$ are two integrals of $f(x)$, then $F(x) = G(x) + c$, where c is a constant.

Power Rule

Let "a" be any real number, "r" any rational number not equal to -1 and "c" an arbitrary constant.

$$\boxed{\text{If } f(x) = ax^r, \text{then } F(x) = \int f(x) = \frac{a}{r+1}x^{r+1} + c.}$$

THEOREM 2

The integral of a sum is the sum of the integrals. If $F_1 = \int f_1(x)$ and $F_2 = \int f_2(x)$,

$$\boxed{\int (f_1 + f_2) = \int f_1 + \int f_2 = F_1 + F_2}$$

Definite Integrals

The **definite integral** evaluates the function $f(x)$ between two definite limits (thus, its name). Therefore, the definite integral can be thought of as the area under the graph of $f(x)$ between two points, such as $x = a$ and $x = b$. Let's look at the logic for determining the definite integral.

For any curve $f(x)$, we can divide the area under the curve into several rectangles of the same width, with a height that is the height of the curve at that point $y = f(x)$, and a width that is the difference between x_{i+1} and x_i. Then the area under the curve can be approximated by the sum of the areas of the rectangles, each with an area $A_i = y_i(x_{i+1} - x_i)$.

But y is varying—it is not the same at x_i as it is at x_{i+1}. Also, if our rectangles are drawn under the curve (inscribed; see Figure 6.20), we will get a different area than if our rectangles are drawn over the curve (circumscribed; see Figure 6.21).

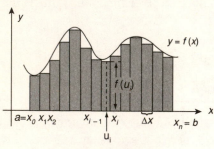

Figure 6.20

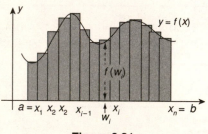

Figure 6.21

So, to improve the approximation, let's make $f(w_i)$ the midpoint value of y in each rectangle. Then the area under a curve between $x_i = a$ and and $x_n = b$ is the sum of all such rectangles within that interval. This leads to the definition of the Riemann sum

$$R = \sum_{i=1}^{n} f(w_i)\Delta x_i$$

and the limit of this sum as the largest of the Δx_i goes to 0 is the definition of the definite integral between points a and b, written as

$$\int_{a}^{b} f(x)dx$$

Rules for Integration of General Functions

$\int af(x)dx = a\int f(x)dx \ \ (a \neq 0, \text{ constant})$

$\int [f(x) + g(x)]dx = \int f(x)dx + \int g(x)dx$

$\int f'(x)g(x)dx = f(x)g(x) - \int f(x)g'(x)dx$

$\int \frac{f'(x)}{f(x)} \ dx = \ln|f(x)| + C$

$\int f'(x)f(x)dx = \frac{1}{2}[f(x)]^2 + C$

$\int [f(x)]^n f'(x)dx = \frac{[f(x)]^{n+1}}{n+1} + C \ \ (\text{for } n \neq -1)$

Integrals of Simple Functions

$\int dx = x + C$

$\int x^n dx = \frac{x^{n+1}}{n+1} + C \ \text{ if } n \neq -1$

$\int \frac{dx}{x} = \ln|x| + C$

$\int \ln x \ dx = x \ln x - x + C$

$\int \log_b x \ dx = x \log_b x - x \log_b e + C$

$\int e^x \ dx = e^x + C$

$\int a^x \ dx = \frac{a^x}{\ln a} + C$

$\int \sin x \, dx = -\cos x + C$

$\int \cos x \ dx = \sin x + C$

$\int \tan x \ dx = -\ln|\cos x| + C$

$\int \cot x \, dx = \ln|\sin x| + C$

$\int \sec x \, dx = \ln|\sec x + \tan x| + C$

$\int \csc x \, dx = \ln|\csc x - \cot x| + C$

$\int \sec^2 x \, dx = \tan x + C$

$\int \csc^2 x \, dx = -\cot x + C$

$\int \sec x \tan x \, dx = \sec x + C$

$\int \csc x \cot x \, dx = -\csc x + C$

PROBLEM

Determine the area under the curve: $y = f(x) = x^2$ between $x = 2$ and $x = 3$.

SOLUTION

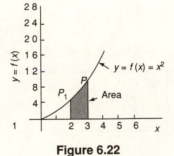

Figure 6.22

It is given that the area to be evaluated is between $x = 2$ and $x = 3$; therefore, these are the limits of the integral that gives us the required area. Area is equal to the integral of the upper function minus the lower function. From Figure 6.22, we see that the required area is between $y = x^2$ as the upper function and $y = 0$ (the x-axis) as the lower function. Therefore, we can write:

$A = \int_2^3 (x^2 - 0)dx$

$\quad = \int_2^3 x^2 dx$

$\quad = \left. \dfrac{x^3}{3} \right]_2^3$

$A = \dfrac{3^3}{3} - \dfrac{2^3}{3} = \dfrac{19}{3}.$

THEOREM 3

If f is continuous on $[a,b]$, then f is integrable on $[a, b]$; that is, the limit $\int_a^b f(x)dx$ exists.

PROBLEM

$\dfrac{dy}{dx} = (a - bx)^n$. What is $y = F(x)$ when $n = 2$?

SOLUTION

$\dfrac{dy}{dx} = (a - bx)^n$ can be rewritten as $dy = (a - bx)^n dx$. We can now write: $\int dy = \int (a - bx)^n dx$, or $y = \int (a-bx)^n dx$.

To integrate, we use u-substitution and consider the formula:

$\int u^n du = \dfrac{u^{n+1}}{n + 1} + C$, with $u = (a - bx)$ and $du = -bdx$.

Applying the formula, we obtain:

$y = \int (a - bx)^n dx = -\dfrac{1}{b} \cdot \dfrac{(a - bx)^{n+1}}{n + 1}$

$\quad = -\dfrac{(a - bx)^{n+1}}{b(n + 1)} + C,$

the integral in the general form.

For $n = 2$,

$$y = \int (a - bx)^2 \cdot dx = -\frac{(a - bx)^3}{3b} + C.$$

Mean Value Theorem for Integrals

If f is continuous on a closed interval $[a, b]$, then there is some number P in the open interval (a, b) such that

$$\int_a^b f(x)dx = f(P)(b - a)$$

To find $f(P)$ we divide both sides of the equation by $(b - a)$, obtaining

$$f(P) = \frac{1}{b - a} \int_a^b f(x)dx$$

PROBLEM

What is the mean value or mean ordinate of the positive part of the curve $y = 2x - x^2$?

SOLUTION

Sketch the graph, as shown in Figure 6.23.

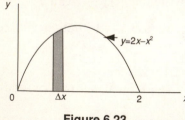

Figure 6.23

First, determine the length of the base to fix the limits of integration for the area by setting y equal to zero, or:

$$0 = 2x - x^2 = x(2 - x).$$

Then, $x_1 = 0$, and $x_2 = 2$.

Now, by the Mean Value Theorem,

$$\bar{y} = \frac{1}{x_2 - x_1} \int y \cdot dx$$

$$= \frac{1}{2 - 0} \int_0^2 (2x - x^2)dx$$

$$= \int_0^2 \left(x - \frac{x^2}{2} \right) dx$$

$$= \left| \frac{x^2}{2} - \frac{x^3}{6} \right|_0^2 = \frac{4}{2} - \frac{8}{6} = \frac{2}{3},$$

the mean ordinate.

Fundamental Theorem of Calculus

Suppose f is continuous on a closed interval $[a, b]$. Then the **Fundamental Theorem of Calculus** states:

(A) If the function G is defined by

$$G(x) = \int^x f(t)dt,$$

for all x in $[a,b]$, then G is an antiderivative of f on $[a, b]$.

(B) If F is any antiderivative of f, then

$$\boxed{\int_a^b f(x)dx = F(b) - F(a)}$$

PROBLEM

Find the mean value of the ordinates of the circle $x^2 + y^2 = a^2$ in the first quadrant.

(a) With respect to the radius along the x-axis

(b) With respect to the arc length

SOLUTION

(a) Noting that the mean value is defined by:

$$f(x_0) = \frac{1}{b-a} \int_a^b f(x)dx, \text{ where } a < x_0 < b$$

We have:

$$f(x_0) = \frac{1}{a-0} \int_0^a \sqrt{a^2 - x^2}\,dx$$

where $f(x) = y = \pm\sqrt{a^2 - x^2}$. We take $y = \sqrt{a^2 - x^2}$ because we are in the first quadrant. Also, noting that:

$$\int \sqrt{a^2 - x^2}\,dx = \frac{1}{2}x\sqrt{a^2 - x^2}$$
$$+\frac{1}{2}a^2 \arcsin \frac{x}{a} + C,$$

we have:

$$f(x_0) = \frac{1}{4}\pi a.$$

(b) The coordinates of any point on the circle can be expressed in terms of θ by the following method. For the point in question, drop a perpendicular line to the x-axis. We have a right triangle with hypotenuse of length a as seen in Figure 6.24.

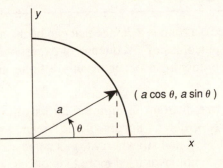

Figure 6.24

$$\cos(\theta) = \frac{x}{a},$$

or

$$x = a \cos(\theta). \qquad \sin(\theta) = \frac{y}{a},$$

or

$$y = a \sin(\theta).$$

Now an element of the arc length is $a\Delta\theta$. (Recall that the length of an arc of a circle is equal to $S = R\theta$ where R is the radius and θ the angle in radians.) Therefore the length of the arc of the circle in the first quadrant is $\frac{1}{2}\pi a$.

By taking the limit, $a\Delta\theta$ becomes $ad\theta$

$$f(\theta) = \frac{1}{\frac{1}{2}\pi a} \int_0^{\frac{\pi}{2}} a\sin\theta\,(ad\theta)$$
$$= \frac{2a}{\pi} \int_0^{\frac{\pi}{2}} \sin\theta\,d\theta = \frac{2a}{\pi}[\cos\theta]_0^{\frac{\pi}{2}}$$
$$= \frac{2a}{\pi}(1-0) = \frac{2a}{\pi}.$$

Discrete/Finite Mathematics

Sets

If S is a collection of objects, then the objects are called the elements of S. We write $x \in S$ to mean x is an element of S, and we write $x \notin S$ to mean x is not an element of S. So, for instance, if S denotes the set of all positive integers $1,2,3,\ldots,n,\ldots$, then $205 \in S$, whereas $-18 \notin S$.

If S and T are two sets such that every element of S is also an element of T, then S is called a subset of T and we write $S \subseteq T$. However, if $S \subseteq T$ and $S \neq T$, then S is called a proper subset of T, and we write $S \subset T$. Thus, if T is the set of all positive integers, and S is the set of all positive even integers, then $S \subset T$. If $S \subseteq T$ and $T \subseteq S$, then S and T are equal sets, that is, $S = T$.

The need also arises for a very peculiar set, namely one having no elements. This is called the empty or null set and is denoted by $\varnothing$; $\varnothing$ has the property that is a subset of every set.

It is helpful to regard all sets under consideration as being subsets of some constant set, called the universal set, U. If S is a subset of U that satisfies a certain property P, we write

$S = \{x \in U : x \text{ satisfies } P\}$ read as "x is an element of U such that x satisfies P".

There are several important ways in which sets may be combined with one another. If S and T are subsets of some universal set, U, then the operations of union, intersection, and difference are defined as follows:

1) Union: $S \cup T = \{x : x \in S \text{ or } x \in T\}$

2) Intersection: $S \cap T = \{x : x \in S \text{ and } x \in T\}$

3) The difference of S and T: $S - T = \{x : x \in S \text{ but } x \notin T\}$

In the particular case when S is a subset of U, then $U - S$ is called the complement of S in U and is written S'. That is,

$$S' = U - S = \{x : x \in U \text{ and } x \notin S\}$$

We represent these three operations pictorially by Venn Diagrams. If S is Ⓢ and T is Ⓣ, then the shaded regions in Figure 6.25 show the union, intersection, and difference of S and T.

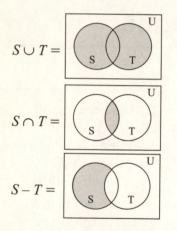

$S \cup T =$

$S \cap T =$

$S - T =$

Figure 6.25

Another construction of new sets from the old is the Cartesian product of two sets, S and T, defined by

$$S \times T = \{(s, t) : s \in S \text{ and } t \in T\}$$

where we define that the ordered pair (s_1, t_1) is equal to the ordered pair (s_2, t_2) if and only if $s_1 = s_2$ and $t_1 = t_2$.

For the sets $S = \{1, 2\}$, and $T = \{5, 10\}$, we have

$$S \times T = \{(1, 5), (1, 10), (2, 5), (2, 10)\}$$

The Fundamental Principle of Counting

Suppose a man has four ways to travel from New York to Chicago, three ways to travel from Chicago to Denver, and six ways to travel from Denver to San Francisco, how many ways can he go from New York to San Francisco via Chicago and Denver?

If we let A_1 be the event "going from New York to Chicago," A_2 be the event "going from Chicago to Denver," and A_3 be the event "going from Denver to San Francisco," then because there are 4 ways to accomplish A_1, 3 ways to accomplish A_2, and 6 ways to accomplish A_3, the number of routes the man can follow is

$$(4) \times (3) \times (6) = 72$$

We can now generalize these results and state them formally as the **fundamental principle of counting**, sometimes called the multiplication rule of counting:

If an operation consists of a sequence of k separate steps of which the first can be performed in n_1 ways, followed by the second in n_2 ways, and so on until the kth can be performed in n_k ways, then the operation consisting of k steps can be performed in

$$n_1 \times n_2 \times n_3 \ldots \ldots n_k$$

ways.

Tree Diagrams

A tree diagram is a device that can be used to list all possible outcomes of a sequence of experiments where each experiment can occur in only a finite number of ways.

The tree diagram in Figure 6.26 lists the different ways three different flavors of ice cream—chocolate (c), vanilla (v), and strawberry (s)—can be arranged on a cone, with no flavor used more than once.

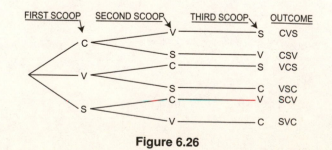

Figure 6.26

The tree starts with three branches in the first stage, representing the three possibilities for first stage. For each outcome at the first stage, there are two possibilities at the second stage. Then, for each outcome in the second stage, there is only one possibility at the third stage. Consequently, there are $3 \times 2 \times 1$, or 6, different arrangements.

Using a tree diagram, we can develop the sample space for an experiment consisting of tossing a fair coin and then rolling a die as shown in Figure 6.27. We see that there are $6 \times 12 = 72$ possible outcomes.

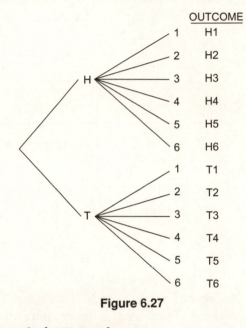

Figure 6.27

Factorial Notation

Consider how many ways the owner of an ice cream parlor can display 10 ice cream flavors in a row along the front of the display case. The first position can be filled in 10 ways, the second position in 9 ways, the third position in 8 ways, and so on. By the fundamental counting principle, there are

$$(10) \times (9) \times (8) \times (7) \times \ldots \times (2) \times (1)$$

or 3,628,800 ways to display the flavors. If there were 16 flavors, there would be $(16) \times (15) \times (14) \times \ldots \times (3) \times (2) \times (1)$ ways to arrange them. In general:

If n is a positive natural number, then the product from 1 to n inclusive is denoted by the symbol $n!$ (read as "n factorial" or as "factorial n"), defined as

$$n! = n(n-1)(n-2) \ldots (3)(2)(1)$$

There are two fundamental properties of factorials:

1. By definition, $0! = 1$
2. $n(n-1)! = n!$

   For example, $(6)(5!) = 6!$

Counting Procedures Involving Order Restrictions (Permutations)

Suppose a class consists of five students. The instructor calls on exactly three students out of the five students during each class period to answer three different questions. To apply the uniform probability model, we need to know how many points there are in the sample space S. Note that each point in S is an ordered triplet; that is, the point $(3, 5, 1)$ is different from the point $(5, 3, 1)$. The same three people are called upon to respond, but the order of response is different. Such an arrangement is referred to as a **permutation**.

A permutation of a number of objects is any arrangement of these objects in a definite order.

For example, if a class consists of three students, then there are $3 \times 2 \times 1 = 6$ ways in which the students might be selected.

In general, if the class had consisted of n students and all of them had been called upon, then the responses could have taken place in

$$n(n-1)(n-2) \ldots (3)(2)(1) = n!$$

ways. Hence, the number of permutations of a set of n distinct objects, taken all together, is $n!$.

In our example of the class consisting of five students, only three students were to be called on to respond; that is, we are interested in an ordered *subset*.

An arrangement of r distinct objects taken from a set of n distinct objects, $r \leq n$, is called a permutation of n objects taken r at a time. The total number of such orderings is denoted by $_nP_r$, and defined as

$$_nP_r = \frac{n!}{(n-r)!}$$

If all n objects are different, this is the same as multiplying the first r factors of $n!$.

In our example, $n = 5$, $r = 3$,

$$_5P_3 = \frac{5!}{(5-3)!} = 5 \times 4 \times 3 = 60$$

Note that this is the same as multiplying the first 3 factors of 5!

If we have n items with r objects alike, then the number of distinct permutations taking all n at a time is

$$\frac{n!}{r!}$$

In general, in a set of n elements having r_1 elements of one type, r_2 elements of a second type, and so on to r_k element of a kth type, then the number of distinct permutations of the n elements, taken all together, is given by

$$\frac{n!}{r_1!r_2!r_3!\ldots r_k!}$$

where $\sum\limits_{i=1}^{k} r_i = n$

For example, the number of ways a group of 10 of which 6 are females and 4 are males can line up for theater tickets, if we are interested only in distinguishing between sexes, is given by

$$\frac{10!}{6!4!} = 210$$

Counting Procedures Not Involving Order Restrictions (Combinations)

Suppose that a class of 12 students selects a committee of three to plan a party. A possible committee is John, Sally, and Joe. In this situation, the order of the three is not important because the committee of John, Sally, and Joe, is the same as the committee of Sally, Joe, and John.

When choosing committee members and in other cases of selection in which order is not important, we are interested in **combinations**, not permutations.

A subset of r objects selected without regard to order from a set of n different objects, $r \leq n$, is called a combination of n objects taken r at a time. The total number of combinations of n things taken r at a time is denoted by $_nC_r$ or $\binom{n}{r}$, and is defined as

$$_nC_r = \binom{n}{r} = \frac{n!}{r!(n-r)!}$$

In our example, the number of possible committees that could plan the party can be calculated by

$$_{12}C_3 = \binom{12}{3} = \frac{12!}{3!(12-3)!} = 220$$

Probability

As we saw in chapter 5, the **probability** of an event occurring is

$$P = \left(\frac{\text{the number of ways the event can occur}}{\text{the number of possible outcomes}} \right)$$

PROBLEM

A deck of playing cards is thoroughly shuffled and a card is drawn from the deck. What is the probability that the card drawn is the ace of diamonds?

SOLUTION

In our case there is one way the event can occur, for there is only one ace of diamonds, and there are 52 possible outcomes (for there are 52 cards in the deck). Hence, the probability that the card drawn is the ace of diamonds is $\frac{1}{52}$.

If two events, A and B, are independent, then the probability that A and B will occur is

$$P(A \text{ and } B) = P(AB) = P(A) \times P(B).$$

Note that two or more events are said to be independent if the occurrence of one event has no effect upon the occurrence or nonoccurrence of the other.

PROBLEM

A bag contains four black and five blue marbles. A marble is drawn and then replaced, after which a second marble is drawn. What is the probability that the first is black and the second blue?

SOLUTION

Let C = event that the first marble drawn is black.

D = event that the second marble drawn is blue.

The probability that the first is black and the second is blue can be expressed symbolically by

$P(C \text{ and } D) = P(CD)$.

In this case the occurrence of choosing a black marble has no effect on the selection of a blue marble and vice versa; because, when a marble is drawn it is then replaced before the next marble is drawn. Therefore, C and D are two independent events.

$P(CD) = P(C) \times P(D)$

$P(C) = \dfrac{\text{number of ways to choose a black marble}}{\text{number of ways to choose a marble}}$

$= \dfrac{4}{9}$

$P(D) = \dfrac{\text{number of ways to choose a blue marble}}{\text{number of ways to choose a marble}}$

$= \dfrac{5}{9}$

$P(CD) = P(C) \times P(D) = \dfrac{4}{9} \times \dfrac{5}{9} = \dfrac{20}{81}$

PROBLEM

A traffic count at a highway junction revealed that out of 5,000 cars that passed through the junction in one week, 3,000 turned to the right. Find the probability that a car will turn (1) to the right and (2) to the left. Assume that the cars cannot go straight or turn around.

SOLUTION

(1) If an event can happen in s ways and fail to happen in f ways, and if all these ways ($s + f$) are assumed to be equally likely, then the probability (P) that the event will happen is

$P = \dfrac{s}{s + f} = \dfrac{\text{successful ways}}{\text{total ways}}$

In this case $s = 3,000$ and $s + f = 5,000$. Hence,

$P = \dfrac{3,000}{5,000} = \dfrac{3}{5}$.

(2) If the probability that an event will happen is $\dfrac{a}{b}$, then the probability that this event will not happen is $1 - \dfrac{a}{b}$. Thus, the probability that a car will not turn right, but left, is $1 - \dfrac{3}{5} = \dfrac{2}{5}$. This same conclusion can also be arrived at by using the following reasoning:

Since 3,000 cars turned to the right, $5,000 - 3,000 = 2,000$ cars turned to the left. Hence, the probability that a car will turn to the left is

$\dfrac{2,000}{5,000} = \dfrac{2}{5}$.

Discrete Mathematics

Sequences and Series

A **sequence** is a function whose domain is the set of all natural numbers. All the sequences described in this section will have a subset in the set of all real numbers as their range. It is common to let a represent the nth term of the sequence. For example, if

$$a_n = 10n$$

then the sequence is 10, 20, 30, 40 . . .

The sum of the first n terms of the sequence,

$$a_1, a_2, a_3, \ldots a_n,$$

is indicated by

$$a_1 + a_2 + a_3 + \ldots + a_n,$$

and the sum of these terms is called a **series**. The Greek letter Σ is used to represent this sum, as indicated below.

$$\sum_{k=1}^{n} a_k = a_1 + a_2 + a_3 + \ldots + a_n$$

For a fixed number a and a fixed number d, the sequence

$$a, a + d, a + 2d, a + 3d, \ldots$$

is called an infinite *arithmetic* sequence, and the nth term of this sequence is given by

$$a_n = a + (n-1)d$$

The number a is called the first term and d is called the common difference. The symbol S_n is used to represent the sum of the corresponding finite series of n elements, and

$$\sum_{k=1}^{n} a + (k-1)d$$

or $S_n = n\left(\dfrac{a_1 + a_n}{2}\right)$

A sequence of the form

$$a, ar, ar^2, \ldots$$

is called an infinite *geometric* sequence, where a is the first term and r is the common ratio. The nth term of such a sequence is

$$a_n = ar^{n-1}$$

The symbol S_n is used to represent the sum of the corresponding finite geometric series of n elements and

$$S_n = \frac{a(1-r^n)}{1-r}.$$

Expressions of the form

$$a + ar + ar^2 \ldots$$

are called infinite geometric series. When $|r| < 1$, the sum S of the infinite geometric series exists and

$$S = \frac{a}{1-r}$$

PROBLEM

In an arithmetic sequence, $a_1 = 29$ and $a_8 = 78$. Find the common difference d and the sixth term, a_6.

SOLUTION

The nth term in an arithmetic sequence is given by $a_n = a + (n-1)d$, where a is the initial term and d is the common difference. Using the given information we first find d.

$$78 = 29 + (8-1)d$$
$$78 = 29 + 7d$$
$$49 = 7d$$
$$7 = d$$

Thus the common difference is 7. We may now use this information to obtain a_6.

$$a_6 = 29 + (6 - 1)(7)$$
$$= 29 + 35$$
$$= 64$$

Thus the sixth term is 64.

Linear Equations and Matrices

Linear Equations

As discussed in Chapter 3, a linear equation is an equation of the form $a_1x_1 + a_2x_2 + \ldots + a_nx_n = b$, where $a_1, \ldots, a_n$ and b are real constants.

- **EXAMPLES**

  (a) $2x + 6y = 9$
  (b) $x_1 + 3x_2 + 7x_3 = 5$
  (c) $\alpha - 2 = 0$

Linear equations in two variables are always straight lines, as shown in Figure 6.28.

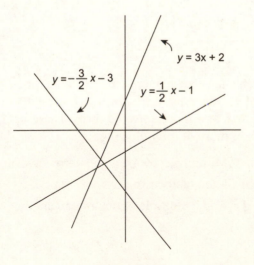

$$y = 3x + 2$$
$$y = -\frac{3}{2}x - 3$$
$$y = \frac{1}{2}x - 1$$

Figure 6.28

A system of linear equations is a finite set of linear equations, all of which use the same set of variables.

- **EXAMPLES**

  (a) $2x_1 + x_2 + 5x_3 = 4$
  $$x_2 + 3x_3 = 0$$
  $$7x_1 + 3x_2 + x_3 = 9$$

  (b) $y - z = 5$
  $$z = 1$$

The solution of a system of linear equations is that set of real numbers which, when substituted into the set of variables, satisfies each equation in the system. The set of all solutions is called the solution set S of the system.

- **EXAMPLE**

  $$y + z = 9 \qquad\qquad S = \{5, 4\}$$
  $$z = 4$$

A consistent system of linear equations has at least one solution, whereas an inconsistent system has no solutions.

- **EXAMPLES**

  (a) $y + z = 9 \qquad S = \{5, 4\}$ (consistent system)
  $$z = 4$$

See Figure 6.29. The solution to both equations is (5,4).

  (b) $x_1 + x_2 = 7 \qquad S = \emptyset$ (inconsistent system)
  $$x_1 = 3$$
  $$x_1 - x_2 = 7$$

See Figure 6.30. There is no solution to all three equations.

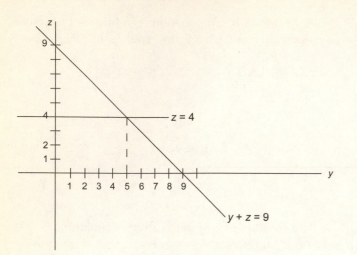

Figure 6.29

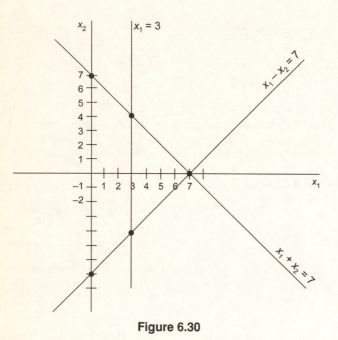

Figure 6.30

Every system of linear equations has either one solution, no solution, or infinitely many solutions. A system of linear equations with infinitely many solutions is called a dependent system of linear equations, all of which are represented by the same line.

Augmented Matrices

The **augmented matrix** for a system of linear equations

$$
\begin{bmatrix}
a_{11} & a_{12} & + & \ldots & a_{1n} = b_1 \\
a_{21} & a_{22} & + & \ldots & a_{2n} = b_2 \\
\vdots & & & & \\
a_{n1} & a_{n2} & + & \ldots & a_{nn} = b_n
\end{bmatrix}
$$

is the matrix of the form:

$$
\left[
\begin{array}{cccc|c}
a_{11} & a_{12} & \ldots & a_{1n} & b_1 \\
a_{21} & a_{22} & \ldots & a_{2n} & b_2 \\
\vdots & & & & \\
a_{m1} & a_{m2} & \ldots & a_{mn} & b_m
\end{array}
\right]
$$

where a_{ij} represents each coefficient in the system and b_i represents each constant in the system.

• **EXAMPLE**

$$
\left[
\begin{array}{ccc|c}
1 & 6 & -2 & 4 \\
3 & 0 & 1 & 7 \\
5 & -3 & 1 & 0
\end{array}
\right]
$$

is the augmented matrix of

$$
\begin{aligned}
x_1 + 6x_2 - 2x_3 &= 4 \\
3x_1 \qquad\quad + x_3 &= 7 \\
5x_1 - 3x_2 + x_3 &= 0
\end{aligned}
$$

Elementary row operations are operations on the rows of an augmented matrix that are used to reduce that matrix to a more solvable form. These operations are one or more of the following:

(a) Multiply a row by a non-zero constant

(b) Interchange two rows

(c) Add a multiple of one row to another row

PROBLEM

By forming the augmented matrix, and reducing rows, determine the solutions of the following system:

$$2x - y + 3z = 4$$
$$3x \quad + 2z = 5$$
$$-2x + y + 4z = 6$$

SOLUTION

The augmented matrix of the system is

$$\begin{bmatrix} 2 & -1 & 3 & | & 4 \\ 3 & 0 & 2 & | & 5 \\ -2 & 1 & 4 & | & 6 \end{bmatrix}$$

Add the first row to the third row:

$$\begin{bmatrix} 2 & -1 & 3 & | & 4 \\ 3 & 0 & 2 & | & 5 \\ 0 & 0 & 7 & | & 10 \end{bmatrix}$$

This is the augmented matrix of:

$$2x - y + 3z = 4$$
$$3x \quad + 2z = 5$$
$$7z = 10$$

The system has been sufficiently simplified now so that the solution can be found.

From the last equation we have $z = \dfrac{10}{7}$. Substituting this value into the second equation and solving for x gives $x = \dfrac{5}{7}$. Substituting $x = \dfrac{5}{7}$ and $z = \dfrac{10}{7}$ into the first equation and solving for y yields $y = \dfrac{12}{7}$. The solution to the system is, therefore,

$$x = \frac{5}{7}, y = \frac{12}{7}, z = \frac{10}{7}.$$

PROBLEM

Solve the following linear system of equations:

$$2x + 3y - 4z = 5$$
$$-2x \quad + z = 7$$
$$3x + 2y + 2z = 3$$

SOLUTION

The augmented matrix for the system is:

$$\begin{bmatrix} 2 & 3 & -4 & | & 5 \\ -2 & 0 & 1 & | & 7 \\ 3 & 2 & 2 & | & 3 \end{bmatrix}$$

which can be reduced by using the following sequence of row operations. There are many sequences that can be used, and not all are as straightforward as that used in the previous solution.

Add the first row to the second row.

$$\begin{bmatrix} 2 & 3 & -4 & | & 5 \\ 0 & 3 & -3 & | & 12 \\ 3 & 2 & 2 & | & 3 \end{bmatrix}$$

Divide the first row by 2 and the second row by 3.

$$\begin{bmatrix} 1 & \frac{3}{2} & -2 & | & \frac{5}{2} \\ 0 & 1 & -1 & | & 4 \\ 3 & 2 & 2 & | & 3 \end{bmatrix}$$

Add –3 times the first row to the third row.

$$\begin{bmatrix} 1 & \frac{3}{2} & -2 & | & \frac{5}{2} \\ 0 & 1 & -1 & | & 4 \\ 0 & -\frac{5}{2} & 8 & | & -\frac{9}{2} \end{bmatrix}$$

Add $\dfrac{5}{2}$ times the second row to the third row.

$$\begin{bmatrix} 1 & \frac{3}{2} & -2 & | & \frac{5}{2} \\ 0 & 1 & -1 & | & 4 \\ 0 & 0 & \frac{11}{2} & | & \frac{11}{2} \end{bmatrix}$$

This is the augmented matrix for the system:

$$x + \frac{3}{2}y - 2z = \frac{5}{2}$$
$$y - z = 4$$
$$\frac{11}{2}z = \frac{11}{2}$$

Now the solution to this system can be easily found. From the last equation we have $z = 1$. Substituting $z = 1$ in the second equation gives $y = 5$. Next, substitute $y = 5$ and $z = 1$ into the first equation. This gives $x = -3$. Therefore, the solution to the system is $x = -3$, $y = 5$, $z = 1$.

PROBLEM

Solve the following system:
$$x + y + 2z = 9$$
$$2x + 4y - 3z = 1$$
$$3x + 6y - 5z = 0$$

SOLUTION

The augmented matrix for the system is

$$\begin{bmatrix} 1 & 1 & 2 & 9 \\ 2 & 4 & -3 & 1 \\ 3 & 6 & -5 & 0 \end{bmatrix}$$

It can be reduced by elementary row operations.

Add -2 times the first row to the second row and -3 times the first row to the third row.

$$\begin{bmatrix} 1 & 1 & 2 & 9 \\ 0 & 2 & -7 & -17 \\ 0 & 3 & -11 & -27 \end{bmatrix}$$

Multiply the second row by $\frac{1}{2}$.

$$\begin{bmatrix} 1 & 1 & 2 & 9 \\ 0 & 1 & -\frac{7}{2} & -\frac{17}{2} \\ 0 & 3 & -11 & -27 \end{bmatrix}$$

Add -3 times the second row to the third row.

$$\begin{bmatrix} 1 & 1 & 2 & 9 \\ 0 & 1 & -\frac{7}{2} & -\frac{17}{2} \\ 0 & 0 & -\frac{1}{2} & -\frac{3}{2} \end{bmatrix}$$

Multiply the second row and the third row by -2 to obtain

$$\begin{bmatrix} 1 & 1 & 2 & 9 \\ 0 & -2 & 7 & 17 \\ 0 & 0 & 1 & 3 \end{bmatrix}$$

This is the augmented matrix for the system:

$$x + y + 2z = 9$$
$$-2y + 7z = 17$$
$$z = 3$$

Solving this system gives $x = 1$, $y = 2$, and $z = 3$.

PROBLEM

For the following system, find the augmented matrix; then, by reducing, determine whether the system has a solution.

$$3x - y + z = 1$$
$$7x + y - z = 6 \qquad (1)$$
$$2x + y - z = 2$$

SOLUTION

The augmented matrix for the system is

$$\begin{bmatrix} 3 & -1 & 1 & | & 1 \\ 7 & 1 & -1 & | & 6 \\ 2 & 1 & -1 & | & 2 \end{bmatrix}$$

This can be reduced by performing the following row operations. Divide the first row by 3.

$$\begin{bmatrix} 1 & -\frac{1}{3} & \frac{1}{3} & | & \frac{1}{3} \\ 7 & 1 & -1 & | & 6 \\ 2 & 1 & -1 & | & 2 \end{bmatrix}$$

Now add -7 times the first row to the second row and -2 times the first row to the third row.

$$\begin{bmatrix} 1 & -\frac{1}{3} & \frac{1}{3} & | & \frac{1}{3} \\ 0 & \frac{10}{3} & -\frac{10}{3} & | & \frac{11}{3} \\ 0 & \frac{5}{3} & -\frac{5}{3} & | & \frac{4}{3} \end{bmatrix}$$

Divide the second row by $\frac{10}{3}$

$$\begin{bmatrix} 1 & -\frac{1}{3} & \frac{1}{3} & | & \frac{1}{3} \\ 0 & 1 & -1 & | & \frac{11}{10} \\ 0 & \frac{5}{3} & -\frac{5}{3} & | & \frac{4}{3} \end{bmatrix}$$

and add $-\dfrac{5}{3}$ times the second row to the third row. The matrix is now

$$\begin{bmatrix} 1 & -\frac{1}{3} & \frac{1}{3} & | & \frac{1}{3} \\ 0 & 1 & -1 & | & \frac{11}{10} \\ 0 & 0 & 0 & | & -\frac{1}{2} \end{bmatrix}$$

The last row implies $0 = -\dfrac{1}{2}$, which is never true, so there is no solution to the given system of equations.

MTEL

Elementary Mathematics (53)

Practice Test

This practice test is also on CD-ROM in our special interactive MTEL Mathematics TEST*ware*®. It is highly recommended that you first take this exam on computer. You will then have the additional study features and benefits of enforced timed conditions and instant, accurate scoring. See page 5 for instructions on how to get the most out of our MTEL book and software.

Answer Sheet

1. Ⓐ Ⓑ Ⓒ Ⓓ   22. Ⓐ Ⓑ Ⓒ Ⓓ   43. Ⓐ Ⓑ Ⓒ Ⓓ   64. Ⓐ Ⓑ Ⓒ Ⓓ   85. Ⓐ Ⓑ Ⓒ Ⓓ

2. Ⓐ Ⓑ Ⓒ Ⓓ   23. Ⓐ Ⓑ Ⓒ Ⓓ   44. Ⓐ Ⓑ Ⓒ Ⓓ   65. Ⓐ Ⓑ Ⓒ Ⓓ   86. Ⓐ Ⓑ Ⓒ Ⓓ

3. Ⓐ Ⓑ Ⓒ Ⓓ   24. Ⓐ Ⓑ Ⓒ Ⓓ   45. Ⓐ Ⓑ Ⓒ Ⓓ   66. Ⓐ Ⓑ Ⓒ Ⓓ   87. Ⓐ Ⓑ Ⓒ Ⓓ

4. Ⓐ Ⓑ Ⓒ Ⓓ   25. Ⓐ Ⓑ Ⓒ Ⓓ   46. Ⓐ Ⓑ Ⓒ Ⓓ   67. Ⓐ Ⓑ Ⓒ Ⓓ   88. Ⓐ Ⓑ Ⓒ Ⓓ

5. Ⓐ Ⓑ Ⓒ Ⓓ   26. Ⓐ Ⓑ Ⓒ Ⓓ   47. Ⓐ Ⓑ Ⓒ Ⓓ   68. Ⓐ Ⓑ Ⓒ Ⓓ   89. Ⓐ Ⓑ Ⓒ Ⓓ

6. Ⓐ Ⓑ Ⓒ Ⓓ   27. Ⓐ Ⓑ Ⓒ Ⓓ   48. Ⓐ Ⓑ Ⓒ Ⓓ   69. Ⓐ Ⓑ Ⓒ Ⓓ   90. Ⓐ Ⓑ Ⓒ Ⓓ

7. Ⓐ Ⓑ Ⓒ Ⓓ   28. Ⓐ Ⓑ Ⓒ Ⓓ   49. Ⓐ Ⓑ Ⓒ Ⓓ   70. Ⓐ Ⓑ Ⓒ Ⓓ   91. Ⓐ Ⓑ Ⓒ Ⓓ

8. Ⓐ Ⓑ Ⓒ Ⓓ   29. Ⓐ Ⓑ Ⓒ Ⓓ   50. Ⓐ Ⓑ Ⓒ Ⓓ   71. Ⓐ Ⓑ Ⓒ Ⓓ   92. Ⓐ Ⓑ Ⓒ Ⓓ

9. Ⓐ Ⓑ Ⓒ Ⓓ   30. Ⓐ Ⓑ Ⓒ Ⓓ   51. Ⓐ Ⓑ Ⓒ Ⓓ   72. Ⓐ Ⓑ Ⓒ Ⓓ   93. Ⓐ Ⓑ Ⓒ Ⓓ

10. Ⓐ Ⓑ Ⓒ Ⓓ   31. Ⓐ Ⓑ Ⓒ Ⓓ   52. Ⓐ Ⓑ Ⓒ Ⓓ   73. Ⓐ Ⓑ Ⓒ Ⓓ   94. Ⓐ Ⓑ Ⓒ Ⓓ

11. Ⓐ Ⓑ Ⓒ Ⓓ   32. Ⓐ Ⓑ Ⓒ Ⓓ   53. Ⓐ Ⓑ Ⓒ Ⓓ   74. Ⓐ Ⓑ Ⓒ Ⓓ   95. Ⓐ Ⓑ Ⓒ Ⓓ

12. Ⓐ Ⓑ Ⓒ Ⓓ   33. Ⓐ Ⓑ Ⓒ Ⓓ   54. Ⓐ Ⓑ Ⓒ Ⓓ   75. Ⓐ Ⓑ Ⓒ Ⓓ   96. Ⓐ Ⓑ Ⓒ Ⓓ

13. Ⓐ Ⓑ Ⓒ Ⓓ   34. Ⓐ Ⓑ Ⓒ Ⓓ   55. Ⓐ Ⓑ Ⓒ Ⓓ   76. Ⓐ Ⓑ Ⓒ Ⓓ   97. Ⓐ Ⓑ Ⓒ Ⓓ

14. Ⓐ Ⓑ Ⓒ Ⓓ   35. Ⓐ Ⓑ Ⓒ Ⓓ   56. Ⓐ Ⓑ Ⓒ Ⓓ   77. Ⓐ Ⓑ Ⓒ Ⓓ   98. Ⓐ Ⓑ Ⓒ Ⓓ

15. Ⓐ Ⓑ Ⓒ Ⓓ   36. Ⓐ Ⓑ Ⓒ Ⓓ   57. Ⓐ Ⓑ Ⓒ Ⓓ   78. Ⓐ Ⓑ Ⓒ Ⓓ   99. Ⓐ Ⓑ Ⓒ Ⓓ

16. Ⓐ Ⓑ Ⓒ Ⓓ   37. Ⓐ Ⓑ Ⓒ Ⓓ   58. Ⓐ Ⓑ Ⓒ Ⓓ   79. Ⓐ Ⓑ Ⓒ Ⓓ   100. Ⓐ Ⓑ Ⓒ Ⓓ

17. Ⓐ Ⓑ Ⓒ Ⓓ   38. Ⓐ Ⓑ Ⓒ Ⓓ   59. Ⓐ Ⓑ Ⓒ Ⓓ   80. Ⓐ Ⓑ Ⓒ Ⓓ   101. —

18. Ⓐ Ⓑ Ⓒ Ⓓ   39. Ⓐ Ⓑ Ⓒ Ⓓ   60. Ⓐ Ⓑ Ⓒ Ⓓ   81. Ⓐ Ⓑ Ⓒ Ⓓ   102. —

19. Ⓐ Ⓑ Ⓒ Ⓓ   40. Ⓐ Ⓑ Ⓒ Ⓓ   61. Ⓐ Ⓑ Ⓒ Ⓓ   82. Ⓐ Ⓑ Ⓒ Ⓓ

20. Ⓐ Ⓑ Ⓒ Ⓓ   41. Ⓐ Ⓑ Ⓒ Ⓓ   62. Ⓐ Ⓑ Ⓒ Ⓓ   83. Ⓐ Ⓑ Ⓒ Ⓓ

21. Ⓐ Ⓑ Ⓒ Ⓓ   42. Ⓐ Ⓑ Ⓒ Ⓓ   63. Ⓐ Ⓑ Ⓒ Ⓓ   84. Ⓐ Ⓑ Ⓒ Ⓓ

Short Constructed-Response Answer Sheets for Questions 101 and 102

Begin your response on this page. If necessary, continue on the next page.

Continue on the next page if necessary.

Continuation of your response from previous page, if necessary.

Continue on the next page if necessary.

Continuation of your response from previous page, if necessary.

MTEL Elementary Mathematics (53) Practice Test

TIME: 4 hours
102 questions

Directions: Read each item and select the best response.

1. In the following figure, O is the center of the circle. If arc ABC has length 2π, what is the area of the circle?

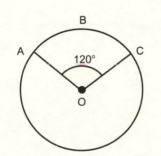

(A) 3π

(B) 6π

(C) 9π

(D) 12π

2. The quotient of $\dfrac{(x^2 - 5x + 3)}{(x + 2)}$ is:

(A) $x - 7 + \dfrac{17}{x + 2}$

(B) $x - 3 + \dfrac{9}{x + 2}$

(C) $x - 7 - \dfrac{11}{x + 2}$

(D) $x - 3 - \dfrac{3}{x + 2}$

3. What is the units digit in the number 3^{2000}?

(A) 1

(B) 3

(C) 7

(D) 9

4. Write a rule that could be used to show the relationship between x and y in the table below.

x	y
-3	9
-1	1
0	0
2	4
3	9
5	25

(A) The value of y is three times the value of x.

(B) The value of y is the square of the value of x.

(C) The value of y is the inverse of the value of x.

(D) The value of y is the square root of the value of x.

5. What is the ratio of 8 feet to 28 inches?

(A) $\dfrac{2}{7}$

(B) $\dfrac{7}{24}$

(C) $\dfrac{24}{7}$

(D) $\dfrac{7}{2}$

6. The measure of an inscribed angle is equal to one-half the measure of its inscribed arc. In the figure shown, triangle ABC is inscribed in circle O, and line $\overline{BD}$ is tangent to the circle at point B. If the measure of angle CBD is 70°, what is the measure of angle BAC?

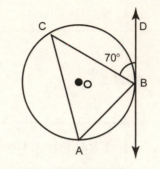

(A) 20°

(B) 35°

(C) 40°

(D) 70°

7. The value of B in the equation $A = \left(\dfrac{h}{2}\right)(B + b)$ is:

(A) $(2A - b)h$

(B) $\dfrac{2h}{A} - b$

(C) $2A - b$

(D) $\dfrac{2A}{h} - b$

8. The greatest area that a rectangle whose perimeter is 52 m can have is

(A) 156 m²

(B) 169 m²

(C) 172 m²

(D) 208 m²

9. What part of three fourths is one tenth?

(A) $\dfrac{1}{8}$

(B) $\dfrac{15}{2}$

(C) $\dfrac{2}{15}$

(D) $\dfrac{3}{40}$

10. In the figure below, which transformation will map $\triangle ABC$ onto $\triangle DEF$?

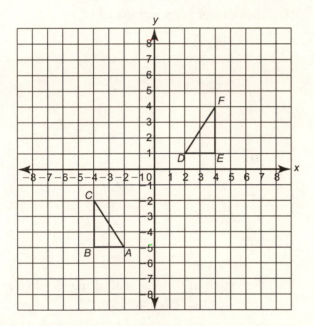

(A) Reflect $\triangle ABC$ over the y-axis and shift up 6 spaces.

(B) Reflect $\triangle ABC$ over the x-axis and shift up 6 spaces.

(C) Reflect $\triangle ABC$ over the y-axis and shift down 6 spaces.

(D) Reflect $\triangle ABC$ over the y-axis, reflect over the x-axis, and shift down 4 spaces.

11. What is the value of the following expression:

$$\frac{1}{1 + \frac{1}{1 + \frac{1}{4}}}$$

(A) $\dfrac{9}{5}$

(B) $\dfrac{5}{9}$

(C) $\dfrac{1}{2}$

(D) 2

12. If in $\triangle ABC$, $AB = BC$ and angle A has measure $46°$, then angle B has measure

(A) $44°$

(B) $46°$

(C) $88°$

(D) $92°$

13. If $\dfrac{3}{x-1} = \dfrac{2}{x+1}$, then $x =$

(A) -5

(B) -1

(C) 1

(D) 5

14. $4\% \times 4\% =$

(A) 0.0016%

(B) 0.16%

(C) 1.6%

(D) 16%

15. The area of $\triangle ADE$ is 12 square units. If B is the midpoint of $\overline{AD}$ and C is the midpoint of $\overline{AE}$, what is the area of $\triangle ABC$?

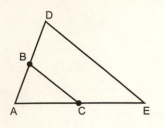

(A) 2 square units

(B) 3 square units

(C) 4 square units

(D) 6 square units

16. Which steps could be used to solve this equation?

$\frac{3}{8}x - 7 = 10$

(A) Multiply both sides by the reciprocal of $\frac{3}{8}$, then add 7 to both sides

(B) Divide both sides by the reciprocal of $\frac{3}{8}$, then add 7 to both sides

(C) Add 7 to both sides, then divide both sides by the reciprocal of $\frac{3}{8}$

(D) Add 7 to both sides, then multiply both sides by the reciprocal of $\frac{3}{8}$

17. The number missing in the series, 2, 6, 12, 20, x, 42, 56 is:

(A) 36

(B) 24

(C) 30

(D) 38

18. A number line is shown below.

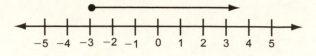

Which of the following statements describes the number represented on this number line?

(A) the number is less than or equal to -3

(B) the number is greater than or equal to -3

(C) the number is less than 3

(D) the number is greater than 3

19. $3\frac{11}{48} - 2\frac{3}{16} =$

(A) $\frac{47}{48}$

(B) $1\frac{1}{48}$

(C) $1\frac{1}{24}$

(D) $1\frac{8}{48}$

20. Find the length of the diagonal of the rectangular solid shown in the following figure.

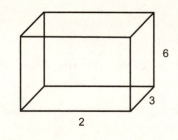

(A) 7

(B) $2\sqrt{10}$

(C) $3\sqrt{5}$

(D) 11

21. A survey asked a group of people to name their favorite pet. The results from this survey are shown in the chart.

FAVORITE PET	
Pet	**Number of People**
Bird	8
Cat	24
Fish	16
Tortoise	5
Dog	20
Hamster	7

If one person were randomly selected from this survey, what is the probability that the person's favorite pet is a dog?

(A) 20%

(B) 25%

(C) 30%

(D) 35%

22. In the figure shown below, line *l* is parallel to line *m*. If the area of triangle *ABC* is 40 cm², what is the area of triangle *ABD*?

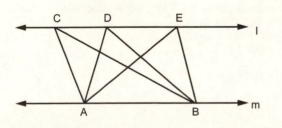

(A) Exactly 40 cm²

(B) Less than 40 cm²

(C) More than 40 cm²

(D) Cannot be determined from the information given

23. The surface area of a cube is 96 square feet. What is the volume of the cube in cubic feet?

(A) 16

(B) 36

(C) 54

(D) 64

24. The graph of a line is shown below.

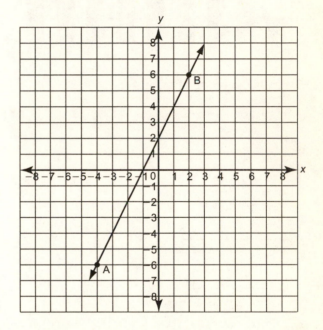

What is the slope of the line shown above?

(A) −2

(B) $-\dfrac{1}{2}$

(C) $\dfrac{1}{2}$

(D) 2

25. How many digits are in the standard numeral for $2^{31} \times 5^{27}$?

(A) 31

(B) 29

(C) 28

(D) 26

26. The graph below shows the frequency of test scores on a history exam.

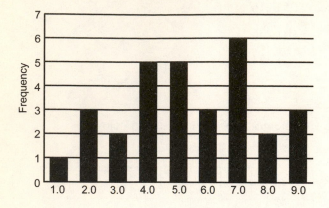

What is the **mode** of the history scores?

(A) 4

(B) 6

(C) 7

(D) 9

27. $1 + \dfrac{y}{x - 2y} - \dfrac{y}{x + 2y} =$

(A) $\dfrac{x^2}{(x - 2y)(x + 2y)}$

(B) $\dfrac{2x - y}{(x - 2y)(x + 2y)}$

(C) $\dfrac{1}{(x - 2y)(x + 2y)}$

(D) 1

28. The sixtieth digit in the decimal representation of $\dfrac{1}{7}$ is

(A) 7

(B) 5

(C) 4

(D) 2

29. If a triangle of base 6 units has the same area as a circle of radius 6 units, what is the altitude of the triangle?

(A) π

(B) 12π

(C) 18π

(D) 36π

30. What is the factorization of $x^2 + ax - 2x - 2a$?

(A) $(x + 2)(x - a)$

(B) $(x - 2)(x + a)$

(C) $(x + 2)(x + a)$

(D) $(x - 2)(x - a)$

31. What is the least natural number that is a multiple of each number from 1 to 10?

(A) 840

(B) 1,260

(C) 2,520

(D) 5040

32. A man buys a book for $20. When he prices it to sell, he wants to offer a discount of 40% on his selling price for the book. Since he wants to make a final profit of 50%, what price should he originally mark it?

(A) $25

(B) $30

(C) $40

(D) $50

33. In the figure shown, all segments meet at right angles. Find the figure's perimeter in terms of r and s.

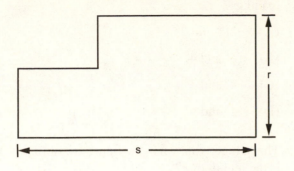

(A) $2r + 2s$

(B) $2r + s$

(C) $2s + r$

(D) $r^2 + s^2$

34. The figure below is constructed from cube blocks. Which drawing—A, B, C, or D—represents the top view of the structure?

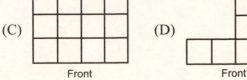

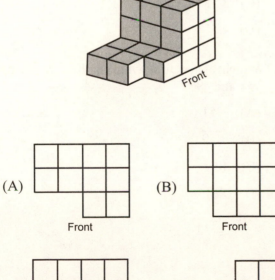

(A)

Front

(B)

Front

(C)

Front

(D)

Front

35. Which of the following is an irrational number?

(A) $\sqrt{3}$

(B) $\sqrt{4}$

(C) $\dfrac{13}{16}$

(D) -1.27

36. Theresa divided 5 by $\dfrac{3}{4}$. Which operation shown below should produce the same result?

(A) $\dfrac{5}{1} \times \dfrac{3}{4}$

(B) $\dfrac{5}{1} \times \dfrac{4}{3}$

(C) $\dfrac{1}{5} \times \dfrac{3}{4}$

(D) $\dfrac{1}{5} \times \dfrac{4}{3}$

37. Read the graph and answer the question.

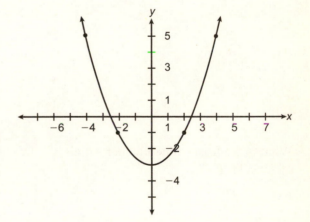

Which equation could be represented by the graph?

(A) $y = \dfrac{1}{2}x^2 + 3$

(B) $y = -\dfrac{1}{2}x^2 - 3$

(C) $y = \dfrac{1}{2}x^2 - 3$

(D) $y = -\dfrac{1}{2}x^2 + 3$

38. Find the area of the shaded portion in the following figure. The heavy dot represents the center of the circle.

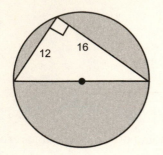

(A) $100\pi - 96$

(B) $400\pi - 96$

(C) $400\pi - 192$

(D) $100\pi - 192$

39. Solve for x.

$$5x + 2y = -5$$
$$-3x + y = 3$$

(A) 0

(B) $-\dfrac{1}{11}$

(C) 1

(D) -1

40. What is the least prime number which is a divisor of $7^9 + 11^{25}$?

(A) 1

(B) 2

(C) 3

(D) 5

41. The winter temperature in a mountain town differed by 9 degrees from one day to the next. Which of the following could be the two temperature readings?

(A) $-10°$ and $2°$

(B) $-5°$ and $4°$

(C) $-4°$ and $3°$

(D) $-1°$ and $9°$

42. The polygons shown in the figure are similar. What is the length of k?

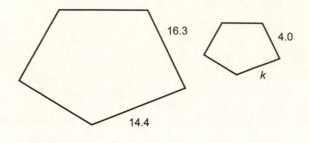

(A) 2.83

(B) 3.76

(C) 3.53

(D) 4.57

43. Which of the following numbers is not between $.8\overline{5}$ and $.\overline{86}$?

(A) $.85\overline{1}$

(B) $.\overline{859}$

(C) $.859$

(D) $.861$

44.

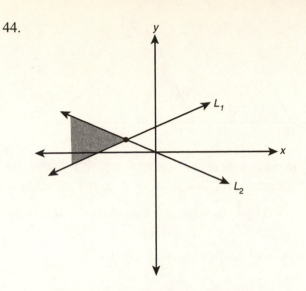

The above graph shows the intersection of two lines L_1 and L_2, and a shaded region. The solution to which of the following systems of inequalities could represent the shaded region?

(A) $x + 2y \geq 0$
 $x - 2y \leq -4$

(B) $x + 2y \leq 0$
 $x - 2y \geq -4$

(C) $x + 2y \leq 0$
 $x - 2y \leq -4$

(D) $x + 2y \geq 0$
 $x - 2y \geq -4$

45. Mary has $29\frac{1}{2}$ yards of material available to make uniforms. Each uniform requires $\frac{3}{4}$ yard of material. How many uniforms can she make and how much material will she have left?

(A) 39 uniforms with $\frac{1}{3}$ yard left over

(B) 39 uniforms with $\frac{1}{4}$ yard left over

(C) 27 uniforms with $\frac{1}{2}$ yard left over

(D) 27 uniforms with $\frac{1}{3}$ yard left over

46.

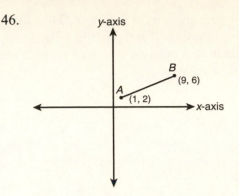

In the graph shown above, if $\overline{AB}$ is reflected about the x-axis, what will be the reflected coordinates of the midpoint of $\overline{AB}$?

(A) $(5, 4)$

(B) $(-5, -4)$

(C) $(5, -4)$

(D) $(-5, 4)$

47. Select the solid figure from the four choices which would result when the flat paper pattern below is folded up.

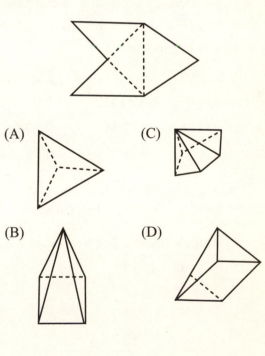

(A)   (C)

(B)   (D)

48. Of the first-year students at a college, 24% failed remedial mathematics. If 360 students failed remedial mathematics, how many first-year students are enrolled at the college?

    (A) 500

    (B) 1200

    (C) 1500

    (D) 3600

49.

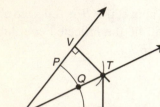

In the diagram above, $\angle PMR$ is acute. At point M, an arc PR is drawn so that $MR = MP$. Arc $\overgroup{PR}$ is then bisected at point Q by the construction shown at point T. The ray joining M, Q, and T is drawn and a perpendicular segment is drawn from T so that $\overline{TV} \perp \overline{MV}$ and $\overline{TW} \perp \overline{MW}$. Which of the following may be *false*?

    (A) $TV = TW$

    (B) $m\angle VMW > m\angle VTM$

    (C) $m\angle VTM = m\angle WTM$

    (D) $MW > MP$

50. The stem and leaf plot below shows Mary's history test scores. What is the median score?

    Mary's History Test Scores

6	1
7	4 7
8	2
9	2 3 6 8 9

    (A) 77   (C) 92

    (B) 82   (D) 96

51.

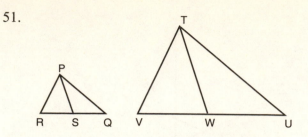

In the figures above, $\Delta PQR \sim \Delta TUV$. Point S is the midpoint of $\overline{QR}$ and point W is the midpoint of $\overline{UV}$. If $\dfrac{PR}{TV} = \dfrac{3}{5}$, what is the value of the following ratio?

(Area of ΔPSR)/(Area of ΔTUV)

    (A) .18

    (B) .30

    (C) .36

    (D) .40

52. Karen invests $2500 into a savings account which pays 8% interest compounded quarterly. To the nearest half-year, in how many years will she earn approximately $800 in interest?

    (A) 5.5

    (B) 4.5

    (C) 3.5

    (D) 2.5

53. How many of the scores 10, 20, 30, 35, 55 are larger than their arithmetic mean score?

    (A) Four

    (B) Three

    (C) Two

    (D) One

54. Sharon wants to conduct a survey to determine if more students say that their favorite school subject is science rather than English. What is the best way to get a random sample of 200 students?

(A) Ask the first 200 students that come out of the library.

(B) Ask 200 students that Sharon knows at school.

(C) Ask all of the students in Sharon's first three classes.

(D) Ask 200 students blindly selected from a list of all students.

55. What is the domain of the function defined by

$$y = f(x) = \sqrt{-x+1} + 5?$$

(A) $\{x \mid x \geq 0\}$

(B) $\{x \mid x \leq 1\}$

(C) $\{x \mid 0 \leq x \leq 1\}$

(D) $\{x \mid x \geq -1\}$

56. Answer the question based on the following:

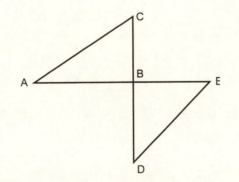

If $\overline{BC} \perp \overline{AE}$, $\overline{DB} \cong \overline{AB}$, and $\angle E = \angle C$, which of the following must be true?

(A) $\overline{AB} = 2\overline{BE}$

(B) $\overline{BC} \cong \overline{AC}$

(C) $\overline{BC} = \frac{2}{3}\overline{BD}$

(D) $\overline{BC} \cong \overline{BE}$

57. $t = -9$ is a root of the equation $t^2 + 4t - 45 = 0$. Which of the following statements is (are) correct for the equation?

I. $t + 9$ is a factor of the equation.

II. Division of the equation by $t - 9$ yields the other factor of the quadratic equation.

III. $t = -5$ is another root of the equation.

(A) I only

(B) II and III only

(C) III only

(D) I, II, and III

58. The volume of a cube changed from 216 cubic centimeters to 64 cubic centimeters. What is the best approximation of the percent change in length for a side of the cube?

(A) 70%

(B) 67%

(C) 50%

(D) 33%

59. What is the range of the function

$$g(x) = \sqrt{16 - x^2}\ ?$$

(A) All numbers between 0 and 4, inclusive

(B) All numbers between −4 and 4, inclusive

(C) All numbers less than or equal to 4

(D) All numbers greater than or equal to 0

60. Which of the following is equivalent to

$$\sqrt{\frac{x^{-7} \cdot x^2}{x^{-3}}}\ ?$$

(A) x^4 (C) $\dfrac{1}{x^2}$

(B) x^6 (D) $\dfrac{1}{x}$

61. Which equation expresses the relationship that the height (h) varies inversely as the square of the base (b)?

    (A) $h = \dfrac{b^2}{k}$

    (B) $kb^2 = h$

    (C) $h = \dfrac{k}{b^2}$

    (D) $kh = b^2$

62. Lines l_1 and l_2 are perpendicular and intersect at $(1, 4)$. If l_1 contains the point $(3, 9)$, which of the following points lies on l_2?

    (A) $(3, -1)$

    (B) $(-9, 8)$

    (C) $(-1, -1)$

    (D) $(6, 6)$

63. If $f(x) = 2x^2 + 4x + k$, what should the value of k be in order to have the graph of this function intersect the x-axis in only one place?

    (A) -2

    (B) 4

    (C) 1

    (D) 2

64. If the length of a rectangle is increased by 30% and the width is decreased by 20%, what is the increase for the area?

    (A) 4%

    (B) 5%

    (C) 10%

    (D) 25%

65. Select the geometric figure that possesses all of the following characteristics:

    I.   Quadrilateral

    II. At least one pair of parallel sides

    III. Diagonals are always perpendicular to each other

    (A) Rectangle

    (B) Rhombus

    (C) Trapezoid

    (D) Parallelogram

66. Let $y = Cp^x$ represent an exponential model for the points $(1, 8)$ and $(3, 18)$. Given that C and p are positive numbers, what is the best approximation to the sum of C and p?

    (A) 5.33

    (B) 5.83

    (C) 6.83

    (D) 7.33

67. Which of the following equations has no solution in real numbers?

    (A) $\sqrt{2x - 5} - 9 = -4$

    (B) $\sqrt{5x - 2} + 8 = 5$

    (C) $\sqrt{2 - 3x} + 6 = 12$

    (D) $\sqrt{7x + 2} - 10 = -10$

68. Age Distribution of People Living in Smallville

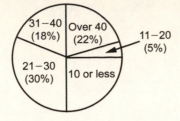

Using the above pie chart, if there are a total of 282 people in Smallville who are under 10 years old or over 40 years old, what is the combined total of people who are between the ages of 11 and 30, inclusive?

(A) 180

(B) 210

(C) 330

(D) 460

69. Two triangles are shown below.

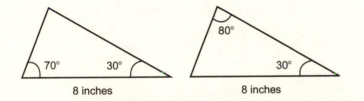

Which of the following statements is true?

(A) The two triangles are congruent.

(B) The two triangles are *not* congruent.

(C) Only one side and one angle are equal.

(D) Both triangles are right triangles.

70. Find a, b for the parabola

$$y = ax^2 + bx + 3$$

if the vertex is (2, 4).

(A) $a = -\dfrac{1}{4}, b = 1$

(B) $a = -1, b = -2$

(C) $a = 1, b = 2$

(D) $a = -\dfrac{1}{3}, b = 1$

71. The base of a right prism, shown here, is an equilateral triangle, each of whose sides measure 4 units. The altitude of the prism is 5 units. Find the volume of the prism.

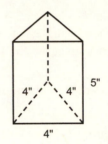

(A) $4\sqrt{3}$

(B) $20\sqrt{3}$

(C) 60

(D) 40

72. Given the equation $Ax + By = C$, if the y-intercept and the slope were doubled, what would be a correct representation of the resulting equation?

(A) $2Ax + 2By = C$

(B) $Ax + 2By = 2C$

(C) $Ax + By = C + 2$

(D) $2Ax + By = 2C$

73.

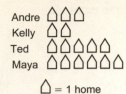

Andre △△△
Kelly △△
Ted △△△△△
Maya △△△△△△

△ = 1 home

Using the chart above, suppose that for this month, Kelly can improve her sales by 50% and Andre can improve his sales by 100%. Assume that Ted's and Maya's sales remain the same. For this month, what fraction of the total number of homes sold by A-Plus realty will Kelly sell?

(A) $\dfrac{1}{5}$ (C) $\dfrac{3}{20}$

(B) $\dfrac{3}{17}$ (D) $\dfrac{1}{8}$

74. The corresponding angles of two geometric figures may be congruent but the sides may not be in proportion.

The above statement could apply to which one of the following?

(A) Two squares

(B) Two rectangles

(C) Two rhombuses

(D) Two triangles

75. Point A has coordinates (2, 5) and point B has coordinates (−3, −3). What is the distance between point A and point B?

(A) 5.6

(B) 9.4

(C) 8.1

(D) 2.4

76. M varies directly as the square of V. When $V = 4$, $M = 24$. What is the value of M when $V = 6$?

(A) 9

(B) $10\dfrac{2}{3}$

(C) 36

(D) 54

77. Given triangle PQR, where points P, Q, and R are located at (−4, 0), (1, 6), and (3, 0), respectively, what is the slope of the median from Q to $\overline{PR}$?

(A) 4

(B) 4.5

(C) 7.5

(D) 9

78. In a certain class, there are twice as many girls as boys. One-half of the boys and two-thirds of the girls are studying physics. What fraction of the entire class is studying physics?

(A) $\dfrac{11}{18}$

(B) $\dfrac{7}{12}$

(C) $\dfrac{9}{20}$

(D) $\dfrac{2}{5}$

79. A jar contains seven white marbles, two red marbles, and three blue marbles. After Joe replaces one white marble with two red marbles, Maria randomly selects one marble from the jar. What is the probability that she will select a red marble?

(A) $\dfrac{1}{3}$

(B) $\dfrac{4}{13}$

(C) $\dfrac{2}{7}$

(D) $\dfrac{1}{4}$

80.

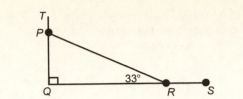

Note: Figure not drawn to scale.

In the right triangle PQR shown above, Q, R, and S are collinear points. Also, T, P, and Q are collinear points. How much larger is $\angle PRS$ than $\angle RPT$?

(A) 24°

(B) 33°

(C) 57°

(D) 90°

81.

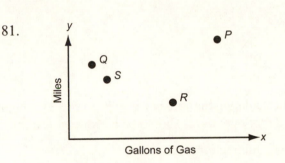

David took 4 different cars for a test drive. These cars are identified as P, Q, R, and S, as shown in the scatter plot above. If these cars were arranged in order from best mileage per gallon to worst mileage per gallon, how would the list appear?

(A) R, P, S, Q

(B) Q, S, P, R

(C) P, Q, S, R

(D) R, S, Q, P

82.

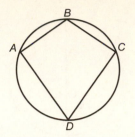

Note: Figure not drawn to scale.

In the figure above, quadrilateral $ABCD$ is inscribed in the circle. If the measure of $\angle B$ is 105° and the measure of $\angle C$ is 95°, what is the measure, in degrees, of arc ABC?

(A) 75°

(B) 80°

(C) 90°

(D) 150°

83. A machine makes 5 bottle caps in 22 seconds. How many bottle caps can it make in 66 minutes?

(A) 15

(B) 290

(C) 900

(D) 1,500

84. Which of the following can be represented by a graph that has the same vertex as the graph of $f(x) = x^2 + 14x + 51$?

(A) $f(x) = 3(x + 7)^2 + 2$

(B) $f(x) = 4(x - 7)^2 + 51$

(C) $f(x) = 7(x - 14)^2 + 2$

(D) $f(x) = 6(x + 14)^2 + 51$

85.

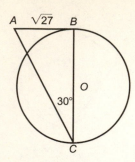

Note: Figure not drawn to scale.

In the figure above, $\overline{AB}$ is tangent to the circle with center O. What is the circumference of circle O?

(A) $3\sqrt{3}\pi$

(B) 9π

(C) $6\sqrt{3}\pi$

(D) 18π

86. A recursive sequence of numbers is defined as follows: $a_1 = 10$, $a_2 = 15$, $a_n = (a_{n-1} - a_{n-2})^2$ for $n > 2$. What is the value of a_5?

(A) 900

(B) 3,125

(C) 5,625

(D) 11,250

87. If the point $(3, 1)$ is rotated $90°$ counterclockwise on an xy-coordinate plane, what is the point's new coordinates?

(A) $(-3, 1)$

(B) $(-3, -1)$

(C) $(1, 3)$

(D) $(-1, 3)$

88. Which one of the following is NOT an example of a direct variation between y and x?

(A) $y = \dfrac{10}{x}$

(B) $y = \dfrac{x}{10}$

(C) $y = 100x$

(D) $\dfrac{y}{x} = \dfrac{1}{100}$

89. Which one of the following is the correct representation of this expression? "Eight less than the quotient of 50 and 5"

(A) $\dfrac{50 - 8}{5}$

(B) $8 - \dfrac{50}{5}$

(C) $\dfrac{(8 - 50)}{5}$

(D) $\dfrac{50}{5} - 8$

90. In calculating the value of $5 + 7^2 \div (9 - 3)$, which order of operations should be performed *last*?

(A) Subtraction

(B) Squaring

(C) Addition

(D) Division

91. The scale drawing of a rectangular floor has a width of three-fourths of an inch and a length of two inches. If the actual width of the floor is 12 feet, what is the perimeter of the floor, in feet?

(A) 88

(B) 96

(C) 132

(D) 144

92. Look at the following table of values:

x	0	3	a	9	12
y	7	1	−5	b	−17

If there is a linear relationship between x and y, what is the value of ab?

(A) −66

(B) −30

(C) −12

(D) −4

93.

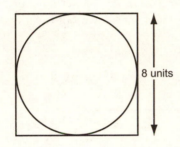

The diagram shown above represents a square dartboard with an inscribed circle. A dart is thrown and lands inside the square. What is the best approximation for the probability that this dart lands inside the circle?

(A) .75

(B) .80

(C) .85

(D) .90

94. A person tosses a coin three times. What is the probability that he will get exactly two tails?

(A) $\dfrac{5}{8}$

(B) $\dfrac{2}{3}$

(C) $\dfrac{3}{8}$

(D) $\dfrac{1}{3}$

95. A class of 40 students is 60% female. If 8 more female students and 2 more male students are added, then the percent of male students in this class will be _____.

(A) 25

(B) $33\dfrac{1}{3}$

(C) 36

(D) 40

96. Which one of the following sets is closed under multiplication?

(A) $\{1, 2\}$

(B) $\{−1, 0\}$

(C) $\{−2, −1, 0\}$

(D) $\{−1, 0, 1\}$

97. $(7)(3 + 2) = (3 + 2)(7)$ is an example of which property of numbers?

(A) Associative

(B) Commutative

(C) Distributive

(D) Inverse

98.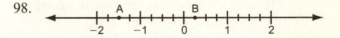

Using the number line shown above, which one of the following is the best approximation to the product of the numbers associated with points A and B.

(A) $-\dfrac{5}{4}$

(B) $-\dfrac{3}{4}$

(C) $-\dfrac{5}{8}$

(D) $-\dfrac{3}{8}$

99. An ordinary six-sided die is thrown once and a coin is tossed twice. What is the probability that the die will show a 5 and the coin will land tails both times?

(A) $\dfrac{1}{24}$

(B) $\dfrac{1}{20}$

(C) $\dfrac{1}{12}$

(D) $\dfrac{1}{10}$

100. Which one of the following has the LOWEST value?

(A) $|-7-5|$

(B) $-|7-(-5)|$

(C) $-|5-7|$

(D) $|-5-(-7)|$

Questions 101 and 102 are open-response questions.

- **Be sure to answer and label all parts of each question.**

- **Show all your work (drawings, tables, or computations) on your Answer Page.**

- **If you do the work in your head, explain in writing how you did the work.**

Write your answers to these questions in the space provided in this book.

101. Tim and Wanda work in a certain company. Tim works a shift of 11 consecutive days, then gets 1 day off. Wanda works a shift of 19 consecutive days, then gets 1 day off.

- If Tim and Wanda both start work on January 1, when is the first day when both will be off work on the same day? Assume 28 days in February.

- If Tim is paid $85 per day, how much per day should Wanda make so that each person will get the same pay per shift? Include the day off as part of the shift.

- Write a chart for each person that shows, in sequence, his or her days off. Extend the chart until it shows both workers off on the same day.

102. The dimensions of a box are shown below.

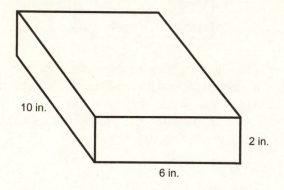

- Find the volume of this box. Show how you found your answer.

- Find the surface area of this box. Show how you found your answer.

- Find the dimensions of a box that has the same volume but less surface area. Show how you found your answer.

Answer Key Practice Test (53) for Elementary Mathematics

Q No.	Correct Answer	Subarea	Q No.	Correct Answer	Subarea
1.	(C)	Geometry	32.	(D)	Operations
2.	(A)	Algebra	33.	(A)	Geometry
3.	(A)	Number Sense	34.	(B)	Geometry
4.	(B)	Relations	35.	(A)	Number Sense
5.	(C)	Measurement	36.	(B)	Operations
6.	(D)	Geometry	37.	(C)	Algebra
7.	(D)	Algebra	38.	(A)	Geometry
8.	(B)	Geometry	39.	(D)	Algebra
9.	(C)	Operations	40.	(B)	Number Sense
10.	(A)	Geometry	41.	(B)	Number Sense
11.	(B)	Number Sense	42.	(C)	Relations
12.	(C)	Geometry	43.	(A)	Number Sense
13.	(A)	Algebra	44.	(C)	Geometry
14.	(B)	Number Sense	45.	(B)	Operations
15.	(B)	Geometry	46.	(C)	Geometry
16.	(D)	Algebra	47.	(A)	Geometry
17.	(C)	Number Sense	48.	(C)	Number Sense
18.	(B)	Number Sense	49.	(B)	Geometry
19.	(C)	Operations	50.	(C)	Data Analysis
20.	(A)	Geometry	51.	(A)	Geometry
21.	(B)	Data Analysis	52.	(C)	Algebra
22.	(A)	Geometry	53.	(C)	Data Analysis
23.	(D)	Geometry	54.	(D)	Data Analysis
24.	(D)	Algebra	55.	(B)	Algebra
25.	(B)	Number Sense	56.	(D)	Geometry
26.	(C)	Data Analysis	57.	(A)	Algebra
27.	(A)	Algebra	58.	(D)	Geometry
28.	(A)	Algebra	59.	(A)	Algebra
29.	(B)	Geometry	60.	(D)	Operations
30.	(B)	Algebra	61.	(C)	Relations
31.	(C)	Number Sense	62.	(B)	Geometry

Q No.	Correct Answer	Subarea	Q No.	Correct Answer	Subarea
63.	(D)	Geometry	83.	(C)	Algebra
64.	(A)	Geometry	84.	(A)	Algebra
65.	(B)	Geometry	85.	(B)	Geometry
66.	(C)	Algebra	86.	(C)	Patterns
67.	(B)	Number Sense	87.	(D)	Geometry
68.	(B)	Data Analysis	88.	(A)	Relations
69.	(A)	Geometry	89.	(D)	Algebra
70.	(A)	Geometry	90.	(C)	Operations
71.	(B)	Geometry	91.	(A)	Measurement
72.	(D)	Algebra	92.	(A)	Algebra
73.	(C)	Data Analysis	93.	(B)	Geometry
74.	(B)	Geometry	94.	(C)	Data Analysis
75.	(B)	Geometry	95.	(C)	Algebra
76.	(D)	Relations	96.	(D)	Algebra
77.	(A)	Geometry	97.	(B)	Operations
78.	(A)	Relations	98.	(D)	Number Sense
79.	(B)	Relations	99.	(A)	Data Analysis
80.	(A)	Geometry	100.	(B)	Algebra
81.	(B)	Data Analysis	101.	–	Open-Response
82.	(D)	Geometry	102.	–	Open-Response

Elementary Math 53
Detailed Explanations of Answers

1.   (C)

Since an arc length of 2π is subtended by a central angle of $120°$, the whole circle, or $360°$, would correspond to an arc length of 6π, which is the circumference of the circle. Then, since $C = 2\pi r$, $6\pi = (2\pi)(\text{radius})$, so the radius $= 3$. Finally, the area of the circle $= \pi r^2$, $(\pi)(3)(3) = 9\pi$.

2.   (A)

The actual polynomial division of $\dfrac{(x^2 - 5x + 3)}{(x + 2)}$ appears as follows:

$$
\begin{array}{r}
x - 7 \\
x + 2 \overline{\smash{\big)}\, x^2 - 5x + 3} \\
\underline{x^2 + 2x} \\
-7x + 3 \\
\underline{-7x - 14} \\
17
\end{array}
$$

Thus, the quotient is $x - 7 + \dfrac{17}{x + 2}$.

3.   (A)

When the number 3 is raised to the powers 1, 2, 3, 4, the units digit is 3, 9, 7, 1, respectively. This pattern continues for each consecutive group of four numbers that are powers of 3. Since 2000 would correspond to the number 4 when placed into a group of four consecutive integers, 3^{2000} has the same units digit as 3^4. Thus, its units digit is 1.

4.   (B)

For each value of x, we can check that the value of y is the value of x squared. Note that $9 = (-3)(-3)$, $1 = (-1)(-1)$, $0 = (0)(0)$, $4 = (2)(2)$, $9 = (3)(3)$, and $25 = (5)(5)$.

5.   (C)

Convert 8 feet to $8 \times 12 = 96$ inches. Then, the ratio $\dfrac{96}{28}$ can be reduced to $\dfrac{24}{7}$ by dividing the numerator and denominator by 4.

6.   (D)

Angle BAC is an inscribed angle for arc BC, and thus its measurement in degrees is one-half of arc BC. Also, the measurement of an angle formed by a chord of a circle and a tangent at the point of contact is one-half of its intercepted arc; this means that $70°$ (angle DBC) is one-half of arc BC. Now, since we know that $BC = 140°$, angle $BAC = \left(\dfrac{1}{2}\right)(140°) = 70°$.

7.   (D)

Divide both sides of the equation by $\dfrac{h}{2}$ to get $\dfrac{A}{\left(\frac{h}{2}\right)} = B + b$, which simplifies to $2\dfrac{A}{h} = B + b$. Finally, subtract b from both sides to get $\dfrac{2A}{h} - b = B$.

8.   (B)

With a given perimeter for a rectangle, the largest possible area would be attained when the rectangle is actually a square. The length of one side of a square with a perimeter of 52 is 13, so its area is $(13)(13) = 169$.

9.   (C)

To determine the part of $\frac{3}{4}$ that $\frac{1}{10}$ is, divide $\frac{1}{10}$ by $\frac{3}{4}$. $\frac{\left(\frac{1}{10}\right)}{\left(\frac{3}{4}\right)} = \left(\frac{1}{10}\right)\left(\frac{4}{3}\right) = \frac{4}{30} = \frac{2}{15}$.

10.   (A)

By reflecting triangle ABC over the y-axis, each x value will change to its opposite, but each y value will remain the same. Then the vertices A, B, and C will become $(2, -5)$, $(4, -5)$, and $(4, -2)$, respectively. When this reflected triangle is shifted up 6 spaces, each x value remains the same, but each y value is increased by 6. The vertices for A, B, and C will now become $(2, 1)$, $(4, 1)$, and $(4, 4)$, respectively. This result is shown by triangle DEF.

11.   (B)

$1 + \frac{1}{4} = \frac{5}{4}$, so the expression reduces to $\frac{1}{1 + \frac{1}{\left(\frac{5}{4}\right)}}$. $\frac{1}{\left(\frac{5}{4}\right)} = \frac{4}{5}$, so the expression then becomes $\frac{1}{1 + \frac{4}{5}}$, or $\frac{1}{\left(\frac{9}{5}\right)}$, which is equivalent to $\frac{5}{9}$.

12.   (C)

This is an isosceles triangle, with m $\angle A$ = m $\angle C = 46°$. Since the sum of all three angles of the triangles is $180°$, m $\angle C = 180° - 46° - 46° = 88°$.

13.   (A)

Multiply the equation by $(x - 1)(x + 1)$, or cross multiply, to get $3(x + 1) = 2(x - 1)$. This becomes $3x + 3 = 2x - 2$, which simplifies to $x + 3 = -2$. Finally, $x = -5$.

14.   (B)

Change each 4% to 0.04. Then, $(0.04)(0.04) = 0.0016 = 0.16\%$.

15.   (B)

The ratio of the areas of the triangles is equal to the square of the ratios of their respective sides. Since $\frac{AB}{AD} = \frac{1}{2}$, $\frac{\text{area of } \triangle ABC}{\text{area of } \triangle ADE} = \left(\frac{1}{2}\right)\left(\frac{1}{2}\right) = \frac{1}{4}$. Thus, the area of triangle $ABC = \left(\frac{1}{4}\right)(12) = 3$ square units.

16.   (D)

The first step in solving is to put all x terms on one side of the equation by adding 7 to both sides. This will simplify the equation to $\left(\frac{3}{8}\right)x = 17$. The final step is to divide each side by $\frac{3}{8}$, which is equivalent to multiplying by the reciprocal of $\frac{3}{8}$, which is $\frac{8}{3}$.

17.   (C)

We notice that $6 - 2 = 4$, $12 - 6 = 6$, $20 - 12 = 8$. The pattern is that for each successive pair of numbers, their difference increases by 2. This means that $x - 20 = 10$, so $x = 30$. Note that 12 will represent the difference between 30 and 42, agreeing with this pattern.

18. (B)

Since the black dot is on -3, the solution must include -3. The arrow points to the right, so this indicates that all numbers greater than -3 are also to be included.

19. (C)

Using the common denominator of 48, $2\frac{3}{16}$ becomes $2\frac{9}{48}$. Then, $3\frac{11}{48} - 2\frac{9}{48} = 1\frac{2}{48}$, which reduces to $1\frac{1}{24}$.

20. (A)

The diagonal of the base of this figure is found by using the Pythagorean Theorem, and is equal to $\sqrt{(2)^2 + (3)^2} = \sqrt{13}$. The diagonal of the solid is computed by using the Pythagorean Theorem with $\sqrt{13}$ and 6, and is equal to $\sqrt{(\sqrt{13})^2 + 6^2} = \sqrt{49} = 7$.

21. (B)

There are a total of 80 people who are surveyed. Since there are 20 people who chose a dog as their favorite pet, the required probability is $\frac{20}{80} = 25\%$.

22. (A)

Triangles ABC and ABD share a common base AB. Their heights would be the same, since each height would be represented by the perpendicular distance from line l to line m. The area of each triangle = $\frac{(\text{base})(\text{height})}{2}$, which would be the same.

23. (D)

The surface area = (6)(area of each surface). Then $\frac{96}{6} = 16$ represents the area of one surface. This means that each edge of the cube is $\sqrt{16} = 4$. The volume = $(4)^3 = 64$.

24. (D)

Choose two points on the graph, for example $(-1, 0)$ and $(0, 2)$. The slope is equal to the change in y values divided by the change in x values = $\frac{(2 - 0)}{(0 - (-1))}$ = $\frac{2}{1} = 2$.

25. (B)

$2^{31} \times 5^{27} = 2^4 \times 2^{27} \times 5^{27}$, but since $2^{27} \times 5^{27} = (2 \times 5)^{27} = 10^{27}$, $2^{31} \times 5^{27}$ is the same as $2^4 \times 10^{27}$, or 16×10^{27}. This is the same as 1.6×10^{28}, which represents a total of 29 digits.

26. (C)

The mode is represented by the number that occurs most frequently. Since 7.0 occurs six times, and this is more frequent than any of the other numbers.

27. (A)

Change each fraction to one with the common denominator of $(x - 2y)(x + 2y)$. The numerators will change to $(x - 2y)(x + 2y)$, $(y)(x + 2y)$, and $(y)(x - 2y)$. The combined answer for the numerator will be $(x - 2y)(x + 2y) + (y)(x + 2y) - (y)(x - 2y)$ $= x^2 - 4y^2 + xy + 2y^2 - xy + 2y^2 = x^2$. Putting this numerator over the common denominator, the final answer is:

$$\frac{x^2}{(x - 2y)(x + 2y)}.$$

28. (A)

When $\frac{1}{7}$ is written as a decimal, we get the repeating group of six digits $.\overline{142857}$. Since $\frac{60}{6} = 10$ with no remainder, we are seeking the digit in position 6, and this digit is 7. Notice that 7 is the $6^{th}, 12^{th}, 18^{th}, 24^{th}$, etc. positions, and each of these numbered positions has no remainder when divided by 6.

29. (B)

The area of a circle with a radius of 6 is 36π. The area of a triangle is $\left(\frac{1}{2}\right)$(base)(altitude). Then $36\pi = \left(\frac{1}{2}\right)$ (6)(height), so $36\pi = $ (3)(height). Solving, height $= 12\pi$.

30. (B)

The answer of $(x - 2)(x + a)$ can be verified by the rules of polynomial multiplication. $(x - 2)(x + a) = (x)(x) + (x)(a) - (2)(x) - (2)(a)$, which equals $x^2 + ax - 2x - 2a$.

31. (C)

Write each number from 2 through 10 in prime factorization form (the number 1 does not have any prime factors). $2 = 2^1, 3 = 3^1, 4 = 2^2, 5 = 5^1, 6 = (2)^1 \cdot (3)^1, 7 = 7^1, 8 = 2^3, 9 = 3^2$, and $10 = (2)^1 \cdot (5)^1$. The least common multiple is the required number, and this is found by taking each different prime factor and using the highest exponent found among these numbers. Thus, the required number is $(2)^3 \cdot (3)^2 \cdot (5)^1 \cdot (7)^1 = 2,520$.

32. (D)

A 50% profit on the cost would be ($20)(1.50) = $30. Thus, $30 will represent the selling price. Since $30 represents a 40% discount from the marked price, $30 is actually 60% of the marked price. The marked price is therefore found by dividing $30 by .60, which is $50.

33. (A)

Although this figure shows indentations, the two unmarked vertical segments have a sum of r. Likewise, the two unmarked horizontal segments have a sum of s. The perimeter is $r + r + s + s = 2r + 2s$.

34. (B)

Viewed from the top, and focusing on the darker faces, this figure would appear as a 4 square by 3 square diagram, with a missing lower left square.

35. (A)

An irrational number is one that cannot be written as a quotient of two integers. Choice (B) is wrong because $\sqrt{4} = 2 = \frac{2}{1}$. Choice (C) is wrong because it is already written as a quotient of two integers. Choice (D) is wrong because $-1.27 = -\frac{127}{100}$. $\sqrt{3}$ cannot be written as a quotient of two integers.

36. (B)

Dividing by a fraction is equivalent to multiplying by its reciprocal. The reciprocal is found by switching the numerator and denominator. Thus, the reciprocal of $\frac{3}{4}$ is $\frac{4}{3}$.

37. (C)

The graph passes through the points $(0, -3)$, $(2, -1)$, $(-2, -1)$, $(4, 5)$, and $(-4, +5)$. Also, the graph is a parabola which faces upward and, therefore, the coefficient of the x^2-term must be positive. These conditions are only satisfied by

$$y = \frac{1}{2}x^2 - 3$$

and, therefore, answer choices (A), (B), and (D) are incorrect.

38. (A)

The hypotenuse of the inscribed right triangle $= \sqrt{12^2 + 16^2} = \sqrt{400} = 20$. This number also represents the diameter of the circle, so the radius equals 10. The area of the circle is $(\pi)(10)(10) = 100\pi$. The area of the triangle is $\left(\frac{1}{2}\right)(12)(16) = 96$. Finally, the area of the shaded portion is the difference of these two areas, which is $100\pi - 96$.

39. (D)

$$5x + 2y = -5$$
$$-3x + y = 3$$

Multiply the bottom equation by -2 so that the terms in the y-column will cancel as follows (in this way if the y-terms cancel you will be solving for x).

$$\begin{array}{ccc} 5x + 2y = -5 & & 5x + 2y = -5 \\ -2(-3x + y) = -2(3) & \Rightarrow & 6x - 2y = -6 \end{array}$$

$$\frac{11x}{11} = \frac{-11}{11}$$
$$x = -1$$

Add the coefficients/terms in the x-column and the constants on the right side. Then divide both sides by 11, the coefficient of the x-term.

Answer choice (A) is incorrect because it solved for the variable y.

$$\begin{array}{rcl} 3(\ 5x + 2y = -5) & = & 15x + 6y = -15 \\ 5(-3x + y = 3) & = & -15x + 5y = 15 \\ \hline & & 11y = 0 \\ & & y = 0 \end{array}$$

Answer choice (B) is incorrect because of an error in adding 2 negative numbers.

$$\begin{array}{c} 5x + 2y = -5 \\ 6x - 2y = -6 \\ \hline 11x = -1, \quad x = -\frac{1}{11} \end{array}$$

Answer choice (C) is incorrect because of an error in signs.

$$\begin{array}{c} 5x + 2y = -5 \\ -6x - 2y = -6 \\ \hline x = 1 \end{array}$$

40. (B)

Each of 7^9 and 11^{25} is an odd number, and the sum of two odd numbers must be an even number. The number 2 is a divisor of every even number.

41. (B)

We need to find two numbers whose difference is 9, and $4 - (-5) = 9$. For each of the other answer choices, the difference between the two given numbers is not 9.

42. (C)

The lengths of corresponding sides are proportional. Thus:

$$\frac{16.3}{4.0} = \frac{14.4}{k}$$
$$k = \frac{4(14.4)}{16.3}$$

$$4 \times 14.4 \div 16.3 = 3.53$$

43. (A)

Since $\overline{.85} = .858585.....$, $\overline{.851} = .851851851....$ is actually less than $\overline{.85}$, so it cannot lie between $\overline{.85}$ and $\overline{.86}$.

44. (C)

$$x + 2y \leq 0$$
$$x - 2y \leq -4$$

The equation $x + 2y = 0$ has a slope of $-\frac{1}{2}$, so it must correspond to line L_2. Likewise, the equation $x - 2y = -4$ has a slope of $\frac{1}{2}$, so it must correspond to line L_1. The shaded area lies below L_2 but above L_1.

45. (B)

Dividing $29\frac{1}{2}$ yards by $\frac{3}{4}$ yard yields $39\frac{1}{3}$. This means she can make 39 complete uniforms, with material for $\frac{1}{3}$ of a uniform left over. Since each uniform requires $\frac{3}{4}$ of a yard of material, $\left(\frac{1}{3}\right)\left(\frac{3}{4}\right) = \frac{1}{4}$ of a yard is left over.

46. (C)

(5, –4)

The midpoint of $\overline{AB}$ is located at (5, 4), which represents the average of the x and y coordinated of the endpoints. When a point is reflected about the x-axis, its x value remains unchanged and its y value simply changes sign.

47. (A)

By folding the given pattern along the dotted lines, we would get a three-dimensional figure that has triangles for all four of its faces.

48. (C)

Divide 360 by 24% $= \dfrac{360}{.24} = 1500$.

49. (B)

$$\text{m} \angle VMW > \text{m} \angle VTM$$

By the construction, $\text{m}\angle VMT = \text{m}\angle WMT$. We already have a right angle in each of triangles VMT and WMT. So, $\text{m}\angle VTM = \text{m}\angle WTM$. Since $\overline{MT}$ is an angle bisector, $TV = TW$. By the construction of the arc $\overgroup{PR}$, we also know that $MP = MR$. Since $MW > MR$, it follows that $MW > MP$. Although it may appear that $\text{m}\angle VMW$ is greater than $\text{m}\angle VTM$, there are no numerical values to verify this statement. We would need to know the relationship between $\text{m}\angle VMT$ and $\text{m}\angle VTM$. We only know that $\text{m}\angle VMT + \text{m}\angle VTM = 90°$.

50. (C)

The nine scores in order are: 61, 74, 77, 82, 92, 93, 96, 98, 99. The median value is the middle, or fifth, score, which is 92.

51. (A)

.18

The ratio of the area of ΔPQR to the area of ΔTUV must be the square of the ratio of corresponding sides $= \left(\dfrac{3}{5}\right)\left(\dfrac{3}{5}\right) = \dfrac{9}{25}$. However, we note that the area of ΔPSR is one-half of the area of ΔPQR. Thus, the correct ratio $= \left(\dfrac{1}{2}\right)\left(\dfrac{9}{25}\right) = \dfrac{9}{50} = .18$.

52. (C)

The appropriate formula is $A = P(1 + R)^x$, where A = Amount, P = Principal, R = Rate per interest period, and x = Number of interest periods. In this example, $A = \$2500 + \$800 = \$3300$, $P = \$2500$, $R = \dfrac{.08}{4} = .02$, and x is unknown. The equation will read as follows: $3300 = 2500(1.02)^x$. Then $\log 3300 = \log 2500 + (x)(\log 1.02)$. Solving, $x \approx 14$ periods, which corresponds to 3.5 years.

53. (C)

The arithmetic mean is found by adding the five scores and dividing by 5. $\dfrac{(10 + 20 + 30 + 35 + 55)}{5} = \dfrac{150}{5} = 30$. Only the scores 35 and 55 are larger than 30.

54. (D)

By selecting any 200 students, we are ensuring that the sample is actually random.

55. (B)

The only restriction for the domain is that $-x + 1$ must be greater than or equal to zero.

$$-x + 1 \geq 0$$
$$\Rightarrow x \leq 1$$

56. (D)

If $\overline{BC} \perp \overline{AE}$, then $\angle ABC$ and $\angle DBE$ are both 90°. In addition, if $\angle E = \angle C$, then ΔABC is similar to ΔDBE by the angle-angle correspondence. Therefore, $\angle A = \angle D$. By Angle-Side-Angle, $\Delta CAB \cong \Delta EDB$. Thus, $\overline{BC} \cong \overline{BE}$ since they are corresponding parts of congruent triangles; so, answer choice (D) is correct.

Answer choices (A) and (C) do not apply since these are relationships between the line segments in the given triangles besides those relationships resulting from congruent triangles. Answer choice (B) is wrong since the hypotenuse of a right triangle must be larger than either of its legs.

57. (A)

Since $t = -9$ is a root of the equation

$$t^2 + 4t - 45 = 0$$

then $(t + 9)$ is a factor. Division of the equation by $(t + 9)$ would therefore yield the other factor of the quadratic, which is $(t - 5)$, giving the second root, $t = 5$.

58. (D)

The respective sides of the cube prior to and after the change are $\sqrt[3]{216} = 6$ cm and $\sqrt[3]{64} = 4$ cm. The percent change from 6 to 4 is $\left(\dfrac{2}{6}\right)(100\%)$, which is approximately 33%.

59. (A)

The graph of $g(x)$ is a semicircle passing through $(-4, 0)$, $(0, 4)$, and $(4, 0)$. The segment connecting $(-4, 0)$ and $(4, 0)$ is the diameter. The lowest y values are found at $(-4, 0)$ and $(4, 0)$, whereas the highest y value is found at $(0, 4)$. Thus, the range is all numbers between 0 and 4, inclusive.

60. (D)

For the fraction under the radical, all factors have the same base, x, so just add exponents for multiplication and subtract exponents for division: $(-7) + 2 - (-3) = -2$. Therefore, the radical reduces to $\sqrt{x^{-2}} = \sqrt{\dfrac{1}{x^2}} = \dfrac{1}{x}$.

61. (C)

If x and y vary inversely as each other and k is the constant of variation, then $xy = k$. So if height (h) varies inversely as the square of the base (b^2) then $hb^2 = k$. Solving for h, we divide both sides of the equation $hb^2 = k$, by b^2 as follows:

$$\frac{h\cancel{b^2}}{\cancel{b^2}} = \frac{k}{b^2}$$

$$h = \frac{k}{b^2}$$

Answer (A) is incorrect because h varies directly as the square of the base,

$$h = \frac{b^2}{k},$$

if h increases then b^2 must also increase. Answer (B) is incorrect because h also varies directly as the square of the base,

$$kb^2 = h,$$

if h increases then b^2 must also increase. Answer (D) is incorrect because it takes the same form as answer (A) so the reasons are the same.

$$kh = b^2$$

$$h = \frac{b^2}{k}$$

62. (B)

The slope of line $\ell_1 = \dfrac{(9-4)}{(3-1)} = \dfrac{5}{2}$. Because the slopes of perpendicular lines are negative reciprocals of each other, the slope of $\ell_2 = -\dfrac{2}{5}$. We know that ℓ_2 contains $(1, 4)$. The only choice among the five points given for which the slope would be $-\dfrac{2}{5}$ is $(-9, 8)$. Note that $\dfrac{(8-4)}{(-9-1)} = -\dfrac{2}{5}$.

63. (D)

The function given is represented graphically by a parabola. A parabola will intersect the x-axis in only one place if both roots are equal, which means *discriminant* $= 0$.

$$discriminant = b^2 - 4ac = +(4)^2 - 4(2)k = 0$$

$$16 - 8k = 0$$

$$16 = 8k \therefore k = 2$$

64. (A)

Let x = original length and y = original width. The new rectangle will have a length of $x + 0.3x = 1.3x$ and a width of $y - 0.2y = 0.8y$. The area of the original rectangle is xy, whereas the area of the new rectangle is $(1.3x)(0.8y) = 1.04xy$. Therefore, $1.04xy$ represents a 4% increases over xy.

65. (B)

A rhombus is a quadrilateral, has at least one pair of parallel sides, and its diagonals are always perpendicular to each other.

66. (C)

By substitution, $8 = Cp$ and $18 = Cp^3$. Dividing the second equation by the first equation, $p^2 = 2.25$, so $p = 1.5$. Now, $y = (C)(1.5)^x$. Using the point $(1, 8)$, $8 = (C)(1.5)$, so $C = 5.33$. Finally, $C + p = 6.83$.

67. (B)

In choice (B), rewrite as $\sqrt{5x-2} = 5 - 8 = -3$. A square root of any real quantity can never be negative, so this equation has no real solution. Incidentally, the answers for choices (A), (C), and (D) are 15, $\frac{34}{3}$, and $\frac{2}{7}$ respectively.

68. (B)

The percent of people age 10 or less is 25%. Thus, 25% + 22% = 47% of the people are either under 10 years old or over 40 years old. If x = the total population of Smallville, $0.47x = 282$. Solving, $x = 600$. Because 5% + 30% = 35% of the population is between the ages of 11 and 30 (inclusive), the actual number of people in this age bracket is $(0.35)(600) = 210$.

69. (A)

First, make use of the fact that the sum of the angles of any triangle is 180 degrees. The missing angle in the second triangle can be found by adding the two angles and then subtracting from 180.

$$80 + 30 = 110$$
$$180 - 110 = 70$$

The missing angle equals 70 degrees. Now compare the two triangles. You can see that both triangles have an angle 70 degrees, a side 8 inches, and an angle 30 degrees. Therefore, by the Angle-Side-Angle postulate, the two triangles are congruent.

70. (A)

If the vertex is (2, 4) we can substitute this value into the equation of the parabola and obtain:

$$\begin{aligned}
4 &= a(2)^2 + b(2) + 3 \\
4 &= 4a + 2b + 3 \\
-3 &= - 3 \\
\hline
1 &= 4a + 2b
\end{aligned} \quad \text{(I)}$$

Also the x-coordinate of the vertex is given by

$$\frac{-b}{2a}$$

so

$$2 = \frac{-b}{2a} \quad \text{(II)}$$

From (I) and (II) we obtain

$$4a + 2b = 1 \quad \text{(I)}$$
$$\frac{-b}{2a} = 2 \quad \text{(II)}$$

From (II), $b = -4a$ and substituting into (I):

$$4a + 2 \times (-4a) = 1$$
$$4a - 8a = 1$$
$$-4a = 1$$
$$a = -\frac{1}{4}$$
$$b = 1$$

71. (B)

We imagine the prism as a stack of equilateral triangles, congruent to the base of the prism. Let each of these triangles be one unit of measure thick. We can then calculate the area of the base, B, and multiply it by the number of bases needed to complete the height of the prism, h, to obtain the volume of the prism. Therefore,

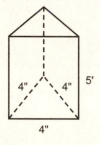

$$V = Bh.$$

All prism volumes can be thought of in this way.

In this particular problem, the base is an equilateral triangle. Therefore

$$B = \frac{s^2 \sqrt{3}}{4},$$

where s is the length of a side of the base. By substitution,

$$B = \frac{(4)^2 \sqrt{3}}{4} = 4\sqrt{3}.$$

Since the prism is 5 units high,

$$V = Bh = (4\sqrt{3})5 = 20\sqrt{3}.$$

Therefore, the volume of the prism is $20\sqrt{3}$ cu. units.

72. (D)

Rewrite the original equation as $By = Ax + C$, which becomes $y = \left(-\dfrac{A}{B}\right)x + \dfrac{C}{B}$. The slope is given by $-\dfrac{A}{B}$ and the y-intercept is given by $\dfrac{C}{B}$. If both these quantities are doubled, the new slope and y-intercept become $-\dfrac{2A}{B}$ and $\dfrac{2C}{B}$, respectively. Then $y = \left(-\dfrac{2A}{B}\right)x + \dfrac{2C}{B}$ becomes the new equation. Multiply by B to get $By = -2Ax + 2C$, which can then be written as $2Ax + By = 2C$.

73. (C)

If Kelly improves her sales by 50%, she will sell $2 + (0.50)(2) = 3$ homes. If Andre improves his sales by 100%, he will sell $3 + (1.00)(3) = 6$ homes. Ted will still sell 5 homes and Maya will still sell 6 homes. A-plus will sell a total of $6 + 3 + 5 + 6 = 20$ homes, and Kelly will sell 3 of them. Kelly will thus sell $\dfrac{3}{20}$ of the total of this month.

74. (B)

The only requirement about the sides of a rectangle is that they must be parallel in pairs and that four right angles must be present. For two squares, two rhombuses, or two triangles, if the corresponding angles are equal, the corresponding sides must be in proportion. Specifically, for any two rhombuses or squares, all sides of any one figure are equal.

75. (B)

Distance d between any two points (x_1, y_1), (x_2, x_2) in the two-dimensional coordinate system is

$$d = \sqrt{(x_1 - x_2)^2 + (y_1 - y_2)^2}$$

The problem can be calculated as:

$$d = \sqrt{(2) - (-3)^2 + (5 - (-3)^2} = \sqrt{89}$$

$\sqrt{89} > \sqrt{81}$ and the only choice greater than 9 is (B).

76. (D)

For this direct variation problem, use the formula $M = kV^2$, where k is a constant. By substituting $M = 24$ and $V = 4$, $24 = k(16)$, so $k = 1.5$. Now $M = 1.5V^2$. If $V = 6$, then $M = (1.5)(36) = 54$.

77. (A)

By definition, the median from Q contains the midpoint of $\overline{PR}$ which is $(-.5, 0)$. The slope of this median is $\dfrac{(6 - 0)}{(1 + .5)} = 4$.

78. (A)

Let x = number of boys, $2x$ = number of girls, and $3x$ = total number of students. The boys studying physics are $\left(\dfrac{1}{2}\right)x$ and the number of girls studying physics is $\left(\dfrac{2}{3}\right)(2x) = \left(\dfrac{4}{3}\right)x$. Then the number of students studying physics is $\left(\dfrac{1}{2}\right)x + \left(\dfrac{4}{3}\right)x = \left(\dfrac{11}{6}\right)x$. The required ratio is $\left(\dfrac{11}{6}\right)x \div 3x = \left(\dfrac{11}{6}\right)\left(\dfrac{1}{3}\right) = \left(\dfrac{11}{18}\right)$.

79. (B)

After Joe replaces one white marble with two red marbles, there are 6 white marbles, 4 red marbles, and 3 blue marbles, with a total of 13 marbles. So the probability of picking a red marble is $\dfrac{4}{13}$.

80. (A)

$\angle PRS = 180° - 33° = 147°$. Also, $\angle QPR = 180° - 90° + 33° = 57°$, because the sum of the angles of any triangle is 180°. Then $\angle RPT = 180° - 57° = 123°$. Finally, $147° - 123° = 24°$.

81. (B)

Each of P, Q, R, and S would be connected to the origin. The best mileage would be indicated by the segment with the steepest slope and the worst mileage would be indicated by the segment with the smallest slope. The segment connecting the origin to Q would have the steepest slope, whereas the segment connecting the origin to R would have the smallest slope. The correct order is then Q, S, P, R.

82. (D)

As inscribed angles, $\angle B = \left(\dfrac{1}{2}\right)(A\widehat{DC})$ and $\angle D = \left(\dfrac{1}{2}\right)(A\widehat{BC})$. If a quadrilateral is inscribed in a circle, then its opposite angles are supplementary. Therefore $\angle B + \angle D = 180°$. The measure of $\angle D$ is $180° - 105° = 75°$. Finally, $75° = \left(\dfrac{1}{2}\right)(A\widehat{BC})$, so $(A\widehat{BC}) = 150°$.

83. (C)

66 minutes = 3,960 seconds. Let x represent the number of bottle caps. Then $\dfrac{5}{22} = \dfrac{x}{3,960}$, so $x = \dfrac{(3,960)(5)}{22} = 900$.

84. (A)

Rewrite the function as $f(x) = (x^2 + 14x + \underline{}) + 51$. To complete the (___) so that it is a perfect square, add 49. (Of course, we must add 49 to the left side as well. Then $f(x) + 49 = (x^2 + 14x + 49) + 51$. This simplifies to $f(x) + 49 = (x + 7)^2 + 51$ and finally to $f(x) = (x + 7)^2 + 2$, which has the same vertex as $f(x) = A(x + 7)^2 + 2$, where A is any real number. Alternate method: For an equation of the form of $f(x) = ax^2 + bx + c$. The vertex is $\left[-\dfrac{b}{2a}, f\left(-\dfrac{b}{2a}\right)\right]$, which is $(-7, 2)$. Recall that if a function $f(x) = A(x - h)^2 + k$, its vetex is located at (h, K). Thus the function in this question has its vertex as $(-7, 2)$. Only answer (A) has its vertex at $(-7, 2)$.

85. (B)

A radius or a diameter dropped to the point of tangent is perpendicular to the tangent line. So, $\triangle ABC$ is a right triangle. In this triangle, $\overline{AB}$ is opposite the 30° angle. Using the rules of a $30° - 60° - 90°$ special triangle

$$\overline{BC} = (\overline{AB}) \cdot \sqrt{3}$$
$$\overline{BC} = \sqrt{27} \cdot \sqrt{3} = \sqrt{81} = 9$$

$\overline{BC} = 9$ is the diameter (d) of the circle. Use this information to find the circumference of the circle O:

$$\text{circumference} = 2\pi r = \pi d = 9\pi$$

86. (C)

$a_3 = (15 - 10)^2 = 5^2 = 25, a_4 = (25 - 15)^2 = 10^2$ $= 100, a_5 = (100 - 25)^2 = 75^2 = 5,625.$

87. (D)

If a point has initial coordinates of (x, y), then after a 90° counterclockwise rotation, its new coordinates will be $(-y, x)$. Thus, the point $(3, 1)$ will become $(-1, 3)$ with this rotation.

88. (A)

A direct variation with y and x can be written in the form $y = kx$, where k is a constant. In choice (B), $k = \frac{1}{10}$. In choice (C), $k = 100$. In choice (D), by cross-multiplication, we get $100y = x$, So $y = \frac{x}{100}$; this means $k = \frac{1}{100}$. Choice (A) cannot be written in the form $y = kx$.

89. (D)

The quotient of 50 and 5 means to divide 50 by 5, written as $\frac{50}{5}$. Eight less than this amount means to subtract 8, which leads to $\frac{50}{5} - 8$.

90. (C)

The sequence of steps is: subtract 3 from 9 to get 6, square 7 to get 49, divide 49 by 6 to get $8\frac{1}{6}$, then finally to add 5 to $8\frac{1}{6}$ to get $13\frac{1}{6}$.

91. (A)

The scale factor is found by dividing 12 feet, which is 144 inches, by $\frac{3}{4}$ inch. $\frac{144}{\left(\frac{3}{4}\right)} = 192$. This means that the actual length of the floor is $(192)(2) = 384$ inches. The perimeter equals $(2)(144) + (2)(384) = 1056$ inches $= 88$ feet.

92. (A)

Using the ordered pairs $(0, 7)$ and $(3, 1)$, the slope of the line containing these points is $\frac{(1 - 7)}{(3 - 0)} = -2$. Using the point-slope formula with the point $(0, 7)$, we have $y - 7 = -2(x - 0)$, which simplifies to $y = -2x + 7$. To find the value of a substitute -5 for y. So, $-5 = -2x + 7$. Simplifying, $-12 = -2x$, and so $x = 6$. Likewise, substitute 9 for x to find the value of b. $y = (-2)(9) + 7 = -11$. Finally, $ab = (6)(-11) = -66$.

93. (B)

The area of the square is $(8)(8) = 64$. Since the diameter of the circle is 8, the radius of the circle is 4. So, the area of the circle is $(\pi)(4)(4) = 16\pi$. The required probability is $\frac{16\pi}{64} \approx .785$, which is approximately .80.

94. (C)

There are $(2)(2)(2) = 8$ different outcomes when tossing a coin three times, namely HHH, HHT, HTH, THH, TTT, TTH, THT, HTT. Of these, the three outcomes that yield exactly two tails are TTH, THT, and HTT. The required probability is $\frac{3}{8}$.

95. (C)

Currently, there are $(.60)(40) = 24$ female students, so there must be $40 - 24 = 16$ male students. With the addition of 8 female students and 2 male students, there will be 32 female students and 18 male students. The percent of male students will be $\dfrac{18}{(32 + 18)} = \dfrac{18}{50} = 36\%$.

96. (D)

If any two elements of $\{-1, 0, 1\}$ are multiplied, the product is one of the elements of this set. For example, $(-1)(1) = -1$, which is an element of $\{-1, 0, 1\}$. Choice (A) is wrong because $(2)(2) = 4$, which is not an element of $\{1, 2\}$. Choice (B) is wrong because $(-1)(-1) = 1$, which is not an element of $\{-1, 0\}$. An example to show why Choice (C) is wrong would be $(-2)(-1) = 2$, which is not an element of $\{-2, -1, 0\}$.

97. (B)

The commutative property of numbers states that $A + B = B + A$ and that $(A)(B) = (B)(A)$. Using the latter equation, 7 replaces A and $3 + 2$ replaces B.

98. (D)

The number associated with point A is $-\dfrac{3}{2}$ and the number associated with point B is $\dfrac{1}{4}$. Then $\left(-\dfrac{3}{2}\right)\left(\dfrac{1}{4}\right) = -\dfrac{3}{8}$.

99. (A)

The probability that the die will show a 5 is $\dfrac{1}{6}$ and the probability that the coin will land tails both times is $\left(\dfrac{1}{2}\right)\left(\dfrac{1}{2}\right) = \dfrac{1}{4}$. Then the probability that both of these events will occur is $\left(\dfrac{1}{6}\right)\left(\dfrac{1}{4}\right) = \dfrac{1}{24}$.

100. (B)

The value of choice (A) is $|-12| = 12$. The value of choice (B) is $-|12| = -12$. The value of choice (C) is $-|-2| = -2$. The value of choice (D) is $|2| = 2$.

101.

- Tim's shift is 12 days, and Wanda's is 20. To find the first time they will both be off work, determine the lowest number that is a multiple of 12 and 20, which is 60. If they started work on January 1, that day will be March 1.

- Tim is paid \$85 per day for 12-day shifts, or \$1020 per shift. If Wanda is to be paid the same for her shift, which is 20 days long, she earns $\dfrac{1020}{20} = \$51$ per day.

Days Off

Tim	Jan. 12	Jan. 24	Feb. 5	Feb. 17	Mar. 1
Wanda	Jan. 20	Feb. 9	Mar. 1		

102.

- Volume $= 10 \times 6 \times 2 = 120$ cubic inches

- Surface area $= 2(10 \times 6 + 10 \times 2 + 6 \times 2) = 184$ square inches

- A new box can be 10 inches by 4 inches by 3 inches.
  Volume of new box: $10 \times 4 \times 3 = 120$ cubic inches
  Surface area of new box: $2(10 \times 4 + 10 \times 3 + 4 \times 3) = 164$ square inches
  Another solution $6 \times 5 \times 4$.

MTEL

Middle School Mathematics (47)

Practice Test

This practice test is also on CD-ROM in our special interactive MTEL Mathematics TEST*ware*®. It is highly recommended that you first take this exam on computer. You will then have the additional study features and benefits of enforced timed conditions and instant, accurate scoring. See page 5 for instructions on how to get the most out of our MTEL book and software.

Formulas

Description	Formula
Sum of the measures of the interior angles in a polygon	$S = (n - 2) \times 180$
Circumference of a circle	$C = 2\pi r$
Area of a circle	$A = \pi r^2$
Area of a triangle	$A = \dfrac{1}{2}bh$
Surface area of a sphere	$A = 4\pi r^2$
Lateral surface area of a right circular cone	$A = \pi r\sqrt{r^2 + h^2}$
Surface area of a cylinder	$A = 2\pi rh + 2\pi r^2$
Volume of a sphere	$V = \dfrac{4}{3}\pi r^3$
Volume of a right cone and a pyramid	$V = \dfrac{1}{3}Bh$
Volume of a cylinder	$V = \pi r^2 h$
Sum of an arithmetic series	$S_n = \dfrac{n}{2}[2a + (n - 1)d] = n\left(\dfrac{a + a_n}{2}\right)$
Sum of a geometric series	$S_n = \dfrac{a(1 - r^n)}{1 - r}$
Sum of an infinite geometric series	$\displaystyle\sum_{n=0}^{\infty} ar^n = \dfrac{a}{1 - r},\ |r| < 1$
Distance formula	$d = \sqrt{(x_2 - x_1)^2 + (y_2 - y_1)^2}$
Midpoint formula	$\left(\dfrac{x_1 + x_2}{2}, \dfrac{y_1 + y_2}{2}\right)$
Slope	$m = \dfrac{\Delta y}{\Delta x} = \dfrac{y_2 - y_1}{x_2 - x_1}$
Law of sines	$\dfrac{a}{\sin A} = \dfrac{b}{\sin B} = \dfrac{c}{\sin C}$
Law of cosines	$c^2 = a^2 + b^2 - 2ab\cos C$
Arc length	$s = r\theta$
Density of an object	$D = \dfrac{m}{V}$
Quadratic formula	$x = \dfrac{-b \pm \sqrt{b^2 - 4ac}}{2a}$

Answer Sheet

1. Ⓐ Ⓑ Ⓒ Ⓓ   22. Ⓐ Ⓑ Ⓒ Ⓓ   43. Ⓐ Ⓑ Ⓒ Ⓓ   64. Ⓐ Ⓑ Ⓒ Ⓓ   85. Ⓐ Ⓑ Ⓒ Ⓓ

2. Ⓐ Ⓑ Ⓒ Ⓓ   23. Ⓐ Ⓑ Ⓒ Ⓓ   44. Ⓐ Ⓑ Ⓒ Ⓓ   65. Ⓐ Ⓑ Ⓒ Ⓓ   86. Ⓐ Ⓑ Ⓒ Ⓓ

3. Ⓐ Ⓑ Ⓒ Ⓓ   24. Ⓐ Ⓑ Ⓒ Ⓓ   45. Ⓐ Ⓑ Ⓒ Ⓓ   66. Ⓐ Ⓑ Ⓒ Ⓓ   87. Ⓐ Ⓑ Ⓒ Ⓓ

4. Ⓐ Ⓑ Ⓒ Ⓓ   25. Ⓐ Ⓑ Ⓒ Ⓓ   46. Ⓐ Ⓑ Ⓒ Ⓓ   67. Ⓐ Ⓑ Ⓒ Ⓓ   88. Ⓐ Ⓑ Ⓒ Ⓓ

5. Ⓐ Ⓑ Ⓒ Ⓓ   26. Ⓐ Ⓑ Ⓒ Ⓓ   47. Ⓐ Ⓑ Ⓒ Ⓓ   68. Ⓐ Ⓑ Ⓒ Ⓓ   89. Ⓐ Ⓑ Ⓒ Ⓓ

6. Ⓐ Ⓑ Ⓒ Ⓓ   27. Ⓐ Ⓑ Ⓒ Ⓓ   48. Ⓐ Ⓑ Ⓒ Ⓓ   69. Ⓐ Ⓑ Ⓒ Ⓓ   90. Ⓐ Ⓑ Ⓒ Ⓓ

7. Ⓐ Ⓑ Ⓒ Ⓓ   28. Ⓐ Ⓑ Ⓒ Ⓓ   49. Ⓐ Ⓑ Ⓒ Ⓓ   70. Ⓐ Ⓑ Ⓒ Ⓓ   91. Ⓐ Ⓑ Ⓒ Ⓓ

8. Ⓐ Ⓑ Ⓒ Ⓓ   29. Ⓐ Ⓑ Ⓒ Ⓓ   50. Ⓐ Ⓑ Ⓒ Ⓓ   71. Ⓐ Ⓑ Ⓒ Ⓓ   92. Ⓐ Ⓑ Ⓒ Ⓓ

9. Ⓐ Ⓑ Ⓒ Ⓓ   30. Ⓐ Ⓑ Ⓒ Ⓓ   51. Ⓐ Ⓑ Ⓒ Ⓓ   72. Ⓐ Ⓑ Ⓒ Ⓓ   93. Ⓐ Ⓑ Ⓒ Ⓓ

10. Ⓐ Ⓑ Ⓒ Ⓓ   31. Ⓐ Ⓑ Ⓒ Ⓓ   52. Ⓐ Ⓑ Ⓒ Ⓓ   73. Ⓐ Ⓑ Ⓒ Ⓓ   94. Ⓐ Ⓑ Ⓒ Ⓓ

11. Ⓐ Ⓑ Ⓒ Ⓓ   32. Ⓐ Ⓑ Ⓒ Ⓓ   53. Ⓐ Ⓑ Ⓒ Ⓓ   74. Ⓐ Ⓑ Ⓒ Ⓓ   95. Ⓐ Ⓑ Ⓒ Ⓓ

12. Ⓐ Ⓑ Ⓒ Ⓓ   33. Ⓐ Ⓑ Ⓒ Ⓓ   54. Ⓐ Ⓑ Ⓒ Ⓓ   75. Ⓐ Ⓑ Ⓒ Ⓓ   96. Ⓐ Ⓑ Ⓒ Ⓓ

13. Ⓐ Ⓑ Ⓒ Ⓓ   34. Ⓐ Ⓑ Ⓒ Ⓓ   55. Ⓐ Ⓑ Ⓒ Ⓓ   76. Ⓐ Ⓑ Ⓒ Ⓓ   97. Ⓐ Ⓑ Ⓒ Ⓓ

14. Ⓐ Ⓑ Ⓒ Ⓓ   35. Ⓐ Ⓑ Ⓒ Ⓓ   56. Ⓐ Ⓑ Ⓒ Ⓓ   77. Ⓐ Ⓑ Ⓒ Ⓓ   98. Ⓐ Ⓑ Ⓒ Ⓓ

15. Ⓐ Ⓑ Ⓒ Ⓓ   36. Ⓐ Ⓑ Ⓒ Ⓓ   57. Ⓐ Ⓑ Ⓒ Ⓓ   78. Ⓐ Ⓑ Ⓒ Ⓓ   99. Ⓐ Ⓑ Ⓒ Ⓓ

16. Ⓐ Ⓑ Ⓒ Ⓓ   37. Ⓐ Ⓑ Ⓒ Ⓓ   58. Ⓐ Ⓑ Ⓒ Ⓓ   79. Ⓐ Ⓑ Ⓒ Ⓓ   100. Ⓐ Ⓑ Ⓒ Ⓓ

17. Ⓐ Ⓑ Ⓒ Ⓓ   38. Ⓐ Ⓑ Ⓒ Ⓓ   59. Ⓐ Ⓑ Ⓒ Ⓓ   80. Ⓐ Ⓑ Ⓒ Ⓓ   101.   —

18. Ⓐ Ⓑ Ⓒ Ⓓ   39. Ⓐ Ⓑ Ⓒ Ⓓ   60. Ⓐ Ⓑ Ⓒ Ⓓ   81. Ⓐ Ⓑ Ⓒ Ⓓ   102.   —

19. Ⓐ Ⓑ Ⓒ Ⓓ   40. Ⓐ Ⓑ Ⓒ Ⓓ   61. Ⓐ Ⓑ Ⓒ Ⓓ   82. Ⓐ Ⓑ Ⓒ Ⓓ

20. Ⓐ Ⓑ Ⓒ Ⓓ   41. Ⓐ Ⓑ Ⓒ Ⓓ   62. Ⓐ Ⓑ Ⓒ Ⓓ   83. Ⓐ Ⓑ Ⓒ Ⓓ

21. Ⓐ Ⓑ Ⓒ Ⓓ   42. Ⓐ Ⓑ Ⓒ Ⓓ   63. Ⓐ Ⓑ Ⓒ Ⓓ   84. Ⓐ Ⓑ Ⓒ Ⓓ

Short Constructed-Response Answer Sheets for Questions 101 and 102

Begin your response on this page. If necessary, continue on the next page.

Continue on the next page if necessary.

Continuation of your response from previous page, if necessary.

Continue on the next page if necessary.

Continuation of your response from previous page, if necessary.

MTEL Middle School Mathematics (47) Practice Test

TIME: 4 hours
102 questions

> **Directions:** Read each item and select the best response.

1. A rectangular piece of metal has an area of $35m^2$ and a perimeter of 24 m. Which of the following are possible dimensions of the piece?

   (A) $8m \times 4m$

   (B) $5m \times 7m$

   (C) $35m \times 1m$

   (D) $6m \times 6m$

2. If the angles of a triangle ABC are in the ratio of $3 : 5 : 7$, then the triangle is:

   (A) acute

   (B) right

   (C) isosceles

   (D) obtuse

3. In a chess match, a win counts 1 point, a draw counts $\frac{1}{2}$ point, and a loss counts 0 points. After 15 games, the winner was 4 points ahead of the loser. How many points did the loser have?

   (A) $4\frac{1}{2}$ (C) 6

   (B) $5\frac{1}{2}$ (D) 7

4. Two pounds of pears and one pound of peaches cost $1.40. Three pounds of pears and two pounds of peaches cost $2.40. How much is the combined cost of one pound of pears and one pound of peaches?

   (A) $1.90

   (B) $1.60

   (C) $1.30

   (D) $1.00

5. What part of three eighths is one tenth?

   (A) $\frac{1}{8}$

   (B) $\frac{15}{2}$

   (C) $\frac{4}{15}$

   (D) $\frac{3}{40}$

6. The figure below shows a number line.

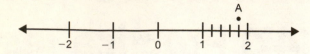

What is the value of A?

(A) 1.4   (C) 1.8

(B) 1.6   (D) 1.9

7. $(\sin\theta \times \cot\theta)^2 + (\cos\theta \times \tan\theta)^2 =$

(A) 1   (C) $2\sin^2\theta$

(B) $2\cos^2\theta$ (D) $2\cot^2\theta$

8. An AP statistics teacher wants to provide her students with a concrete example of a data set that illustrates the normal curve. Select her best choice from the examples below.

(A) The shoe sizes of the 15 students in her class.

(B) The weight of all the 17 year olds in the country.

(C) The number of times of one hundred that a flipped penny will land on its head.

(D) The height of the students in the high school.

9. If the probability of a certain team winning is $\frac{3}{4}$, what is the probability that this team will win its first 3 games and lose the fourth?

(A) $\frac{3}{256}$ (C) $\frac{27}{256}$

(B) $\frac{9}{256}$ (D) $\frac{81}{256}$

10. The input-output table below shows values for x and y.

Input (x)	Output (y)
−2	−6
0	2
2	10
3	14

Which equation could represent the relationship between x and y?

(A) $y = 4x + 2$ (C) $y = -x - 2$

(B) $y = 2x + 1$ (D) $y = x + 4$

11. If $f(x) = 3x - 5$ and $g(f(x)) = x$, then $g(x) =$

(A) $\frac{x-5}{3}$.   (C) $\frac{2x+5}{3}$.

(B) $\frac{x+5}{3}$.   (D) $\frac{x+5}{4}$.

12. The area between the line $y = x$ and the curve $y = \frac{1}{2}x^2$ is

(A) 1   (C) $\frac{2}{3}$

(B) $\frac{1}{2}$ (D) $\frac{3}{2}$

13. The following ratio: 40 seconds: $1\frac{1}{2}$ minutes: $\frac{1}{6}$ hour, can be expressed in lowest terms as

(A) $4:9:60$ (C) $40:90:60$

(B) $4:9:6$ (D) $40:9:6$

14. What is the smallest positive number that leaves a remainder of 2 when the number is divided by 3, 4 or 5?

(A) 22   (C) 62

(B) 42   (D) 82

15. $\sin\left(\dfrac{1}{2}\pi + t\right) =$

(A) $\sin\dfrac{\pi}{2} + \sin t$ (C) $\sin t$

(B) $\cos t$ (D) $\cos 2t$

16. If $f(x) = x^3 - x - 1$, then the set of all c for which $f(c) = f(-c)$ is

(A) {all real numbers}.

(B) {0}.

(C) {0, 1}.

(D) {−1, 0, 1}.

17. $\lim\limits_{h\to 0}\dfrac{e^{x+h} - e^x}{h}$ equals

(A) 0   (C) $+\infty$

(B) e^x (D) $-\infty$

18. Which of the following groups of data has two modes?

(A) 2, 2, 3, 3, 4, 4, 5, 6, 7

(B) 2, 2, 2, 3, 3, 4, 4, 4, 5

(C) 2, 3, 3, 4, 4, 4, 5, 5, 6

(D) 2, 3, 3, 3, 3, 4, 5, 6, 6

19. An owner of a delicatessen is thinking of constructing a parking lot in back of his store. He would like to have 35 parking spaces, and will need 2 pounds of cement for each parking space. If he buys 40 more pounds of cement than he expects to use, how many pounds of cement does he buy?

(A) 110 pounds   (C) 30 pounds

(B) 70 pounds   (D) 1,470 pounds

20. At what value of x does $f(x) = \dfrac{x^3}{3} - x^2 - 3x + 5$ have a relative minimum?

(A) −1 only   (C) +1 only

(B) −1 and 3   (D) 3 only

21. Look at the following summary of the students in a small college.

	Freshmen	Sophomores	Juniors	Seniors
Males	75	90	150	125
Females	105	170	200	85

The name of each student is put on a slip of paper and put into a jar. One slip of paper is randomly drawn. Given that the name drawn is that of a female student, what is the probability that the individual is a sophomore or a junior?

(A) .71   (C) .61

(B) .66   (D) .56

22. $1 + 2 + 3 + 4 + \ldots + 99 =$

(A) 4800   (C) 4900

(B) 4850   (D) 4950

23. Given the triangle below, what is the value of θ?

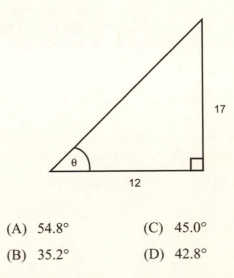

(A) 54.8°   (C) 45.0°

(B) 35.2°   (D) 42.8°

24. Triangle *ABC* is similar to triangle *ADE*. If the area of triangle *ABC* is 324, the area of triangle *ADE* is 441, and *AC* = 36, what is the length of $\overline{CE}$?

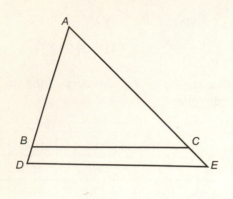

(A) 3   (C) 9

(B) 6   (D) 12

25. If the hypotenuse of a right triangle is $x + 1$ and one of the legs is x, then the other leg is

(A) $\sqrt{2x + 1}$ (C) $\sqrt{x^2 + (x + 1)^2}$

(B) $\sqrt{2x} + 1$ (D) $\sqrt{2x - 1}$

26. The decimal $.12\overline{4}$ expressed as a fraction is

(A) $\dfrac{6}{25}$ (C) $\dfrac{124}{999}$

(B) $\dfrac{41}{330}$ (D) $\dfrac{31}{250}$

27. In July 2004 there were approximately 293,000,000 people living in the United States. How is this number written in scientific notation?

(A) 29.3×10^7 (C) 2.93×10^8

(B) 293.0×10^6 (D) 29.3×10^9

28. What is the smallest positive even number that is the product of five different prime numbers?

(A) 15,015   (C) 2310

(B) 10,395   (D) 1890

29. The mean of a group of 20 numbers is 9. If one number is removed, the mean of the remaining numbers is 7. What is the value of the removed number?

(A) 16   (C) 40

(B) 25   (D) 47

30. Which of the graphs below represents the function $y = 2 + \sin(x - \pi)$?

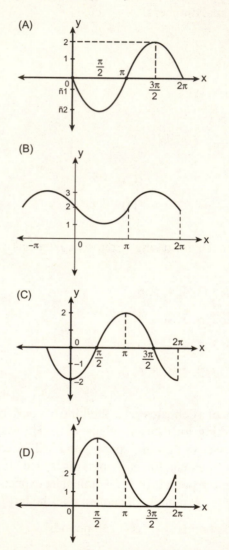

31.

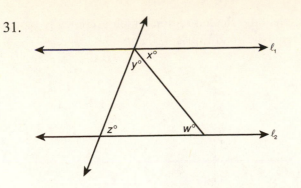

In the figure shown above, $x° = y°$. Which additional information would be sufficient to conclude that line ℓ_1 is parallel to line ℓ_2?

(A) $z = 180 - 2x$ (C) $z = 90 - w$

(B) $w = 180 - y - z$ (D) $w = z - x$

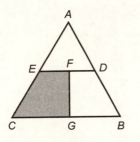

32. The figure above represents a dartboard in which $\triangle ABC$ is equilateral, E is the midpoint of $\overline{AC}$, D is the midpoint if $\overline{AB}$, F is the midpoint of $\overline{ED}$, and G is the midpoint of $\overline{BC}$. If a dart is thrown and lands on the dartboard, what is the probability that it lands in the shaded area?

(A) $\dfrac{1}{4}$ (C) $\dfrac{1}{3}$

(B) $\dfrac{3}{10}$ (D) $\dfrac{3}{8}$

33. Let a_i, $i = 1, 2, 3, \ldots$ represent a recursive sequence so that $a_1 = 3$, $a_i = a_{i-1}^2 + 5$. What is the value of $a_3 + a_4$?

(A) 40,205   (C) 40,607

(B) 40,406   (D) 40,808

34. If the radius of a sphere is increased by a factor of 3, then the volume of the sphere is increased by a factor of

(A) 3   (C) 9

(B) 6   (D) 27

35. Given that $X = $ {all prime numbers between 10 and 20} and $X \cup Y = $ {all positive odd numbers less than 20}, what is the *minimum* number of elements in Y?

(A) 5   (C) 7

(B) 6   (D) 8

36. 456 is 80% of three times what number?

(A) 121.6   (C) 273.6

(B) 190   (D) 570

37. The fraction

$$\frac{\dfrac{2}{b^2 a^2}}{\dfrac{1}{b^2 - 2b}}$$

may be expressed more simply as

(A) $\dfrac{2a}{b}$ (C) $\dfrac{2b - 4}{a^2 b}$

(B) $\dfrac{b - 4}{b}$ (D) $\dfrac{b - a}{a}$

38. If $f(x) = 2x + 4$ and $g(x) = x^2 - 2$, then $(f \circ g)(x)$, where $(f \circ g)(x)$ is a composition of functions, is

(A) $2x^2 - 8$ (C) $2x^2$

(B) $2x^2 + 8$ (D) $2x^3 + 4x^2 - 4x - 8$

39. What is the solution for x in the inequality $2x^2 - x - 3 < 0$?

(A) $-1 < x < \dfrac{3}{2}$ (C) $-\dfrac{3}{2} < x < 1$

(B) $x > \dfrac{3}{2}$ or $x < -1$ (D) $x > 1$ or $x < -\dfrac{3}{2}$

40. A runner along a track starts slowly and increases his speed gradually to the finish. Which graph below illustrates this process?

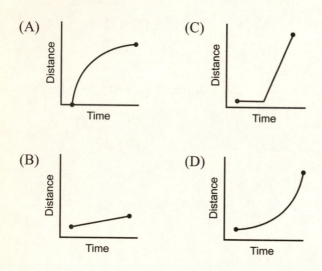

41. Select the shaded region which graphically represents the conditions $x \geq 0$ and $-3 < y < 3$.

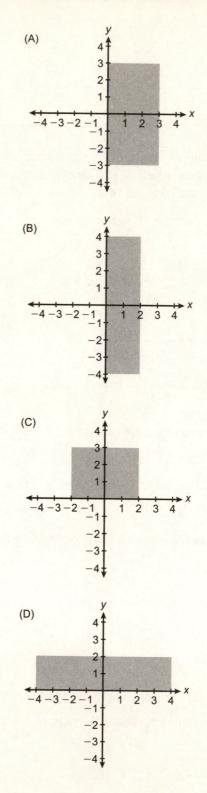

42. If m $\overset{\frown}{ABC}$ is $\dfrac{3}{2}\pi$ radians, then y is equal to

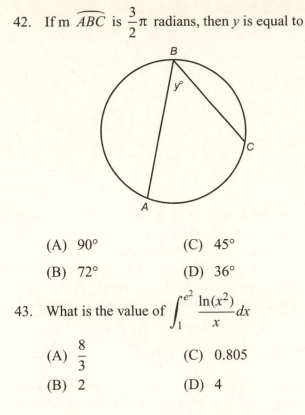

(A) 90°   (C) 45°

(B) 72°   (D) 36°

43. What is the value of $\displaystyle\int_{1}^{e^2}\dfrac{\ln(x^2)}{x}dx$

(A) $\dfrac{8}{3}$ (C) 0.805

(B) 2   (D) 4

44. What is the range of values for which $|6x-5|\le 8$ is satisfied?

(A) $-\dfrac{1}{2}\le x\le\dfrac{1}{2}$ (C) $-1\le x\le\dfrac{1}{2}$

(B) $0\le x\le\dfrac{5}{6}$ (D) $-\dfrac{1}{2}\le x\le\dfrac{13}{6}$

45. Which of the following equations is correct?

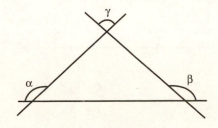

(A) $\alpha+\beta+\gamma=180°$

(B) $\gamma-\alpha+180°=\beta$

(C) $\alpha=\beta+\gamma$

(D) $\gamma=\alpha+\beta$

46. What is the units digit for 4^{891}?

(A) 2   (C) 6

(B) 4   (D) 8

47. If $y=\dfrac{3}{\sin x+\cos x}$ then $\dfrac{dy}{dx}=$

(A) $\dfrac{3(\sin x-\cos x)}{1+2\sin x\cos x}$ (C) $\dfrac{3}{\cos x-\sin x}$

(B) $\dfrac{6\sin x}{1+2\sin x\cos x}$ (D) $\dfrac{-3}{(\sin x+\cos x)^2}$

48. A circular region rotated 360° around its diameter as an axis generates a

(A) cube.   (C) cone.

(B) cylinder.   (D) sphere.

49. The cost of a cab ride with the Built-Rite Taxi Company is as follows: An initial cost of $2.50, plus $0.15 for each $\dfrac{1}{4}$ mile. If Mike takes a cab ride for a distance of 20 miles, which equation could be used to calculate his total cost?

(A) T = ($2.50 + $0.15)(20)

(B) T = ($2.50 + $0.60)(20)

(C) T = $2.50 + ($0.15)(20)

(D) T = $2.50 + ($0.60)(20)

50. The ratio of boys to girls in a pottery class is 2 to 3. If there are 15 girls in this class, how many boys are there?

(A) 5   (C) 15

(B) 10   (D) 20

51.

x	1	2	3	4
y	24	17	−2	−39

In the table shown above, which expression best represents the relationship between x and y?

(A) $y = -13x + 37$ (C) $y = -x^3 + 25$

(B) $y = -7x + 31$ (D) $y = -7x^2 + 14x + 17$

52. These figures form a pattern.

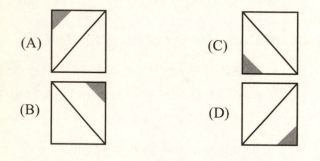

Which of the figures below best continues this pattern?

(A)   (C)

(B)   (D)

53. The population of bacteria that begins with a count of X and triples every n years is given by the formula $Y = (X)(3^{\frac{t}{n}})$, where t represents the number of years of growth and Y represents the growth after t years. Suppose the bacteria population in the year 1895 was 150, and it grew to 36,450 by the year 1935. In what year was the population equal to 1,350?

(A) 1932   (C) 1911

(B) 1919   (D) 1903

54. In the cube *ABCDEFGH* with side $AB = 2$, what is the length of diagonal *AF*?

(A) $2\sqrt{6}$

(B) $2\sqrt{5}$

(C) $2\sqrt{3}$

(D) $2\sqrt{2}$

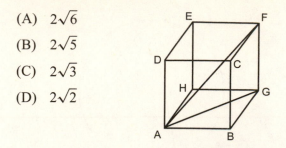

55. In a linear programming problem involving ordered pairs (x, y), the restraints yield feasible solutions in a region where the corner points are (0, 0), (0, 10), (16, 8), and (40, 0). Which one of the following objective functions would *not* have a unique point on this region that corresponds to a maximum P value?

(A) $P = 20x + 70y$ (C) $P = 40x + 100y$

(B) $P = 30x + 90y$ (D) $P = 30x + 350y$

56. In triangle *ABC*, angle *A* is a right angle, and the length of *BC* is 7. What are the lengths of sides *AB* and *AC*?

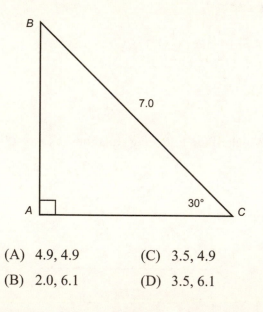

(A) 4.9, 4.9   (C) 3.5, 4.9

(B) 2.0, 6.1   (D) 3.5, 6.1

57. Which of these numbers is the greatest prime number less than 40?

(A) 39   (C) 33

(B) 37   (D) 31

58. If $0 < w < y < \dfrac{1}{2}$, which of the following must be greater than 1?

    (A) $w + y$ (C) $\dfrac{y}{w}$

    (B) $y - w$ (D) $\dfrac{w}{y}$

59. If x is divisible by 3 and y is divisible by 6, which of the following *must* be divisible by 4?

    (A) $\dfrac{x}{2y}$ (C) $3xy$

    (B) $\dfrac{y}{x}$ (D) $8x + 2y$

60. The four exam scores for each of five students are given in the chart below. If student #3 takes a fifth exam, what score is needed so that this student achieves an average score of 90?

Student	Exam Scores				Total
#1	75	85	80	92	332
#2	67	80	75	82	304
#3	83	88	95	90	356
#4	94	82	87	77	340
#5	83	70	78	85	316

    (A) 90   (C) 94

    (B) 92   (D) 96

61. Each point of the graph of $f(x) = (x + 3)^2 - 5$ is moved 4 units in a positive horizontal direction and 6 units in a negative vertical direction. If this new graph is called $g(x)$, which of the following describes $g(x)$?

    (A) $g(x) = (x - 1)^2 - 11$

    (B) $g(x) = (x - 1)^2 + 1$

    (C) $g(x) = (x + 7)^2 - 11$

    (D) $g(x) = (x + 7)^2 + 1$

62. The equation $x^2 + 2x + 7 = 0$ has

    (A) two complex conjugate roots.

    (B) two real rational roots.

    (C) two real equal roots.

    (D) two real irrational roots.

63. D varies inversely as the square root of F. When $F = 16$, $D = 9$. What is the value of D when $F = 100$?

    (A) 0.003   (C) 4.44

    (B) 3.6   (D) 22.5

64.

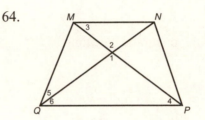

Note: Figure not drawn to scale.

In the figure shown above, $MNPQ$ is an isosceles trapezoid, with $\overline{MN} \parallel \overline{QP}$. Which of the following is *not necessarily* true?

    (A) $\angle 3 \cong \angle 4$ (C) $\angle 1 \cong \angle 2$

    (B) $\angle 5 \cong \angle 6$ (D) $\angle 4 \cong \angle 6$

65. Let T be a transformation function, $T(x, y) = (3.5x, 6.3y)$. Suppose the vertices of a rectangle of area 5 undergo the transformation $T(x, y)$. What is the area of the transformed rectangle?

    (A) 19.6   (C) 110.25

    (B) 22.05   (D) 259.7

66. What is the equation of the line which is parallel to $6x + 3y = 4$ and has a y-intercept of -6?

    (A) $y = 2x - 6$ (C) $y = -2x - \dfrac{4}{3}$

    (B) $y = 2x + \dfrac{4}{3}$ (D) $y = -2x - 6$

67. Which of the following functions has its highest point at $(-1, 5)$?

    (A) $f(x) = -2(x - 1)^2 - 5$

    (B) $f(x) = 2(x + 1)^2 - 5$

    (C) $f(x) = -2(x - 1)^2 + 5$

    (D) $f(x) = -2(x + 1)^2 + 5$

68. If $x + y = 8$ and $xy = 6$, then $\dfrac{1}{x} + \dfrac{1}{y} =$

    (A) $\dfrac{1}{8}$ (C) $\dfrac{1}{4}$

    (B) $\dfrac{1}{6}$ (D) $\dfrac{4}{3}$

69. Solve the following quadratic equation.

    $2x^2 - 1 = 3x$

    (A) $\dfrac{3 \pm \sqrt{17}}{2}$ (C) $\dfrac{3 \pm \sqrt{17}}{4}$

    (B) $1, \dfrac{1}{2}$ (D) $\dfrac{-3 \pm \sqrt{17}}{4}$

70. The graph of which one of the following equations has no x-intercept?

    (A) $5y = 10$ (C) $2x + 5y = 10$

    (B) $2x = 10$ (D) $5x - 2y = 10$

71. If $27^x = 9$ and $2^{x-y} = 64$, then $y =$

    (A) -5 (C) $-\dfrac{2}{3}$

    (B) -3 (D) $-\dfrac{16}{3}$

72. What is the range of the function $f(x) = -x^2 - 3x + 4$?

    (A) All numbers less than or equal to -1.5

    (B) All numbers between -1 and 4, inclusive

    (C) All numbers less than or equal to 6.25

    (D) All numbers between -4 and 1, inclusive

73. What is the area of the shaded portion of the rectangle? The heavy dot represents the center of the semicircle.

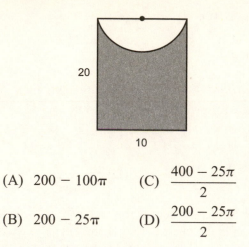

    (A) $200 - 100\pi$ (C) $\dfrac{400 - 25\pi}{2}$

    (B) $200 - 25\pi$ (D) $\dfrac{200 - 25\pi}{2}$

74. Exclusive of the numbers 1 and 1176, how many factors are there for the number 1176?

    (A) 20   (C) 24

    (B) 22   (D) 26

75. Given the seven numbers 26, 30, 32, 32, 28, 21, 21, which one of the following can be added to this group of numbers so that the median of all eight numbers is 27?

    (A) 23   (C) 29

    (B) 27   (D) 31

76. The sum of the multiplicative inverses of 2 and 3 is equal to the multiplicative inverse of which number?

    (A) $\dfrac{2}{3}$ (C) $\dfrac{6}{5}$

    (B) $\dfrac{5}{6}$ (D) $\dfrac{3}{2}$

77. Robyn was completing an algebra problem in which she was solving for the variable x. At the last step, she mistakenly subtracted $\frac{1}{2}$ instead of dividing by $\frac{1}{2}$. If her answer was $x = -6$, what was the correct value of x?

(A) -3 (C) -6.5

(B) -5.5 (D) -11

78. Which one of the following is equivalent to 100^{18}?

(A) $(100^6)^3$ (C) $(10^6)^3$

(B) $100^6 \cdot 100^3$ (D) $10^6 \cdot 10^3$

79. If Larry walks at the rate of 5 miles per hour, what is his rate in feet per minute?

(A) 88 (C) 440

(B) 300 (D) 1048

80. For rectangle PQRS, point P is located at $(1, 0)$ and point Q is located at $(8, -3)$. What is the slope of $\overline{QR}$?

(A) $\frac{7}{3}$ (C) $-\frac{1}{3}$

(B) $\frac{1}{3}$ (D) $-\frac{7}{3}$

81. Look at the triangle shown below:

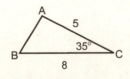

Note: Figure not drawn to scale

What is the BEST approximation to the length of $\overline{AB}$?

(A) 4.2 (C) 4.6

(B) 4.4 (D) 4.8

82. In a group of five women and four men, three people will be randomly chosen. What is the probability that all three people chosen will be women?

(A) $\frac{3}{5}$ (C) $\frac{125}{729}$

(B) $\frac{1}{3}$ (D) $\frac{5}{42}$

83. Given the set $\{5, 6, 7, 8, \ldots, 20\}$, how many proper subsets are there?

(A) 81,917 (C) 49,152

(B) 65,535 (D) 32,768

84. A 7-sided die is rolled twice. The numbers on the die are 1 through 7. What is the probability that the die will show a prime number on the first roll or an even number on the second roll, or both of these results?

(A) $\frac{8}{49}$ (C) $\frac{37}{49}$

(B) $\frac{2}{7}$ (D) $\frac{6}{7}$

85. For which one of the following linear equations does the change of 3 units for the x value correspond to the change of 4 units for the associated y value?

(A) $3x - 4y = 1$

(B) $4x - 3y = 1$

(C) $3x + 4y = 7$

(D) $4x + 3y = 7$

86. Which one of the following has the same value as $-|-8 - (-5)|$?

(A) $|-8 - 5|$ (C) $-|5 - (-8)|$

(B) $|-8 - (-5)|$ (D) $-|-8 + 5|$

87. For the rhombus $ABCD$, the point A is located at $(-1, 5)$ and the point B is located at $(5, 3)$. Which one of the following could represent the coordinates of point C?

    (A) $(3, -4)$ (C) $(7, -3)$

    (B) $(5, -1)$ (D) $(9, -2)$

88. Which one of the following groups of data describes the stem-and-leaf plot shown below?

$$\begin{array}{c|ccccc} 0 & 5 & 3 & 8 & 5 & 1 \\ 1 & 2 & 6 & 9 & 9 & 9 \\ 2 & 4 & 3 & 4 & 3 & \end{array}$$

    (A) 1, 3, 5, 8, 12, 16, 19, 23, 23, 24, 24

    (B) 1, 3, 5, 5, 8, 12, 16, 19, 19, 23, 24, 24

    (C) 1, 3, 5, 5, 8, 12, 16, 19, 19, 19, 23, 23, 24, 24

    (D) 1, 3, 5, 8, 12, 16, 19, 19, 19, 23, 24

89. Suppose the length of a rectangle is doubled and the width is tripled. By what percent will the area increase?

    (A) 600%   (C) 400%

    (B) 500%   (D) 300%

90. Which one of the following identities uses *both* the distributive and commutative properties of numbers?

    (A) $(4)(7 + 9) = (4)(9) + (4)(7)$

    (B) $(5)(8 + 6) = (5)(8) + (5)(6)$

    (C) $(6)(2 + 4) = (2 + 4)(6)$

    (D) $(7)(1 + 5) = (7)(1) + 5$

91. The volume of a cone is 72π cubic inches. If the height is 12 inches, what is the length, in inches, of the radius?

    (A) $\sqrt{6}$ (C) $\sqrt{18}$

    (B) $\sqrt{12}$ (D) $\sqrt{24}$

92. Look at the following geometric proof.

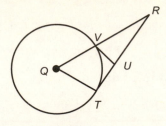

Note: Figure not drawn to scale.

Given: A circle with Q as the center, $\overline{RT}$ is tangent to the circle at point T, and $\overline{UV}$ is perpendicular to $\overline{RT}$.

Prove: m $\angle RVU = $ m $\overset{\frown}{VT}$

Statements	Reasons
1. A circle with Q as the center, $\overline{RT}$ is tangent to the circle at point T, and $\overline{UV}$ is perpendicular to $\overline{RT}$.	1. Given
2. m $\angle QTR = 90°$	2. A tangent to a circle is perpendicular to a radius at the point of contact.
3. m $\angle VUR = 90°$	3. Definition of perpendicular lines.
4. $QT \parallel \overline{UV}$	4. Two lines perpendicular to the same line are parallel.
5.	5.
6.	6.
7. m $\angle RVU = $ m $\overset{\frown}{VT}$	7. Substitution.

Which one of the following pairs of statements and reasons would be the most appropriate in Steps 5 and 6?

(A)

Statement	Reason
5. $\angle R \cong \angle R$	5. Identity
6. $\triangle RVU \backsim \triangle RQT$	6. AAA postulate

(B)

Statement	Reason
5. m $\angle Q$ = m $\angle RVU$	5. When parallel lines are crossed by a transversal, the corresponding angles are equal.
6. m $\angle Q$ = m $\overset{\frown}{VT}$	6. An interior angle of a circle has the same measure as its intercepted arc.

(C)

Statement	Reason
5. $\angle R \cong \angle R$	5. Identity
6. m $\angle Q$ = m $\overset{\frown}{VT}$	6. An interior angle of a circle has the same measure as its intercepted arc.

(D)

Statement	Reason
5. m $\angle Q$ = m $\angle T$	5. Base angles of an isosceles triangle are equal.
6. m $\angle Q$ = m $\overset{\frown}{VT}$	6. AAA postulate

93. In calculating the value of $3 + 6^2 \div (7 \cdot 2 - 2) \cdot 4$, which one of the following operations would NOT be used?

(A) Dividing 36 by 12

(B) Subtracting 2 from 14

(C) Multiplying 12 by 4

(D) Adding 3 to 36

94. What is the sum of the infinite series $0.3 + 0.24 + 0.192 + 0.1536 + \ldots$?

(A) 1.5   (C) 1.3

(B) 1.4   (D) 1.2

95. A group of n data, where n is an odd number, is arranged in ascending order. The position of the first quartile is given by $\frac{(n + 1)}{4}$, and the position of the third quartile is given by $\frac{(3n + 3)}{4}$. If the 66th number is the third quartile, which number is the first quartile?

(A) 6th   (C) 22nd

(B) 11th   (D) 33rd

96. There are 30 slips of paper in a jar. The slips are numbered 1 through 30. An experiment consists of drawing three slips of paper, one at a time, with *no* replacement. If event E consists of all outcomes in which the first two numbers drawn are even and the third number is odd, how many outcomes are there in E?

(A) 5880   (C) 3150

(B) 3375   (D) 2730

97. Ten people are to be seated in a row with 10 seats in a movie theatre. Two of the 10 people do not want to sit in either of the two end seats of this row. In how many accommodating ways can all ten people be seated?

(A) 20,120   (C) 2,257,920

(B) 40,320   (D) 3,628,800

98. Consider the function $F(x)$ defined as follows:

$$F(x) = \begin{cases} -x + 3, & \text{if } x < 0 \\ 2x + 3, & \text{if } 0 < x < 3 \\ 3x, & \text{if } x > 3 \end{cases}$$

What is the value of $F(-3) + F(2) - F(4)$?

(A) 2   (C) -1

(B) 1   (D) -2

99.

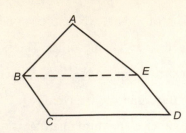

Note: Figure not drawn to scale

In the figure above, *BCDE* is a parallelogram. The distance from point *A* to $\overline{BE}$ is 9 and the distance from point *A* to $\overline{CD}$ is 16.5. If the area of *ABCDE* is 136.8, what is the length of $\overline{CD}$?

(A) 16.55

(C) 8.45

(B) 11.40

(D) 6.50

100. For which one of the following box plots is the value of the median one-half the sum of the values of the first and third quartiles?

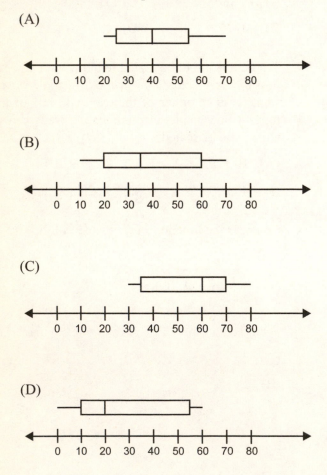

Questions 101 and 102 are open-response questions.

- **Be sure to answer and label all parts of each question.**

- **Show all your work (drawings, tables, or computations) in your Answer Booklet.**

- **If you do the work in your head, explain in writing how you did the work.**

Write your answers to these questions in the space provided in your Answer Booklet.

101. Marcy has been saving to buy some furniture. The chart below shows the prices for each piece that she needs.

Furniture Prices	
Item	**Price**
Couch	$750
Loveseat	$500
End Table	$125
Lamp	$85

- A furniture store is offering a 25% discount. *Not* including taxes, how much would the loveseat cost after the discount?

- Marcy must pay 5% sales tax for her total purchase. Including the 25% discount, how much will it cost to purchase all four pieces of furniture?

- Marcy has a coupon that will allow her to take an additional 15% off of the discounted price of the loveseat. If Marcy uses the coupon to buy the loveseat, what is the final price of the loveseat before tax is added?

102. Two trucks leave a warehouse at the same time. Truck *A* travels east at 50 mph and Truck *B* travels north at 60 mph.

- If Truck *A* reaches its destination in 2 hours and Truck *B* reaches its destination in 3 hours, how many miles apart will they be?

- Suppose Truck *C* will travel from Truck *A*'s destination to Truck *B*'s destination. If Truck *C* travels at 40 mph for half the distance of this trip, how fast will it need to travel for the remaining distance in order to complete its entire trip in 4 hours? (Figure to the nearest $\frac{1}{10}$ mph.)

- Using the first quadrant of an *xy*-coordinate system, draw a representation of the trip of each truck. Use the *y*-axis to represent the path of truck *B* and the *x*-axis to represent the path of truck *A*. Each axis should be labeled: *Miles*.

Answer Key Practice Test (47) for Middle School Mathematics

Q No.	Correct Answer	Subarea	Q No.	Correct Answer	Subarea
1.	(B)	Geometry	32.	(D)	Geometry
2.	(A)	Geometry	33.	(C)	Discrete Math
3.	(B)	Algebra	34.	(D)	Geometry
4.	(D)	Algebra	35.	(B)	Discrete Math
5.	(C)	Number Sense	36.	(B)	Algebra
6.	(C)	Number Sense	37.	(C)	Algebra
7.	(A)	Trigonometry	38.	(C)	Functions
8.	(D)	Statistics	39.	(A)	Algebra
9.	(C)	Probability	40.	(D)	Data Analysis
10.	(A)	Algebra	41.	(A)	Algebra
11.	(B)	Functions	42.	(C)	Geometry
12.	(C)	Calculus	43.	(D)	Calculus
13.	(A)	Number Sense	44.	(D)	Algebra
14.	(C)	Number Sense	45.	(B)	Geometry
15.	(B)	Trigonometry	46.	(B)	Number Sense
16.	(D)	Functions	47.	(A)	Calculus
17.	(B)	Calculus	48.	(D)	Geometry
18.	(B)	Statistics	49.	(D)	Algebra
19.	(A)	Number Sense	50.	(B)	Number Sense
20.	(D)	Calculus	51.	(C)	Algebra
21.	(B)	Data Analysis	52.	(A)	Patterns
22.	(D)	Algebra	53.	(C)	Algebra
23.	(A)	Trigonometry	54.	(C)	Geometry
24.	(B)	Geometry	55.	(B)	Functions
25.	(A)	Geometry	56.	(D)	Geometry
26.	(B)	Number Sense	57.	(B)	Number Sense
27.	(C)	Number Sense	58.	(C)	Algebra
28.	(C)	Number Sense	59.	(D)	Algebra
29.	(D)	Statistics	60.	(C)	Statistics
30.	(B)	Functions	61.	(A)	Functions
31.	(A)	Geometry	62.	(A)	Algebra

Q No.	Correct Answer	Subarea	Q No.	Correct Answer	Subarea
63.	(B)	Algebra	83.	(B)	Discrete Math
64.	(B)	Geometry	84.	(C)	Probability
65.	(C)	Geometry	85.	(B)	Algebra
66.	(D)	Algebra	86.	(D)	Algebra
67.	(D)	Functions	87.	(C)	Geometry
68.	(D)	Algebra	88.	(C)	Statistics
69.	(C)	Algebra	89.	(B)	Geometry
70.	(A)	Algebra	90.	(A)	Operations
71.	(D)	Algebra	91.	(C)	Geometry
72.	(C)	Functions	92.	(B)	Geometry
73.	(C)	Geometry	93.	(D)	Operations
74.	(B)	Number Sense	94.	(A)	Discrete Math
75.	(A)	Statistics	95.	(C)	Algebra
76.	(C)	Operations	96.	(C)	Probability
77.	(D)	Algebra	97.	(C)	Probability
78.	(A)	Number Sense	98.	(B)	Functions
79.	(C)	Number Sense	99.	(B)	Geometry
80.	(A)	Geometry	100.	(A)	Statistics
81.	(D)	Trigonometry	101.	–	Open-Response
82.	(D)	Probability	102.	–	Open-Response

Middle School Math (47)
Detailed Explanations of Answers

1.   (B)

The perimeter (P) = (2)(length) + (2)(width). For answer choice (B), the perimeter = (2)(7) + (2)(5) = 24 and its area = (7)(5) = 35. For answer choice (A), the perimeter = 24, but the area = 32. For answer choice (C), the area = 35, but the perimeter = 72. For answer choice (D), the perimeter = 24, but the area = 36.

2.   (A)

The three angles can be represented by $3x$, $5x$, and $7x$. Their sum is 180°, so $3x + 5x + 7x = 180$. Solving, $x = 12$. The values of the three angles are (3)(12), (5)(12), and (7)(12) = 36°, 60°, and 84°. Since each angle is less than 90°, the triangle is acute.

3.   (B)

The total number of points for both players after 15 games must equal 15. Let x = the number of points for the loser and let $x + 4$ = the number of points for the winner. Then $x + x + 4 = 15$. Simplifying this equation, $2x = 11$. Then $x = 5.5$ or $5\frac{1}{2}$.

4.   (D)

Let x = the price per pound for pears and let y = the price per pound for peaches. Then, $2x + y = \$1.40$ and $3x + 2y = \$2.40$. Multiply the first equation by 2 to get $4x + 2y = \$2.80$. Now subtract the original second equation to get $x = \$0.40$. By substituting this value of x into the original first equation, we get (2)(\$0.40) + $y = \$1.40$. This results in $y = \$0.60$. Finally, \$0.40 + \$0.60 = \$1.00.

5.   (C)

Divide $\frac{1}{10}$ by $\frac{3}{8}$, which becomes $\left(\frac{1}{10}\right)\left(\frac{8}{3}\right) = \frac{8}{30}$. This reduces to $\frac{4}{15}$.

6.   (C)

The interval between 1 and 2 is broken up into 5 equal intervals. Each interval is equal to $\frac{1}{5}$ or 0.2. Therefore, point A is located at 1.8 on the number line.

7.   (A)

$$(\sin\theta \times \cot\theta)^2 + (\cos\theta\tan\theta)^2$$

$$= \left(\sin\theta\left(\frac{\cos\theta}{\sin\theta}\right)\right)^2 + \left(\cos\theta\left(\frac{\sin\theta}{\cos\theta}\right)\right)^2$$
$$= \cos^2\theta + \sin^2\theta = 1$$

8.   (D)

The students in the statistics class have a reasonable chance at being able to sample a large enough portion of the students at their high school to get a reasonable estimate of the population and the data collected would produce a normal curve under these circumstances. Therefore the choice is concrete and mathematically correct. Choice (A) is incorrect because there are not enough students and the data being collected is unlikely to yield a normal curve over such a small, homogeneous sample. Choice (B) does not work because there is no way to get the data. An internet source may provide a sample but the problem then becomes abstract — a mind exercise. Choice (C) is incorrect because the data collected would not produce a normal curve.

9. (C)

Let's call the event of winning A and that of not winning $\overline{A}$. We want the probability P given by the expression below:

$$P = P(A) \times P(A) \times P(A) \times P(\overline{A})$$
$$= \frac{3}{4} \times \frac{3}{4} \times \frac{3}{4} \times \frac{1}{4} = \frac{27}{256}$$

10. (A)

Using the ordered pair (0, 2), each of answer choices (B), (C), and (D) can be shown to be incorrect. Each of the ordered pairs satisfies the equation in (A).

11. (B)

$f(x) = 3x - 5$ and $g(f(x)) = x$

We want to know what value of x (in terms of x) would cause $g(3x - 5)$ to equal x. To distinguish one x from the other, we can represent the x from $3x - 5$ with a y. This will result in:

$$3y - 5 = x$$
$$3y = x + 5$$
$$y = \frac{x + 5}{3}$$
$$g(y) = g(3x - 5) = \frac{3x - 5 + 5}{3} = x$$

Note: $g(x)$ is the inverse of $f(x)$, since $g(f(x)) = f(g(x)) = x$.

12. (C)

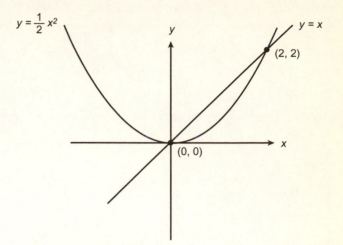

The curve is below the line, so

$$\text{Area} = \int_0^2 \left(x - \frac{1}{2}x^2 \right) dx = \left(\frac{x^2}{2} - \frac{x^3}{6} \right) \Big|_0^2 = 2 - \frac{8}{6} = \frac{2}{3}.$$

13. (A)

Change all quantities to seconds. 40 seconds remains unchanged; 1.5 minutes = (1.5)(60) = 90 seconds; $\frac{1}{6}$ hour = $\left(\frac{1}{6}\right)$ (60)(60) = 600 seconds. The required answer is $40:90:600$, which reduces to $4:9:60$.

14. (C)

First find the Least Common Multiple (LCM) of 3, 4, and 5. Since these numbers have no common factor, other than 1, the LCM = (3)(4)(5) = 60. This number is the smallest number that can be divided by 3, 4, and 5 and leave no remainder. Thus, 62 would leave a remainder of 2 when divided by 3, by 4, or by 5.

15. (B)

$$\sin\left(\frac{\pi}{2}+t\right)=\sin\frac{\pi}{2}\cos t+\cos\frac{\pi}{2}\sin t$$

But $\qquad \sin\frac{\pi}{2}=1$ and $\cos\frac{\pi}{2}=0$

$\therefore \qquad \sin\left(\frac{\pi}{2}+t\right)=\cos t.$

16. (D)

$$f(c) = c^3 - c - 1,$$
$$f(-c) = -c^3 + c - 1$$
$$c^3 = c$$
$$\therefore c = -1, 0, \text{ or } 1$$

17. (B)

$\lim\limits_{h\to 0}\dfrac{e^{x+h}-e^x}{h}$ equals the derivative of e^x by using the definition of the derivative

$$f'(x)=\lim\limits_{h\to 0}\frac{f(x+h)-f(x)}{h}$$
$$= e^x \quad \text{for} \quad f(x)=e^x$$

18. (B)

2, 2, 2, 3, 3, 4, 4, 4, 5

The two modes are 2 and 4. Answer choice (A) is wrong since it has three modes. Answer choice (C) is wrong since 4 is the only mode. Answer choice (D) is wrong since 3 is the only mode.

19. (A)

2 pounds of cement/parking space $\times$ 35 parking spaces = 70 pounds of cement

70 pounds of cement + 40 extra pounds of cement = 110 pounds of cement

Answer choice (B) is incorrect because it does not add on the 40 extra pounds of cement.

2 pounds of cement/parking space $\times$ 35 parking spaces = 70 pounds

Answer choice (C) is incorrect because it subtracts the 40 extra pounds of cement.

(2 pounds of cement/parking space $\times$ 35 parking spaces) − 40 pounds = 30 pounds

Answer choice (D) is incorrect because it shows

(40 pounds + 2 pounds) $\times$ 35 parking spaces = 1,470 pounds

20. (D)

$$f'(x) = x^2 - 2x - 3 = (x + 1)(x - 3)$$

$(x + 1)(x - 3) = 0 \Rightarrow x = -1$ and 3 are critical values.

The numbers -1 and 3 divide the x-axis into 3 intervals, from $+\infty$ to -1, -1 to 3, and 3 to $+\infty$.

$f(x)$ has a relative minimum value at $x = x_1$, if and only if $f'(x_1) = 0$ and the sign of $f'(x)$ changes from $-$ to $+$ as x increases through x_1.

If $-1 < x < 3$, then $f'(x) = -$

If $x = 3$, then $f'(x) = 0$

If $x > 3$, then $f'(x) = +$

Therefore, $f(3)$ is a relative minimum.

Note that when $x < -1$, $f'(x) = +$. If $x = -1$, $f'(x) = 0$. If $-1 < x < 3$, $f'(x) = -$.

Thus, $f(-1)$ is a relative maximum, not minimum.

21. (B)

There are a total of 560 female students. Of that total, 370 are either sophomores or juniors. Then $\dfrac{370}{560} = .66$ (nearest hundredth).

22. (D)

The sum of an arithmetic series, in which there is a common difference between terms is given by the formula $S = \left(\dfrac{N}{2}\right)(A + L)$. N is the number of terms, A is the first term, and L is the last term. For this example,

$$S = \left(\dfrac{99}{2}\right)(1 + 99) = 4950$$

23. (A)

$$\tan\theta = \dfrac{\text{opp}}{\text{adj}} = \dfrac{17}{12}$$

$$\theta = \tan^{-1}\left(\dfrac{17}{12}\right)$$

$$\theta = \tan^{-1}1.41\overline{6}$$

$$\theta \approx 54.8°$$

24. (B)

The ratio of the area of two similar polygons is equal to the square of the ratio of the lengths of any two corresponding sides. Thus:

$$\dfrac{\text{Area } \Delta ABC}{\text{Area } \Delta ADE} = \left(\dfrac{AC}{AE}\right)^2$$

$$(AE)^2 = \dfrac{(AC)^2(\text{Area } \Delta ADE)}{\text{Area } \Delta ABC}$$

$$AE = \sqrt{\dfrac{(AC)^2(\text{Area } \Delta ADE)}{\text{Area } \Delta ABC}}$$

$$= \sqrt{36^2\left(\dfrac{441}{324}\right)}$$

$$= 36\left(\dfrac{21}{18}\right) = 42$$

Thus, $AE = 42$. Since $AC + CE = AE$, then

$$CE = AE - AC$$

$$= 42 - 36$$

$$= 6$$

25. (A)

If a, b, c are the sides of a right triangle, with c as the hypotenuse, the Pythagorean Theorem states that $a^2 + b^2 = c^2$. Substitute x for a and substitute $x + 1$ for c. Then $x^2 + b^2 = (x + 1)^2$. This simplifies to $x^2 + b^2 = x^2 + 2x + 1$. So $b^2 = 2x + 1$. Finally, taking the square root of each side, $b = \sqrt{2x + 1}$

26. (B)

Let $N = .1\overline{24}$. Then $100\,N = 12.4\overline{24}$. By subtraction, $99N = 12.3$, so $N = \dfrac{12.3}{99} = \dfrac{123}{990}$. This reduces to $\dfrac{41}{330}$.

27. (C)

The number 293,000,000 equals 2.93×10^8 in scientific notation. Moving the decimal point 8 places to the left until it leaves only the 2 in the ones place does this.

28. (C)

The required number is $(2)(3)(5)(7)(11) = 2310$.

29. (D)

47

The sum of the original group of 20 numbers was $(9)(20) = 180$. The sum of the new group of 19 numbers is $(7)(19) = 133$. The removed number is the difference of 180 and 133.

30. (B)

There are three steps to build this graph.

First Step: Draw the graph $y = \sin x$

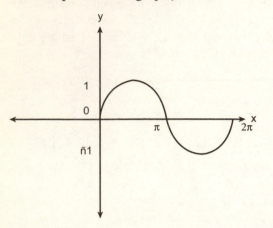

Second Step: Move the graph two units up, because it is $y = \sin(x - \pi) + 2$.

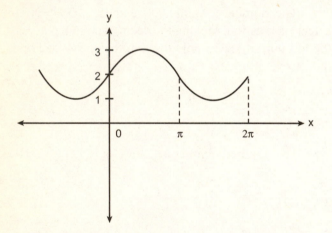

Third Step: Move the graph π units because it is $y = \sin(x - \pi) + 2$.

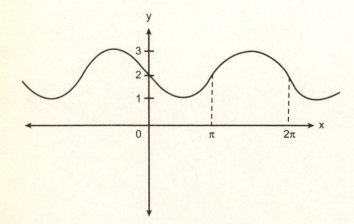

31. (A)

If $z = 180 - (x + y)$, we would have parallel lines, since interior angles of the same side of the transversal would be supplementary. Since $x = y$, the expression $180 - (x + y)$ is equivalent to $180 - 2x$. The statement in answer choice (B) would always be true, since the sum of the angles of any triangle is $180°$. The statement in answer choice (C) would be impossible since this would mean that each of x and y equals 90, and the transversal would coincide with line ℓ_1. The statement in answer choice (D) would imply that since $z = w + x = w + y$, $z = 90$. Each of x and y would be the same value less than 90, but would not imply that $\ell_1 \parallel \ell_2$.

32. (D)

Because $\triangle ABC$ is equilateral, $\angle A = \angle B = \angle C = 60°$. If we assign the following numerical values for the length of the sides, $\overline{AC} = \overline{AB} = \overline{CB} = 2$, then $\overline{AE} = \overline{AD} = \overline{CG} = \overline{GB} = 1$. In addition, we can find the height of $\triangle ABC$ to be $\sqrt{3}$ when a perpendicular bisector is dropped from A; note that a 30–60–90 triangle is formed. Thus the area of $\triangle ABC = \left(\frac{1}{2}\right)(2)(\sqrt{3}) = \sqrt{3}$. Using the same process we find the area of $\triangle ADE = \left(\frac{1}{2}\right)(1)\left(\frac{\sqrt{3}}{2}\right) = \left(\frac{\sqrt{3}}{4}\right)$. To find the area of the shaded region, we can subtract half of the area of $\triangle ADE$ from half of the area of $\triangle ABC = \left[\left(\frac{1}{2}\right)(\sqrt{3})\right] - \left[\left(\frac{1}{2}\right)\left(\frac{\sqrt{3}}{4}\right)\right] = \left(\frac{\sqrt{3}}{2}\right) - \left(\frac{\sqrt{3}}{8}\right) = \left(\frac{3\sqrt{3}}{8}\right)$. To find the probability, divide the area of the shaded region by the area of $\triangle ABC$: $\frac{3\sqrt{3}}{8} \div \sqrt{3}$, or or $\left(\frac{3\sqrt{3}}{8}\right)\left(\frac{1}{\sqrt{3}}\right) = \frac{3}{8}$.

33. (C)

$a_2 = (a_1)^2 + 5 = 9 + 5 = 14$, $a_3 = (14)^2 + 5 = 201$, $a_4 = (201)^2 + 5 = 40,406$. Then $a_3 + a_4 = 201 + 40,406 = 40,607$.

34. (D)

The Volume (V) of a sphere $= \left(\dfrac{4}{3}\right)(\pi)(R^3)$, where R is the radius. If R is increased by a factor of 3, it becomes $3R$ and the new volume is

$$V = \left(\frac{4}{3}\right)(\pi)(3R)^3$$

$$= \left(\frac{4}{3}\right)(\pi)(27)(R^3)$$

which is 27 times the original sphere, no matter what 'R' is.

35. (B)

X contains four elements, namely, 11, 13, 17, and 19, $X \cup Y$ contains ten elements, namely, 1, 3, 5, 7, 9, 11, 13, 15, 17, and 19. Then Y must contain *at least* the six elements 1, 3, 5, 7, 9, and 15.

36. (B)

Let x equal the unknown number. Then, $(0.8)(3x) = 456$ and $2.4x = 456$. Therefore, $x = 190$.

37. (C)

The fraction is a complex fraction. To simplify, we must multiply both the numerator and denominator by $b^2 - 2b$:

$$\frac{\dfrac{2}{a^2b^2}}{\dfrac{1}{b^2 - 2b}} \times \frac{b^2 - 2b}{b^2 - 2b} = \frac{2(b^2 - 2b)}{a^2b^2}$$

Multiplying through in the numerator:

$$\frac{2b^2 - 4b}{a^2b^2}$$

The numerator is factored and like terms are cancelled:

$$\frac{b(2b - 4)}{a^2b^2} = \frac{2b - 4}{a^2b}$$

38. (C)

$$(f \circ g)(x) = f(x) \circ g(x) = f(g(x)).$$

This is the definition of the composition of functions. For the functions given in this problem we have

$$2(g(x)) + 4 = 2(x^2 - 2) + 4$$

$$= 2x^2 - 4 + 4 = 2x^2.$$

39. (A)

Factor the left side of the inequality to get $(2x - 3)(x + 1) < 0$. If $2x - 3 > 0$ and $x + 1 < 0$, we get $x > \dfrac{3}{2}$ and $x < -1$, which is impossible. If $2x - 3 < 0$ and $x + 1 > 0$, we have the actual solution of $-1 < x < \dfrac{3}{2}$.

40. (D)

Speed is the slope of the distance versus time curve. The condition of starting slowly and increasing the speed gradually implies a smooth curve. Graph (A) does not meet the condition, because it would illustrate a condition of decreasing the speed, instead of increasing. Graph (B) does not meet the condition, because it would illustrate that the rate is constant. Graph (C) does not meet the condition, because it illustrates a combination of two constant rates. Graph (D) meets the required condition, because it illustrates an increasing rate.

41. (A)

The inequality $x \geq 0$ identifies the region to the right of the y-axis, eliminating choices (C) and (D). The double inequality of $-3 < y < 3$ represents dotted horizontal lines passing through 3 and -3 on the y-axis with the area between the lines shaded. Of the two remaining choices, (A) is the only one which satisfies this constraint.

42. (C)

From a theorem we know that the measure of an inscribed angle is equal to $\dfrac{1}{2}$ the intercepted arc.

We are told that $m\,\overarc{ABC}$ is $\dfrac{3}{2}\pi$ radians. There are 2π radians in a circle. Therefore, the intercepted arc is the remaining $\dfrac{\pi}{2}$ radians.

Converting to degrees:

$$\left(\frac{\pi}{2}\right)\left(\frac{180}{\pi}\right) = 90°.$$

The angle y is half of this:

$$y = \frac{90°}{2} = 45°.$$

43. (D)

Since $\ln(x^2) = 2 \ln x$, we have

$$\int_1^{e^2} \frac{\ln(x^2)}{x}\,dx = 2\int_1^{e^2} \frac{\ln x}{x}\,dx.$$

This integral can be evaluated by using the substitution $u = \ln x$. The integrand becomes, u, with $du = \dfrac{dx}{x}$, and the limits of integration change to

$$u(1) = \ln 1 = 0$$

$$u(e^2) = \ln(e^2) = 2.$$

We get

$$2\int_0^2 u\,du = u^2\Big|_0^2$$

$$= 2^2 - 0 = 4$$

44. (D)

When given an inequality with an absolute value, recall the definition of absolute value:

$$|x| \equiv \begin{cases} x \text{ if } x \geq 0 \\ -x \text{ if } x < 0 \end{cases}$$

$6x - 5 \leq 8$ if $6x - 5 \geq 0$.

$-6x + 5 \leq 8$ if $6x - 5 < 0$.

If $6x - 5 \leq 8$, then $6x \leq 13$, so $x \leq \dfrac{13}{6}$.

If $-6x + 5 \leq 8$, then $-6x \leq 3$, so $x \geq -\dfrac{1}{2}$.

45. (B)

Label the triangle as shown below:

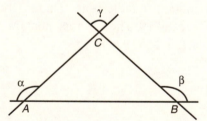

For the interior angles of $\triangle ABC$, the angle at point A is supplementary to α, so that its value is $180 - \alpha$. The angle at point B is supplementary to β, so that its value is $180 - \beta$. The angle at point C is vertical to γ, so that its value is γ. The sum of the interior angles of a triangle is $180°$, so $180 - \alpha + 180 - \beta + \gamma = 180$. Simplifying, $-\alpha + 180 - \beta + \gamma = 0$, which is equivalent to $\gamma - \alpha + 180 = \beta$.

46. (B)

Note that $4^1 = 4$, $4^2 = 16$, $4^3 = 64$, $4^4 = 216$, $4^5 = 1024$, $4^6 = 4096$, …… Thus, when 4 is raised to an odd exponent, the units digit is 4; when 4 is raised to an even digit, the units digit is 6. Since 891 is odd, 4^{891} has a units digit of 4.

47. (A)

$$y = \frac{3}{\sin x + \cos x} = \frac{3}{u} \text{ where } u = \sin x + \cos x$$

So $\dfrac{dy}{dx} = 3(-1)u^{-1-1}\dfrac{du}{dx}$ using the derivative of a power and chain rule theorems.

Thus,

$$\frac{dy}{dx} = \frac{-3}{(\sin x + \cos x)^2}(\cos x - \sin x)$$

$$= \frac{3(\sin x - \cos x)}{\sin^2 x + 2\sin x \cos x + \cos^2 x}$$

$$\frac{dy}{dx} = \frac{3(\sin x - \cos x)}{1 + 2\sin x \cos x},$$

using the identity $\sin^2 x + \cos^2 x = 1$

48. (D)

A sphere is formed when a circle is rotated $360°$ about its diameter.

49. (D)

$$T = \$2.50 + (\$0.60)(20)$$

$0.15 per one-fourth mile is equivalent to $0.60 per mile. Since Mike is traveling 20 miles, his total cost would be $2.50 + ($0.60)(20).

50. (B)

$$\frac{2}{3} \times \frac{15}{1} = \frac{30}{3} = 10 \text{ boys}$$

51. (C)

$$y = -x^3 + 25$$

Each pair of values in the table will check this equation. Answer choice (A) is wrong since (2, 17) and (4, –39) do not check the equation. Answer choice (B) is wrong since (3, –2) and (4, –39) do not check the equation. Answer choice (D) is wrong since (3, –2) does not check the equation.

52. (A)

The figures show a pattern of a counterclockwise rotation of the dark corner. The figure that best continues this pattern has the dark corner in the upper-left side.

53. (C)

In this example, $X = 150$, $Y = 36{,}450$, and $t = 1935 - 1895$. Then we have $36{,}450 = (150)\left(3^{\frac{40}{n}}\right)$. Divide both sides by 150 to get $243 = 3^{\frac{40}{n}}$. By inspection, $3^5 = 243$, so $\dfrac{40}{n} = 5$. This leads to $n = 8$, which means that the population triples every 8 years. Now use the equation $1{,}350 = (150)\left(3^{\frac{t}{8}}\right)$. Divide both sides by 150 to get $9 = 3^{\frac{t}{8}}$. This can be written as $3^2 = 3^{\frac{t}{8}}$. Equating exponents, $\dfrac{t}{8} = 2$, so $t = 16$. The required year is then $1895 + 16 = 1911$.

54. (C)

Note that each edge of the cube $= 2$. $\triangle ABC$ is a right triangle, so by using the Pythagorean Theorem, $AB^2 + BG^2 = AG^2$, $2^2 + 2^2 = AG^2$. Simplifying, $8 = AG^2$, so $AG = \sqrt{8}$. $\triangle AFG$ is also a right triangle, so that $AG^2 + FG^2 = AF^2$. By substitution, $(\sqrt{8})^2 + 2^2 = AF^2$. Simplifying, $12 = AF^2$, so $AF = \sqrt{12} = 2\sqrt{3}$.

55. (B)

In order for an objective function not to have a unique point that corresponds to a maximum P value, the slope of this function must be the same as one of the lines that form the boundary of this region. The slope of the x-axis is zero and that of the y-axis is undefined. The slope of the line containing $(0, 10)$ and $(16, 8)$ is $-\frac{1}{8}$; the slope of the line containing $(40, 0)$ and $(16, 8)$ is $-\frac{1}{3}$. The only objective function among these four answer choices with either of these slope values is $P = 30x + 90y$. This objective function has a slope of $-\frac{30}{90} = -\frac{1}{3}$.

56. (D)

This is a $30°$, $60°$, and $90°$ triangle. The hypotenuse (BC) is twice the length of the shorter leg (AB), and the length of the longer leg (AC) is the length of the shorter leg multiplied by $\sqrt{3}$.

$$2AB = BC$$
$$AB = \frac{BC}{2}$$
$$AB = \frac{7.0}{2} = 3.5$$

and

$$AC = \sqrt{3} \times AB$$
$$= \sqrt{3} \times 3.5$$
$$\sqrt{3} \times 3.5 = 6.1$$

57. (B)

A prime number is a number that can only be divided by 1 and itself. The greatest prime number less than 40 is 37 (B). In choice (A) the number 39 is not prime because it can be divided by 13. In choice (C) the number 33 can be divided by 11. In choice (D) the number 31 is a prime number, but it is less than 37 and the question asks for the greatest prime number less than 40.

58. (C)

The most efficient way to solve this question is to substitute values for w and y. Let $w = \frac{1}{4}$ and $y = \frac{2}{3}$. The answers for (A), (B), (C), and (D) are $\frac{7}{12}$, $\frac{1}{12}$, $\frac{4}{3}$ and $\frac{3}{4}$. Only choice (C) yields a number greater than 1. Another way to solve this is to remember that any positive number divided by another positive number less than itself is always greater than 1.

59. (D)

If x is divisible by 3, then $x = 3k_1$, where k_1 is a constant. If y is divisible by 6, then $y = 6k_2$, where k_2 is a constant. Now, $8x + 2y = 2(4x + y) = 2(4 \times 3k_1 + 6k_2) = 4(6k_1 + 3k_2)$. This last expression can be divided by 4 to yield $6k_1 + 3k_2$. To show why the other choices are incorrect, let $x = 3$ and $y = 6$. Then choices (A), (B) and (C) would have values of 21, 2 and 54, respectively; none of these numbers is divisible by 4.

60. (C)

The total score for four exams is given in the table as 356. To that amount, add the score x of the fifth exam, and then average the result over five exams as follows:

$$\frac{356 + x}{5} = 90; \ 356 + x = 90(5) = 450$$

and $x = 450 - 356 = 94$

61. (A)

For a parabolic function $f(x) = A(x - h)^2 + k$, the vertex is located at (h, k). When this function is moved in a positive horizontal direction, the value of h increases; when the function is moved in a negative vertical direction, the value of k decreases. In this example, the original values of h and k are -3 and -5, respectively. The new value of h is $-3 + 4 = 1$, and the new value of k is $-5 - 6 = -11$. So, the function $g(x) = (x - 1)^2 - 11$.

62. (A)

To solve this quadratic equation, we invoke the quadratic formula:

$$x = \frac{-b \pm \sqrt{b^2 - 4ac}}{2a}$$

The equation is $x^2 + 2x + 7 = 0$.

So $a = 1$, $b = 2$, and $c = 7$.

Substituting into the formula:

$$x = \frac{-2 \pm \sqrt{2^2 - 4(1)(7)}}{2(1)}$$

$$= \frac{-2 \pm \sqrt{4 - 28}}{2} = -1 \pm \sqrt{-6}$$

Since $i = \sqrt{-1}$, $x = -1 \pm i\sqrt{6}$.

These roots are complex conjugates of each other.

63. (B)

$D = \dfrac{k}{\sqrt{F}}$, where k is a constant. By substitution,

$9 = \dfrac{k}{\sqrt{16}} = \dfrac{k}{4}$. solving, $k = 36$.

Then $D = \dfrac{36}{\sqrt{100}} = \dfrac{36}{10} = 3.6$.

64. (B)

$\angle 5$ and $\angle 6$ together form the base angle at point Q, but they need not be congruent. $\angle 3 \cong \angle 4$, since they are alternate interior angles of parallel lines. $\angle 1 \cong \angle 2$, since they are vertical angles. Triangles MPQ and NQP can be shown to be congruent by side-side-side. (Note that the diagonals of an isosceles trapezoid are congruent.) Then $\angle 4 \cong \angle 6$, since they are corresponding parts of congruent triangles.

65. (C)

The width will be multiplied by 3.5 and the length by 6.3, so the area will be $3.5 \times 6.3 = 22.05$ times the original area $= 22.05 \times 5 = 110.25$.

66. (D)

We employ the slope intercept form for the equation to be written, since we are given the y-intercept. Our task is then to determine the slope.

We are given the equation of a line parallel to the line whose equation we wish to find. We know that the slopes of two parallel lines are equal. Hence, by finding the slope of the given line, we will also be finding the unknown slope. To find the slope of the given equation

$$6x + 3y = 4$$

we transform the equation $6x + 3y = 4$ into slope intercept form.

$$6x + 3y = 4$$
$$3y = -6x + 4$$
$$y = -\frac{6}{3}x + \frac{4}{3}$$
$$y = -2x + \frac{4}{3}$$

Therefore, the slope of the line we are looking for is –2. The y-intercept is –6. Applying the slope intercept form,

$$y = mx + b,$$

to the unknown line, we obtain,

$$y = -2x - 6$$

as the equation of the line.

67. (D)

When a quadratic function is written in the form $f(x) = A (x - h)^2 + k$, the vertex is located at (h, k). This vertex is the highest point, when A is negative, and the lowest point when A is positive. Since we seek a highest point, A must be negative. The values of h and k are -1 and 5, respectively. Thus, $f(x) = A(x - [-1])^2 + 5 = A(x + 1)^2 + 5$. Only choice (D) satisfies all the requirements.

68. (D)

$$\frac{1}{x} + \frac{1}{y} = \frac{(y+x)}{xy} = \frac{8}{6}, \text{ which reduces to } \frac{4}{3}.$$

69. (C)

It is necessary to first write the quadratic in standard form: $2x^2 - 3x - 1 = 0$. This quadratic does not factor, so it is necessary to use the quadratic formula to find the solutions. The quadratic formula is as follows:

$$x = \frac{-b \pm \sqrt{b^2 - 4ac}}{2a} \text{ with } a = 2, b = -3, \text{ and } c = -1.$$

$$x = \frac{3 \pm \sqrt{9 - 4(2)(-1)}}{2(2)} = \frac{3 \pm \sqrt{17}}{4}$$

(A), (B), and (D) all contain errors in the use of the formula or with simplifying.

70. (A)

If a graph of a line has no x-intercept, it must be parallel to the x-axis. This means that the general form of the equation is $y = k$, where k is a constant. The equation $5y = 10$ can be reduced to $y = 2$, so it represents a line which is parallel to the x-axis.

71. (D)

$$27^x = (3^3)^x = 3^{3x}$$
$$9 = 3^2$$

Thus, we have $3^{3x} = 3^2$, which implies $3x = 2$ or $x = \frac{2}{3}$ because the power function is one-to-one, which means that if

$$a^{x1} = a^{x2} \text{ then } x_1 = x_2.$$

Now $2^{x-y} = 64 = 2^6$

so $x - y = 6$ or $\frac{2}{3} - y = 6$.

Hence, $y = \frac{2}{3} - 6 = -\frac{16}{3}$.

72. (C)

The x-value of the vertex of this parabola is given by $-\frac{(-3)}{[(2)(-1)]} = -1.5$. The corresponding y-value $= -(-1.5)^2 - 3(-1.5) + 4 = 6.25$. Since the coefficient of x^2 is negative, this parabola will have its highest point at the vertex, which is $(-1.5, 6.25)$. Thus, the range will be all numbers less than or equal to the y-value of the vertex, which is 6.25.

73. (C)

The area of the rectangle $= (20)(10) = 200$. The area of the semicircle $= \left(\frac{1}{2}\right)(\pi)(R^2)$, where R is the radius. Since the diameter $= 10$, the radius $= 5$. Thus the area of the semicircle $= \left(\frac{1}{2}\right)(\pi)(5^2) = \left(\frac{25}{2}\right)(\pi)$. The shaded area is the difference between the area of the rectangle and the area of the semicircle $= 200 - \left(\frac{25}{2}\right)(\pi)$, which is equivalent to $= \frac{(400 - 25\pi)}{2}$.

74. (B)

22

The number 1176 can be written as $2^3 \cdot 3^1 \cdot 7^2$. The total number of factors is given by the product of the value of the exponents increased by 1, which becomes $(4)(2)(3) = 24$. However, this number includes the factors of 1 and 1176. Remove these two numbers to get 22 factors.

75. (A)

When 23 is added, the numbers will appear, in ascending order, as follows: 21, 21, 23, 26, 28, 30, 32, 32. The median will equal the mean of the two middle numbers 26 and 28 $= 27$. Choice (B) is wrong because the median would be 27.5. Choice (C) is wrong because the median would be 28.5. Choice (D) is wrong because the median would be 29.

76. (C)

The multiplicative inverses of 2 and 3 are $\frac{1}{2}$ and $\frac{1}{3}$, respectively. Their sum is $\frac{3}{6} + \frac{2}{6} = \frac{5}{6}$. This number is the multiplicative inverse of $\frac{6}{5}$.

77. (D)

Robyn's incorrect answer of $x = -6$ must have been derived from mistakenly subtracting $\frac{1}{2}$ from -5.5. She should have divided -5.5 by $\frac{1}{2}$, so the correct answer should be $x = \frac{(-5.5)}{\frac{1}{2}} = -11$.

78. (A)

When an expression involving a base and an exponent is raised to an exponent, the base remains unchanged and the exponents are multiplied. Thus, $(100^6)^3 = 100^{18}$.

79. (C)

Five miles per hour is equivalent to $(5)(5280) = 26{,}400$ feet per hour. To calculate the feet per minute, divide 26,400 by 60. $\frac{26{,}400}{60} = 440$.

80. (A)

The slope of $\overline{PQ} = \frac{(-3 - 0)}{8 - 1} = -\frac{3}{7}$. Since $\overline{QR}$ is perpendicular to $\overline{PQ}$, its slope must be the negative reciprocal of $-\frac{3}{7}$, which is $\frac{7}{3}$.

81. (D)

By the Law of Cosines, $\overline{AB}^2 = 8^2 + 5^2 - (2)(8)(5)(\cos 35°) = 89 - (80)(\cos 35°) \approx 23.46$. Then $\overline{AB} = \sqrt{23.46} \approx 4.8$.

82. (D)

The number of combinations of 3 people chosen from 9 is given by $_9C_3 = \frac{[(9)(8)(7)]}{[(3)(2)(1)]} = 84$. The number of combinations of 3 women chosen from 5 women is given by $_5C_3 = \frac{[(5)(4)(3)]}{[(3)(2)(1)]} = 10$. Thus, the required probability is $\frac{10}{84}$, which reduces to $\frac{5}{42}$.

83. (B)

The given set has $20 - 5 + 1 = 16$ elements. $2^{16} = 65{,}536$ total subsets, which includes the set itself. Thus, there are 65,535 proper subsets.

84. (C)

The prime numbers between 1 and 7, inclusive, are 2, 3, 5, and 7; so the probability of getting a prime number on the first roll is $\frac{4}{7}$. Since the even numbers are 2, 4, and 6, the probability of getting an even number on the second roll is $\frac{3}{7}$. The probability of getting at least one of these outcomes (and possibly both) is given by $\frac{4}{7} + \frac{3}{7} - \left(\frac{4}{7}\right)\left(\frac{3}{7}\right) = \frac{37}{49}$.

85. (B)

The slope of any line is represented by the change in y values divided by the corresponding change in x values between any two points on the line. So we need an equation where the slope of the line is $\frac{4}{3}$. By rewriting $4x - 3y = 1$ as $y = \left(\frac{4}{3}\right)(x) - \frac{1}{3}$, the slope is identified as $\frac{4}{3}$. The slopes for answer choices (A), (C), and (D) are $\frac{3}{4}$, $-\frac{3}{4}$, and $-\frac{4}{3}$, respectively.

86. (D)

The value of the item in the stem is $-|-8+5| = -|-3| = -3$. Answer choice (D) also has a value of -3. The values of answer choices (A), (B), and (C) are 13, 3 and -13, respectively.

87. (C)

The distance of

$$\overline{AB} = \sqrt{[(5-(-1)]^2 + (3-5)^2} = \sqrt{36+4} = \sqrt{40}.$$

Point C must be at a location such that the distance of $\overline{BC}$ is also $\sqrt{40}$. Note that the distance of

$$BC = \sqrt{(7-5)^2 + (-3-3)^2} = \sqrt{4+36} = \sqrt{40}.$$

For answer choice (A), the distance would be $\sqrt{53}$. For answer choice (B), the distance would be $\sqrt{16}$. For answer choice (D), the distance would be $\sqrt{41}$.

88. (C)

By just reading the values from left to right of the stem-and-leaf shown, we have: 5, 3, 8, 5, 1, 12, 16, 19, 19, 24, 23, 24, 23. This list corresponds to choice (C) when the numbers are arranged in ascending order.

89. (B)

If L is the original length and W is the original width, the original area is LW. The new length will be $2L$ and the new width will be $3W$, so the new area will be $6LW$. The increase in area is $5LW$. This increase as a percent is $\left(\dfrac{5LW}{LW}\right)(100\%) = 500\%$.

90. (A)

The Distributive Property states that $(a)(b+c) = ab + ac$. The Commutative Property states that $m + n = n + m$. By substituting 4 for a, 7 for b, and 9 for c, we can see that answer choice (A) satisfies the Distributive Property. Now, by substituting $(4)(7)$ for m and $(4)(9)$ for n, we can see that answer choice (A) also satisfies the Commutative Property. In each case, these properties are satisfied for the operation related to addition. Answer choice (B) satisfies only the Distributive Property. Answer choice (C) satisfies only the Commutative Property. Answer choice (D) satisfies neither of these two properties, and is actually an incorrect statement.

91. (C)

The volume of a cone is given by $V = \left(\dfrac{1}{3}\right)(\pi)(R^2)(H)$, where R is the radius and H is the height. By substitution, $72\pi = \left(\dfrac{1}{3}\right)(\pi)(R^2)(12)$. This simplifies to $R^2 = 18$, so $R = \sqrt{18}$.

92. (B)

After establishing that $\overline{QT}$ is parallel to $\overline{UV}$, the next step should be to state that corresponding angles are equal. Then to prove that m $\angle RVU =$ m $\overparen{VT}$, it is necessary to establish that m$\angle Q =$ m $\overparen{VT}$. This is done by noting that a central angle's measurement is equal to that of its intercepted arc.

93. (D)

First, calculate $7 \times 2 - 2 = 14 - 2 = 12$. Second, calculate $6^2 = 36$. Third, divide 36 by 12 to get 3. Fourth, multiply 3 by 4 to get 12. Finally, add 3 to 12 to get 15. In none of these steps is 3 added to 36.

94. (A)

The sum of an infinite geometric series is given by the formula $S = \dfrac{A}{(1-R)}$, where A is the first number and R is the ratio. In this example, $A = 0.3$ and $R = \dfrac{0.24}{0.3} = 0.8$. Then $S = \dfrac{0.3}{0.2} = 1.5$.

95. (C)

If the 66th number is the third quartile, $\dfrac{(3n+3)}{4} = 66$. Multiplying both sides by 4, $3n + 3 = 264$. Then $3n = 261$, so $n = 87$. The first quartile's position is given by $\dfrac{(87+1)}{4} = 22$.

96. (C)

There are 15 even numbers, and since there is no replacement, the number of ways to draw two even numbers is $(15)(14) = 210$. There are also 15 odd numbers available for the third number. Then the number of outcomes in $E = (210)(15) = 3150$.

97. (C)

The number of ways to assign the left-most seat is 8, since two people cannot be seated there. The number of remaining ways to assign the right-most seat is 7, since one person has already been assigned to the left-most seat and the two people who could not be assigned to the left-most seat cannot be assigned to the right-most seat. Since there are no restrictions on the assignment of the remaining 8 seats, there are $8! = (8)(7)(6)(\ldots)(1) = 40,320$ ways of making this seating arrangement. The number of ways to seat all the people $= (8)(8!)(7) = 2,257,920$.

98. (B)

$F(-3) = -(-3) + 3 = 6$. $F(2) = (2)(2) + 3 = 7$. $F(4) = (3)(4) = 12$. $6 + 7 - 12 = 1$.

99. (B)

The height of parallelogram $BCDE$ is $16.5 - 9 = 7.5$. If x is length of $CD = BE$, then the area of parallelogram $BCDE$ can be represented by $7.5x$. Likewise, the area of $\triangle ABE$ can be represented by $\dfrac{1}{2}(x)(9) = 4.5x$.

Then, $7.5x + 4.5x = 136.8$

Solving, $x = \dfrac{136.8}{12} = 11.40$.

100. (A)

The median is given by the value corresponding to the vertical segment inside the box, which is 40. The left-most vertical segment and the right-most segment of the box represent the first and third quartiles, respectively. For Choice (A), their values are 25 and 55.

$40 = \left(\dfrac{1}{2}\right)(25 + 55)$. This relationship is not true for the other answer choices.

101. • First, calculate the discount.

$500 \times 0.25 = \$125$

Then, subtract the discount from the regular price.

$500 - 125 = \$375$

• All of the items added together equals

$750 + 500 + 125 + 85 = \$1,460$

The 25% discount equals

$1,460 \times 0.25 = \$365$

Subtracting the discount from the regular price gives

$1,460 - 365 = \$1,095$

The tax will be

$1,095 \times 0.05 = 54.75$

Adding the cost of the discounted cost of the furniture and the tax comes to

$1,095.00 + 54.75 = \$1,149.75$

- The 25% discount on the loveseat is

  $500 \times 0.25 = \$125$

Subtracting the discount from the regular price gives

  $500 - 125 = \$375$

The coupon discount is

  $375 \times 0.15 = 56.25$

Subtracting this coupon discount gives

  $375 - 56.25 = \$318.75$

102.

- Truck A travels $(50)(2) = 100$ miles east.
  Truck B travels $(60)(3) = 180$ miles north.
  Distance apart:

  $$\sqrt{100^2 + 180^2} = \sqrt{42,400} \approx 206 \text{ miles},$$

- Truck C travels at 40 mph for 103 miles, which requires 2.575 hrs.

  Then

  $4 - 2.575 = 1.425$ hrs to cover the remaining miles.

  Finally, $\dfrac{103}{1.425} = 72.3$ miles/hr.

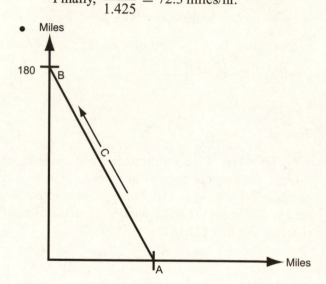

MTEL

Mathematics (09)

Practice Test

This practice test is also on CD-ROM in our special interactive MTEL Mathematics TEST*ware*®. It is highly recommended that you first take this exam on computer. You will then have the additional study features and benefits of enforced timed conditions and instant, accurate scoring. See page 5 for instructions on how to get the most out of our MTEL book and software.

Formulas

Description	Formula
Sum of the measures of the interior angles in a polygon	$S = (n - 2) \times 180$
Circumference of a circle	$C = 2\pi r$
Area of a circle	$A = \pi r^2$
Area of a triangle	$A = \dfrac{1}{2}bh$
Surface area of a sphere	$A = 4\pi r^2$
Lateral surface area of a right circular cone	$A = \pi r \sqrt{r^2 + h^2}$
Surface area of a cylinder	$A = 2\pi rh + 2\pi r^2$
Volume of a sphere	$V = \dfrac{4}{3}\pi r^3$
Volume of a right cone and a pyramid	$V = \dfrac{1}{3}Bh$
Volume of a cylinder	$V = \pi r^2 h$
Sum of an arithmetic series	$S_n = \dfrac{n}{2}[2a + (n-1)d] = n\left(\dfrac{a + a_n}{2}\right)$
Sum of a geometric series	$S_n = \dfrac{a(1 - r^n)}{1 - r}$
Sum of an infinite geometric series	$\displaystyle\sum_{n=0}^{\infty} ar^n = \dfrac{a}{1 - r},\ |r| < 1$
Distance formula	$d = \sqrt{(x_2 - x_1)^2 + (y_2 - y_1)^2}$
Midpoint formula	$\left(\dfrac{x_1 + x_2}{2}, \dfrac{y_1 + y_2}{2}\right)$
Slope	$m = \dfrac{\Delta y}{\Delta x} = \dfrac{y_2 - y_1}{x_2 - x_1}$
Law of sines	$\dfrac{a}{\sin A} = \dfrac{b}{\sin B} = \dfrac{c}{\sin C}$
Law of cosines	$c^2 = a^2 + b^2 - 2ab\cos C$
Arc length	$s = r\theta$
Density of an object	$D = \dfrac{m}{V}$
Quadratic formula	$x = \dfrac{-b \pm \sqrt{b^2 - 4ac}}{2a}$

Answer Sheet

1. Ⓐ Ⓑ Ⓒ Ⓓ   22. Ⓐ Ⓑ Ⓒ Ⓓ   43. Ⓐ Ⓑ Ⓒ Ⓓ   64. Ⓐ Ⓑ Ⓒ Ⓓ   85. Ⓐ Ⓑ Ⓒ Ⓓ

2. Ⓐ Ⓑ Ⓒ Ⓓ   23. Ⓐ Ⓑ Ⓒ Ⓓ   44. Ⓐ Ⓑ Ⓒ Ⓓ   65. Ⓐ Ⓑ Ⓒ Ⓓ   86. Ⓐ Ⓑ Ⓒ Ⓓ

3. Ⓐ Ⓑ Ⓒ Ⓓ   24. Ⓐ Ⓑ Ⓒ Ⓓ   45. Ⓐ Ⓑ Ⓒ Ⓓ   66. Ⓐ Ⓑ Ⓒ Ⓓ   87. Ⓐ Ⓑ Ⓒ Ⓓ

4. Ⓐ Ⓑ Ⓒ Ⓓ   25. Ⓐ Ⓑ Ⓒ Ⓓ   46. Ⓐ Ⓑ Ⓒ Ⓓ   67. Ⓐ Ⓑ Ⓒ Ⓓ   88. Ⓐ Ⓑ Ⓒ Ⓓ

5. Ⓐ Ⓑ Ⓒ Ⓓ   26. Ⓐ Ⓑ Ⓒ Ⓓ   47. Ⓐ Ⓑ Ⓒ Ⓓ   68. Ⓐ Ⓑ Ⓒ Ⓓ   89. Ⓐ Ⓑ Ⓒ Ⓓ

6. Ⓐ Ⓑ Ⓒ Ⓓ   27. Ⓐ Ⓑ Ⓒ Ⓓ   48. Ⓐ Ⓑ Ⓒ Ⓓ   69. Ⓐ Ⓑ Ⓒ Ⓓ   90. Ⓐ Ⓑ Ⓒ Ⓓ

7. Ⓐ Ⓑ Ⓒ Ⓓ   28. Ⓐ Ⓑ Ⓒ Ⓓ   49. Ⓐ Ⓑ Ⓒ Ⓓ   70. Ⓐ Ⓑ Ⓒ Ⓓ   91. Ⓐ Ⓑ Ⓒ Ⓓ

8. Ⓐ Ⓑ Ⓒ Ⓓ   29. Ⓐ Ⓑ Ⓒ Ⓓ   50. Ⓐ Ⓑ Ⓒ Ⓓ   71. Ⓐ Ⓑ Ⓒ Ⓓ   92. Ⓐ Ⓑ Ⓒ Ⓓ

9. Ⓐ Ⓑ Ⓒ Ⓓ   30. Ⓐ Ⓑ Ⓒ Ⓓ   51. Ⓐ Ⓑ Ⓒ Ⓓ   72. Ⓐ Ⓑ Ⓒ Ⓓ   93. Ⓐ Ⓑ Ⓒ Ⓓ

10. Ⓐ Ⓑ Ⓒ Ⓓ   31. Ⓐ Ⓑ Ⓒ Ⓓ   52. Ⓐ Ⓑ Ⓒ Ⓓ   73. Ⓐ Ⓑ Ⓒ Ⓓ   94. Ⓐ Ⓑ Ⓒ Ⓓ

11. Ⓐ Ⓑ Ⓒ Ⓓ   32. Ⓐ Ⓑ Ⓒ Ⓓ   53. Ⓐ Ⓑ Ⓒ Ⓓ   74. Ⓐ Ⓑ Ⓒ Ⓓ   95. Ⓐ Ⓑ Ⓒ Ⓓ

12. Ⓐ Ⓑ Ⓒ Ⓓ   33. Ⓐ Ⓑ Ⓒ Ⓓ   54. Ⓐ Ⓑ Ⓒ Ⓓ   75. Ⓐ Ⓑ Ⓒ Ⓓ   96. Ⓐ Ⓑ Ⓒ Ⓓ

13. Ⓐ Ⓑ Ⓒ Ⓓ   34. Ⓐ Ⓑ Ⓒ Ⓓ   55. Ⓐ Ⓑ Ⓒ Ⓓ   76. Ⓐ Ⓑ Ⓒ Ⓓ   97. Ⓐ Ⓑ Ⓒ Ⓓ

14. Ⓐ Ⓑ Ⓒ Ⓓ   35. Ⓐ Ⓑ Ⓒ Ⓓ   56. Ⓐ Ⓑ Ⓒ Ⓓ   77. Ⓐ Ⓑ Ⓒ Ⓓ   98. Ⓐ Ⓑ Ⓒ Ⓓ

15. Ⓐ Ⓑ Ⓒ Ⓓ   36. Ⓐ Ⓑ Ⓒ Ⓓ   57. Ⓐ Ⓑ Ⓒ Ⓓ   78. Ⓐ Ⓑ Ⓒ Ⓓ   99. Ⓐ Ⓑ Ⓒ Ⓓ

16. Ⓐ Ⓑ Ⓒ Ⓓ   37. Ⓐ Ⓑ Ⓒ Ⓓ   58. Ⓐ Ⓑ Ⓒ Ⓓ   79. Ⓐ Ⓑ Ⓒ Ⓓ   100. Ⓐ Ⓑ Ⓒ Ⓓ

17. Ⓐ Ⓑ Ⓒ Ⓓ   38. Ⓐ Ⓑ Ⓒ Ⓓ   59. Ⓐ Ⓑ Ⓒ Ⓓ   80. Ⓐ Ⓑ Ⓒ Ⓓ   101. —

18. Ⓐ Ⓑ Ⓒ Ⓓ   39. Ⓐ Ⓑ Ⓒ Ⓓ   60. Ⓐ Ⓑ Ⓒ Ⓓ   81. Ⓐ Ⓑ Ⓒ Ⓓ   102. —

19. Ⓐ Ⓑ Ⓒ Ⓓ   40. Ⓐ Ⓑ Ⓒ Ⓓ   61. Ⓐ Ⓑ Ⓒ Ⓓ   82. Ⓐ Ⓑ Ⓒ Ⓓ

20. Ⓐ Ⓑ Ⓒ Ⓓ   41. Ⓐ Ⓑ Ⓒ Ⓓ   62. Ⓐ Ⓑ Ⓒ Ⓓ   83. Ⓐ Ⓑ Ⓒ Ⓓ

21. Ⓐ Ⓑ Ⓒ Ⓓ   42. Ⓐ Ⓑ Ⓒ Ⓓ   63. Ⓐ Ⓑ Ⓒ Ⓓ   84. Ⓐ Ⓑ Ⓒ Ⓓ

Short Constructed-Response Answer Sheets for Questions 101 and 102

Begin your response on this page. If necessary, continue on the next page.

Continue on the next page if necessary.

Continuation of your response from previous page, if necessary.

Continue on the next page if necessary.

Continuation of your response from previous page, if necessary.

MTEL Mathematics
Practice Test 09

TIME: 4 hours
102 questions

> <u>**Directions:**</u> Read each item and select the best response.

1.

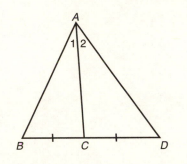

Note: Figure not drawn to scale.

In the figure shown above, $BC = CD$. Which additional information would *not* be sufficient to conclude that $\overline{AC}$ is perpendicular to $\overline{BD}$?

(A) $\angle B \cong \angle D$

(B) Triangle ABC is equilateral

(C) $AB = AD$

(D) $\angle 1 \cong \angle 2$

2. In an apartment building there are 9 apartments having terraces for every 16 apartments. If the apartment building has a total of 144 apartments, how many apartments have terraces?

(A) 137   (C) 63

(B) 81   (D) 102

3.

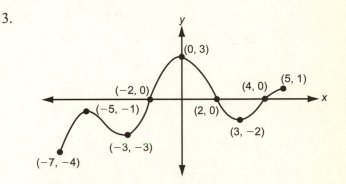

The graph of $g(x)$ is shown above. How many zeros would exist for the graph created by shifting $g(x)$ vertically downward by two units?

(A) 0   (C) 2

(B) 1   (D) 3

4. If $f(x) = |9 - 2x|$, for which values of x will $f(x) < 3$?

(A) $3 < x < 6$

(B) $-3 < x < 6$

(C) $-6 < x < -3$

(D) $-6 < x < 3$

5. In order to be accepted into a program at West Point, a person must score in the top 2% of a standardized test on general knowledge. Historically, the mean score for this test is 70, with a standard deviation of 3. What would be the *minimum* integer score on this test in order for a person to be accepted into this program?

(A) 83

(B) 81

(C) 79

(D) 77

6. A sample of drivers involved in motor vehicle accidents was categorized by age. The results appear as:

Age	Number of Accidents
16–25	28
26–35	13
36–45	12
46–55	8
56–65	19
66–75	20

What is the value of the median age?

(A) 43

(B) 46

(C) 50

(D) 59

7. The height of an object is given by the equation $z = -16t^2 + 144t$, where z is the distance in feet and t is the time in seconds. After how many seconds will this object reach its maximum height?

(A) 3

(B) 4.5

(C) 7.5

(D) 9

8. Events A and B are dependent, where $P(B) = .20$, $P(B \mid A) = .40$, and $P(A \cup B) = .29$. What is the value of $P(A)$? Note: $P(A)$ means the probability of event A.

(A) .09

(B) .15

(C) .29

(D) .31

9. $\int_1^e x \ln x \, dx = ?$

(A) e

(B) $\dfrac{e^2 - 1}{2}$

(C) $\dfrac{e^2 + 1}{4}$

(D) $\dfrac{e - 1}{2}$

10. $\lim\limits_{x \to 1} \dfrac{\dfrac{1}{x+1} - \dfrac{1}{2}}{x - 1} =$

(A) $-\dfrac{1}{4}$ (C) $\dfrac{1}{4}$

(B) -1 (D) 0

11.

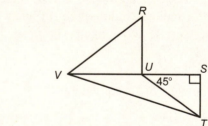

Note: Figure not drawn to scale.

In the figure above, $\overline{RU} = \overline{UV} = \overline{TU}$. If $\overline{RV} = 8$, what is the length of $\overline{TV}$?

(A) 9.66   (C) 11.32

(B) 10.5   (D) 12.0

12.

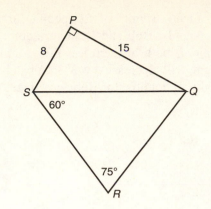

Note: Figure not drawn to scale.

In the figure shown above, what is the length of QR? Your answer should be to the nearest tenth.

(A) 16.2

(B) 15.7

(C) 15.2

(D) 14.7

13. A sequence of P values is defined as follows: $P_1 = 1$, $P_2 = 2$, $P_i = (2)(P_{i-1})$ if i is even, and $P_i = P_{i-1} + 1$ if i is odd. What is the value of $P_5 + P_6$?

(A) 11   (C) 17

(B) 15   (D) 21

14. If $x = 3 + 2i$ and $y = 1 + 3i$, where $i^2 = -1$, then $\dfrac{x}{y} =$

(A) $\dfrac{9}{10} - \dfrac{2}{3}i$.

(B) $\dfrac{9}{10} - \dfrac{7}{10}i$.

(C) $\dfrac{9}{10} + \dfrac{2}{3}i$.

(D) $3 - \dfrac{7}{10}i$.

15.

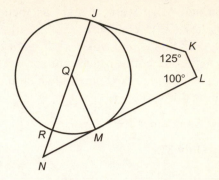

Note: Figure not drawn to scale.

In the figure above, Q is the center of the circle. JK and LM are tangents to the circle. J, Q, N, and R are collinear. Also, L, M, and N are collinear. If $JQ = 6$, what is the length of RN?

(A) $6\sqrt{2} - 6$

(B) $6\sqrt{3} - 6$

(C) $6 - \sqrt{2}$

(D) $6\sqrt{2} - 3$

16. Which one of the following sets is closed under division?

(A) $\{0, 1\}$

(B) $\{-1, 1, 2\}$

(C) $\{-1, 1\}$

(D) $\{-1, 0, 1\}$

17.

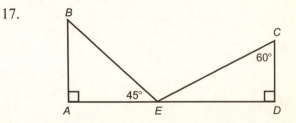

Note: Figure not drawn to scale

In the figure above, $\overline{BE} = 10$ and $\overline{CE} = 8$. What is the *best* approximation to the length of $\overline{AD}$? (A, E, D are collinear points.)

(A) 12   (C) 14

(B) 13   (D) 15

18. Lisa and Mike work at night as security guards for the *WXYZ* company. Lisa is off work once every 12 nights and Mike is off work once every 14 nights. If both of them are off work on April 15th, when is the next date on which both of them will be off work?

    (A) September 15th

    (B) July 8th

    (C) June 24th

    (D) May 11th

19.

CALORIE CHART — BREADS

Bread	Amount	Calories
French Bread	2 oz	140
Bran Bread	1 oz	95
Whole Wheat	1 oz	115
Oatmeal Bread	0.5 oz	55
Raisin Bread	1 oz	125

Use the Calorie Chart shown with the following items: Julie has decided to sample the breads shown in the above Calorie Chart, but she wants to consume no more than 1500 calories. She decides to eat 4 ounces of French bread, 1 ounce of bran bread, 3 ounces of whole wheat bread, and 2 ounces of oatmeal bread. What is the *maximum* integral number of ounces of raisin bread that she can eat?

    (A) 5

    (B) 4

    (C) 3

    (D) 2

20. The mean weight of 20 people in a room is 130 pounds. Bob and Diane are among these 20 people. If both of them leave the room, the mean weight will decrease by 3%. What is the mean weight, in pounds, for Bob and Diane?

    (A) 162

    (B) 165

    (C) 168

    (D) 171

21. In a large survey, it was discovered that 1 out of every 5 adults visits Disney World every year. If 30 adults are randomly selected, what is the probability that exactly 7 of them will visit Disney World this year?

    (A) .233

    (B) .167

    (C) .154

    (D) .125

22. The surface area of a cube is exactly the same as the lateral surface area of a cylinder with a radius of $\dfrac{6}{\pi}$ and a height of 15. What is the best approximation of the volume of the cube?

    (A) 135

    (B) 150

    (C) 165

    (D) 180

23. Read the graph below, then answer the question.

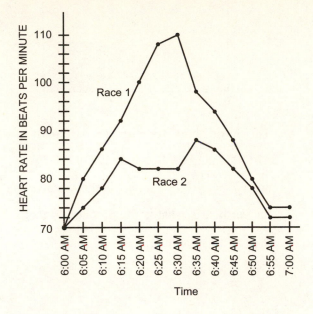

A runner has her heartbeat recorded for two 10.1-mile races run in the same park near her home, held on different days, and both starting at 6:00 a.m.

Which of the following is true at 6:20 a.m. for the recorded heart rates for Race #1 and Race #2?

(A) Both recorded heart rates are increasing.

(B) Both recorded heart rates are decreasing.

(C) The recorded heart rate for Race #1 is increasing, and the recorded heart rate for Race #2 is stable.

(D) The recorded heart rate for Race #1 is stable, and the recorded heart rate for Race #2 is increasing.

24. What is the *least* integer value for n in order that

$$\left(\frac{2}{3}\right)^n < \left(\frac{1}{2}\right)^3 ?$$

(A) 6

(B) 5

(C) 4

(D) 3

25.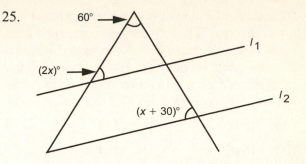

Note: Figure is not drawn to scale.

In the figure above, line l_1 is parallel to line l_2. What is the value of x?

(A) 30

(B) 25

(C) 20

(D) 15

26. In the figure shown, m$\angle A = 130°$, m$\angle B = 95°$, and m$\angle C = 90°$. Point O is the center of a circle with a radius of 12. The area bounded by the polygon $ABCO$ is 30% larger than the shaded area. What is the value of the shaded area?

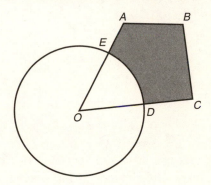

Note: Figure is not drawn to scale.

(A) 18π

(B) 24π

(C) 42π

(D) 60π

27. An amount of N dollars was placed into an account 6 months ago. This account pays compound interest at an annual rate of 16% compounded quarterly. Currently, this account has $2000. Assuming that no money has been withdrawn from or added to this account, what is the value of N? (Nearest dollar)

    (A) $1843   (C) $1847

    (B) $1845   (D) $1849

28. Define the symbol ♠ as follows:

    if $x < y$, $x ♠ y = y^3 - 3x$

    if $x \geq y$, $x ♠ y = x^2 + y^2$

    What is the value of $(2 ♠ 3) ♠ 4$?

    (A) 403

    (B) 425

    (C) 457

    (D) 481

29. A function contains the points $(8, 3)$, $(-1, -3)$, $(-2, 6)$, and $(7, 6)$. Which one of the following must be a point belonging to the inverse of this function?

    (A) $(3, -8)$

    (B) $(1, 3)$

    (C) $(-2, 7)$

    (D) $(6, 7)$

30. A number is considered "perfect" if it is the sum of all its positive integer factors, except itself. For example, 6 is a "perfect" number, since $6 = 1 + 2 + 3$. Which one of the following is a "perfect" number?

    (A) 36

    (B) 28

    (C) 20

    (D) 12

31.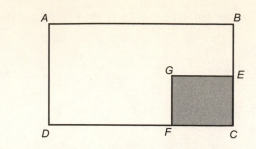

    The figure above represents a dartboard in which $ABCD$ and $ECFG$ are rectangles. $EC = \frac{1}{2}BC$ and $CF = \frac{1}{3}CD$. If a dart is thrown and lands on the dartboard, what is the probability that it lands in the *unshaded* area?

    (A) $\frac{1}{6}$

    (B) $\frac{1}{5}$

    (C) $\frac{3}{5}$

    (D) $\frac{5}{6}$

32. In the triangle shown below, $\cos\omega$ is equal to

    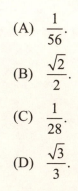

    (A) $\frac{1}{56}$.

    (B) $\frac{\sqrt{2}}{2}$.

    (C) $\frac{1}{28}$.

    (D) $\frac{\sqrt{3}}{3}$.

33.

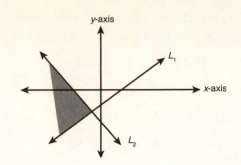

The shaded region could represent the graphical solution to which pair of inequalities?

(A) $2x + 3y \geq -6$
      $x - y \leq -1$

(B) $2x - 3y \geq 6$
      $x + y \geq -1$

(C) $2x + 3y \leq -6$
      $x - y \leq 1$

(D) $2x - 3y \leq 6$
      $x + y \geq 1$

34. $(9^3)^2$ has the same value as which one of the following?

(A) 27^2

(B) $9^3 \cdot 9^2$

(C) 3^{12}

(D) 81^6

35. For which of the following intervals is the graph of $y = x^4 - 2x^3 - 12x^2$ concave down?

(A) $(-2, 1)$

(B) $(-1, 2)$

(C) $(-1, -2)$

(D) $(-\infty, -1)$

36. If $0° < x < 180°$, what values of x, to the nearest degree, are the solutions to the equation $2\tan^2 x + 5\tan x - 12 = 0$?

(A) 56° and 104°

(B) 34° and 104°

(C) 56° and 166°

(D) 34° and 166°

37. In the accompanying figure of a circle centered about point O, the measure of arc AB is $\dfrac{\pi}{5}$ radians. Find $\angle OBA$.

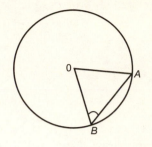

(A) 36°

(B) 144°

(C) 90°

(D) 72°

38.

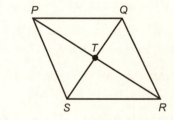

In the figure above, which of the following describes sufficient conditions in order for $PQRS$ to be classified as a rhombus?

(A) $\overline{PQ} = \overline{QR} = \overline{RS} = \overline{SP}$

(B) $\overline{SP}$ is parallel to $\overline{QR}$ and $\overline{PQ}$ is parallel to $\overline{RS}$

(C) $\overline{PR}$ and $\overline{QS}$ are perpendicular bisectors of each other

(D) $\angle QPS \cong \angle QRS$ and $\angle PSR \cong \angle PQR$

39. At the ACE Security Company, each ID badge has 3 letters which appear consecutively and alphabetically in order, followed by 3 digits from 1 through 7 with no repetition and in any order. How many different ID badges are possible?

   (A) 8918

   (B) 8232

   (C) 5460

   (D) 5040

40. An ice cream parlor claims that 40% of its customers prefer chocolate, 35% prefer vanilla, 15% prefer strawberry, and the remaining 10% prefer other flavors. In an actual survey of 100 people, 49 preferred chocolate, 29 preferred vanilla, 17 preferred strawberry, and the remaining people preferred other flavors. Using the 5% level of significance with the chi-square goodness of fit test, which of the following is completely correct?

   (A) The test chi-square value is 8.13 and the claim should be rejected.

   (B) The test chi-square value is 8.13 and the claim should not be rejected.

   (C) The test chi-square value is 5.82 and the claim should be rejected.

   (D) The test chi-square value is 5.82 and the claim should not be rejected.

41. Any Mercenne prime can be written in which form?

   (A) A number of the form $2^n - 1$, where n is composite.

   (B) A number of the form $3^n - 1$, where n is prime.

   (C) A number of the form $2^n - 1$, where n is prime.

   (D) A number of the form $3^n - 1$, where n is composite.

42. For which one of the following situations must events A and B be mutually exclusive?

   Note: P(A) means the probability of event A.

   (A) $P(A) = .30$, $P(B) = .40$, $P(A \cup B) = .50$

   (B) $P(A) = .40$, $P(B) = .35$, $P(A \cup B) = .75$

   (C) $P(A) = .60$, $P(B) = .40$

   (D) $P(A) = .70$, $P(A \cap B) = .30$

43. Consider the function $f(x) = mnx^2$, where m and n are constants. Which of the following sequences is geometric?

   (A) $f(2), f(6), f(8)$

   (B) $f(1), f(2), f(3)$

   (C) $f(2), f(4), f(8)$

   (D) $f(3), f(5), f(7)$

44. Find the coordinates of the vertex of the parabola $y = x^2 - 8x + 15$.

   (A) $(2, 0)$

   (B) $(0, -1)$

   (C) $(4, -1)$

   (D) $(5, 0)$

45.

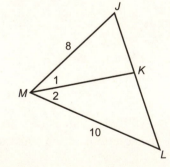

Note: Figure not drawn to scale.

In the figure above, $\angle 1 \cong \angle 2$. If $\overline{JK} = 6$, what is the length of $\overline{KL}$?

   (A) 1.5   (C) 7.5

   (B) 4.8   (D) 12.8

46. What is the period of the function $f(x) = \left(\frac{1}{2}\right)\left(\sin\frac{2x}{3}\right) + \frac{1}{4}$?

    (A) 3π

    (B) $\frac{3\pi}{2}$

    (C) $\frac{4\pi}{3}$

    (D) $\frac{2\pi}{3}$

47. In order to evaluate $3^2 - \left(\frac{7}{3}\right) \div \left(\frac{1}{4}\right) + \left(\frac{1}{2}\right)\left(\frac{1}{6}\right)$, for which number would the calculation of its reciprocal be required?

    (A) $\frac{7}{3}$

    (B) $\frac{1}{2}$

    (C) $\frac{1}{4}$

    (D) $\frac{1}{6}$

48. The area enclosed by the graphs of $y = x^2$ and $y = 2x + 3$ is

    (A) $\frac{38}{3}$

    (B) $\frac{40}{3}$

    (C) $\frac{32}{3}$

    (D) $\frac{16}{3}$

49. If $f(x) = (x - 2)^2$ and $g(x) = x^2 - 2$, what is the value of $g(f[-2])$?

    (A) 260

    (B) 258

    (C) 256

    (D) 254

50. If the graph of $px - 4y = 12$ is perpendicular to the graph of $5x + 6y = 24$, what is the value of p?

    (A) 5.4

    (B) 4.8

    (C) 3.75

    (D) 3.33

51. Which functions(s) below is (are) symmetric with respect to the origin?

    I. $f(x) = x^3 - x$

    II. $f(x) = 2x + x^5$

    III. $f(x) = 2x + 4$

    (A) I and II

    (B) I only

    (C) I and III

    (D) II and III

52. According to Pierre Fermat's Last Theorem, if x, y, z, and n are positive integers, and $x^n + y^n = z^n$, what are the correct restrictions on n?

    (A) n must be 1

    (B) n must be 1 or 2

    (C) n must be 2

    (D) n must be greater than 2

53. Given that sin $(x + y) = 0.9$, sin $x = 0.3$, and cos $y = 0.8$, what is the value of $(2)(\sin y)(\cos x)$?

    (A) 0.66

    (B) 0.74

    (C) 1.20

    (D) 1.32

54. A job placement counselor claims that at the 5% level of significance, the mean entry-level salary of an accountant is $30,000 per year. In a sample of 8 entry-level accountants, it is discovered that their mean salary is $28,000 per year with a standard deviation of $1500. Assuming a normal distribution and using the small sample t-test for means, which of the following is completely correct?

    (A) The critical t-test value is -3.77 and the claim should be rejected.

    (B) The critical t-test value is -3.77 and the claim should not be rejected.

    (C) The critical t-test value is -1.33 and the claim should be rejected.

    (D) The critical t-test value is -1.33 and the claim should not be rejected.

55. An equation of the line normal to the graph of $y = x^4 - 3x^2 + 1$ at the point where $x = 1$ is

    (A) $2x - y + 3 = 0$

    (B) $x - 2y + 3 = 0$

    (C) $2x - y - 3 = 0$

    (D) $x - 2y - 3 = 0$

56. Look at the following figure:

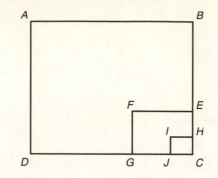

Note: Figure is not drawn to scale.

$ABCD$ is a square with area 9. $EFGC$ is a square in which $EC = \left(\dfrac{1}{3}\right)(BC)$. $HIJC$ is a square in which $HC = \left(\dfrac{1}{3}\right)(EC)$. If this pattern is continued so that there are a total of ten squares with a common vertex at C, and in which each square lies inside its predecessor, what is the area of the tenth square?

    (A) 9^{-12} (C) 9^{-9}

    (B) 9^{-10} (D) 9^{-8}

57. Given parallelogram $KLMN$, where points K, L, M, N are located at $(2, 5)$, (b, c), $(7, 1)$, $(0, 1)$ respectively, which of the following is equivalent to c?

    (A) $b - 12$ (C) $2b - 13$

    (B) $b + 5$ (D) $2b + 4$

58. According to the Fundamental Theorem of Calculus, if f is a continuous function on the closed interval $[c, d]$, then $F(x) = \int_c^x f(t)\,dt$ has what property at every point x in $[c, d]$?

    (A) It may not be defined nor differentiable at a finite number of values of x.

    (B) It is differentiable but may not be defined at each x.

    (C) It is defined and differentiable at each x.

    (D) It is defined but may not be differentiable at each x.

59. Age Distribution of University Faculty Members

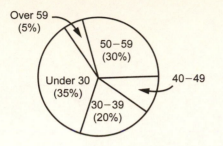

If there are 88 faculty members between the ages of 30 and 39, what is the combined total of faculty members who are at least 40 years old?

(A) 198

(B) 213

(C) 227

(D) 242

60. Given the numbers 2 and 3, how much larger is the sum of their multiplicative inverses than the multiplicative inverse of their sum?

(A) $\dfrac{1}{6}$

(B) $\dfrac{19}{30}$

(C) $\dfrac{5}{6}$

(D) $\dfrac{31}{30}$

61.

In the figure above, $\overline{AC} = \overline{CE}$ and $\overline{AB} = \overline{DE}$. Which of the following statements must be true?

I. $\overline{AB} = \overline{FE}$

II. $\angle ABE \cong \angle EDA$

III. $\triangle ACD \cong \triangle ABE$

(A) I only

(B) II only

(C) II and III only

(D) I, II, and III

62. If $f(x) = e^{\frac{x^3}{3} - x}$, then $f(x)$

(A) increases in the interval $(-1, 1)$

(B) decreases for $|x| > 1$

(C) increases in the interval $(-1, 1)$ and decreases in the intervals $(-\infty, -1) \cup (1, \infty)$

(D) increases in the intervals $(-\infty, -1) \cup (1, \infty)$ and decreases in the interval $(-1, 1)$

63. Which of the following triangles $A'\ B'\ C'$ is the image of triangle ABC that results from reflecting the triangle ABC across the y-axis?

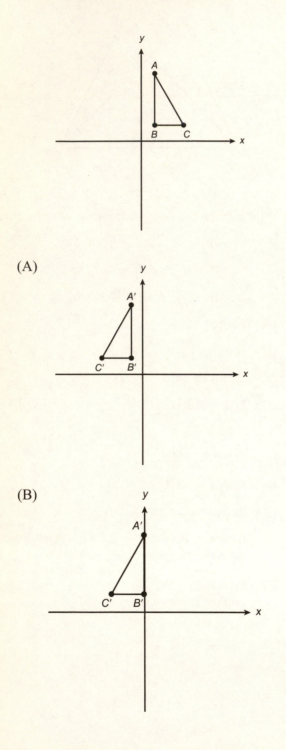

(A)

(B)

(C)

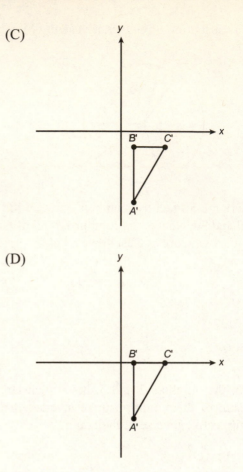

(D)

64. Which of the graphs below represents the equation $\dfrac{x^2}{9} - \dfrac{y^2}{9} = 1$?

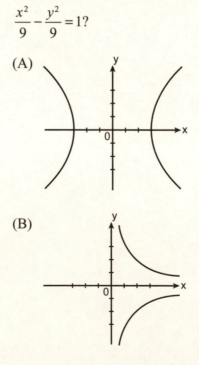

(A)

(B)

(C)

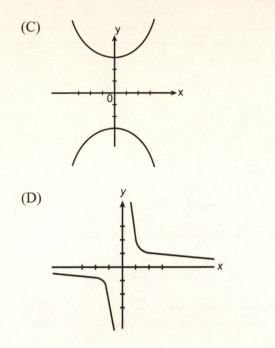

(D)

65. At a local high school, the teacher-student ratio is 1:25. The school has 900 students. If no new students are added, how many additional teachers are needed to change the teacher-student ratio to 1:15?

(A) 60

(B) 48

(C) 36

(D) 24

66. Suppose that P varies directly as the square root of Q and inversely as the cube of R. How does Q vary with P and R?

(A) Directly as the square root of P and the cube root of R

(B) Directly as the square of P and the sixth power of R

(C) Inversely as the square of P and the cube root of R

(D) Inversely as the square root of P and directly as R

67.

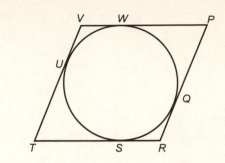

Note: Figure is not drawn to scale.

In the figure above, $\overline{PR}$, $\overline{RT}$, $\overline{TV}$, and $\overline{VP}$ are tangents to the circle at points Q, S, U, and W, respectively. The perimeter of $PRTV$ is 28 and $PW = 4$. Which of the following must be true?

(A) $PR = RT$

(B) $VW = 3$

(C) $PR + TV = 14$

(D) $m\angle P = m\angle T$

68. The sum of the first 50 terms of an arithmetic series is 100. If the common difference is 2, what is the first term?

(A) 47

(B) 48

(C) −48

(D) −47

69. At a certain company, each employee has received a 5% increase in salary each year for the past six years. Anna was earning $30,000 per year six years ago, while Marty is now earning $50,000 per year. To the nearest dollar, how much higher was Marty's annual salary than Anna's annual salary three years ago?

(A) $8,463

(B) $11,393

(C) $14,322

(D) $17,252

70. What is the domain of the function $\dfrac{(2x^2+13x-15)}{(2x^2-x-15)}$?

   (A) All numbers except $-\dfrac{13}{2}$ and 1

   (B) All numbers except $\dfrac{5}{2}$ and -3

   (C) All numbers except $-\dfrac{5}{2}$ and 3

   (D) All numbers except $\dfrac{15}{2}$ and -1

71.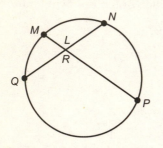

   Note: Figure is not drawn to scale.

   Chords $\overline{MP}$ and $\overline{NQ}$ intersect at point R, which is not the center of the circle. If arc $QM = 50°$ and $\angle MLN = 110°$, what is the degree measure of arc NP?

   (A) 70°

   (B) 90°

   (C) 105°

   (D) 110°

72. If $2^n = x$ and $3^n = y$, which of the following is the correct expression for 6^{n-1}?

   (A) $\dfrac{xy}{6}$

   (B) $xy - 1$

   (C) $xy - 6$

   (D) $6xy$

73. The radius of the base of a cone is 2 cm and its total surface area is 70 cm². What is the best approximation, in cm, for its slant height?

   (A) 9.14

   (B) 7.95

   (C) 6.76

   (D) 5.57

74. Which one of the following represents an experiment for which the probability is equal to $\dfrac{1}{221}$?

   (A) Drawing two aces, one at a time, with no replacement, from a deck of 52 cards.

   (B) Drawing two jacks, one at a time, with replacement, from a deck of 52 cards.

   (C) Drawing two slips of paper, numbered 13 and 17, one at a time, with no replacement, from a jar with 17 slips of paper numbered 1 through 17.

   (D) Drawing two slips of paper, numbered 13 and 17, one at a time, with replacement, from a jar with 30 slips of paper numbered 1 through 30.

75. What is the slope of the tangent to the curve $y = x^2 + 11x - 2$ at the point where $x = -3$?

   (A) -44

   (B) -36

   (C) 3

   (D) 5

76. A sphere and a cylinder have equal volumes. If the height of the cylinder is twice its radius, what ratio represents the cube of the radius of the sphere to the cube of the radius of the cylinder?

    (A) $\dfrac{2}{3}$

    (B) $\dfrac{3}{4}$

    (C) $\dfrac{4}{3}$

    (D) $\dfrac{3}{2}$

77. Which one of the following geometric figures has neither a horizontal nor vertical line of symmetry?

    (A) Isosceles triangle

    (B) Parallelogram

    (C) Rectangle

    (D) Circle

78. Which one of the following sets is not a group?

    (A) Integers under the operation of subtraction

    (B) Rational numbers under the operation of division

    (C) Positive real numbers under the operation of multiplication

    (D) Negative integers under the operation of addition

79. What is the value of $(-1 + i)^{10}$?

    (A) $8\sqrt{2} - 8i\sqrt{2}$

    (B) $16\sqrt{2} - 16i\sqrt{2}$

    (C) $-16\sqrt{2} + 16i\sqrt{2}$

    (D) $-8\sqrt{2} + 8i\sqrt{2}$

80. For the expanded expression equivalent to $(x + 3y)^{20}$, which one of the following is the coefficient of the term containing x^{16}?

    (A) 1,177,335

    (B) 392,445

    (C) 58,140

    (D) 4,845

81. Including 1 and the number itself, how many total positive factors are there for the number $8^3 \cdot 35 \cdot 27^2$?

    (A) 280

    (B) 210

    (C) 168

    (D) 54

82. If plane P is perpendicular to plane Q, and plane R is perpendicular to plane Q, which one of the following is the correct conclusion concerning the relationship between plane P and plane R?

    (A) Plane P must be perpendicular to plane R

    (B) Plane P may be perpendicular to plane R

    (C) Plane P may be skew to plane R

    (D) Plane P must be skew to plane R

83. The first term of an infinite geometric series is 1.8. If the sum of this series is 4.5, what is the sum of the first three terms?

    (A) 2.88

    (B) 3.528

    (C) 3.6

    (D) 4.176

84. Point Q is located at $(2, -3)$. If this point is rotated $90°$ clockwise about the origin, what will be the new coordinates of Q?

    (A) $(3, 2)$

    (B) $(2, 3)$

    (C) $(-2, -3)$

    (D) $(-3, -2)$

85. Which one of the following matrices represents the product $\begin{bmatrix} 3 & 2 & -1 \\ -2 & 1 & 0 \end{bmatrix} \begin{bmatrix} 1 & -3 \\ 2 & 1 \\ -2 & -1 \end{bmatrix}$?

    (A) $\begin{bmatrix} 5 & 6 \\ 0 & -7 \end{bmatrix}$

    (B) $\begin{bmatrix} 5 & -6 \\ 7 & 0 \end{bmatrix}$

    (C) $\begin{bmatrix} 9 & -6 \\ 0 & 7 \end{bmatrix}$

    (D) $\begin{bmatrix} 9 & 6 \\ -7 & 0 \end{bmatrix}$

86. Let a, b represent positive integers less than 19 for which $19 \equiv a \pmod 3$ and $27 \equiv b \pmod 4$. What is the *maximum* value of $a - b$?

    (A) 18

    (B) 17

    (C) 14

    (D) 13

87. The average rate of change for y with respect to x over the closed interval $[-2, 4]$ is 6. Which one of the following equations satisfies this condition?

    (A) $y = 4x^2 + 1$

    (B) $y = 3x^2 - 2$

    (C) $y = 2x^2 + 3$

    (D) $y = x^2 - 4$

88. Given a group of n data, the percentile score of a particular number P in this data is given by $(100)\dfrac{B + (0.5)(E)}{n}$, where $B = $ number of data below P, and $E = $ number of data equal to P. Suppose that in a group of 60 data, 45 is one of the numbers. If there are eight 45's and the percentile score for 45 is 40, how many numbers are greater than 45?

    (A) 20

    (B) 32

    (C) 36

    (D) 52

89. Suppose set M is a proper subset of set N. Set M has 15 elements and set N has 25 elements. The Universal Set, which contains sets M and N, has 45 elements. If set P is also a proper subset of the Universal Set, but contains no elements from set N, what is the *maximum* number of elements in P?

    (A) 5

    (B) 10

    (C) 20

    (D) 25

90. A linear translation on a coordinate plane is defined as follows: $(x, y) \to (x - 4, y + 8)$. If the point $(-7, -1)$ represents the image of a linear translation for point P, what are the coordinates of P?

    (A) $(-11, 7)$

    (B) $(-5, 1)$

    (C) $(-3, -9)$

    (D) $(-1, -7)$

91. Which one of the following functions has no horizontal asymptote?

    (A) $f(x) = \dfrac{(3x^2 + x - 7)}{(4x^2 + x + 1)}$

    (B) $f(x) = \dfrac{(x - 4)}{(5x^3 + 3x - 1)}$

    (C) $f(x) = \dfrac{(x^4 + x^3 - x + 3)}{(x^5 - x^4 + 2)}$

    (D) $f(x) = \dfrac{(x^3 + 7x^2 - 2)}{(2x^2 - 5)}$

92. A vector **v** is described by $<5, -12>$. Which of the following describes a vector of length $\dfrac{1}{2}$ unit in the direction of **v**?

    (A) $\left\langle \dfrac{5}{26}, -\dfrac{6}{13} \right\rangle$

    (B) $\left\langle \dfrac{10}{13}, -\dfrac{24}{13} \right\rangle$

    (C) $\left\langle \dfrac{5}{7}, -\dfrac{12}{7} \right\rangle$

    (D) $\left\langle \dfrac{5}{2}, -6 \right\rangle$

93. If $(x + 3y)^2 = 100$ and $(3x + y)^2 = 196$, what is the value of $\left(\dfrac{1}{3}\right)(x^2 - y^2)$?

    (A) 3

    (B) 4

    (C) 6

    (D) 9

94. A person wishes to place nine books on a shelf that has nine slots. There are four math books, two history books, and three English books. In how many ways can these books be arranged so that all books of the same subject are placed together?

    (A) 288   (C) 15,552

    (B) 1,728   (D) 362,880

95. If $\log_3\left(\dfrac{1}{27}\right) = x$ and $y^x = -64$, what is the value of $\log_{\frac{9}{16}} xy$?

    (A) -2

    (B) $-\dfrac{1}{2}$

    (C) $\dfrac{1}{2}$

    (D) 2

96. Suppose Z varies jointly as W and X. If $Z = 18$ when $W = 9$ and $X = 3$, what is the value of W when $Z = 15$ and $X = \dfrac{1}{3}$?

    (A) 3.5   (C) 30.0

    (B) 10.8   (D) 67.5

97. What is the area of a circle whose equation is given by $x^2 + 8x + y^2 + 12y + 3 = 0$?

    (A) 98π (C) 49π

    (B) 64π (D) 14π

98. A polynomial function $g(x)$ of degree 5 has a zero of $2 - i$ and a zero of $4 + i$. What is the maximum number of real zeros for $g(x)$?

    (A) 0   (C) 2

    (B) 1   (D) 3

99. Which one of the following represents a function whose graph has a single vertical asymptote at $x = -3$?

    (A) $\dfrac{(x + 3)}{2x^2 + 5x - 3}$

    (B) $\dfrac{(9x + 1)}{x^3 - 9x}$

    (C) $\dfrac{(3x - 1)}{(x^3 + 3x^2 + 2x + 6)}$

    (D) $\dfrac{(x - 3)}{x^2 + 3x + 9}$

100. The position function of a particle moving on a coordinate line is given by the equation $s(t) = t^3 + 4t^2 - 2$, where $s(t)$ represents feet and t represents seconds. What is the acceleration of this particle when $t = 5$?

    (A) 18 ft/sec²

    (B) 38 ft/sec²

    (C) 75 ft/sec²

    (D) 115 ft/sec²

Open-Response Item Assignments (101, 102)

Directions: Prepare a legibly written response of one to two pages on the problem below. Plan, write, review, and edit your response. Your response will not be judged on writing ability, but must be communicated clearly and will be scored on a scale of 1 to 4. It will be evaluated on the following:

Purpose: Fulfill the charge of the assignment.

Application of Content: Accurately and effectively apply the relevant knowledge and skills.

Support: Support the response with appropriate examples and/or sound reasoning reflecting an understanding of the relevant knowledge and skills.

101. A small housing community consists of three dwellings, as shown below.

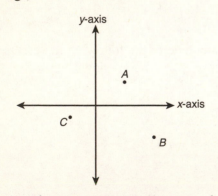

The town planner wants to construct a clubhouse which is equidistant from each dwelling.

• If you had only a straightedge and a compass, how would you determine the exact location of the clubhouse?

• If the coordinates of the dwellings are (4, 3), (–3, –1), and (7, –6), what are the coordinates of the clubhouse?

• A direct walkway will be built between the clubhouse and each dwelling. Each walkway is rectangular in shape and will be 4 feet wide. The length of each walkway is 20 feet times the distance in units on the graph from each dwelling to the clubhouse. If the cost of the walkway is $15 per square foot, what is the total cost of all three walkways?

• Using your straight edge and your compass, construct the location of the clubhouse.

102. At the Sleep-Easy Motel, a senior citizen is given a $10-per-night discount, calculated by taking the cost of each night's lodging, adding an 8% sales tax, then deducting $10 per night. At the Rest-Well Motel, a senior citizen is also given a $10-per-night discount. The discount is first applied to the cost of each night's lodging; then the 8% sales tax is added. At either motel, one night's lodging (before discounts) costs $90.

• What is the cost for a senior citizen to stay at the Sleep-Easy Motel for 4 nights?

• What is the cost for a senior citizen to stay at the Rest-Well Motel for 4 nights?

• In order for the cost to be the same at each motel, how much of a discount, in dollars and cents, should be offered at the Rest-Well Motel?

• Using the first quadrant of an xy-coordinate system, draw a linear representation for the cost of staying at each motel for each of the first 4 nights. Label the x-axis as "Number of Nights" and label the y-axis as "Total Cost."

Answer Key Practice Test (09) for Mathematics

Q No.	Correct Answer	Subarea	Q No.	Correct Answer	Subarea
1.	(D)	Geometry	32.	(A)	Trigonometry
2.	(B)	Number Sense	33.	(C)	Algebra
3.	(C)	Algebra	34.	(C)	Number Sense
4.	(A)	Algebra	35.	(B)	Algebra
5.	(D)	Statistics	36.	(A)	Trigonometry
6.	(A)	Statistics	37.	(D)	Geometry
7.	(B)	Algebra	38.	(C)	Geometry
8.	(B)	Discrete Math	39.	(D)	Algebra
9.	(C)	Calculus	40.	(D)	Statistics
10.	(A)	Calculus	41.	(C)	Number Sense
11.	(B)	Geometry	42.	(B)	Probability
12.	(C)	Geometry	43.	(C)	Discrete Math
13.	(D)	Discrete Math	44.	(C)	Algebra
14.	(B)	Algebra	45.	(C)	Geometry
15.	(A)	Geometry	46.	(A)	Functions
16.	(C)	Discrete Math	47.	(C)	Number Sense
17.	(C)	Geometry	48.	(C)	Calculus
18.	(B)	Number Sense	49.	(D)	Discrete Math
19.	(B)	Data Analysis	50.	(B)	Algebra
20.	(B)	Statistics	51.	(A)	Functions
21.	(C)	Probability	52.	(B)	Number Sense
22.	(C)	Geometry	53.	(D)	Trigonometry
23.	(C)	Data Analysis	54.	(A)	Statistics
24.	(A)	Algebra	55.	(D)	Calculus
25.	(A)	Geometry	56.	(D)	Geometry
26.	(D)	Geometry	57.	(C)	Geometry
27.	(D)	Algebra	58.	(C)	Calculus
28.	(C)	Algebra	59.	(A)	Data Analysis
29.	(D)	Functions	60.	(B)	Number Sense
30.	(B)	Number Sense	61.	(B)	Geometry
31.	(D)	Geometry	62.	(D)	Calculus

Q No.	Correct Answer	Subarea	Q No.	Correct Answer	Subarea
63.	(A)	Geometry	83.	(B)	Discrete Math
64.	(A)	Geometry	84.	(D)	Geometry
65.	(D)	Number Sense	85.	(C)	Discrete Math
66.	(B)	Algebra	86.	(D)	Algebra
67.	(C)	Geometry	87.	(B)	Algebra
68.	(D)	Discrete Math	88.	(B)	Statistics
69.	(A)	Algebra	89.	(C)	Discrete Math
70.	(C)	Functions	90.	(C)	Geometry
71.	(B)	Geometry	91.	(D)	Algebra
72.	(A)	Algebra	92.	(A)	Algebra
73.	(A)	Geometry	93.	(B)	Algebra
74.	(A)	Probability	94.	(B)	Discrete Math
75.	(D)	Calculus	95.	(C)	Algebra
76.	(D)	Geometry	96.	(D)	Algebra
77.	(B)	Geometry	97.	(C)	Geometry
78.	(B)	Operations	98.	(B)	Algebra
79.	(C)	Trigonometry	99.	(C)	Algebra
80.	(B)	Algebra	100.	(B)	Calculus
81.	(A)	Number Sense	101.	–	Open-Response
82.	(B)	Geometry	102.	–	Open-Response

Math 09
Detailed Explanations of Answers

1. **(D)**

If $\angle 1 \cong \angle 2$, the triangles ABC and ACD would have two pairs of congruent sides and a pair of non-inclusive congruent angles. This would be insufficient to prove that these triangles are congruent, which means that we cannot conclude that $\angle ACB \cong \angle ACD$. Thus, we cannot conclude that $\overline{AC}$ is perpendicular to $\overline{BD}$. Answer choice (A) would imply that triangles ABC and ACD are congruent by side-angle-angle, so $\angle ACB \cong \angle ACD$ by corresponding parts. This would imply that $\overline{AC}$ is perpendicular to $\overline{BD}$. Answer choice (B) would already establish that since $\angle B \cong \angle D$, $\angle ACB \cong \angle ACD$. Thus we would conclude that $\overline{AC}$ is perpendicular to $\overline{BD}$. Answer choice (C) would imply that triangles ABC and ACD are congruent by side-side-side, so $\angle ACB \cong \angle ACD$ by corresponding parts. This would imply that $\overline{AC}$ is perpendicular to $\overline{BD}$.

2. **(B)**

$$\frac{9 \text{ apartments with terraces}}{16 \text{ apartments}} = \frac{?}{144 \text{ apartments}}$$

Solving this proportion for the "?"

$$? = \frac{9 \text{ apartments} \times 144 \text{ apartments}}{16 \text{ apartments}}$$

$$= \frac{1296 \text{ apartments}}{16 \text{ apartments}} = 81 \text{ apartments}$$

Answer (A) is incorrect because the apartments were subtracted.

$$144 - (16 - 9) = 144 - 7 = 137 \text{ apartments}$$

Answer (C) is incorrect because the number of apartments with terraces is 9, not $16 - 9$.

$$(144 \div 16) \times (16 - 9) = 9 \times 7 = 63$$

Answer (D) is incorrect due to a multiplication factor guess of 6.

$$144 - [(16 - 9) \times 6] = 102$$

3. **(C)**

Real zeros of a function are represented by x-intercepts. Each point of $g(x)$ would have its y value decreased by 2. The only two places where there would be x-intercepts are: a point on $g(x)$ between $(-2, 0)$ and $(0, 3)$; and a point on $g(x)$ between $(0, 3)$ and $(2, 0)$. Note that any point on $g(x)$ between $(4, 0)$ and $(5, 1)$ would lie below the x-axis after the downward shift of 2 units.

4. **(A)**

If $f(x) < 3$, then $|9 - 2x| < 3$, which means $-3 < 9 - 2x < 3$. Subtracting 9, we get $-12 < -2x < -6$. Now, divide by -2, remembering to reverse the order of inequality, to get $6 > x > 3$, which is equivalent to $3 < x < 6$.

5. **(D)**

Using the Normal Distribution, the critical z value is 2.05. The corresponding raw score is $(3)(2.05) + 70 = 76.15$. Since we need a minimum integer score, the correct answer is 77.

6.   (A)

We seek the $\dfrac{100}{2}$ = 50th number, which appears in the third class (36 − 45). The only answer choice in this interval is 43.

To calculate the answer: The total number of accidents is 100. The median is the $\dfrac{100}{2}$ = 50th number when the numbers are arranged in ascending order. (In this case, we have intervals of numbers instead of just numbers.) The two age intervals 16–25 and 26–35 total 41 accidents. Therefore, we need nine numbers from the next interval age 36–45. Use the lower boundary of this interval 36–45, which is 35.5, and add $\dfrac{9}{12}$ of the width of the interval (10, which equals 45.5 − 35.5). Then

$$35.5 + \frac{9}{12}(10) = 43$$

7.   (B)

The maximum height of any parabola given in the form $y = Ax^2 + Bx + C$, where A is negative, is given by the y value of the vertex. In this example, z replaces y, and t replaces x. The x value of the vertex is given by $-\dfrac{B}{2A} = \dfrac{144}{-32} = 4.5$, and this is the required time in seconds.

8.   (B)

.15

Using the formula $P(A \cup B) = P(A) + P(B) - P(A \cap B)$, and replacing $P(A \cap B)$ with $P(A) \cdot P(B \mid A)$, we get $.29 = P(A) + .20 - P(A) \cdot .40$. This equation simplifies to $.09 = .60 \cdot P(A)$. So $P(A) = \dfrac{.09}{.60} = .15$.

9.   (C)

Use integration by parts with

$u = \ln x$	$du = \dfrac{1}{x}\,dx$
$dv = x$	$v = \dfrac{x^2}{2}$

$$\int_1^e x \ln x \, dx = \frac{x^2}{2}\ln x - \int_1^e \frac{x}{2}\,dx$$
$$= \left(\frac{x^2}{2}\ln x - \frac{x^2}{4} \right)\Big|_1^e$$
$$= \frac{e^2 + 1}{4}$$

10.   (A)

$$\lim_{x \to 1} \frac{\dfrac{1}{x+1} - \dfrac{1}{2}}{x-1}$$

Obtain a common denominator in the main numerator.

$$\lim_{x \to 1} \frac{\dfrac{2-(x+1)}{2(x+1)}}{x-1} = \lim_{x \to 1} \frac{1-x}{2(x+1)(x-1)}$$
$$= \lim_{x \to 1} \frac{-1}{2(x+1)}$$
$$= \frac{-1}{2(1+1)} = -\frac{1}{4}$$

Note: $\dfrac{1-x}{x-1} = -1$ for $x \neq 1$

11.   (B)

Triangles RUV and STU are both $45°$–$45°$–$90°$ right triangles. Let $\overline{RU} = \overline{UV} = x$. Because $\overline{RV} = 8$, $x^2 + x^2 = 8^2$. Then $2x^2 = 64$, so $x = \sqrt{32}$. This means that $\overline{UT} = \sqrt{32}$. Let $\overline{ST} = \overline{SU} = y$. Then $y^2 + y^2 = (\sqrt{32})^2 = 32$, so $2y^2 = 32$, $y^2 = 16$, and thus $y = 4$. Now in $\triangle STV$, $\overline{ST} = 4$ and $\overline{SV} = \overline{UV} + \overline{US} = \sqrt{32} + 4$. Finally, in $\triangle STV$ $\overline{VT}^2 = \overline{SV}^2 + \overline{ST}^2 = 9.657^2 + 4^2 \approx 109.26$. Therefore, $\overline{VT} = \sqrt{109.26} \approx 10.5$.

12.   (C)

Using the Pythagorean Theorem, $QS = \sqrt{8^2 + 15^2}$ $= \sqrt{289} = 17$. Using the Law of Sines on triangle QRS, $\dfrac{17}{\sin 75°} = \dfrac{QR}{\sin 60°}$. Then, $QR = \dfrac{17 \sin 60°}{\sin 75°} \approx 15.2$

13.   (D)

$P_3 = P_2 + 1 = 3$. $P_4 = (2)(P_3) = 6$, $P_5 = P_4 + 1 = 7$, $P_6 = (2)(P_5) = 14$. Then $P_5 + P_6 = 7 + 14 = 21$.

14.   (B)

$$\frac{x}{y} = \frac{3 + 2i}{1 + 3i}$$
$$= \frac{3 + 2i}{1 + 3i} \times \frac{1 - 3i}{1 - 3i}$$
$$= \frac{3 - 9i + 2i - 6i^2}{1^2 - 3^2 i^2}$$
$$= \frac{9 - 7i}{1 + 9}$$
$$= \frac{9}{10} - \frac{7}{10}i$$

15.   (A)

$\angle QJK$ and $\angle QML$ are each $90°$ because tangents to a circle form right angles at points of tangency. In any 5-sided figure, the sum of the interior angles is $(180°)(5 - 2) = 540°$. So $\angle JQM = 540° - 90° - 90° - 125° - 100° = 135°$; this means that $\angle MQN = 180° - 135° = 45°$. This means that $\angle N = 45°$, by noting that the sum of the angles of $\triangle QMN$ is $180°$. Because $\triangle QMN$ is a $45°$–$45°$–$90°$ right triangle, $\overline{QN} = (\overline{QM})(\sqrt{2}) = 6\sqrt{2}$. Now $\overline{RN} = \overline{QN} - \overline{QR}$, and because $\overline{QR}$ is a radius, $\overline{RN} = 6\sqrt{2} - 6$.

16.   (C)

If either one of -1 or 1 is divided by itself or the other number, the result is either -1 or 1. An example to show why answer choice (A) is wrong is $\dfrac{1}{0}$, which is undefined. An example to show why answer choice (B) is wrong is $\dfrac{2}{-1} = -2$, which is not an element of this set. An example to show why answer choice (D) is wrong is $-\dfrac{1}{0}$, which is undefined.

17.   (C)

$\triangle ABE$ is an isosceles right triangle, so $\overline{AE} = \dfrac{10}{\sqrt{2}} \approx 7.07$. $\triangle CDE$ is a right triangle with acute angles of $30°$ and $60°$, so $\overline{ED} = 4\sqrt{3} \approx 6.93$. Thus, $\overline{AD} \approx 7.07 + 6.93 = 14$.

18.   (B)

The least common multiple of 12 and 14 is 84. We need to count 84 days from April 15th. There are 15 days left for April, so $84 - 15 = 69$. The month of May has 31 days, so $69 - 31 = 38$. The month of June has 30 days, so $38 - 30 = 8$. Thus, the required date is the 8th day of July.

19. (B)

First, determine how many calories Julie has already allocated: French bread (280), bran bread (95), whole wheat (345), plus oatmeal (220). That totals 940 calories, leaving $1500 - 940 = 560$ calories for the raisin bread. At 125 calories per ounce, Julie could eat $\frac{560}{125} = 4.48$, or 4 ounces of raisin bread.

20. (B)

The original total weight of all the people in the room is $(20)(130) = 2600$ pounds. After Bob and Diane leave the room, the mean weight of the remaining 18 people will be $(130)(.97) = 126.1$ pounds. This means that the total weight for these 18 people is $(18)(126.1) \approx 2270$ pounds. Then $2600 - 2270 = 330$ pounds is the total weight for Bob and Diane. Finally, the mean weight for Bob and Diane is $\frac{330}{2} = 165$ pounds.

21. (C)

Use the Binomial Distribution, which states Probability of x successes in n trials $= ({}_nC_x)(p^x)(1-p)^{n-x}$. In this formula, ${}_nC_x =$ the number of combinations of x successes in n trials $= (n)(n-1)(n-2)(\ldots)\frac{(n-x+1)}{x!}$, and $p =$ probability of success on any single trial. Here, $n = 30, x = 7, p = .2$, and ${}_{30}C_7 = \frac{(30)\,29\,(28)(\ldots)(24)}{7!}$. Thus, the required probability $= (2{,}035{,}000)(.2)^7\,(.8)^{23} \approx .154$.

22. (C)

The surface area of a cube is given by the expression $6s^2$, where s is the length of one side. The lateral surface area of a cylinder is given by the expression $2\pi rh$, where r is the radius and h is the height. Equating these expressions, we get $6s^2 = (2)(\pi)\left(\frac{6}{\pi}\right)(15)$. Simplifying, we get $6s^2 = 180$, so $s = \sqrt{30} \approx 5.48$. This means that the volume of the cube is $(5.48)^3 \approx 165$.

23. (C)

In the interval of 6:20 AM to 6:30 AM, one observes on the graph that for Race #1 the heart rate in beats per minute is increasing from 100 beats/minute to 110 beats/minute, as follows: (6:20, 100) (6:25, 108), (6:30, 110); while for Race #2 the heart rate in beats per minute is stable at 82 beats/minute, as follows: (6:20, 82), (6:25, 82), (6:30, 82).

Answer choice (A) is incorrect because the heart rate for Race #2 is steady. Answer choice (B) is incorrect because the heart rate for Race #1 is increasing, and the heart rate for Race #2 is steady. Answer choice (D) is incorrect because the answers are reversed: Race #2 is stable, and Race #1 is increasing.

24. (A)

$\left(\frac{1}{2}\right)^3 = \frac{1}{8}$. By substitution, $\left(\frac{2}{3}\right)^3 = \frac{8}{27}$, $\left(\frac{2}{3}\right)^4 = \frac{16}{81}$, $\left(\frac{2}{3}\right)^5 = \frac{32}{243}$, and $\left(\frac{2}{3}\right)^6 = \frac{64}{729}$. Among these fractions, only $\frac{64}{729} < \frac{1}{8}$.

25. (A)

The third angle in the small triangle, which lies on l_1, has a measure of $(x + 30)°$ because it represents a corresponding angle on l_2. The sum of the angles of any triangle is $180°$, so using the three angles of the small triangle, $(2x) + (x + 30) + 60 = 180$; $3x + 90 = 180$, $3x = 90$, so $x = 30$.

26. (D)

The central angle of sector $EOD = 360° - 130° - 95° - 90° = 45°$. Then the area of sector $EOD = \left(\dfrac{45°}{360°}\right)(\pi)(12)^2 = 18\pi$. Let $x =$ shaded area. The area of polygon $ABCO = 1.30x$. So $1.30x - x = 18\pi$. Solving, $x = 60\pi$.

27. (D)

$1849

An annual rate of 16% compounded quarterly means 4% every three months. A period of 6 months is equivalent to two compounding periods. Use the formula $(N)(1.04)^2 = \$2000$. Solving, $N \approx \$1849.11$, which rounds off to $1849.

28. (C)

Because $2 < 3$, use the equation $2 \spadesuit 3 = 3^3 - (3)(2) = 27 - 6 = 21$. Likewise, because $21 > 4$, $21 \spadesuit 4 = 21^2 + 16 = 441 + 16 = 457$.

29. (D)

The inverse of the graph of any function is found by reflecting the graph across the line $y = x$. This means that for any point (x, y) on the original graph, the point (y, x) must be on the inverse graph. The point $(6, 7)$ is a point on the graph of the inverse since $(7, 6)$ is on the graph of the original function.

30. (B)

The factors of 28, other than itself, are 1, 2, 4, 7, and 14. Note that $1 + 2 + 4 + 7 + 14 = 28$. Answer choice (A) is wrong because $36 \neq 1 + 2 + 3 + 4 + 6 + 9 + 12 + 18$. Answer choice (C) is wrong because $20 \neq 1 + 2 + 4 + 5 + 10$. Answer choice (D) is wrong because $12 \neq 1 + 2 + 3 + 4 + 6$.

31. (D)

Let $x =$ length of BC and $y =$ length of CD. The area of $ABCD$ is xy and the area of $ECFG = \left(\dfrac{x}{2}\right)\left(\dfrac{y}{3}\right) = \dfrac{xy}{6}$. Thus the unshaded area is $xy - \dfrac{xy}{6} = \left(\dfrac{5}{6}\right)(xy)$. The probability that a dart lands in the unshaded area is $\dfrac{\frac{5}{6}xy}{xy} = \dfrac{5}{6}$.

32. (A)

To solve, we use the law of cosines:

$$c^2 = a^2 + b^2 - 2ab\cos(\text{included angle}).$$

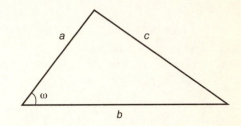

In the figure given, $a = 4$, $b = 7$, $c = 8$, and ω is the included angle.

We solve the law of cosine relation for $\cos\omega$:

$$c^2 = a^2 + b^2 - 2ab\cos\omega.$$

Transposing a^2 and b^2 and dividing through by $-2ab$, we obtain:

$$\dfrac{c^2 - a^2 - b^2}{-2ab} = \cos\omega.$$

Substituting for a, b, and c we obtain

$$\cos\omega = \dfrac{8^2 - 4^2 - 7^2}{-2(4)(7)} = \dfrac{64 - 16 - 49}{-56} = \dfrac{-1}{-56} = \dfrac{1}{56}.$$

33. (C)

The equation $2x + 3y = 6$ has a slope of $-\dfrac{2}{3}$, so it must be represented by L_2. Similarly, the equation $x - y = 1$ has a slope of 1, so it must be represented by L_1. The inequality $2x + 3y \leq -6$ can be rewritten as $y \leq \left(-\dfrac{2}{3}\right)x - 2$, so we are looking for a region below L_2. Likewise, the inequality $x - y \leq 1$ can be rewritten as $y \geq x - 1$, so we are also looking for a region above L_1. The given shaded region satisfies both of these requirements.

34. (C)

$(9^3)^2$ can be written as $9^6 = (3^2)^6 = 3^{12}$. Answer choice (A) is wrong because $27^2 = 3^6$. Answer choice (B) is wrong because $9^3 \cdot 9^2 = 9^5 = 3^{10}$. Answer choice (D) is wrong because $81^6 = 3^{24}$.

35. (B)

$$y = x^4 - 2x^3 - 12x^2$$
$$y' = 4x^3 - 6x^2 - 24x$$
$$y'' = 12x^2 - 12x - 24$$
$$= 12(x - 2)(x + 1)$$

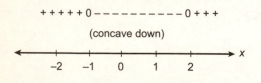

$$+ + + + + 0 - - - - - - - - - - 0 + + +$$

(concave down)

36. (A)

Factoring the left side of the equation, we get $(2\tan x - 3)(\tan x + 4) = 0$. If $2\tan x - 3 = 0$, $x = \text{Arctan}\left(\dfrac{3}{2}\right) \approx 56°$. If $\tan x + 4 = 0$, $x = \text{Arctan}(-4) \approx 104°$.

37. (D)

From a theorem, we know that a central angle is equal in measurement to the arc it intercepts. The arc measurement is given as

$$m\widehat{AB} = \frac{1}{5}\pi \text{ radians.}$$

Converting this to degrees, we obtain

$$\left(\frac{1}{5}\pi\right)\left(\frac{180}{\pi}\right) = 36°.$$

Note that points A, O, and B form a triangle. Two sides of this triangle are equal to the radius of the circle. Thus, they are equal sides, and $\triangle AOB$ is isosceles (we know that the base angles of an isosceles triangle are equal). The vertex angle is 36°, and there are 180° in a triangle. The relation that is set up is

$$36° + 2 \text{ (base angle)} = 180°.$$

Solving for the base angle:

$$\text{base angle } = \frac{180° - 36°}{2} = 72°.$$

Thus, $\angle OBA = 72°$.

38. (C)

If $\overline{PR}$ and $\overline{QS}$ are perpendicular bisectors of each other, then all four angles at T are right angles. By using the side-angle-side (SAS) theorem, it can be shown that all four nonoverlapping triangles are congruent to each other. Since corresponding parts of congruent triangles are congruent, $\overline{PQ} = \overline{QR} = \overline{RS} = \overline{SP}$. Thus, $PQRS$ must be a rhombus.

39. (D)

The first letter can be any of 24 letters from A through X. Once the first letter is selected, there is only one choice for each of the second letter and the third letter. The reason is because each of the second and third letters must follow the first letter, both alphabetically and in order. For example, if Q is the first letter, then R must be the second letter and S must be the third letter. There are 7 choices for the first digit, 6 choices for the second digit, and 5 choices for the third digit. The number of different ID badges is $(24)(1)(1)(7)(6)(5) = 5040$.

40. (D)

The observed values of the 4 flavors are: 49, 29, 17, and 5.

The expected values of the 4 flavors are: 40, 35, 15, and 10.

Note that the expected values are simply the percents multiplied by the actual number of people, which is 100.

The chi-square value is calculated by the formula

$$\sum \frac{(O_i - E_i)^2}{E_i},$$ where each O_i is an observed value

and each E_i is an expected value. Then, the chi-square value $= \frac{81}{40} + \frac{36}{35} + \frac{4}{15} + \frac{25}{10} \approx 5.82$

The next step would be to locate the critical chi-square value in a table. Here, the number of degrees of freedom is 3. (One less than the number of pairs of data.) At the 5% level of significance, the critical chi-square value is 7.815. Since $5.82 < 7.815$, the claim should not be rejected.

41. (C)

The definition of a Mercenne prime is any number of the form $2^n - 1$, where n is prime.

42. (B)

Two events A and B are mutually exclusive if $P(A \cap B) = 0$. The following formula applies to any two events A and B: $P(A \cup B) = P(A) + P(B) - P(A \cap B)$. Using the numbers from answer choice (B), $.75 = .40 + .35 - P(A \cap B)$. Solving, $P(A \cap B) = 0$. Answer choices (A), (C), and (D) are wrong because $P(A \cap B)$ does not equal zero.

Note: For choice (C), $P(A \cap B)$ *may* be zero, but is not necessarily zero.

43. (C)

Calculate $f(x)$ for the values of the variable given in each option as follows:

(A) $f(2) = 4mn, f(6) = 36mn, f(8) = 64mn$

(B) $f(1) = mn, f(2) = 4mn, f(3) = 9mn$

(C) $f(2) = 4mn, f(4) = 16mn, f(8) = 64mn$

(D) $f(3) = 9mn, f(5) = 25mn, f(7) = 49mn$

Among the options given, only terms of (C) form a geometric sequence, because $(16\,mn)^2 = (4mn)(64mn)$.

44. (C)

$$y = x^2 - 8x + 15$$

The above equation is of the general quadratic form:

$$f(x) = ax^2 + bx + c,$$

here $a = 1$, and $b = -8$.

$$x = \frac{-b}{2a}$$

is the equation for the axis of symmetry of the parabola. Hence $x = -\frac{8}{2} = 4$ is the x value at the turning point.

When $x = 4$, we find y to be:

$$y = 4^2 - 8(4) + 15 = -1.$$

Hence the coordinates of the turning point are $(4, -1)$.

45. (C)

Let x = length of $\overline{KL}$. An angle bisector always divides the side to which it is drawn into two parts whose ratio is equal to the ratio of the two sides forming the angle bisector. So, $\dfrac{8}{10} = \dfrac{6}{x}$. Then $8x = 60$, and $x = 7.5$.

46. (A)

The period of a function given by $y = A \sin Bx + C$, where A, B, C are constants is $\dfrac{2\pi}{B} = \dfrac{2\pi}{\left(\frac{2}{3}\right)} = 3\pi$.

47. (C)

The number $\dfrac{7}{3}$ is divided by $\dfrac{1}{4}$, which requires using the reciprocal of $\dfrac{1}{4}$.

48. (C)

First determine where the graphs $y = x^2$ and $y = 2x + 3$ intersect.

$$x^2 = 2x + 3$$
$$x^2 - 2x - 3 = 0$$
$$(x - 3)(x + 1) = 0$$
$$x = 3, -1$$
$$A = \int_{-1}^{3} \left(2x + 3 - x^2\right) dx$$
$$= \int_{-1}^{3} \left\{(2x + 3) - x^2\right\} dx$$
$$= \left(x^2 + 3x - \frac{1}{3}x^3\right)\Bigg|_{-1}^{3}$$
$$= 3^2 - (-1)^2 + 3(3 - (-1)) - \frac{1}{3}(3^3 - (-1)^3)$$
$$= 9 - 1 + 3(4) - \frac{1}{3}(27 + 1)$$
$$= 20 - \frac{28}{3}$$
$$= \frac{32}{3}$$

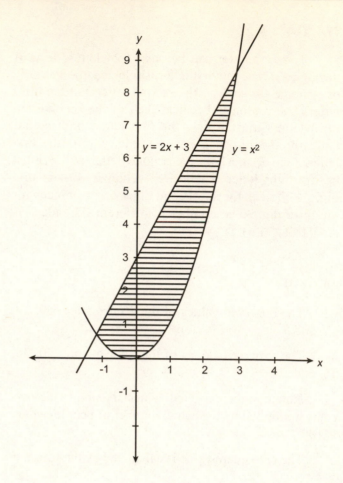

49. (D)

$f(-2) = (-2 - 2)^2 = (-4)^2 = 16$. Then $g(16) = 16^2 - 2 = 256 - 2 = 254$.

50. (B)

The slope of the graph of $5x + 6y = 24$ is $-\dfrac{5}{6}$, so the slope of the graph of $px - 4y = 12$ must be $\dfrac{6}{5}$. Then $\dfrac{6}{5} = \dfrac{p}{4}$. Solving, $p = \dfrac{24}{5} = 4.8$.

51. (A)

A function is symmetric with respect to the origin if replacing x by $-x$ and y by $-y$ produces an equivalent function.

(I) $y = f(x) = x^3 - x$

$(-y) = (-x)^3 - (-x)$

$-y = -x^3 + x$

$y = x^3 - x$

(I) is symmetric.

(II) $y = f(x) = 2x + x^5$

$-y = 2(-x) + (-x)^5$

$-y = -2x - x^5$

$y = 2x + x^5$

(II) is symmetric.

(III) $y = f(x) = 2x + 4$

$-y = 2(-x) + 4$

$-y = -2x + 4$

$y = 2x - 4$

(III) is not symmetric.

52. (B)

The equation $x^n + y^n = z^n$, where x, y, z, and n are positive integers, has solutions only if $n \le 2$. For $n > 2$, solutions are possible only if at least one of x, y, z is equal to zero.

53. (D)

Using the formula $\sin(x + y) = (\sin x)(\cos y) + (\sin y)(\cos x)$, we get $0.9 = (0.3)(0.8) + (\sin y)(\cos x)$. This simplifies to $(\sin y)(\cos x) = 0.66$. Thus, $(2)(\sin y)(\cos x) = 1.32$.

54. (A)

In a table of t values, using the number of degrees of freedom as 7 you would find that the critical t values are 2.365. The test value of t is given by the formula $t = \dfrac{(\bar{x} - \mu)}{\left(\frac{s}{\sqrt{n}}\right)}$, where $\bar{x}$ is the sample mean, μ is the

population mean, s is the sample standard deviation, and n is the size of the sample. By substitution,

$$t = \frac{(28,000 - 30,000)}{\left(\frac{1500}{\sqrt{8}}\right)} \approx -3.77.$$ Since $-3.77 < -2.65$,

the claim should be rejected.

55. (D)

The normal line is the line that is perpendicular to the curve at the given point. Its equation is $y = y_0 + m(x - x_0)$ where (x_0, y_0) is the given point and m is the slope. At the point where $x = 1$,

$y = x^4 - 3x^2 + 1$

$= (1)^4 - 3(1)^2 + 1$

$= -1$

Thus, $(x_0, y_0) = (1, -1)$. The slope m of the normal line is the negative reciprocal of the slope of the tangent line, which is the value of the derivative at the given point;

i.e., $\quad m = \dfrac{-1}{\left.\dfrac{dy}{dx}\right|_{x=1}}$

Since $\dfrac{dy}{dx} = \dfrac{d}{dx}(x^4 - 3x^2 + 1)$

$= 4x^3 - 6x,$

$m = \dfrac{-1}{\left. (4x^3 - 6x) \right|_{x=1}}$

$= \dfrac{-1}{(4 - 6)}$

$= \dfrac{-1}{-2}$

$= \dfrac{1}{2}$

Thus, the equation of the normal line is:

$$y = y_0 + m(x - x_0)$$
$$y = -1 + \frac{1}{2}(x - 1)$$
$$2y = -2 + (x - 1)$$
$$2y = x - 3$$
$$x - 2y - 3 = 0$$

56. (D)

The area of the first square = 9, the area of the second square = $\left(\dfrac{1}{9}\right)(9) = 1$. Each subsequent square will have an area equal to $\dfrac{1}{9}$ of its predecessor. The tenth term is given by $(9)\left(\dfrac{1}{9}\right)^9 = 9^{-8}$.

57. (C)

The slope of the line segment connecting $(2, 5)$ and $(0, 1)$, which is 2, must equal the slope of the line segment connecting $(7, 1)$ and (b, c). Thus, $2 = \dfrac{(c - 1)}{(b - 7)}$. This becomes $2b - 14 = c - 1$, so $c = 2b - 13$. Another approach would be to realize that the segment connecting $(0, 1)$ and $(7, 1)$ has a distance of 7 and a slope of zero. This would mean that point (b, c) is really $(2 + 7, 5) = (9, 5)$. This would match the relationship shown in answer choice (C), since $5 = (2)(9) - 13$.

58. (C)

By definition, since $f(x)$ is continuous on the closed interval $[c, d]$, the integral of $f(x)$ over some interval within $[c, d]$, which is denoted by $F(x)$, must be defined and differentiable at each x.

59. (A)

Because 88 faculty members represent the age bracket 30 to 39, there must be a total of $\dfrac{88}{0.20} = 440$ faculty members. The age bracket 40 to 49 represents $100\% - 30\% - 35\% - 20\% - 5\% = 10\%$ of the total, so that 45% of the faculty is at least 40 years old. (Total of the age brackets 40 to 49, 50 to 59, and over 59). Thus, $(440)(0.45) = 198$ faculty members are at least 40 years old.

60. (B)

The sum of their multiplicative inverses is $\dfrac{1}{2} + \dfrac{1}{3} = \dfrac{5}{6}$. The multiplicative inverse of their sum is $\dfrac{1}{(3 + 2)} = \dfrac{1}{5}$. Then $\dfrac{5}{6} - \dfrac{1}{5} = \dfrac{19}{30}$.

61. (B)

All that is given is $\overline{AC} = \overline{CE}$ and $\overline{AB} = \overline{DE}$. It may be tempting to look at the figure and draw other conclusions (such as "$\triangle ACE$ looks like an equilateral triangle" or "$\overline{BE}$ and $\overline{AD}$ look like angle bisectors"). By working with only the information given, we can see that $\triangle ABE$ and $\triangle AED$ are congruent because they have a Side-Angle-Side relationship. Therefore, corresponding angles $\angle ABE \cong \angle EDA$. The other two statements are not necessarily true.

62. (D)

$$f(x) = e^{\frac{x^3}{3} - x}$$

$$\Rightarrow f'(x) = (x^2 - 1)e^{\frac{x^3}{3} - x},$$ by the chain rule.

We see $f(x) = e^{\frac{x^3}{3} - x} > 0$ for every real number x, and $x^2 - 1 = (x + 1)(x - 1)$

$$\Rightarrow x^2 - 1 < 0 \text{ when } x \in (-1, 1) \text{ and}$$
$$x^2 - 1 > 0 \text{ when } |x| > 1.$$

Hence,

$$f'(x) = (x^2 - 1)e^{\frac{x^3}{3} - x} < 0 \text{ for } x \in (-1, 1) \text{ and}$$

$$f'(x) = (x^2 - 1)e^{\frac{x^3}{3} - x} > 0 \text{ for } |x| > 1.$$

(D) is the answer.

63. (A)

Find the *y*-axis. Find the side of the figure closest to the *y*-axis and measure the distance that this side is from the *y*-axis. A reflection of the figure will put this side the same distance from the *y*-axis, but on the other side.

Also, notice the point labeled *C*. A reflection of this point across the *y*-axis will also be the same distance from the *y*-axis, but on the other side.

64. (A)

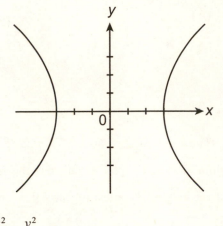

$$\frac{x^2}{9} - \frac{y^2}{9} = 1$$

is an equation of the form:

$$\frac{x^2}{a^2} - \frac{y^2}{b^2} = 1$$

with $a = 3$ and $b = 3$.

Therefore the graph is a hyperbola. The *x*-intercepts are found by setting $y = 0$:

$$\frac{x^2}{9} - \frac{0^2}{9} = 1$$
$$x^2 = 9$$
$$x = \pm 3.$$

Thus, the *x*-intercepts are at $(-3, 0)$ and $(3, 0)$. There are no *y*-intercepts since for $x = 0$ there are no real values of *y* satisfying the equation.

65. (D)

The current number of teachers at this school is $\frac{900}{25} = 36$. If the teacher-student ratio is changed to 1:15, there would be $\frac{900}{15} = 60$ teachers. Thus, $60 - 36 = 24$ additional teachers are needed.

66. (B)

If *k* is a nonzero constant, then $P = \frac{k\sqrt{Q}}{R^3}$ would represent the given relationship. To solve for *Q*, multiply both sides by R^3 to get $PR^3 = k\sqrt{Q}$. Divide by *k* to get $\frac{PR^3}{k} = \sqrt{Q}$. Now square both sides to get $\frac{(PR^3)^2}{k^2} = (\sqrt{Q})^2$, which can be written as $\frac{1}{k^2}(P^2R^6) = Q$. Note that $\frac{1}{k^2}$ is simply another constant. Thus, *Q* varies directly as the square of *P* and the sixth power of *R*.

67. (C)

Given an external point from a circle, two tangents drawn to the circle from that point must be equal. So $PQ = PW$, $QR = RS$, $ST = TU$, $UV = VW$. Then $PQ + QR + TU + UV$ must represent one-half the perimeter of *PRTU*, or 14. By substitution, we get $PR + TV = 14$. Note that *PRTV* is not any specific kind of quadrilateral.

68. (D)

The sum of n terms in arithmetic series with first term t_1, and common difference d is given by

$$S_n = \frac{n}{2}[2t_1 + (n-1)d]$$

In this problem $S_n = 100$, $n = 50$, $d = 2$, thus,

$$100 = \frac{50}{2}(2t_1 + (50-1)2)$$
$$100 = 25(2t_1 + 98)$$
$$\frac{100}{25} = 2t_1 + 98$$
$$4 = 2t_1 + 98$$
$$2t_1 = 4 - 98 = -94$$
$$t_1 = -\frac{94}{2} = -47$$

69. (A)

Anna's salary three years ago was ($30,000)(1.05)^3 \approx \$34,728.75$, whereas Marty's salary three years ago was ($50,000)/(1.05)^3 \approx \$43,191.88$. To the nearest dollar, the difference between these two numbers is $8,463.

70. (C)

The domain is determined solely by the denominator. If the denominator is not zero, then the function has a real value. Thus, $2x^2 - x - 15 = 0$ will yield the excluded values of x. $2x^2 - x - 15 = (2x + 5)(x - 3)$. Solving $2x + 5 = 0$ yields $x = -\frac{5}{2}$. Solving $x - 3 = 0$ yields $x = 3$. These two numbers represent the excluded values of the domain.

71. (B)

Because $\angle MLN = 110°$, $\angle MRQ = 70°$. A theorem states that $\angle MRQ = \left(\frac{1}{2}\right)(\overset{\frown}{QM} + \overset{\frown}{NP})$. Let arc $NP = x°$. Then $70 = \left(\frac{1}{2}\right)(50 + x)$. Simplifying, $70 = 25 + \left(\frac{1}{2}\right)x$, and thus $x = (70 - 25)(2) = 90$.

72. (A)

$6^n = (2^n)(3^n) = xy$. However, $6^{n-1} = \frac{6^n}{6} = \frac{xy}{6}$.

73. (A)

The total surface area of a cone is given by the formula $A = \pi rs + \pi r^2$, where r is the radius and s is the slant height. By substitution, $70 = (\pi)(2)(s) + 4\pi$. Solving, $s = \frac{(70 - 4\pi)}{2\pi} \approx 9.14$.

74. (A)

The probability for the experiment in choice (A) is $\left(\frac{4}{52}\right)\left(\frac{3}{51}\right)$, which reduces to $\frac{1}{221}$. For choice (B), the probability would be $\left(\frac{4}{52}\right)\left(\frac{4}{52}\right) = \frac{1}{169}$. For choice (C), the probability would be $\left(\frac{2}{17}\right)\left(\frac{1}{16}\right) = \frac{1}{136}$. For choice (D), the probability would be $\left(\frac{2}{30}\right)\left(\frac{2}{30}\right) = \frac{1}{225}$.

75. (D)

The correct answer is 5.

The slope of any tangent line to this curve is given by $\frac{dy}{dx} = 2x + 11$. Substituting $x = -3$, $\frac{dy}{dx} = 5$.

76. (D)

Let R_1 represent the radius of the cylinder, let R_2 represent the radius of the sphere, and let H represent the height of the cylinder. Then $\pi R_1^2 H = \left(\frac{4}{3}\right)\pi R_2^3$. Since $H = 2R_1$, we can rewrite this equation as $(\pi R_1^2)(2R_1) = \left(\frac{4}{3}\right)\pi R_2^3$. Simplifying, we get $2\pi R_1^3 = \left(\frac{4}{3}\right)\pi R_2^3$. Then $\frac{R_2^3}{R_1^3} = \frac{2}{\left(\frac{4}{3}\right)} = \frac{3}{2}$.

77. (B)

A parallelogram has neither a horizontal nor vertical line of symmetry. Choice (A) is wrong because a perpendicular line from the vertex to the base would be a vertical line of symmetry. Choices (C) and (D) are wrong because a vertical line through the center or horizontal line through the center would be a vertical or horizontal line of symmetry, respectively.

78. (B)

The rational numbers under the operation of division is not closed, so it is not a group. As an example, $\frac{5}{0}$ is undefined.

79. (C)

$$-1 + i = \sqrt{2}\left[\cos\left(\frac{3\pi}{4}\right) + i\sin\left(\frac{3\pi}{4}\right)\right].$$

So $(-1 + i)^{10} = \sqrt{2}^{10}\left[\cos\left(\frac{15\pi}{2}\right) + i\sin\left(\frac{15\pi}{2}\right)\right]$

$$= \sqrt{2}^{10}\left(\frac{-1}{\sqrt{2}} + (i)\frac{1}{\sqrt{2}}\right)$$

$$= -\left(\frac{2^5}{\sqrt{2}}\right) + (i)\left(\frac{2^5}{\sqrt{2}}\right) = -16\sqrt{2} + 16i\sqrt{2}.$$

80. (B)

The term of this expanded expression that contains x^{16} is $(_{20}C_4)(x^{16})(3y)^4 = 392{,}445x^{16}y^4$.

Note: $_{20}C_4 = \frac{[(20)(19)(18)(17)]}{[(4)(3)(2)(1)]} = 4845.$

81. (A)

$8^3 = (2^3)^3 = 2^9, 35 = (5)(7), 27^2 = (3^3)^2 = 3^6$. Thus, the original number can be written as $(2^9)(5^1)(7^1)(3^6)$. The total number of factors is found by adding 1 to each exponent of the prime factorization, then multiplying. We get $(9 + 1)(1 + 1)(1 + 1)(6 + 1) = 280$.

82. (B)

Two planes perpendicular to the same plane may intersect, but they need not be perpendicular to each other. Only lines in space may be skew to each other.

Note: P and R may be parallel to each other.

83. (B)

The formula for the sum of an infinite geometric series is $S = \frac{A}{(1 - R)}$, where A = the first term and R = the common ratio. In this example, $A = 1.8$ and R is unknown. By substitution, $4.5 = \frac{1.8}{(1 - R)}$. Then $1 - R = \frac{1.8}{4.5} = 0.4$. So, $R = 0.6$. The second term must be $(1.8)(0.6) = 1.08$ and the third term must be $(1.08)(0.6) = 0.648$. So, the sum of the first three terms is $1.8 + 1.08 + 0.648 = 3.528$.

84. (D)

If a point located at (x, y) is rotated 90° clockwise about the origin, its new location is given by $(y, -x)$. Thus, the point $(2, -3)$ becomes $(-3, -2)$.

85. (C)

The term in the first row, first column is given by $(3)(1) + (2)(2) + (-1)(-2) = 9$. The term in the second row, first column is given by $(-2)(1) + (1)(2) + (0)(-2) = 0$. The term in the first row, second column is given by $(3)(-3) + (2)(1) + (-1)(-1) + -6$. The term in the second row, second column is given by $(-2)(-3) + (1)(1) + (0)(-1) = 7$.

86. (D)

The maximum value of $a - b$ can be determined by finding the largest value of a and the smallest value of b. Since $19 - a$ is a multiple of 3 and $a < 19$, the largest value of a is 16. Since $27 - b$ is a multiple of 4 and $b < 19$, the smallest value of b is 3. Finally, $a - b = 16 - 3 = 13$.

87. (B)

In choice (B), when $x = -2$, $y = 10$, and when $x = 4$, $y = 46$. The average rate of change is $\frac{(46 - 10)}{(4 - [-2])} = \frac{36}{6} = 6$. For choice (A), the average rate of change is $\frac{(65 - 17)}{(4 - [-2])} = 8$. For choice (C), the average rate of change is $\frac{(35 - 11)}{(4 - [-2])} = 4$. For choice (D), the average rate of change is $\frac{(12 - 0)}{(4 - [-2])} = 2$.

88. (B)

By substitution, $40 = (100)\frac{[B + (0.5)(8)]}{60}$. Then $2400 = 100B + 400$. Solving, $B = 20$. We now know that there are twenty numbers below 45 and eight numbers equal to 45. Thus, there must be $60 - 20 - 8 = 32$ numbers greater than 45.

89. (C)

Since no elements of P are elements of N, P and M also share no elements. There are $45 - 25 = 20$ elements in the universal set not belonging to M or N, and this is the maximum number of elements in P.

90. (C)

Since $(-7, -1)$ represents the image of point P, we need to reverse the order for finding each of the coordinates of P. Mathematically, $x - 4 = -7$ and $y + 8 = -1$. Solving, $x = -3$ and $y = -9$.

91. (D)

If a rational function $f(x) = \frac{P(x)}{Q(x)}$ has no horizontal asymptote, then the degree of $P(x)$ must be greater than the degree of $Q(x)$. In choice (D), the degree of $P(x)$ is 3, whereas the degree of $Q(x)$ is 2. Thus, there is no horizontal asymptote. For choice (A), the degree of $P(x)$ equals the degree of $Q(x)$; its horizontal asymptote is $y = \frac{3}{4}$. For each of choices (B) and (C), the degree of $P(x)$ is less than the degree of $Q(x)$; the horizontal asymptote for each of these answer choices is $y = 0$.

92. (A)

$|v| = \sqrt{5^2 + (-12)^2} = \sqrt{169} = 13$. A unit vector in the direction of y is $\left\langle \frac{5}{13}, -\frac{12}{13} \right\rangle$. Thus, a vector that has a length of $\frac{1}{2}$ unit in this direction is $\left\langle \frac{5}{26}, -\frac{6}{13} \right\rangle$.

93. (B)

$(x +3y)^2 = x^2 + 6xy + 9y^2 = 100$. Also, $(3x + y)^2 = 9x^2 + 6xy + y^2 = 196$. By subtraction, $8x^2 - 8y^2 = 96$. Then, $x^2 - y^2 = 12$. Therefore, $\left(\dfrac{1}{3}\right)(x^2 - y^2) = 4$.

94. (B)

The number of ways of arranging all the math books first, all the history books second, and all the English books last is $(4!)(2!)(3!) = 288$. However, there are $(3)(2)(1) = 6$ different ways to arrange the ordering of these three subjects. Thus there are $(6)(288) = 1{,}728$ ways of arranging the nine books so that all books of the same subject are together.

95. (C)

Since $\log_3\left(\dfrac{1}{27}\right) = x$, $3^x = \dfrac{1}{27} = 3^{-3}$. So $x=-3$. So $y^x = y^{-3} = \dfrac{1}{y^3} = -64$, and $\dfrac{1}{y} = -4$, which means that $y = -\dfrac{1}{4}$. Let $\log_{\frac{9}{16}} xy = z$. Then, $\log_{\frac{9}{16}}\left(\dfrac{3}{4}\right) =z$. So, $\left(\dfrac{9}{16}\right)^z = \left(\dfrac{3}{4}\right)^{2z} = \left(\dfrac{3}{4}\right)$. Therefore, $2z = 1$, and $z = \dfrac{1}{2}$.

96. (D)

Since Z varies jointly as W and X, $Z = kWX$ for some constant k. By substitution, $18 = (k)(9)(3)$, so $k = \dfrac{18}{27} = \dfrac{2}{3}$. Now we know that $Z = \left(\dfrac{2}{3}\right) WX$. Again, by substitution, $15 = \left(\dfrac{2}{3}\right)(W)\left(\dfrac{1}{3}\right)$. Simplifying, $15 = \left(\dfrac{2}{9}\right) W$, so $W = (15)\left(\dfrac{9}{2}\right) = 67.5$.

97. (C)

Rewrite the equation as $(x^2 + 8x + 16) + (y^2 + 12y + 36) = -3 + 16 + 36$. Then, $(x + 4)^2 + (y + 6)^2 = 49$. A circle with this equation will have a center at $(-4, -6)$ and a radius of $\sqrt{49} = 7$. Thus, its area is $(\pi)(7)^2 = 49\pi$.

98. (B)

Since both $2 - i$ and $4 + i$ are zeros of $g(x)$, their conjugates, $2 + i$ and $4 - i$, respectively, must also be zeros of $g(x)$. This means that there are 4 complex zeros of $g(x)$, so there can only be a maximum of 1 real zero because $g(x)$ is of degree 5.

99. (C)

For polynomial functions, vertical asymptotes are found by setting the denominator equal to zero. Since, $x^3 + 3x^2 + 2x + 6 = (x^2 +2)(x + 3)$, the vertical asymptotes would be found using the equations $x^2 + 2 = 0$ and $x + 3 = 0$. The first of these equations has no real solution, and the second equation has the solution $x = -3$. Choice (A) is wrong because the denominator factors as $(x + 3)(2x - 1)$, so it has vertical asymptotes of $x = -3$ and $x = \dfrac{1}{2}$. Choice (B) is wrong because the denominator factors as $(x)(x - 3)(x + 3)$, so it has vertical asymptotes of $x = 0$, $x = 3$, and $x = -3$. Choice (D) is wrong because its denominator has no real roots, so it has no vertical asymptotes.

100. (B)

The acceleration is found by determining the second derivative of this function. The first derivative, denoted as $s'(t)$, is $3t^2 + 8t$. The second derivative, denoted as $s''(t)$, is $6t + 8$. Substituting $t = 5$, we get $(6)(5) + 8 = 38$.

101.

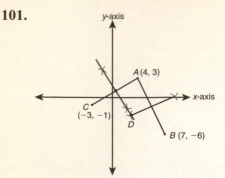

- Draw line segments $\overline{AC}$ and $\overline{AB}$. Construct the perpendicular bisector of each of these segments, as shown above. The point of intersection, D, of these perpendicular bisectors is equidistant from A, B, and C. Point D is the center of the circle which contains points A, B, and C.

- The equation of $\overline{AC}$ can be determined as $y = \left(\dfrac{4}{7}\right)x + \dfrac{5}{7}$. The perpendicular bisector of $\overline{AC}$ would have a slope of $-\dfrac{7}{4}$ and would pass through the midpoint of $\overline{AC}$, which is $(0.5, 1)$; its equation would be given by $y = \left(-\dfrac{7}{4}\right)x + \dfrac{15}{8}$.

Likewise, the equation of $\overline{AB}$ can be determined as $y = -3x + 15$. The perpendicular bisector of $\overline{AB}$ would have a slope of $\dfrac{1}{3}$ and would pass through the midpoint of $\overline{AB}$, which is $(5.5, -1.5)$; its equation would be given by $y = \left(\dfrac{1}{3}\right)x - \dfrac{10}{3}$.

We need to find the intersection of these two perpendicular bisectors. We can write $\left(-\dfrac{7}{4}\right)x + \dfrac{15}{8} = \left(\dfrac{1}{3}\right)x - \dfrac{10}{3}$. Multiplying this equation by 24, we get $-42x + 45 = 8x$

$- 80$. Solving, $x = 2.5$. We can now determine that using either of these two equations $y = -2.5$

- The clubhouse is located at $(2.5, -2.5)$.

- We need to find the distance between D and any of A, B, or C. The distance between A and D equals $\sqrt{(4-2.5)^2 + (3+2.5)^2} = \sqrt{32.5} \approx 5.7$. So, the length of the walkway between A and D is $(20)(5.7) = 114$ feet, and its area is $(114)(4) = 456$ square feet. The cost of this walkway is $(\$15)(456) = \$6840$. Since three walkways will be constructed, the total cost is $\$20,520$.

Another possible solution for the second bullet.

Let (x, y) represent the point which is equidistant from points A, B, and C. The distance from A to $D = \sqrt{(x-4)^2 + (y-3)^2}$ and the distance from B to $D = \sqrt{(x-7)^2 + (y+6)^2}$. Equating these distances and squaring both sides, we get $x^2 - 8x + 16 + y^2 - 6y + 9 = x^2 - 14x + 49 + y^2 + 12y + 36$. This simplifies to $6x - 18y = 60$, or $x - 3y = 10$. The distance from C to $D = \sqrt{(x+3)^2 + (y+1)^2}$. Equating this distance with the distance from A to D and squaring both sides, we get $x^2 - 8x + 16 + y^2 - 6y + 9 = x^2 + 6x + 9 + y^2 + 12y + 36$. This simplifies to $14x + 8y = 15$. Solving the equations $x - 3y = 10$ and $14x + 8y = 15$ simultaneously, we get $x = 2.5$ and $y = -2.5$. Thus, the clubhouse is located at $(2.5, -2.5)$.

102.

- At the Sleep-Easy Motel, 4 nights would cost $(4)(90)(1.08) - 40 = \$348.80$.

- At the Rest-Well Motel, 4 nights would cost $(4)(90-10)(1.08) = \$345.60$.

- One night at the Sleep-Easy costs, $(90)(1.08) - 10 = 87.20$. Let x = dollar discount at Rest-Well. Then: $(90 - x)(1.08) = 87.20$. Solving, $x = \$9.26$, approximately.

- The actual coordinates for the Rest-Well Motel include:

  $(1, 86.4), (2, 172.8), (3, 259.2), (4, 345.6)$.

  The actual coordinates for the Sleep-Easy Motel include:

  $(1, 87.2), (2, 174.4), (3, 261.6), (4, 348.8)$.

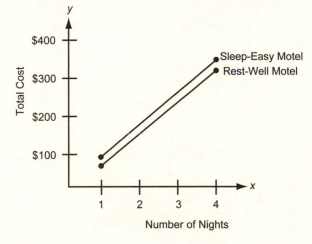

Index

A

absolute inequality, 55
absolute value, 13–14, 80
  absolute value equations, 54
acute angle, 81
acute triangle, 98
addition
  addition property of inequality, 56
  and subtraction formulas, 146
  associative property of, 27
  closure property of, 26
  commutative property of, 27
  identity property of, 27
  inverse property of, 28
adjacent angles, 81
algebra vocabulary, 33
  algebraic expressions, simplifying, 36–38
  binomial, 33
  coefficient, 33
  constant, 33
  expression, 33
  monomial, 33
  polynomial, 33
  trinomial, 33
  variable, 33
altitude of triangle, 99
angle bisector of a triangle, 100
angle difference postulate, 87
angle sum postulate, 86
angles, 79–90
  acute angle, 81
  adjacent angles, 81
  complementary angles, 82
  congruent angles, 82
  obtuse angle, 82
  reflex angle, 82
  right angle, 81
  straight angle, 82
  supplementary angles, 82
  vertical angles, 81
angles and trigonometric functions, 143–144
  addition and subtraction formulas, 146
  basic identities, 145–146
  cosine, 143
  cotangent, 143
  double-angle formulas, 146
  half-angle formulas, 146
  inverse trigonometric functions, 148–149
  product formulas of sines and cosines, 147
  sine, 143
  sum and difference formulas, 147
  tangent, 143
antiderivatives, 163
antidifferentiation, power rule for, 163
arc of the circle, 108
area
  of a circle, 110
  of a triangle, 99
arithmetic mean, definition of, 132
associative property
  of addition, 27
  of multiplication, 27

B

bar graph, 123
base of the triangle, 97
bell-shaped or symmetrical curve, 127–128
binomial, 33
bisector of a line segment, 81
box-and-whiskers plot, 125–126

C

calculator usage, 5
calculus
  fundamental theorem of, 166
  limits, 154–155, *see also separate entry*
Cartesian coordinate system, 65
central angle, 109
central tendency, measures of, 132–134
  definition of the mode, 134
  median, definition, 135
chord of the circle, 108
circles, 108–112
  arc of, 108
  area of, 110
  central angle, 109
  chord of, 108
  circumference of, 109
  circumscribed circle, 109
  concentric circles, 110
  congruent circles, 109

diameter of, 108

inscribed angle, 109

line of centers, 108

point of tangency, 109

radius of, 108

secant, 108

closure property

of addition, 27

of multiplication, 27

coefficient, 33

collinear points, 79

combinations, 170

commutative property

of addition, 27

of multiplication, 27

complementary angles, 82

complex fraction, 17

complex numbers, 28–29

imaginary part, 28

real part, 28

composite function, 62

computing methods, of probabilities, 130–131

addition, 130

dependent events, 131

independent events, 130

multiplication, 130

mutually exclusive events, 130

nonmutually exclusive events, 130

concentric circles, 110

concurrent lines, 100

conditional inequality, 55

congruent angles, 82

and congruent line segments, 90–94

definitions, 90

postulates, 91

theorems, 90–91

congruent circles, 109

congruent segments, 80

constant, 33

continuity, 154–156

theorems of, 155–156

coordinate geometry, 115–116

coordinate axes, 115

horizontal axis, 115

vertical axis, 115

coplanar points, 81

correlation, 127

negative correlation, 127

positive correlation, 127

zero correlation, 127

cosine, 143

cotangent, 143

counting, 168–171

combinations, 170

factorial notation, 169

permutations, 169–170

principle of, 168

sampling and counting, 169

tree diagrams, 168–169

cubes, cylinders, 112

D

data analysis, statistics and probability, 123–142

graphs, 123–127, *see also separate entry*

probability, 129, *see also separate entry*

day of the MTEL Mathematics test, 7–8

after the test, 8

before the test, 7

during the test, 8

decimals, 18–19

decimal point, 18

operations with decimals, 18–19, *see also separate entry*

definite integral, 164

antiderivatives, 163

antidifferentiation, power rule for, 163

fundamental theorem, definition of, 163

mean value theorem for integrals, 166

denominator, 14

dependent equations, 41

dependent variable, 61

derivative, 156–163

at a point, 158–159

definition and Δ-method, 156–157

rate of change and related rates, 162–163

rectilinear motion, 160–162

rules for finding the derivatives, 159–160

diameter of the circle, 108

discrete/finite mathematics, 167, 172–173

sequences, 172–173

series, 172

sets, 167–168

dispersion of the data, 138

distributive property, 28

domain, 61

double-angle formulas, 146

E

elementary functions, 61–63
  composite function, 62
  dependent variable, 61
  domain, 61
  function, 61
  independent variable, 61
  inverse of a function, 62
  range, 61
equality, real number properties of, 27
  reflexive property, 27
  symmetric property, 27
  transitive property, 27
equilateral triangle, 97
equivalent inequalities, 56
estimation, 25–26
even integers, 12
exponential function, 63
exponents, 22–24
  base, 22
  exponent or power, 22
  general laws of, 23
  power of a power, 24
expression, 33
exterior angle of a triangle, 100

F

factoring, 15
  prime factor, 15
fractions, 14–17
  complex fraction, 17
  denominator, 14
  improper fraction, 14
  mixed number, 14
  numerator, 14
  operations with fractions, 14–17, *see also separate entry*
frequency curves, types, 127–129
  bell-shaped or symmetrical, 127
  J-shaped curve, 128
  multimodal (bimodal) frequency curve, 128
  skewed to the left (negative skew), 128
  skewed to the right (positive skew), 128
  U-shaped curve, 128
function, 61
fundamental theorem, 166–167

G

geometry and measurement, 79–121
  circles, 100–103, *see also separate entry*
  congruent angles and congruent line segments, 90–94
  coordinate geometry, 115–116
  definitions, 79–83
  postulates, 84–87
  quadrilaterals, 103–107, *see also separate entry*
  solid geometry, 112–115, *see also separate entry*
  theorems, 87–90
graphs, 41, 123–126, *see also* correlation; frequency curves
  bar graph, 123–125
  box-and-whiskers plot, 125–126
  graphing a function, 65–67
    Cartesian coordinate system, 65
    drawing the graph, 65–67
  polynomial functions and their graphs, 67–70
  rational functions and their graphs, 68–69
  scatter-plot, 126–127
  special functions and their graphs, 69–70
  stem-and-leaf plot, 126
greatest common divisor (GCD), 15
greatest common factor (GCF), 36

H

half-angle formulas, 146
half-line, 79

I

identity property
  of addition, 27
  of multiplication, 27
imaginary part, of complex numbers, 28
improper fraction, 14
independent variable, 61
inequalities, 55–57
  absolute inequality, 55
  addition property of, 56
  conditional inequality, 55
  equivalent inequalities, 56
  properties of, 56
inscribed angle, 109
integers, 11–12
  even integers, 12
  odd integers, 12
intercept form of a linear equation, 39

interquartile range, 138–139
intersecting planes, 112
inverse of a function, 62
inverse property
  of addition, 28
  of multiplication, 28
inverse trigonometric functions, 148–149
irrational numbers, 12–13
isosceles trapezoid, 106
isosceles triangle, 97

J

J-shaped curve, 128

L

least common multiple (LCM), 36
limits, 154–155
  continuity, 154–155
  definition, 154
line of centers, 108
line postulate, 84
line segment, 79
  length of, 80
  perpendicular bisector of, 82
  projection of, 83
linear equations, 38
  and matrices, 173–176
  in two variables are always straight lines, 173
  intercept form of, 39
  slope-intercept form of, 39
  two linear equations, 41–44, *see also separate entry*
  two-point form of, 39
linear pair, 82
lines, 79–90
  perpendicular lines, 82
logarithms and exponential functions and equations, 63
lowest common denominator, (LCD), 15

M

matrices, 173–176
mean value theorem for integrals, 166
median
  definition, 135
  of the triangle, 99
midline of the triangle, 100
midpoint of a segment, 80

mixed number, 14
mode, definition of, 134
monomial, 33
multimodal (bimodal) frequency curve, 128
multiplication
  associative property of, 27
  closure property of, 27
  commutative property of, 27
  identity property of, 27
  inverse property of, 28
mutually exclusive events, 130

N

natural numbers, 11
negative numbers, 11
non-mutually exclusive events, 130
number sense and operations, 32
  absolute value, 13–14
  decimals, 18–19, *see also separate entry*
  estimation, 25–26
  fractions, 14–17, *see also separate entry*
  numbers, 11–13, *see also separate entry*
  operations, order of, 14
  percentages, 19–21
  radicals, 21–22, *see also separate entry*
  scientific notation, 24
  significant digits, 26–27
numbers, 11–13
  complex numbers, 28–29, *see also separate entry*
  equivalent forms of, 20–21
    decimal to a fraction conversion, 20
    fraction to a decimal conversion, 20
    number to a percent conversion, 20
    percent to a decimal conversion, 20
  natural numbers, 11
  negative numbers, 11
  prime numbers, 12
  rational and irrational numbers, 12–13
  real numbers, 11–12
  whole numbers, 11
numerator, 14

O

obtuse angle, 82
obtuse triangle, 98
odd integers, 12

operations
  order of, 14
  with decimals, 18–19
    to add numbers containing decimals, 18
    to divide numbers with decimals, 18
    to multiply numbers with decimals, 18
  with fractions, 14–17
    improper fraction to a mixed number, 17
    mixed number to an improper fraction, 16
    product of two or more fractions, 16
    quotient of two fractions, 16
    simplify a fraction, 16
    sum of the two fractions having different
      denominators, 15
    sum of two fractions having a common
      denominator, 14
  with radicals, 22
    to add two or more radicals, 22
    to divide radicals, 22
    to multiply two or more radicals, 22
opposite rays, 80

P

parallel lines, 83
parallelograms, 103
parameters, 140
patterns, relations, and algebra, 33–77
percentages, 19–20
  number, equivalent forms of, 21–21, *see also separate entry*
percentiles, 138–139
perimeter of a triangle, 97
periodicity, 147
perpendicular bisector, 82, 100
perpendicular lines, 82
plane postulate, 86
plane separation postulate, 86
points, 79–90
  distance between those two points, 80
  point betweenness postulate, 84
  point of tangency, 109
  point uniqueness postulate, 84
  points-in-a-plane postulate, 86
  point-slope form, 39
  projection of a given point, 83
polygons
  apothem and radius of, 95
  equiangular polygon, 94

equilateral polygon, 94
  regular polygons (convex), 94–95, *see also separate entry*
  similar polygons, 95–96, *see also separate entry*
polynomials, 33
  operations with, 33–36
    addition, 33
    division of a monomial by a monomial, 34
    division of a polynomial by a polynomial, 34
    multiplication of a polynomial by a monomial, 34
    multiplication of a polynomial by a polynomial, 34
    multiplication of two or more, 34
    subtraction, 34
  polynomial functions and their graphs, 67
population parameters, 140
prime factor, 15, 36
prime numbers, 12
probability, 129–131
  methods of computing, 131–132, *see also under* computing methods
  probability tables, 131
    cell probabilities, 131
    marginal probabilities, 131
    total row, 131
  properties of, 129–130
product formulas of sines and cosines, 147
projection
  of a given point, 83
  of a segment on a given line, 83
proportion, 57–59
  real-world problems involving, 59–60

Q

quadratic equations, 44–54
  in two unknowns and systems of equations, 50
  roots, 45
    factoring, 45
    solving direct solution, 45
quadratics, *see also* quadratic equations
  quadratic formula, 46–47
  quadratic functions, 49–50
  solving systems of equations involving, 51–53
quadrilaterals, 103–108
  parallelograms, 103
  rectangles, 104
  rhombi, 104
  squares, 105
  trapezoids, 105–106, *see also separate entry*

R

radicals, 21–22
  operations with, 22, *see also separate entry*
  radical equation, 47–49
  radical sign, 21
  radicand, 21
radius of a circle, 108
random sampling, 141
range, 61, 138
rate of change and related rates, 162–163
ratio, 57–59
rational functions and their graphs, 68
rational numbers, 12–13
ray, 79
real numbers, 11–12
  and their components, 27–28, *see also under* equality
  real number operations and their properties, 27–28
real part, of complex numbers, 28
rectangles, 104
rectilinear motion, 160–162
reflex angle, 82
reflexive property of equality, 27
regular polygons (convex), 94–95
  perimeter of, 95
repeating decimal, 12
rhombi, 104
right angle, 81
right triangle, 98
right-triangle problems, trigonometry to solve, 149–151

S

sampling, 140–142
  population parameters or parameters, 140
  random sampling, 141
  sampling distributions, 142
  with and without replacement, 141
scalene triangle, 97
scatter-plot, 126–127
scientific notation, 24–25
scoring the MTEL tests, 6–7
  multiple-choice questions, 6
  open-response questions, 6
  score results, 7
  test-taking tips, 7–8
segments
  bisector of, 80

congruent segments, 80
  midpoint of, 80
sequences, 172–173
series, 172–173
sets, 167
significant digits, 26–27
similar polygons, 95–96
  definition, 95
  theorems, 95–96
sine, 143
skewed curves, 128
slope of the line, 38–40
  point-slope form, 39
slope-intercept form of a linear equation, 39
solid geometry, 112–115
  cubes, cylinders, 112
  intersecting planes, 112
  volume and surface area, 112–115
special functions and their graphs, 69
square root of a number, 21
squares, 105
standard deviation, 139
statistics, 132–138
  arithmetic mean, definition of, 132
stem-and-leaf plot, 126
straight angle, 82
substitution, 41
sum and difference formulas, 147
supplementary angles, 82
symmetric property of equality, 27

T

tangent, 143
terminating decimal, 12
tests, MTEL Mathematics, 3–8
  about, 3–5
  administers of, 5
  calculators, 5
  day of the test, 7–8, *see also separate entry*
  eligibility for, 5
  format of, 6
  preparation, commencement, 5
  registration fee, 5
  retaking, 5
  review sections, 6
  scoring the, 6–7, *see also separate entry*

studying for, 6

Tests Overview Charts, 4

test-taking tips, 7–8

transitive property of equality, 27

trapezoids, 105–108

  altitude of, 106

  bases, 106

  isosceles trapezoid, 106

  median of, 105

tree diagrams, 168–169

triangles, 97–103

  acute triangle, 98

  altitude of, 99

  angle bisector of, 100

  area of, 99

  base of, 97

  exterior angle of, 100

  interior angle of, 100

  isosceles triangle, 97

  median of, 99

  midline of, 100

  obtuse triangle, 98

  perimeter of, 97

  perpendicular bisector of, 100

  right triangle, 98

  scalene triangle, 97

  vertices of, 97

trigonometry, 143–177

  angles and trigonometric functions, 143–153, *see also separate entry*

  inverse trigonometric functions, 148–149

  periodicity, 147–148

  to solve right-triangle problems, 149–150

  trigonometric functions, properties and graphs of, 147

trinomial, 33

two linear equations, 41–44

  ways to solve systems of, 41–44

    addition or subtraction, 41

    graph, 41

    substitution, 41

two-point form of a linear equation, 39

U

U-shaped curve, 128

V

variability, measures of, 138–140

  interquartile range, 138–139

  range and percentiles, 138–139

  standard deviation, 139

  variance, 139–140

variable, 33

variance, 139–140

variation, 57–58, 129

vertical angles, 81

vertices of the triangle, 97

volume and surface area, 112–115

W

whole numbers, 11

INSTALLING REA's TEST*ware*®

SYSTEM REQUIREMENTS

Pentium 75 MHz (300 MHz recommended) or a higher or compatible processor; Microsoft® Windows 98 or later; 64 MB available RAM; Internet Explorer 5.5 or higher.

INSTALLATION

1. Insert the MTEL Mathematics TEST*ware*® CD-ROM into the CD-ROM drive.

2. If the installation doesn't begin automatically, from the Start Menu choose the RUN command. When the RUN dialog box appears, type d:\setup (where d is the letter of your CD-ROM drive) at the prompt and click OK.

3. The installation process will begin. A dialog box proposing the directory "Program Files\REA\ MTEL_Math" will appear. If the name and location are suitable, click OK. If you wish to specify a different name or location, type it in and click OK.

4. Start the MTEL TEST*ware*® application by double-clicking on the icon.

REA's MTEL TEST*ware*® is **EASY** to **LEARN AND USE**. To achieve maximum benefits, we recommend that you take a few minutes to go through the on-screen tutorial on your computer. The "screen buttons" are also explained here to familiarize you with the program.

TECHNICAL SUPPORT

REA's TEST*ware*® is backed by customer and technical support. For questions about **installation or operation of your software**, contact us at:

> **Research & Education Association**
> **Phone: (732) 819-8880 (9 a.m. to 5 p.m. ET, Monday–Friday)**
> **Fax: (732) 819-8808**
> **Website: *http://www.rea.com***
> **E-mail: info@rea.com**

Note to Windows XP Users: In order for the TEST*ware*® to function properly, please install and run the application under the same computer administrator-level user account. Installing the TEST*ware*® as one user and running it as another could cause file-access path conflicts.